Curriculum Based Instruction for Special Education Students

Curriculum Based Instruction for Special Education Students

JUNE BIGGE

San Francisco State University

MAYFIELD PUBLISHING COMPANY

Mountain View, CA

Copyright © 1988 by Mayfield Publishing Company

Library of Congress Cataloging-in-Publication Data

Bigge, June L.
    Curriculum based instruction for special education students.

    Bibliography: p.
    Includes index.
    1. Special education—Teacher training—United States.   I.
Title.
LC3981.B54   1988   371.9   87-31295
ISBN 0-87484-694-3

Manufactured in the United States of America

10 9 8 7 6 5 4 3 2 1

Mayfield Publishing Company
1240 Villa Street
Mountain View, California 94041

Sponsoring editor, Franklin C. Graham; production editor, Linda Toy; manuscript editor, L. Jay Stewart; text designer, Adriane Bosworth; cover designer, Cynthia Bassett. The text was set in 10/12 Sabon by TCSystems and printed on 50# Maple Opaque by The Maple Vail Book Manufacturing group.

Text credits: Page 121   From "Hearing Impaired Students in Regular Education" by M. Waldron, T. Diebold, and S. Rose, *Exceptional Children* 52(1), 1985, p. 41. Copyright (c) 1985 by The Council for Exceptional Children. Reprinted with permission. Page 192   From *The Conditions of Learning,* 3/e, by Robert M. Gagnè. Copyright (c) 1977 by Holt, Rinehart & Winston. Copyright (c) 1965, 1970 by Holt, Rinehart & Winston, Inc. Reprinted by permission of CBS College Publishing.

Photo credits: pages 86, 93 Marvin Silverman; pages 89, 90 Curtis Fukuda; page 91 courtesy of Communication Engineering; page 97 courtesy of American Printing House for the Blind; page 98 Ellen Driscoll; pages 99, 114, 115 courtesy of Sensory Aids; pages 100, 117 Allan D. Darrow, II; pages 101, 102 courtesy of ABLENET, Larry Roepke.

Contents

Preface

This book is designed for teachers, administrators, consultants, supervisors, and others who are responsible for curriculum, assessment, and instruction of students receiving special education and related services. Although directed primarily to special education personnel, much of the content will be useful to regular education personnel, especially teachers who often find themselves responsible for educating students with special needs. This text will also be valuable for school principals who need to know how the curriculum of special education students in their school relates to the regular school curriculum.

In writing this preface I would like to share some of what led to writing this text. I hope this book helps with defining all curriculum components for each student in special education and that it successfully guides efforts in providing these students as much participation in an appropriate curriculum as possible.

As a professor of special education responsible for training special education teachers, I spend part of each year working in the field with teachers and students. In doing so, I frequently find myself puzzled by the inequalities in curriculum guides and resources available to teachers in special education compared to those available to teachers in regular education. This divergence is what moved me to spend three years writing a textbook.

Teachers of regular education generally have state guidelines, specified courses of study, curriculum guides, and overall district support in terms of books and instructional supplies. In contrast, special education is a relatively new field. Provision of board-adopted curriculum is not common practice. Each special education teacher must strive to develop curriculum and materials appropriate to individual students and to the special education program each year. And because each teacher in special education may be doing something different, local education agencies cannot be systematically alerted to needs for instructional resources. Teachers develop a certain curriculum for students who spend most of their instructional time in special education classes and modify other curricula for students enrolled in regular classes part time and design curricula for students being prepared for transition to regular class enrollment. In addition to curricula of varied content, special education teachers are frequently responsible for curriculum, assessment, and modifications of instruction for students of different ages. This "starting from scratch" process, moreover, is repeated each year when new students arrive and presents an almost insurmountable challenge to teachers.

As a result, many special education teachers are becoming masters in curriculum development, and I encourage them to pursue and formalize their endeavors. This text will be a major resource in that process. But special education teachers need and deserve consistent curricular guidelines and the attendant support.

This book takes a broader point of view than just discussing special education curriculum; it helps develop attitudes and strategies to augment all components of the curriculum for students receiving special education and related services. Descriptions and related specifics are included for all the possible components that might make up individual courses of study for students in special education regardless of how much actual special education they receive.

This text organizes curriculum, assessment, and instructional interventions according to the generalized and functional needs of students. When applicable, disability-specific interventions are introduced. This text uses regular education core-curriculum as the central reference point in looking at curriculum and instruction for special education students. Each special education curriculum can include one or more of the following options each year:

- *Identical* curriculum and instruction (same objectives at same level of complexities as board-adopted regular education objectives
- *Parallel* curriculum and instruction (same objectives as regular education but at reduced level of complexity)
- *Practical academic* curriculum and instruction (different objectives in the same disciplines as regular objectives but more practical in nature)
- *Life management* curriculum and objectives (unique to individuals and groups in special education that may or may not be related to regular education disciplines)

For every concept and strategy described in this text, several practical examples are presented. Illustrations cross disability identifications and intellectual and age ranges. Step-by-step procedures are presented and illustrated.

This book is a major resource for sample modifications in student response methods, teacher presentation modalities, and special conditions for students in special education. These modifications range from simple and inexpensive to complex and expensive. Although expensive equipment may seem prohibitive to schools, it can have a strong positive impact, and various sources of funds can be explored.

This is not a text that recommends student educational placements. The suggested curriculum options relate to student assessment information and curriculum and instruction needs. These are not correlated with *where* students are taught.

Every chapter builds on a strong skill basis presented in earlier chapters. Recommended teacher actions in each chapter can guide teachers to effective professional practices in working with their students.

Chapter One identifies four recommended features of curriculum for students in special education, explaining the advantages of each: a curriculum that is *powerful,* or designed to have great empowering influence on individuals; a *de-*

scribable curriculum written in some standard vernacular so everyone involved has the same frame of reference for planning and communicating; an *assessment-linked* curriculum that fosters systematic evaluation of student progress and rapidly instituted strategies to offset problems resulting from student handicaps; and a curriculum *accessible* to students with disabilities so they can both learn and show what they know and can do.

Chapter Two addresses the relationships between curriculum, assessment, and instruction, describing approaches to finding present performance levels of students in special education. It explores ways of discerning the impact of handicaps on students' education performance and cautions about the necessary considerations when assessing students with disabilities. This chapter details specific assessment methods for students with disabilities and shows how to translate assessment results into curriculum goals and objectives. The chapter concludes with instructions on how to write instructional objectives that are consistent with federal laws and regulations.

Chapter Three explains how to pinpoint actual or potential needs for modifications in student response methods so they can learn and show what they are learning. A specific technique for inventorying current student responses enables the teacher to identify needed modifications. This chapter's highlight is an overview of student response methods organized by functional need according to participation in various school activities. Suggested modifications range from simple adaptations to the usual methods of student response methods to highly technological innovations.

Chapter Four discusses procedures for modifying teacher presentation modalities. This can greatly enhance how much and how well information is transmitted. Included are examples of materials designed specifically for use by students with certain disabilities. Modifications in teaching approach range from the simple such as reducing the amount of visual material presented on a page to the more complex such as adjustments in staffing patterns or changing to community-based instruction.

Chapter Five presents an overview of effective strategies for instruction. These strategies include traditional instruction, task analysis, content- and application-centered instruction, curriculum-based assessment and instruction, direct instruction, academic learning time modification, curriculum-based instruction, community-intensive instruction, and transitional instructional strategy.

Chapter Six teaches thinking skills described on a continuum according to complexity. The chapter reviews learning theory, which it translates into practical applications for teachers. The chapter suggests a teaching sequence to help students who have problems in the area of thinking skills. Examples carefully illustrate each type of thinking skill and the movement between thinking skills.

Chapter Seven meets a great challenge in educating students with problems in learning as it explains a strategy for reducing complexities of schoolwork for students unable to work at the regular complexity level. This chapter demonstrates how to teach core curriculum objectives but at reduced levels of complexity as well as when and how to systematically derive objectives that are related, but different from, the original ones. The chapter also details how to create practical academic objectives for students who need to incorporate them into life-skill attainment activities.

Chapter Eight presents examples of existing courses of study designed specifically to meet the needs of special education students. Included are courses of study paralleling the regular education curriculum and one that is practical or applied in nature. Readers are also introduced to the few resources for existing courses of study.

Chapter Nine illustrates alternate approaches to life management curriculum. Two examples demonstrate district-adopted curricula to prepare special education students for full or partial participation in major life areas. A secondary emphasis is to prepare the students to participate fully in curricula. Disability-specific curriculum and instruction examples include intensive training in methods of responding to and receiving information. This chapter presents strategies for determining goals and objectives unique to individuals that will do the most to help them now and in the future. A case study illustrates this process.

Chapter Ten illuminates issues of evaluation and grading special education students and documenting their courses of study. A literature review covers ways students in special education are evaluated and graded and their participation in minimal competency testing programs. Issues of promotion and graduation are investigated. The chapter concludes with an innovative approach to describing and documenting both regular and special education aspects of a student's curriculum. This approach embodies most of the concepts and practices presented in the text for purposes of providing ongoing consistency and to prevent unnecessary gaps in student programs.

Acknowledgments

I would like to express my deep appreciation to those who helped bring this text to fruition. Many of the ideas incorporated here emerged from work with graduate students in the Department of Special Education at San Francisco State University. These students are by now special education teachers or teachers with special education students in their classes. Major contributors are also listed at the end of the relevant chapter. They are Eileen Vukicevich, Shana Carol A. Robinson, Shannon Wakeman, and Leslie Anido.

Other graduate students who contributed material for the book are Susan Boyd, Tammy Lee McCulloch, Holly McCulloch, Virginia Wong, Jean Ma, Cheryl Garavaglia, Michelle Olmsted, Carmen Ko, Terri Stewart-Schwarz, Elizabeth Murphy, Jonathan Roselin, Mary Shirley, Nancy Palmieri, Jill Kaufler, Lynda Kneifel, Sally Muhley, Leah V. Movillion, Marsha Olsen, and Lynne Kubota. Nancy Palmieri and Jonathan Lord, research assistants, conducted library searches for difficult-to-find information.

Professionals who responded to my requests for assistance in obtaining the latest data and viewpoints are Edward Gickling, Lawrence A. Scadden, Norm Erkin, and William D. Rohwer. Professionals who responded to requests for reviews and input into particular chapters are Carolyn L. Compton and Jean Fleischner. They contributed to Chapter Two on linking assessment, curriculum, and instruction.

The arduous task of completing the manuscript was made easier with the help of professionals who rewrote short sections to increase clarity, including family members Morris L. Bigge (father and author of several education texts) and Jeanette Bigge (aunt and former teacher trainer and middle-school teacher). Pat Nordin typed the manuscript; Ruth Bigge (stepmother and former secretary to a local education agency) typed the revisions. These people along with Pauline Adams, Winifred Baker, H. O. Bigge, Rich Holm, Penny Musante, Charlotte Thompson, and Linda Warner helped and encouraged me throughout the arduous process of writing.

Reviewers from both regular and special education interests helped me significantly. My thanks to Ann Corn, David Gordon, Marilyn Hammond, Laura Keller-Gautsch, Charles Kokaska, Robert Gaylord-Ross, Spencer Salend, Tomassine Sellers, and Gerald Wallace. I also thank Gil Guerin who reviewed an early manuscript and encouraged me. Finally, a special thanks to Jane Scandary and Dru Stainback who provided invaluable assistance.

Vanessa Coveau, Kenny Trant, Pamela Grist, Anne Perkins, Courtland Lomax, Taunnie Howery, and Sara Desumala allowed us to photograph elements of their daily lives to illustrate points in the book.

Largely responsible for helping prepare the manuscript for publication were Jay Stewart, developmental editor, and Linda Toy, production editor, who kept track of the multitude of details involved.

Finally, a special word of appreciation to Frank Graham of Mayfield Publishing Company, who had confidence in my efforts to produce a text in keeping with the latest advances in the field. With extreme patience he provided the necessary moral and service support. Without his contribution, this book would not have been written.

I sincerely thank all who helped in this endeavor.

June Bigge

This book is dedicated to
all those teachers who make the changes that allow
special education students to learn and to show
what they know and can do.

Curriculum Based Instruction for Special Education Students

1

Curriculum for Students Requiring Special Education: An Introduction

Curriculum is an essential organizing tool in any educational institution. Curriculum is the total content of instruction, an overall structure that provides continuity, sequenced challenges, and meaningful learning that meets the needs of both students and society. Curriculum designers provide for special interests and skills, individual differences and the demands of society. The curriculum for students receiving special education should be *powerful, describable, assessment-linked,* and *accessible.*

A *powerful curriculum* has a forceful influence on its students. It empowers students with handicaps to participate as fully as possible in current and future life activities. A *describable curriculum* provides effective communication about curriculum for students involved in special education. Different components of the curriculum for each student in special education can relate to the regular education core curriculum. An *assessment-linked* curriculum is based on the students' present levels of performance. Teachers need to identify broad curriculum goals and objectives as well as specific areas calling for specialized instruction and services. To be sure that a curriculum's goals and objectives will indeed offset or reduce handicapping problems, the curriculum needs to be *assessment-linked.* An *accessible curriculum* assures that students with different kinds of disabilities can participate in all appropriate curriculum activities. It allows students, through modifications, to receive instruction fully, express what they know, and show what they can do.

A Powerful Curriculum

Teachers need to go beyond the mechanics of writing educational goals to recognize the characteristics of curriculum objectives that will have the greatest overall positive impact on students. This entails the concept of a "powerful curriculum." What is the nature of a powerful curriculum for students receiving special education? Why are powerful objectives suggested for students with special education and related service needs?

Developing students' current and future capabilities in a range of situations at home, in school, and in the community is a primary goal of curriculum choices for all students (Brown et al. 1978, Brolin and Kokaska 1979 and Clark 1979). Everyone involved with schools wants the students to be able to function and succeed as fully as possible in school and out in the world. The greatest challenge the people establishing the curriculum for students in special education face is to choose the goals and objectives that are the most powerful—that is, have the greatest empowering influence for the students. This introduces the concept of the *power principle*. Borrowed from Papert's work, *Mindstorms: Children, Computers and Powerful Ideas* (1980), the power principle for students with special needs means that goals and objectives should lead to empowering interventions. Specifically such interventions empower students to perform activities that are meaningful to them and could not be done without those interventions. *Meaningful activities* are those that students with disabilities can participate in as fully as possible that are the same as their nonhandicapped peers do in school and outside of school.

To prepare most students with disabilities for partial or full participation in a broad range of situations, curriculum goals and objectives for special education students should be carefully and wisely determined. A crisp clear determination of goals and objectives will gain "the most mileage" for students. These are what will best empower them.

In writing goals and objectives, teachers influence the quality and the functionality written into each. *Functional skills* are those required to operate in normal daily life. With relation to special education and rehabilitation, Brown et al. (1978) suggest that if a student does not perform an everyday action and it must be done for him, this is considered a disability in a functional skill. Billingsley (1984) notes that curriculum objectives are considered *functional* if the "specified behavior would potentially be demanded by, or used in, community, domestic, vocational, or recreational settings and would permit participation in nontraining environment activities" (p. 188).

Billingsley does not stop there. He helps us realize that though functionality is desirable, it alone may not make objectives as powerful as they could be. *Performance generality*, as an outcome of instruction described in a study by Billingsley

(1984), empowers individuals even more. *Performance generality* is the ability to use information, skills, and activities in *different* natural settings, or situations, and in the presence of persons *other than the* teachers and other trainees (Billingsley 1984; Brown et al. 1976; Stokes and Baer 1977; Streifel and Cadez 1983).

A Describable Curriculum

To communicate effectively about curriculum and coordinate programs of individual students receiving special education services, teachers need to work from a curriculum that is *describable* in some standard vernacular and to coordinate efforts in behalf of individual students. Relevant issues include these questions: How do teachers describe the curriculum components of any given student requiring special education services? How do teachers describe the relationship of the special education student's curriculum to the core curriculum?

When regular education students transfer from one school to another or from one district to another, teachers can identify their program or course of study including the major subjects and the major objectives accomplished within each subject. Teachers and other educational personnel can use the core curriculum as a basis for summarizing the content each student experienced. Substitutions and additions can be added to the summary, and even students can describe parts of their own curriculum, stating the classes they took in high school or the subjects they studied in elementary school.

A Unique Curriculum Problem

In contrast, the curriculum of students in special education can be difficult to describe. Teachers of special education students and their students do not always progress systematically through a clearly identified course of study. In addition, local educational agencies may not have identified specially designed courses of study for students not participating in the regular education course of study. And then, some programs are so individualized that each must be described separately. Teachers rarely have the opportunity each year to develop a comprehensive well-articulated curriculum for their own use and as a description of what they finally do teach. Teachers must use curriculum resources from other educational units or find time to develop their own.

Certain special education students—particularly those in special classes for most of the day—do not talk with their age-mates about classes that they are taking or planning to take. Often, their day is not even clearly divided into periods and subjects. Due to the unique program each student has and the lack of precision in program description and long-term planning, students have little chance to reinforce their academic goals through natural social interactions with other students. For example, they seldom say, "What do you have next period?" "Who do you have for geography?" "See you, I've got math now." "I'm supposed to decide whether to take keyboard literacy, drama, or band next year." "What are you taking?"

Regular education students have many chances to become aware of milestones they have passed and those ahead that will be challenges. Studying increasingly difficult levels of the same material also notifies students of what they are accomplishing and have yet to master. Preparing for tests continually reminds students of what they need to learn. Then the feedback teachers give after the test-assessments again reinforces what the students have learned and lets them know what they haven't yet learned. Semester exams, periodic grades in each subject area, and grade-level proficiencies are all roughly consistent at each level and age for regular education students.

The situation can be dramatically different for special education students and their teachers. Each student with some kind of special education can have a program so specialized that the curriculum milestones would be pinpointed entirely differently from other curricula. This means that describing what each student has had and is yet to study can become a monumental task for special education teachers. Often this task is not accomplished.

When no appropriate overall curriculum serves as a framework or no recommended courses of study with specific skill and concept objectives exist, special education students can experience a fragmented program. For example, teachers rarely have access to distinct adapted reading curriculum and so do not build on learned reading skills or provide a systematic transition from one reading skill to the next. Consequently, special education programs can resemble patchwork quilts. Each teacher may see a different area to stress, and each teacher is the sole determiner of what and how the student is taught for a year with little assurance of ongoing consistency. For instance, a teacher that is highly competent in teaching reading using DISTAR, could do a great job one year only to have her student's gains lost because next year the student is taught by a teacher who does not know the DISTAR methodology and chooses to teach another reading curriculum.

When no way to communicate about a student's curriculum exists, teachers put themselves, students, parents, and even local education agencies at a disadvantage. Everyone involved needs some clear way to describe both the totality and the components of special educational programming. Yet the vernacular generally used to describe the nature and content of a special education curriculum is often confusing and inconsistent, much less clear than the regular education curriculum. It is essential to find *some* easily communicated system to describe curriculum for students receiving special education and related services.

Core Curriculum as a Frame
of Reference

One approach to describing curriculum for students in special education is to anchor it to the local regular education curriculum. Then the regular education curriculum functions as a "frame of reference" that can enhance communication and planning.

As an example, let's take an education document, *Academic Preparation for College*, (1983), prepared by College Board Publications, as a model for describing basic academic *competencies* and *subjects* in a school curriculum. The basic academic competencies are skills—reading, written expression, and mathematics (and perhaps speaking and listening, reasoning, and studying). These "are the broad intellectual skills essential to effective work across all disciplines" (*Academic Preparation for College* 1983, 3). Such competencies are interdependent with the basic academic subjects of English, the arts, mathematics, science, social science, and—in secondary school—foreign languages.

Basic academic competencies are detailed in the curriculum as competency statements that describe what students must do in each subject to achieve an acceptable standard (Rowntree 1981). *Competency* refers to the skills or knowledges to be measured, and *proficiency* refers to the levels of complexity at which these skills and knowledges will be measured. In a broader sense proficiency also means progress, attaining higher levels of skill and knowledge.

Competency standards and expectations stem from state, local, or commercially developed testing protocols. Programs testing student competence take several forms:

1. Minimal basic skills test
2. Basic skills test
3. Grade-level checkpoint tests
4. Statewide basic skills tests
5. Eighth-grade basic skills test for proceeding to high school
6. Basic essentials skills test
7. Functional test in the basics of reading, writing, mathematics, and citizenship.

Proficiency standards defining the minimum levels of competency required for high school graduation are identified as many things including: (1) minimum competency testing standards for graduation requirements, (2) minimum competency tests, (3) proficiency tests, (4) rigorous (not minimum) competencies, and (5) exit competencies.

A proficiency *standard* then is a statement of a skill to be measured (statement of competence) and a description of the level of complexity at which the skill or competency will be measured. Proficiency standards can be built into competency statements.

Local school districts often describe basic skills or competencies in terms of specific proficiencies. For example, sixth graders should be able to read at the fifth-grade level; do operations of addition, subtraction, and multiplication; and be able to write legibly for a paragraph at least three sentences long. Such proficiencies, which are minimal standards, give direction to the curriculum. More and more, "a passing score on identified basic academic competencies" in a minimum competency test (MCT) is also a graduation requirement.

Establishing minimal proficiency standards, at various grade levels or for high school graduation, enables a school district to periodically assess whether its educational goals are being met. But the stated proficiencies represent only part of a much larger curriculum. Almost all local education agencies have publicly stated educational goals, which are translated into grade-level proficiencies. These can then be measured in basic skills tests at various times in a child's schooling.

These curriculum goals in turn reflect the society's values and needs because the schools are preparing students to participate as adults and citizens in society. For high school students, the graduation standards relate directly to their fast-approaching adulthood and adult responsibilities. Standards for elementary students usually lead into the high school proficiencies so students progress successfully through an established and hopefully logical sequence of learning.

Basic academic subjects become important at the secondary levels. To graduate, students in many states must pass specified competencies in certain academic *subjects* as well as mastering basic academic competencies. Graduation can also depend on demonstrating proficiencies in academic subjects established and mandated by the state board of education and the local school board as well as taking and passing certain classes and course work. English, math, social science, health, and science are common areas state law mandates that are adopted by boards of education. Proficiency requirements for additional subjects such as government, computer science, and economics are also being phased into graduation requirements.

The educational objectives for basic academic competencies and subjects form the structure of the general education curriculum. Whatever else is thought important, enriching, or stimulating, these primary educational objectives form the major components, or structural members, of the curriculum. They form "the core." The entire course of study is built up around them, then added to, or enlarged upon.

All this is to say that there is a logic and a stepped sequence in learning and curriculum planning that relates directly to the goals and objectives of public education. The curriculum provides information to the teacher, bears upon instruction, and guides teachers and administrators toward helping their students attain established educational goals. As such, the standard curriculum for any local education agency is a resource that details the expectations and proficiencies of that local educational system for its students.

Graduation proficiencies are a local responsibility (National Commission on Excellence in Education 1983). Yet states can propose requirements for (1) minimum skills required for graduation and (2) designated years of study in each of several specific subjects or designated number of units required for graduation. State legislatures may also direct state boards of education to require that high school students pass a *state* proficiency test in order to receive a regular diploma.

Graduation proficiencies represent cumulative objectives from lower age and grade levels. Competency in mathematics starts with recognizing simple numbers and learning the counting sequence. These, in turn, are the subskills needed to learn how to add one-digit numbers. And this is a subskill of adding two- and three-digit numbers, which is, in turn, a precursor and subskill of a graduation proficiency in multiplication.

Graduation proficiencies are not, however, synonymous with the students' postgraduation goals. Graduation proficiency and course requirements are *minimum requirements* and are not necessarily adequate for all students' goals following graduation. Minimum proficiencies in a college-preparatory program are more stringent. Often they include the usual high school graduation proficiencies plus the added knowledge and skills college entrants will need.

Special Education Curriculum

If a school district's regular curriculum works as a map routing students toward a specific set of goals (the district proficiencies), then a course of study designed for students with special needs is another route going in the same general direction. Ultimately both head toward the same destination because the goals established for regular students are also important for special students, who may be able to reach some or all of them by the same or alternate routes. Thus the regular curriculum is like a series of freeways, denoting the fastest, most direct route toward the goals and objectives decreed necessary. Curricular options worked out for students with special needs can be identical or alternate routes. Some, like local roads running parallel to the freeways, are identical to regular education destinations reached with no intervention. Others are reached by routes identical to regular education but with special services provided along the way. Then still others go only part way, hitting as many priority destinations as possible for as far as they go. Finally, others veer considerably to arrive at destinations already reached very easily by most students. Several of these options can be used by any one student in any one year.

The curriculum for special education students is focused on implementing the goals and objectives stated in each student's individualized educational program (IEP). Individualized educational programs are the basic curricular map for special education students, detailing the goals and objectives for each student who has *special education* and *related services needs.*

MEANINGS OF KEY CONCEPTS

Special education means "specially designed instruction, at no cost to the parent, to meet the unique needs of a handicapped child, including classroom instruction, instruction in physical education, home instruction, and instruction in hospitals and institutions. Special education means those instructional services provided by teaching personnel which are specially designed to meet the unique needs of handicapped persons. Special education may include speech pathology, and/or any other related services, if the service consists of specially designed instruction, at no cost to the parents, to meet the unique needs of a handicapped child, and is considered 'special education' rather than 'related service' under state standards" (U.S. Office of Education 1977, 42479).

Special education also includes *vocational education* programs. These are "organized educational programs which are directly related to the preparation of individuals for paid or unpaid employment, or for additional preparation for a career requiring other than a baccalaureate or advanced degree" (U.S. Office of Education 1977, 42480).

Related services means "transportation and such developmental, corrective, and other supportive services as are required to assist a handicapped child to benefit from special education . . ." (U.S. Office of Education 1977, 42479). Basically, related services are nonclassroom services. Commonly included are mobility and orientation, transportation, educational evaluation, speech and language, and specialized therapies such as occupational therapy and school psychological services. People who provide these services are referred to as *service providers.* Each local education agency determines which services are special education and which are related services. These can differ from unit to unit.

Options for Special Education Curricula

Six approaches or options exist as baseline strategies for describing special education curriculum components. These approaches also assist teachers plan assessments, curriculum, and instruction. The options are based on the need some students in special education have for different standards of achievement (California State Department of Education 1978). These options for establishing differential proficiency standards can provide a systematic framework for describing the special education components of the curriculum for students in special education. Options include:

1. Using the regular education curriculum and meeting the same standards and expectations as regular students do but with special and/or related services.

2. Using the regular education curriculum and accompanying objectives but reducing the level of complexity.
3. Using a lower grade-level curriculum.
4. Using different but related curriculum objectives derived by substituting skills enroute to the regular objective.
5. Using a unique curriculum and objectives.
6. Using other curriculum and objectives.

A curricular program, or course of study, combines a variety of curriculum components into a whole. Each component represents something to be studied (subject, course, unit, discipline) and the level at which it is to be studied. Special education curriculum components are characterized by their relationship to the content of the regular education curriculum and the levels and nature of instructional objectives for general education students. Similarities to and differences from the general education curriculum and objectives are determined by doing assessments and gathering other information that identifies the unique needs of handicapped students.

Regular curriculum at regular complexity (identical curriculum) is appropriate for students who can accomplish the regular curriculum objectives at the regular level of complexity. *Identical curriculum* is a label often used to identify this kind of curriculum. The main difference between the identical curriculum option and the regular education nonhandicapped students pursue is that handicapped students are provided special education and related services. These services focus on:

- Modifications in student response methods
- Modifications in instructional or presentation methods
- Modifications in other conditions
- Other specially designed instruction and related support services

Modifications in response methods include helping students answer questions aloud or write text answers in other ways when they cannot do these things using the usual response methods. Modifying the instructional method or mode means changing the way instructional material is presented, received, and studied and how the student is assessed. Such modifications allow students with disabilities to receive and process stimuli fully. Modifications, other specialized instruction and related services enable certain special education students to study regular lessons at regular levels of complexity.

Regular curriculum at reduced levels of complexity (parallel curriculum), the second option, is organized so that students meet many of the same or similar objectives but at a less complex level. This option is often called *parallel curriculum*. Any components of a modified curriculum that highly resemble the regular education curriculum and objectives but are simpler become *parallel components*. Within this option, basic academic competencies, basic academic subjects, and other curricular activities are again referenced to the regular curriculum. The content, though, is changed, reducing the complexity to a simpler level so the student is able to learn the required curriculum. This strategy involves reducing complexity in instruction, learning, studying, and testing situations.

Other specialized education and related services such as the modifications mentioned earlier can also be required, and this is true of all the options. Parts of different options can be combined to form a curriculum that best benefits the student.

Lower grade-level curriculum is in effect another way to reduce complexity. The curriculum for students at lower grade levels may provide the basis for some or all the special education curriculum for given students. When this curricular option is used, components identified as *lower grade curriculum* are often accompanied by designation of the grade level and skill or subject area: for example, the math curriculum component on Harry Lee's program is the *lower grade level curriculum of fourth grade math.* For certain students like Harry Lee this option is best. The value of this option is that students are assured of receiving systematic instruction in the designated curricular area, and they have evidence they have attained a broadly recognized standard of proficiency reflecting a reasonable level of competence.

A *different but related curriculum* (practical academic curriculum) is used when it is determined that students will probably not be able to learn the critical skills for succeeding in the regular curriculum. This curricular option, identified by the *practical academic component(s),* includes *practical* skills, those available, or valuable, in practice or action. A common synonym for practical is *applied.*

In this option, skills enroute to age-appropriate objectives in the basic skills of reading, writing, and computation are selected for their practicability. They are not, though, simpler versions of the same objectives; they are different objectives. Using the practical academic skill option, one or more enroute skills to regular education objectives may be chosen as substitutes. For example, to "write simple sentences" is a language skill prerequisite, or an enroute skill, to the regular-education objective, "summarize main events and supporting details in literary works." This particular skill may be more critical and practical to certain students with hearing impairment than any of the other enroute skills. If so, enroute curriculum objectives such as this one are then elevated to become the curriculum content and focus of instruction. In this approach, the curriculum itself is different, but the general area of curriculum is the same as in regular education. Thus different but related curriculum objectives replace regular objectives.

Another approach within this option involves using curriculum specially designed for students in special education in which the objectives are related to regular education because they are within similar context or skill areas. For example, studying specialized aspects of consumerism and the laws related to disabilities could replace the regular-education "civics" objectives. Different objectives within disciplines can be chosen for their usefulness to students for whom learning is difficult.

This different but related option is selected when it is determined, using the best information available, that it is unreasonable to expect certain individuals to succeed in the identical or parallel curriculum and objectives even with specialized instruction and other services. In these cases, handicapping conditions interfere with abilities to learn the key *critical* or *salient* subskills even at a reduced level of complexity.

Unique curriculum objectives (life management curriculum) include options considered unique. Sometimes these curriculum objectives are unique to groups, but most frequently they relate to individuals. In fact most of these objectives stem from individual instructional plans for particular handicapped students. These may or may not encompass the same skill areas as the board-adopted regular objectives. It is often possible, and powerful, to incorporate practical academic skills into a functional context to form unique curriculum objectives. For example, an objective in a subject such as handwriting could be taught students with intellectual impairment in the context of copying the letters on their favorite cereal box as a way of requesting that cereal at a store. Life management options are considered unique because they focus on intensive *functional* and *generalized* preparation for participating in major life areas. Life management preparation facilitates skills and activities essential to participation in the diverse everyday situations that most citizens enjoy. Some life-management curriculum components are disability specific. This is usually highly specialized instruction or related services that assist students with a particular disability (e.g., orientation and mobility instruction for students who are blind).

What constitutes major life areas varies depending on the source of the description, but they usually include (1) domestic and family living, (2) education, (3) community living including recreation and leisure, (4) work, and (5) communication. Concepts similar to major life areas are also identified by different authorities as *domains* (Brown et al. 1979), *environments* (Clark 1979, Schwartz 1980), *competency areas* (Brolin 1976, Brolin and Kokaska 1979), and *life situations* (Bigge 1982).

This component is unique compared to regular education but not because these goals are undesirable for regular education students. All students need to master many of these skills, but it is the kind and amount of programming devoted to teaching the fundamentals that makes a difference. This option is unique because the students involved need a high degree of curriculum concentration and intense specialized training to learn basic life management skills. Most regular students do not require this.

Other curriculum objectives include situations in which curriculum components cannot be described in a previously mentioned option. Career education is one example. It might not be taught as a separate subject or program but rather infused in a total curriculum. Kokaska and Brolin (1985) give an example: "Career education concepts, materials and experiences can be integrated into traditional subject matter. For example when teaching mathematics concepts, the teacher should use practical examples of how to relate mathematics to productive

work activities in the home, community, job and avocational situations"
(p. 59).

In other situations, teachers take advantage of their students' special interests
or else special events in their lives to spontaneously develop a component of
curriculum that would then fall into this category. Students in special education
might also receive other supplemental services such as a program for limited
English proficient students (LEP program) or programs for gifted students. An
intensive personal social skills curriculum is another example of something that
might be taught under this option either as a separate subject or diffused throughout the curriculum.

People can talk more easily about curriculum components that they can name
and describe consistently. *Regular education curriculum components* are readily
described in terms of subject area and grade level, graduation and grade-level
proficiencies, and designated courses of study. Components of a special education
curriculum can also be readily identified and described using these options relating to the regular education curriculum and objectives (see Table 1.1).

Regular education with no special education or related services can comprise
one or more components of a curriculum for students in special education. Those
components for which special education and/or related services are provided can
also be readily identified and described using these options related to the regular
education curriculum and objectives. When the components of curriculum for
each special education student are describable, the total curriculum becomes
describable. This lends to clarity and consistency of planning in terms of any
given student's past, present, and future curriculum.

An Assessment-Linked Curriculum

The educational and related services to be provided to students
with handicaps, and the nature of those services, emerge from assessments of the
student's present performance level. Federal requirements assure that curriculum
is assessment linked. The federal government also requires certain components in
individualized educational programs (IEPs) for students who need special education and related services.

On November 29, 1975, President Gerald Ford signed into law P.L. 94-142,
which has since become known as the Bill of Education Rights for Handicapped
Children. In reality, this legislation was a comprehensive revision of Part B of the
Education of the Handicapped Act (Title VI of P.L. 91-239). It was the product of a
movement led by parents and educators to require that a free appropriate public
educational program be provided to all handicapped children. (Michigan State Board
of Education 1984, 1).

Table 1.1 Curriculum Component Options for Students in Special Education

CURRICULUM COMPONENT	DESCRIPTION
Regular Education	
Regular education curriculum without special education	Regular curriculum, receiving no special education or related services.
Special Education	
Identical curriculum	Regular education curriculum, meeting the same standards and expectations at same complexities as students not in special education, but receiving special education and/or related services.
Parallel curriculum	Regular education curriculum, using regular education objectives, meeting the objectives at reduced levels of complexity and receiving special education and/or related services.
Lower grade level curriculum	Lower grade-level curriculum, using lower grade-level objectives, receiving special education and/or related services.
Practical academic curriculum	Different but related to regular education curriculum, using different but related objectives derived by substituting skills and knowledges enroute to the regular education objectives (or other similar objectives), receiving special education and/or related services.
Life management curriculum	Unique curriculum with unique objectives stemming from student needs for intensive preparation for participation in major life areas rather than from regular education curriculum and objectives, receiving special education and/or related services. Disability-specific curriculum such as augmentative and alternative communication training or orientation and mobility instruction.
Other curriculum	Diffused curriculum such as career education, curriculum resulting from specially funded services in addition to special education, other curriculum that does not fit other components, receiving special education and related services.

Consequently, statements of present levels of educational performance, annual goals, and short-term instructional objectives are federally required for students with special education and related service needs (U.S. Office of Education 1977). The statements of present performance levels are gathered from assessments and other kinds of information on a student's educational performance. Curilcular goals and objectives are then based on this information.

According to P.L. 94-142, specific educational goals and objectives are part of the required individualized educational program (IEP). An *individualized educational program* is a written statement of the program for a particular child developed by a collaborative multidisciplinary group effort usually at one or more "IEP meetings."

Participants at IEP meetings must include at least:

1. A representative of the public agency, other than the child's teacher, who is qualified to provide or supervise provision of special education
2. The child's teacher
3. One or both of the child's parents, subject to Section 121a.345
4. The child, when appropriate
5. Other individuals at the discretion of the parent or agency (U.S. Office of Education 1977, Sections 121a.344; 121a.345)

Once a student has been evaluated, additional participants are required including:

1. Member(s) of the evaluation team or
2. A representative of the public agency, the child's teacher, or some other person who knows the evaluation procedures used with the child and is familiar with the results of the evaluation (U.S. Office of Education, 1977 Section 121a.344).

Brown et al. (1980) summarizes the six required components of an IEP. State education agencies (SEAs) and local education agencies (LEAs) can also provide more specific information.

Component 1: A statement containing a description of present levels of educational performance
Component 2: A statement containing a description of annual goals and short-term objectives
Component 3: A statement containing a description of the specific education and related services that will be provided
Component 4: A statement containing a description of the extent to which the handicapped student will participate in educational programs for non-handicapped children
Component 5: A statement containing the projected dates for the initiation of services and the anticipated duration of the services
Component 6: A statement containing a description of appropriate and objective evaluation procedures (p. 200)

Formulating the IEP

These components of the IEP then become the foundation for each student's special education curriculum and instruction. Because the IEP is so important, it is valuable to explore how an IEP is formulated and what it includes.

The Michigan State Board of Education developed a document called *A Resource Guide to Developing Annual Goals, Short-term Instructional Objectives and Performance Objectives* (1984) that defines aspects of the IEP process. Following are portions of the Michigan State Board of Education resource guide that provide (1) a history of the terms, (2) an overview, (3) descriptions of annual goals and short-term instructional objectives, and (4) performance objectives. This guide is broadly representative of resources available in many states.

Michigan rules (as well as P.L. 94-142) partially define special education as specifically designed instruction to meet the unique needs of the handicapped child. Each student's unique needs are inferred from the statement of the student's *present level of educational performance*. From this information, the Individual Educational Planning Committee (IEPC) develops *annual goals and short-term instructional objectives* that identify the specific individual skills which are the focus of the student's educational program until the next IEP is developed. [*Performance objectives* may be developed by the service providers from the annual goals and short-term instructional objectives.] (p. 3)

While the annual goals, short-term instructional objectives, and performance objectives reflect individual needs, they do not reflect all of the educational activities in which the student will participate. They do not reflect the total classroom programming. They are not intended to be an administrative or parental tool for keeping track of teacher and related support service time. Rather, they are designed to:

- Be a vehicle for communication among service providers and parents
- Address the unique needs of the student
- Take the student from his/her present level of educational performance to the completion of the annual goal
- Be a written record of reasonable expectations of student progress
- Be useful for both parents and school personnel in reviewing student progress toward meeting those goals and objectives (p. 3)

The term *educational activities* is not to be confused with *program or service*. Every special education program and service also must be reflected on the IEP. While each individual service provider (e.g., teacher, occupational therapist, physical therapist, school social worker, teacher of the speech and language impaired) may recommend individual goals and objectives, the IEP must reflect a coordinated effort. There should be only one IEP meeting even when more than one special education service is provided. The intent is to identify the goals and objectives for the whole child in an integrated manner and then to specify the types of special education programs and services required to meet them. Committee members use the student's present level of educational performance to identify areas of need, develop the appropriate goals and objectives, and from there, the IEPC determines programs and services. [Remember these do not reflect all educational activities and programming.]

The IEPC may be reconvened at any time at the request of the parent or school to review or modify the placement, service, or instructional program.

The IEP must be understood by all participants so its language should be clear. It should also be self-contained and not require extensive interpretation or explanation. (A Department of Education, Office of Special Education Policy Paper on individualized educational programs published in the *Federal Register* clarifies the law, including policies relating to present levels of educational performance, annual goals, and short-term instructional objectives; U.S. Department of Education 1981.)

Drawing from the Michigan *Resource* and the *Federal Register*, let's look at how each describes some very specific objectives in addition to *annual goals* and *short-term objectives*. The *Federal Register* calls these more specific objectives "objectives in instructional plans," while the State of Michigan document refers to them as *performance* objectives. They function as the same thing, dealing with highly specific outcomes that "are to be accomplished on a daily, weekly, or monthly basis (U.S. Department of Education 1981, 5470).

STATEMENT OF EACH CHILD'S PRESENT LEVELS
OF EDUCATIONAL PERFORMANCE

1. The statement should accurately describe the effect of the child's handicap on the child's performance in any area of education that is affected, including (1) academic areas (reading, math, communication, etc.) and (2) nonacademic areas ("daily life activities," "mobility," etc.).
2. The statement should be written in objective measurable terms, to the extent possible. Data from the child's evaluation would be a good source of such information. Test scores that are pertinent to the child's diagnosis might be included, where appropriate. However, the scores should be (1) self-explanatory (i.e., they can be interpreted by all participants without the use of test manuals or any other aids), or (2) an explanation should be included. Whatever test results are used should reflect the impact of the handicap on the child's performance. Thus, raw scores would not usually be sufficient.
3. There should be a direct relationship between the present levels of educational performance and the other components of the IEP. Thus, if the statement describes a problem with the child's reading level and points to a deficiency in a specific reading skill, these problems and needs should be addressed under both (1) goals and objectives and (2) specific special education and related services to be provided to the child (Department of Education 1981, 5470).

ANNUAL GOALS

The annual goals in the IEP are statements which describe what a handicapped child can reasonably be expected to accomplish within a twelve-month period in the child's special education program. There should be a direct relationship between the annual goals and the present levels of educational performances (U.S. Department of Education 1981, 5470).

SHORT-TERM INSTRUCTIONAL OBJECTIVES

"Short-term instructional objectives" (also called IEP objectives) are measurable, intermediate steps between a handicapped child's present levels of educational performance and the annual goals that are established for the child. The objectives are developed based on a logical breakdown of the major components of the annual goals and can serve as milestones for measuring progress toward meeting the goals (U.S. Department of Education 1981, 5470).

IEP goals and objectives are concerned primarily with meeting a handicapped child's need for special education and related services and are not required to cover other areas of the child's education. Stated another way, the goals and objectives in the IEP should focus on offsetting or reducing the problems resulting from the child's handicap which interfere with learning and educational performance in school (U.S. Department of Education 1981, 5470).

The IEP's goals and objectives, stating student needs for special education and related services, are tools to reduce a student's handicap-related problems with learning and performance in school. Linking assessment, curriculum, and instruction within the IEP by means of these goals and objectives serves to integrate all aspects of a student's curriculum.

An Accessible Curriculum

Curriculum accessibility is particularly important to special education professionals. Educational performance is affected because students' impairments or disabilities affect student performance methods and the way information is transmitted to and received by them. Thus students with certain handicaps do not have ready access to the regular curriculum.

Curriculum activities stem from the perspective of the nonhandicapped majority, and many components present access barriers to students with disabilities. What does the concept of accessibility mean when applied to curriculum? What are some reasons for allowing other means than usual of accessing the curriculum? How can we analyze accessibility needs? What are valuable access modifications to curriculum activities?

Student accessibility to curriculum is primarily the responsibility of special education teachers, though regular classroom teachers share the job. Accessibility is gained when students have physical access to, and opportunity to participate in, the same or similar curriculum situations as do regular education students.

Challenges to Accessibility

Certain students have impairments or disabilities that adversely affect their educational performances and present a challenge to curricular accessibility. This challenge is successfully met when special education personnel and programs help these students find and learn satisfactory ways of accessing the education program. Hearing impairments, severe emotional disturbance, and specific learning disabilities are three examples of conditions that can interfere with educational performance. When impairments are so severe that students cannot process linguistic information through hearing (U.S. Office of Education 1977), they are said to be "hearing impaired." Characteristic behavior that interferes with social performance or functioning in school exemplifies students with emotional disturbances. A specific learning disability is a disorder in "one or more of the basic psychological processes involved in understanding or in using language, spoken or written, which may manifest itself as an imperfect ability to listen, think, speak, read, write, spell, or to do mathematical calculations (U.S. Office of Education 1977, 42478). Specialized instruction and related services are directed toward finding and teaching the best alternative methods of learning and teaching so that school performance is no longer adversely affected by handicapping conditions.

Analyzing Current and Future Curriculum Activities

Curriculum accessibility is enhanced when educators meet the unique needs of students with disabilities who require modifications in the regular curriculum to achieve partial or full participation in curricular activities. Certain students cannot participate in the curriculum using customary response methods, or they cannot learn when teachers instruct using the customary methods, media, and conditions. Something has to be modified to establish an effective teacher-student link. To make curriculum accessible, special education teachers first need to analyze the nature and requirements of different curriculum activities. Before a teacher can determine which specific modification may be best for a student, the teacher must first learn what activities the regular student is able to do to participate fully in school. More precisely, the teacher needs to explore what kinds of activities and interactions are expected of similar-age students now and in the future. These activities change with time but are usually cumulative, building upon one another. For example, coloring inside lines, an activity expected of a kindergartner, evolves into manuscript printing and then cursive writing in later grades. Teachers can analyze current and projected activities by curriculum areas and then institute modifications as needed for special education students.

It is also helpful to take the long view across curriculum areas as well as vertically within areas and then project usual or modified response abilities the student needs to succeed. In doing this, a teacher is able to help the student learn adaptations, alternatives, or augmentations as needed for long-term success in schooling. As an example, take a local sixth-grade proficiency standard in language arts that involves delivering an oral report in class. Knowing this sixth-grade proficiency requirement, a special education teacher might realize that his student, Zena, who cannot talk, will need some modification or help to be able to perform this and other similar proficiencies three and five years "down the road." So he works with the IEP team to determine a strategy that will eventually enable Zena to "tell" about things, and to do this without physical assistance or context prompts from others. The team asks, Which alternative or augmentative method(s) of communicating can we start now and perfect over the next years, or Which access skills should we teach Zena to reach this goal? When they come up with an approach, they will teach Zena a basic multipurpose ability. She will then be able to communicate her answers to teacher's questions, initiate telling the class her ideas, express her feelings to friends, and finally—in the sixth grade—give an oral report on the agricultural products of Zimbabwe. And all this became possible because of her special education teacher's foresight!

Regular and special education teachers commonly focus primarily on helping students attain *current* objectives. Though valid and important, this is only a part of what special education students need. If Zena's teacher had followed this current-focus-only strategy, he might have just concentrated on teaching her to recognize letters and write them, while "down playing" her speech limitation. At the first-grade level, Zena may not seem so handicapped by her inability to express herself in class. But by sixth-grade, this limitation would prevent Zena from taking part in many aspects of the regular school curriculum. Her teacher's long-range vision, extending well beyond current objectives, enabled Zena to participate in lessons and other activities with her nondisabled age mates years after he was her teacher.

Students using different means to access lessons need to learn skills and activities that will give them the "greatest mileage," the ones that make the most educationally economical use of their time. To help them do this, special education teachers need to locate, analyze, and refine the basic learning activities required of nondisabled students. This approach suggests that well before a teacher can start altering and improving the modes of teaching and learning, she or he has to define what skills a student needs in order to learn effectively now and in the future. What are the primary access activities or skills? What nuggets can the teacher pass on to a particular child that will best endow that child with what it takes to perform in school and society?

Access to Curriculum Activities

Modifications to better access the curriculum include (1) changing the methods the student uses to respond or perform in curricular and extracurricular activities and (2) changing the teacher's instructional methods and conditions. *Modifications in methods of student response or performance* include (a) adapting regular methods, (b) using alternative methods, or (c) using augmentations. *Modifying instructional methods and conditions* includes altered presentation methods, instructional procedures, or instructional material and conditions.

Modifications in Student Response Method(s).

The usual student response methods include talking, pointing, gesturing, and writing. Teachers and other specialists have to assess whether the student will need something other than usual response modes for broad curriculum accessibility. Once teachers have identified the most common kinds of tasks in a student's current and projected education, collaborating with relevant team members including the parents is helpful in deciding what modifications, if any, are in order.

Student response modifications can include: *adapting usual methods* of response (for example, writing with a dark felt-tip pen for a student who has some visual impairment and needs to see her work); *alternative methods* of response (such as using a microcomputer instead of handwriting when a learning disability causes illegible handwriting); *augmentation* or aided-response methods (for example, substituting a wallet-sized letter board for partially intelligible speech when students have severe articulation impairment and cannot express themselves well verbally).

Modification in Instructional Methods.

Instructional methods are the ways a teacher uses information and materials to instruct and help students learn. Presentation methods depend directly on the students' input modalities because certain methods of presentation in teaching/learning situations require certain modalities. If a student can't see, she can't see the vocabulary words written on the board. *Modalities* are the sensory channels (i.e., visual, auditory, tactile) through which students receive information.

Certain presentation methods are inherent in the regular curriculum. For example, educational films depend on visual and auditory modalities to be "received." Alternative presentation methods are something teachers or others such as interpreters *do*. Examples are when the teacher writes on the board using larged-size print, or an interpreter accompanies a student to class and does signing for him.

Reasons for alternative modes of presentation include any physical or sensory impairment in a student's receptive modality. Additional reasons are perceptual problems and other learning disabilities so that students see or hear the information but do not "make of it what most people make of it" (Bigge 1982, 185–86). And then certain students just perform better in school with alternatives to the customary presentation modalities.

Modification in Conditions.

Some students may be able to participate in the curriculum using customary response methods and responding to customary presentation strategies, but they will learn more given certain conditions. Finding the conditions that improve such variables as the quality, rate, and amount of learning gives teachers another way to increase curriculum accessibility. Changing conditions includes making spatial and temporal changes and using reinforcements to encourage desired performance. An example would be moving an easily distracted student in an open-classroom situation from a group table to a personal desk. Condition manipulations, reflecting recent developments in the field of special education, result from (1) academic learning time (ALT) strategies, (2) staffing strategies (community-based instruction), and (3) use of school and adult services.

Academic learning time (ALT) is the amount of time a student spends in relevant content performing with high success (Denham and Lieberman 1980, 8). A main premise of ALT is that students exhibit higher performances under certain conditions, and to maximize ALT, these conditions must be identified for each student in each situation.

Changes in curriculum focus for students with severe handicaps have resulted in *different staffing patterns* to cover special student education in the community setting. More and more, such programs call for teachers to provide the condition of community-based instruction.

Insuring a well-articulated transition from school to postschool programs for youngsters with special needs is only possible when *school and adult services* are coordinated. Vocational education access in particular depends upon conditions stemming from specific well-integrated collaborations of school and adult service providers.

Student access to assessment, curriculum, and instruction are high-priority goals and objectives on student individualized educational programs. To achieve these worthwhile goals, special education teachers can practice procedures for determining the unique needs of their special education students. When these needs are met by special instruction, training, and practice, students gain optimal access to curriculum activities. Then specially designed instruction teaches students to learn or perfect alternative response methods for use when needed in varied curriculum-related situations. All appropriate special instruction and modification contributes to curriculum assessability.

Summary and Conclusions

Within the many possible curriculum goals and objectives for students requiring specialized interventions, this chapter emphasizes making interventions that create a *powerful* curriculum or one that greatly empowers the special education student. To enhance communication among participants about the curriculum for students in special education, the curriculum should be *describable* using some standard vernacular. In order for curriculum goals and objectives to offset or reduce the problems resulting from a student's handicap that adversely affect educational performance in school, teachers need to assure that the chosen curriculum is *assessment-linked*. For students with differing disabilities to benefit most from their educational opportunities, assessment processes and the curriculum itself must be *accessible* to those students.

References

Academic preparation for college: What students need to know and be able to do. 1983. Princeton, N.J.: College Board Publications.

Bigge, J. 1982. *Teaching individuals with physical and multiple disabilities.* 2d ed. Columbus, Ohio: Charles E. Merrill.

Billingsley, F. 1984. Where are the generalized outcomes? An examination of instructional objectives. *JASH* 9(3): 186–92.

Bracey, G. W. 1983. On the compelling need to go beyond minimum competency. *Phi Delta Kappan* 64(10): 712–17.

Brolin, D. E. 1976. *Vocational preparation of retarded citizens.* Columbus, Ohio: Charles E. Merrill.

Brolin, D. E., and Kokaska, C. 1979. *Vocational preparation of handicapped children and youth.* Columbus, Ohio: Charles E. Merrill.

Brown, L., Branston, M., Hamre-Nietupski, S., Pumpian, I., Certo, N., and Gruenwald, L. 1978. A strategy for developing chronological age-appropriate and functional curricular content for severely handicapped adolescents and young adults. *Journal of Special Education* 13(1): 81–90.

Brown, L., Branston-McClean, M., Baumgart, D., Vincent, L., Falvey, M., and Schroeder, J. 1979. Using the characteristics of current and subsequent least restrictive environments in the development of curricular content for severely handicapped students. *AAESPH Review* 4(4): 404–24.

Brown, L., Falvey, M., Vincent, L., and Kaye, N. 1980. Strategies for generating comprehensive, longitudinal, and chronological-age appropriate individualized education programs for adolescent and young-adult severely handicapped students. *Journal of Special Education* 14(2): 199–215.

Brown, L., Nietupski, J., and Hamre-Nietupski, S. 1976. Criterion of ultimate functioning. In *Hey, don't forget about me: Education's investment in the severely, profoundly and multiply handicapped,* edited by M. A. Thomas. Reston, Va.: Council for Exceptional Children, pp. 2–15.

California State Department of Education. 1978. Developing proficiency standards for pupils in special education programs. Sacramento, Calif.: Department of Education, p. 42479.

Clark, G. 1979. *Career education for the handicapped child in the elementary school.* Denver, Colo.: Love Publishing Co.

Denham, C., and Lieberman, A., eds. 1980. *Time to learn.* Washington, D.C.: U.S. Department of Education, National Institute of Health.

Kokaska, C., and Brolin, D. 1985. *Career education for handicapped individuals.* 2d ed. Columbus, Ohio: Charles E. Merrill.

McCormick, L., and Shane, H. 1984. Augmentative communication. In *Early language intervention,* edited by L. McCormick and R. Schiefelbusch. Columbus, Ohio: Charles E. Merrill, pp. 325–56.

Michigan State Board of Education. 1984. *A resource guide to developing annual goals, short-term instructional objectives and performance objectives.* Lansing, Mich.: Office of Special Education Services.

National Commission on Excellence in Education. 1983. *A nation at risk: The imperative of educational reform.* Washington, D.C.: U.S. Department of Education.

Papert, S. 1980. *Mindstorms: Children, computers and powerful ideas.* New York: Basic Books.

Rowntree, D. 1981. *Developing courses for students.* London: McGraw-Hill.

Schwartz, S., ed. 1980. *Participant's guide: Institute on career education for the handicapped.* Project RETOOL, University of Alabama.

Stokes, T. P., and Baer, D. M. 1977. An implicit technology of generalization. *Journal of Applied Behavior Analysis* 10: 349–67.

Streifel, S., and Cadez, M. J. 1983. Serving children and adolescents with developmental disabilities in the special education classroom: Proven methods. Baltimore, Md.: Paul Brookes.

U.S. Department of Education, Office of Special Education, 34 CFR Pt. 300. 1981. Assistance to states for education of handicapped children; interpretation. *Federal Register* (12): 5460–74.

U.S. Office of Education, Department of Health, Education, and Welfare. 1977, Pt. II. Education of handicapped children, implementation of Part B of the Education of the Handicapped Act. *Federal Register* 42(163): 42474–518.

2

Linking Assessment to Curriculum and Instruction

Assessment Is Primary

Preliminary to building a curriculum, teachers need to know about linking assessment to the curriculum and subsequent instruction. Formulating a curriculum without adequate and accurate assessment is like building a house without a blueprint. What vehicle links assessment information to specific curriculum goals and objectives for students in special education? What are the characteristics of goals and short-term instructional objectives on IEPs? How are these goals and objectives formulated and written? What are some ways to evaluate the impact of students' handicaps on their educational performance? What are considerations for assessing students with disabilities? What are approaches to finding present performance levels of students in special education?

Assessment is the process of collecting, summarizing, and organizing a variety of information that (1) specifies and verifies student academic, cognitive, adaptive, behavioral, and physical problems and (2) aids in decision making about individual students. Assessment, used to explore all areas related to suspected student disabilities, helps identify those who are candidates for special education and related services. Statements of current educational performance come from several different assessment procedures. These statements characteristically describe the effect the child's handicap has on educational performance including (1) academics such as reading, math, and communication and (2) nonacademics such as mobility and daily life activities or life management skills.

Function of Assessment

Tucker (1985) identifies two assessment functions of particular importance in special education: "(1) diagnosis of a handicapping condition for the purpose of placement or eligibility, and (2) the collection of the data which are essential for planning an effective instructional program of the individual being assessed" (p. 201).

A rich literature offers information on assessment as it relates to diagnosis and placement or screening and eligibility for special education. Eligibility criteria vary, and state education departments and local education agencies define eligibility criteria for special education and related services. In general, "eligibility is typically established by reference to scores on standardized tests of intelligence or achievement" (Wilcox 1986, 2). Assessment for diagnosis and/or placement is not covered in this text.

Here assessment is viewed as a means of collecting information for developing a relevant curriculum and effective instruction. Teachers need as much information as possible on the types of assessment information because assessment influences their teaching and curriculum programming for special education students. They also benefit from understanding how to use the IEP as a vehicle for translating assessment results into instructional objectives. These objectives in turn shape a meaningful curriculum and relevant instruction.

Phases of Assessment

Assessment of students thought to have handicapping conditions falls into a logical sequence. The phases of educational assessment are (1) screening, (2) determining eligiblity, (3) program planning, (4) monitoring student progress, and (5) evaluating the program (McLoughlin and Lewis 1981, and Salvia and Ysseldyke 1985).

Screening. Screening is performed to identify students with suspected handicaps who may need special education and related services. P.L. 94-142 requires that each school district or other educational unit providing education for students employ reliable and time-saving procedures to identify students in need of further assessment. Checklists and rating forms are often distributed to preschool and regular-education teachers for preliminary screening. These teachers are also asked to complete checklists on students they suspect have problems. Teacher interviews with parents, former teachers, and others are another valuable source of information. School records, the results of group testing, and report cards offer further screening information for this first stage of assessment that takes place within the regular classroom (McLoughlin and Lewis 1981).

Determining Eligibility for Special Education.   Educational assessments assist in determining student eligibility, using eligibility requirements based upon P.L. 94-142 and established by state departments of education. A student's qualification for special education is determined by "whether the child has a school performance problem and whether it is related to a handicap . . . If the student's performance data and the other data gathered meet the standards, the student is eligible for special education or related services. In addition, the school may be eligible to receive federal government funds to help pay for the special services" (McLoughlin and Lewis 1981, 8).

Program Planning.   Educational assessments help organize programs for exceptional students "on the basis of demonstrated *skill deficits,* rather than global disability syndromes or labels . . . Programs are based on needed services rather than the *type* of handicap. In other words, special educators use assessment to determine that Jim is two grades behind his age-peers in reading, rather than to say he is 'dyslexic' " (McLoughlin and Lewis 1981, 8). Specifically, for students with vision and hearing impairment, teachers use educational assessment to look at a child's functional abilities with and without various prosthetic devices such as enhanced lighting or amplified speech. Assessments can also include the need for special education or related services for students with different disabilities who excel in certain areas (e.g., a gifted but visually impaired student). The annual goals and short-term objectives derived from educational assessments lead to informed program planning for students in special education.

Monitoring Student Progress.   Teachers monitor student progress by gathering data about the immediate and long-range effects of instruction. Different assessment procedures are used to determine student progress in terms of the level and kind of achievement detailed in the curriculum goals and objectives. Teachers and others involved in the interdisciplinary effort rely on educational assessment for any information "that can be used to make necessary modifications in the program" (McLoughlin and Lewis 1981, 9).

Evaluating a Program.   As mandated in P.L. 94-142, program evaluation takes place at least annually. School personnel and parents are required to examine the results of the student's program over the past year collaboratively. The program, described by the IEP, is evaluated to determine if the special service program for the student in special education should be continued as is, modified, or eliminated. This annual review also requires documentation of any changes in student performance from the time the operating goals and objectives were established.

Personnel Involved

A variety of professionals, the parents, the student with a disability (when appropriate), and others all contribute to a multifaceted assessment process. The professionals involved in assessment often include counselors, teachers with expertise in teaching students with particular disabilities, physical and occupational therapists, speech and language specialists, and psychologists. These professionals provide leadership in the assessment process, interpret assessment results, and solicit information from parents or other significant persons. They collaborate with the parents or guardians in addressing assessment results to see what implications these have for intervention.

In certain situations, it is particularly desirable to have the parent or guardian as part of the effort. The parent knows about the student's abilities and anxieties in a variety of situations, and this knowledge could apply to the testing situation. For example, in one case a sixth-grade student tested as reading at the low fifth-grade level, up from mid fourth the year before. The boy's mother, at the meeting with others of the IEP team, expressed surprise at the assessment results. The boy was reading Tolkien's *Lord of the Rings* trilogy, an adult-level book, on his own at home, she reported. One of the counselors present requested the results of another test given in the regular classroom rather than in a special testing room by the school psychologist. In this classroom test, the same student showed a reading and comprehension ability at mid ninth-grade level. Though different and administered under differing circumstances, both tests were given within a short period of time. Yet on these two tests, the student showed a difference in reading ability of more than four years of schooling! If the visiting counselor had not requested the additional information, a placement would have been made based only on the first test. Which was more valid? No one at the meeting seemed to have a ready answer. The moral guideline is to be cautious with assessments of special education students and invite input from parents and significant others as well as teachers, special related service providers, and former education teachers.

Such a mix of people requires successful teamwork to develop a truly collaborative effort. There are several recognized styles for teamwork commonly described as *multidisciplinary, interdisciplinary,* and *transdisciplinary. Multidisciplinary* is a generic term meaning that people from different disciplines and parents all work in behalf of the same child. Technically a multidisciplinary style is one in which professionals from different disciplines work in relative isolation—they remain in their separate areas of expertise. With an *interdisciplinary* style, professionals, parents, and others communicate with each other about how they work with particular students. A case manager provides a structure to prevent fragmentation of services and coordination of assessment efforts and results. Using a *transdisciplinary* style, personnel share and exchange knowledge and expertise across disciplines. Persons doing this experience more role release than do people working within the other systems (Lyon and Lyon 1980).

Quality Assessment

What makes for a good assessment differs depending on the kind of decisions that need to be made about each student. Teachers have questions, parents have questions, administrators have questions, and some questions are better formulated than others. Knowing what questions to ask is the key to making any good assessment. Wilcox (1986) says that to conduct a solid assessment, people must know what question is being asked, what type of information will answer that question, and what are the characteristics an assessment instrument or procedure must have to generate that information.

The team's first step is to delineate the questions to be answered and decisions to be made. These can include:

1. Is this student likely to need special education services?
2. Is this student eligible for special education?
3. What does this student need to learn? What is most important for a student to learn?
4. Where should the student be placed?
5. How can this student be taught most effectively?
6. Is this student making progress on his/her program? Should teaching procedures be changed? (Wilcox 1986, 2).

Wilcox cautions against using information collected to address one kind of question for answering other assessment questions. Questions about eligibility, about *what* to teach, and about *how* to teach might each require different types of data gathered from different sources. Information gathered for the purpose of eligibility will not necessarily work for deciding what to teach. For example, a student might consistently fail academic tests, but this does not indicate that the student needs to study academic subjects. Further assessments may be needed to determine what the student can and should learn. The assessment team always needs to know what it is assessing for and how the results relate back to intended use.

The IEP: A Linking Mechanism

The individualized educational program is a major vehicle for translating assessment results into instructional objectives for students requiring special education. The specific mechanisms that make this vehicle work are statements of the student's present levels of educational performance, the goals, and the instructional and performance objectives. These unite assessment with the curriculum and instruction. The IEP in effect becomes a support document for a special education student's program of study.

Special education teachers, other resource personnel, parents, and others collaborate to develop and write goals and instructional objectives for individualized educational programs. It is imperative to write the goals and objectives for the part of a student's schooling designated as special education and related services using the IEP process. At times, performance objectives, or similar kinds of descriptive information, are not included in the IEP but are used as support data in case specific questions arise. Goals and objectives for any regular curriculum will be addressed in the same ways they are addressed for nonhandicapped students.

Developing an individualized educational program involves writing out annual goals, short-term objectives, performance objectives, and instructional plans about progress on short term instructional objectives. Again, the Michigan State Board of Education resource guide (1984) provides important information.[1]

Annual Goals

Annual goals (AGs) are general statements relating to a skill area without specific reference to observable behaviors. They provide purpose and focus for individual programming. Generally, annual goals are not directly measurable and must be translated into instructional objectives in order to be measured. Annual goals may be written at different levels of specificity depending on the functioning level of the student. For example, "Mary will improve computation skills" could be an annual goal for one student, while "John will improve in counting objects to 10" might be a more appropriate goal for a lower functioning student.

Annual goals are determined from the statement of the present level of educational performance. The annual goals address specific skills needs.

Short-term Instructional Objectives

Short-term instructional objectives (IOs) describe what the student is to learn and how to measure when that learning has occurred. The IOs define each annual goal in terms of the specific skill or behavior the student is to learn. The IOs define how each annual goal is reached and are, therefore, more detailed. An instructional objective defines a behavior or skill that the student should be expected to learn within the school year. In some cases there may be only one instructional objective for each AG, but usually there are several. When the IOs listed for each annual goal are completed, that AG is completed for that IEP.

Short-term instructional objectives and annual goals are mandated components of the IEP that must be determined by the IEPC [Individual Educational Planning Committee]. Both are based on information about the student's present level of educational performance. The sources of information for determining the annual goals and instructional objectives include the multidisciplinary evaluation team (MET) report, parent input, ongoing assessment, and expectations of future life activities.

Annual goals (AGs) and short-term instructional objectives (IOs) are interdependent. Annual goals are necessary for the development of IOs as they provide the general direction for programming. IOs are the measurable steps toward achieving the annual goals. Instructional objectives may be worked on sequentially or simultaneously. Completion of the short-term instructional objectives listed for an annual goal represents completion of the AG for that IEP.

Criteria for short-term instructional objectives, evaluation procedures, and schedules of evaluation are required on the IEP.

Criteria specify *how* the skill is to be measured; *evaluation procedures* define *what* method is to be used to measure achievement of the skill; and the *evaluation schedules* specify *when* the evaluation procedures occur.

Criteria determine successful completion of the short-term instructional objectives and may be established in a variety of ways. Criteria may be written as:

Grade level—increased achievement such as "will improve reading comprehension from 3.6 to 4.0 grade level"

Grades—improvement of grades earned in the regular classroom such as "will complete all class assignments with a grade of C or better"

Percentage or number of skills or POs [performance objectives] acquired—the number of tasks, skills, or performance objectives to be learned such as "will learn 80% of selected addition facts," "will learn 100% of selected POs related to addition," or "will learn at least 10 addition skills"

The above measures are not exhaustive. Other criteria for measuring achievement of the IOs may be used. Sometimes use of more specific criteria such as those described in the section on performance objectives may be appropriate.

Evaluation procedures describe what method is to be used to measure achievement. They include such methods as standardized achievement tests, pre- and post-tests which accompany existing curricula, systematic observation of behavior or informal teacher-made tests. When the criterion for an IO is a percentage or number of selected performance objectives, the evaluation procedure may be determined by the method of assessment established for each PO, and the procedure should appear on the IEP. If using a prepared curriculum which contains evaluation procedures, these procedures should be stated on the IEP, e.g., "Specified in the TMI [trainable mentally impaired] curriculum."

Evaluation schedules define when the measurement occurs. They indicate the frequency of evaluation such as "October and May," "by April 1984," "regularly throughout the year," "at semester end," or "each card marking period."

Performance Objectives

Performance objectives (POs) are specific steps leading to the completion of the short-term instructional objective. POs break each short-term instructional objective down into small steps which are the focus of the educational programming for the student. Each performance objective must be measurable. POs are developed by the individual service provider rather than the IEPC as a whole. Each individual service provider must have POs related to specific short-term instructional objectives. The POs must be available for review. However, POs can be changed, added or deleted at the discretion of the individual service provider without convening an IEPC.

There is considerable confusion as to how short-term instructional objectives (IOs) differ from performance objectives (POs) in content and format. The relationship between IOs and POs is similar to the relationship between AGs and IOs. Short-term instructional objectives are manageable steps toward the achievement of an annual goal. Similarly, performance objectives are manageable steps toward the achievement of the short-term instructional objective. Performance objectives are more specific than the short-term instructional objective.

. . . In a review of the literature on the component parts of a performance objective, Roberts (1982) concludes that from three to eight components are suggested. Based on this review, it is recommended that most POs include three components [described by Mager 1975]. They are:

1. the behavior or skill to be learned,
2. the criteria used to determine accomplishment of the behavior or skill,
3. the conditions under which the student is to perform the behavior or skill, where appropriate.

Service providers [e.g., teachers, teacher of the speech and language impaired] may write performance objectives that include more detailed information and contain more components. However, these three components are recommended [as a minimum].

Component One: Behavior or Skill to Be Learned

The behavior or skill to be learned is the observable performance that demonstrates that the learner has acquired the behavior or skill. The stated behavior or skill must reliably communicate what the service provider [teacher] is to observe the student doing. Typically, there are two parts to the statement of behavior or skill. The first part identifies the knowledge to be learned. The second part defines the action necessary to demonstrate the knowledge learned.

Examples of knowledge are:

Verbal learning, such as vocabulary lists, names of people;
Procedures, such as how to line up, the steps in long division, how to use the library;
Concepts, such as roundness, number sets, principles of economics, pluralization.

Examples of actions are:

the student will *list* . . . , the student will *write* . . . ,
the student will *say* . . . , the student will *sort* . . . ,
the student will *point* . . .

Component Two: Criteria to Determine Accomplishment

Criteria are the measures used to determine when the student has accomplished the behavior or skill. The method selected depends on the student *and* the behavior or skill being taught. When using prepared objectives which contain criteria, it may be necessary to modify the criteria to meet the needs of the individual student.

There are many ways to state the criteria used to measure the behavior or skill. The following are commonly used criteria.

Accuracy refers to the number of times a behavior or skill occurs within a given number of opportunities for the behavior or skill to occur. It may be expressed in terms of a percentage or the number of successful trials, such as 80%; 14 out of 15 times; 10 consecutive times.

Cumulative counts refers to the number of times a behavior occurs without a times reference, such as "waves goodbye on 5 occasions; "reads 3 books"; "completes 5 art projects"; "requests assistance from the teacher on 3 occasions."

Duration refers to the amount of time a specific behavior or skill occurs. It may be used to measure an increase or decrease in the amount of time it takes the student to perform the task, such as "attends to task for 15 minutes"; "walks to next class within the 5 minute class change period."

Rate refers to the number of times the behavior or skill occurs within a time reference. Time is used with the cumulative count to express rate, such as "is not tardy more than 2 times per week"; "uses bathroom independently 3 times per day"; "writes 3 sentences in 30 minutes."

There are other criteria which may be used to determine accomplishment of the behavior or skill. One less frequently used measure is distance such as "walks 10 feet." Different criteria can be combined, such as "walks 10 feet within 2 minutes (distance and time); "attends to task for 5 minutes on 10 occasions" (duration and cumulative count); "catches a ball 80% of the time on 3 occasions" (accuracy and cumulative count).

Component Three: Conditions Under Which the Student Will Perform

Conditions are the circumstances under which the student must perform the behavior or skill or demonstrate the knowledge. Conditions are not necessary for every performance objective, but should be used to further clarify the PO when appropriate. Conditions may include one or more of the following:

Level of assistance needed, such as "independently"; "with a prompt."

Materials used, such as "presented with flashcards with 3-inch letters"; "given an auditory signal"; "when shown pictures of animals."

Special appliances needed, such as "using a tape recorder"; "with a Bliss board"; "using a wheelchair"; "using his calculator."

Location where the behavior will occur, such as "in the classroom"; "in his seat"; "in the lunchroom"; "at the grocery store."

In some cases, the condition is assumed and need not be stated. For example, a performance objective states that "the student will write the numbers from 1 to 10 in sequence on three occasions." This PO implies several conditions—using a pencil and piece of paper; writing the numbers from memory and not from dictation. In another situation, a PO might read "the student will write the numbers 1 to 10 correctly from dictation within one minute on three occasions." In this situation, the condition ("from dictation") needs to be specified.

Performance objectives may contain additional information when it is deemed appropriate by the service provider. When mastery of a particular skill by a certain date is critical, that information may be part of the performance objective. However, an expected date of achievement for each PO is not required. Evaluation procedures may be written into performance objectives if needed for clarification. However, as long as evaluation procedures and schedules for evaluating the short-term instructional objectives are clearly written in the IEP, it is not necessary to include them in the performance objectives.

Whether annual goals, short-term instructional objectives, and performance objectives are selected from existing curricula or written individually for each student, it is the responsibility of the special education staff to assure that the AGs, IOs, and POs for each student are appropriately tailored to his/her particular needs.

The specific goals and objectives (AGs, POs) tie information about a student's current and anticipated performances to special instructional needs. Knowing what different kinds of assessment approaches can indicate about deficit areas lets teachers begin to think about the content of appropriate goals and objectives.

Altering Standard Assessment Techniques for Special Education Use

Modifications in Presentation and Response

The most direct approach to assessing special education students is to use tests designed for nonhandicapped students. To do so, however, teachers may need to make certain modifications.

Two kinds of test modifications are regularly made in assessment of handicapped students: modification of the stimulus demands and modifications of the response requirements. . . . Very often diagnostic personnel change the way in which items are administered in an effort to accommodate the student's physical or sensory limitations. Verbal directions are often signed or pantomimed to hearing-impaired or deaf students; written items are read to visually impaired or blind students. Similarly, examiners often modify response requirements, such as by requiring multiple-choice pointing responses for students who evidence severe language disabilities and elimination of time requirements for motorically disabled students (Salvia and Ysseldyke 1985, 31–32).

Five types of basic changes, or accommodations, alter the measurement techniques but do not interfer with the standard content (California State Department of Education 1978). These five, affecting stimulus demands or response requirements, are changes in:

1. sensory modality
2. written format
3. time constraints
4. test conditions
5. performance method

Changes in Sensory Modality.   Students who are impaired in motor or sensory capacities may need a change in the stimulus presentation. The student could be deaf, blind, or orthopedically disabled. An appropriate change involves administering psychological, educational, and other assessment procedures unaltered in content, but presented in sign language, braille, or whatever the student's primary modality of receptive communication is. Sensory modality changes also include using large type, taped material, magnifying equipment, and other implements to help the student process test stimuli. Students with perceptual-motor problems such as difficulties in fine motor or eye-hand coordination may require particular adaptations.

To be able to assess and make the right changes in sensory modality, the teacher must know some of the alternatives to the usual paper-and-pencil or oral presentation test materials. The test mode the teacher chooses should parallel the special student's usual instructional learning modality (e.g., sign language or braille). Changes should also be consistent with the intent of the assessment, and those not consistent with the intent of the assessment should be avoided. If, for example, the intention is to assess reading vocabulary, the items should not be read aloud to visually impaired students because the answers are partially given in the presentation.

Changes in the Written Format.   Changing the written format of a test affects stimulus demands in different ways. For instance, the physical layout of the test can be altered in a way that helps the student without changing the content. Or the item types or item construction can be changed, from selection-type items such as true/false to supply-type items such as short answers.

With experience, the special education teacher will learn how perceptual problems can affect a student's ability to perform on standard written tests and how to modify the test layout so the student can take the test. A student might have problems such as being distracted by too much material on a page, keeping his place while working on a page, an inability to keep attention focused on the task, organizing work put on the page, or a difficulty generalizing knowledge and skills in different assessment formats. Below is a list of possible modifications in the written formats of assessments:

1. Reduce the number of questions per page.
2. Allow more space between problems or between columns on a page of problems.
3. Enlarge the print.
4. Use alternative answer sheets.
5. Use original or realistic facsimiles of forms the student usually comes in contact with and allow student to write on that form.
6. Put all the materials necessary to answer the test questions on the same page rather than requiring the student to turn to a map or earlier reference.
7. Use graph paper for math problems.

To make a sensitive modification, try to view test items from the student's perspective. For example, with an item that says, "Put an X on top of the circle," the sighted student will place it "on top" in reference to the page; the blind student will place it "on top" of a portion of the raised circle. In another example, the teacher gives two blocks to the student and asks if they are the same. To the sighted observer, they are (i.e., look) the same; for the blind student, one block might have a slightly irregular surface, be sticky, or have some other attribute that would make them "different."

Changing the wording, item types, and construction in an assessment can do more than alter the stimulus modality. Such changes can alter the thinking processes required to respond to a test item. The answer might be the same, but the process used to get the answer may be totally different. Teachers need to have some idea of what the question is testing and the level of thinking that is desired before making changes. Refer to Gronlund (1982) to review technical considerations such as validity and reliability that can be affected by changes in test items and item construction.

Changes in the Time Constraints.   Some students may be able to do the assessment activities as indicated, but they need more time—either to process questions and information or to respond. In addition, students with limited attention spans or motivational problems can require time accommodations to standard tests. Changes in the time constraints of assessments include:

1. Administering tests in more than one session.
2. Allowing a longer time for each test.
3. Presenting more breaks within the test session.
4. Building the test or test items into the teaching program (remember, however, that to function as a test, the specific item can only be given once).

With standardized tests, any departures from standard procedures such as a time extension should be described in any report of the results. If a teacher extends the time limits, it helps to mark where on the page the student is at the regular test time, and then allow the student to continue. By comparing these two, the teacher may gain additional information on how the student would fare with regular time constraints.

Changes in Test Conditions. Changing test conditions to meet the needs of special students usually involves departing from the common strategy of administering standardized tests to a large group of students with standard instructions that control student and test administrator interaction. This traditional setting presents problems for some students, and teachers can make the following accommodations:

1. Test is administered individually or to a small number of students.
2. The directions are read aloud to the student.
3. Directions are repeated or rephrased until the student indicates understanding.
4. Extra examples are given along with instructions.
5. Individual instruction (or an example) is given when asked for.

The special education teacher should strive to create assessment situations, whether through the conventional modality or adaptations to it, that provide the student with clear and efficient access. What a student does with the assessment situation once the best access has been devised or discovered gives a much more accurate picture of the student's abilities. The best-accessed assessment provides the desired goal of a reliable evaluation and leads to appropriate related instruction.

Changes in Response Method. Students unable to demonstrate mastery in areas being assessed because they cannot use a conventional method such as paper and pencil may need a response or performance modification. For example, multiple-choice pointing responses can be an adequate response substitution when students have impairments that interfer with writing or talking.

Changes in method of response may be accompanied by the need to modify the stimulus. For example, braille can be a method of response, stimulus, or both. Students with learning disabilities may be better able to show what they do and do not know if verbal directions are read to them, and they may be able to respond better by saying the letter that represents their choice rather than marking it on an IBM answer sheet.

In short, it is not fair to assess students and make recommendations about their educational needs and abilities until examiners are certain that they have addressed necessary stimulus demands and response requirements accurately. Students have to be able to participate in assessment situations that most appropriately indicate their ability, knowledge, and mastery and yet maintain the integrity of the results. This guideline applies to all kinds and levels of evaluation: psychological tests, educational tests, grade-level proficiency tests, graduation tests, testing in daily classroom activities, and even testing functional skills in natural environments such as the local shopping center.

Teachers should only introduce modifications of stimulus and response modes after scrutinizing the effects these changes could have on the interpretation of results. In certain kinds of testing situations, after making modifications, score interpretations must be undertaken with caution. It helps to keep several considerations in mind when assessing students with special needs.

Considerations for Assessing Students in Special Education

Making assessments of students with a variety of special needs also requires unusual considerations. These special considerations vary with the individual student and the particulars of the assessment situation. The following are the areas that commonly require extra consideration when assessing special education students:

1. Knowing test conventions
2. Interpreting scores after modification
3. Assessment bias
4. Hearing and visual acuity and functional use
5. Reliability of response

Knowing Test Conventions

It is the job of the special education teacher to learn how to prepare students with disabilities to respond as fully as they can in assessment situations. For example, certain students may be able to use the conventional response mode but not understand the test conventions, such as "point to" or "mark your choice." Sometimes simply rehearsing the assessment materials and conditions helps students learn the conventions.

Usually a collaborative group determines which are the best or most appropriate modes, vehicles, and conditions for the assessment and instruction of particular disabled students. In this way persons from different disciplines and areas of expertise can help create the most complete understanding of the student's capabilities and a realization of how to measure them. Professionals on the team generally include special education specialists, speech and language pathologists, the student's teacher or teachers, technology specialists, and perhaps persons specializing in visual, aural, or physical rehabilitation. These individuals all have specific information on the assessment conventions within their areas of expertise. They are a resource for the special education teacher who quickly needs to learn about special assessment conventions.

Interpreting Scores After Modifications

Standardized tests contain "empirically selected materials, with specific directions for administration, scoring, and interpretation. They provide data on validity and reliability" (Compton 1984, 332). Salvia and Ysseldyke (1985) remind us that tests are no longer standardized when modifications of stimulus demands and/or response requirements have been made to facilitate students with handicaps. When this is done, the conditions under which the tests were normed have been altered. "Consequently, it is no longer appropriate for test users to attempt to make norm-referenced interpretations of the 'scores' handicapped students earn. The norms are no longer relevant" (Salvia and Ysseldyke 1985, 32).

In attempting to accommodate students with disabilities, teachers consciously adapt the administration of standardized tests. In essence they are adapting the assessment medium. As an example, Varnhagen and Gerber (1984) report research on the testing of spelling. One version of a standardized spelling test was given in the traditional paper-and-pencil medium; the other was administered and scored by a microcomputer. Results caused the researchers to state that "if scores are intended to assist in making instructional decisions, computer use may lead to potentially harmful placement or prescriptive errors" (p. 269). In this example, both stimulus demands and response requirements were modified, and the researchers found spelling to be sensitive to the assessment medium. They suggest caution, hypothesizing that the change may have introduced interference with the cognitive processes being assessed due to increased letter-search time needed for the microcomputer.

Ongoing research by the Educational Testing Service, College Entrance Examination Board, and Graduate Record Examination Board (Bennett, Ragosta and Stricker 1984, Ragosta and Kaplan 1986, and Bennett and Ragosta 1984) has implications for testing of all school-age students. Bennett and Ragosta (1984), for instance, found that test results overpredicted success in college for students with learning disabilities who used the regular version of the Scholastic Achievement Test (SAT) and were given extended time. This data, if generalized to public schools, suggests that time extensions may invalidate test results. Thus, when students use extended time to take a standardized test, the tests may no longer measure what they purport to measure.

The need to study the impact of standardizing modifications for specific disability groups is evident. If this were done, students who use different stimulus presentations, such as braille for instance, would have a norm group for performance comparisons. Even though examiners cannot at present make norm-referenced interpretations of assessment results, they can obtain valuable information. Through even modified assessments, they obtain samples of behavior that can tell what skills a student does and does not have. Such information about academic problems can guide the content of needed instruction. The kinds of errors that show up on standard assessments can suggest valid remedial approaches. Even the student's behavior during the test-taking situation can render insights about problems that might hinder learning. The way students perform with modifications gives clues about the impact their physical disability has on showing others what they know and can do.

Assessment Bias

Batschke (1986a) defines *assessment bias* along three dimensions: content, atmosphere, and use.

Content bias means that not all students have had equal exposure to materials the test items cover.

Atmosphere bias focuses on the child's behavior and examiner-child interaction patterns.

Bias in use occurs when the examiner misuses the test and makes poor decisions as a result.

Certain procedural guidelines can help professionals involved in the assessment process to control bias. The procedural guidelines described here, and adopted by the Illinois Board of Education, point out important considerations and model procedures (Batschke 1986b).

1. The language used to evaluate a child shall be consistent with the child's language use pattern.

2. Tests given to a child whose primary language is other than English shall be relevant, to the maximum extent possible, to his or her culture.

3. If the child's receptive and/or expressive communication skills are impaired due to hearing and/or language deficits, the district shall utilize test instruments and procedures which do not stress spoken language.

4. Each local district shall ensure that testing and evaluation materials and procedures used for evaluation and placement of exceptional children must be selected and administered so as not to be racially or culturally discriminatory.

5. Tests and other evaluation materials: are provided and administered in the child's native language or other mode of communication unless it is clearly not feasible to do so; have been validated for the specific purpose for which they are used; and are administered by trained personnel in conformance with the instructions provided by their producer.

6. Tests and other evaluation materials include those tailored to assess specific areas and not merely those which provide a single general intelligence quotient.

7. When tests are administered to a child with impaired sensory, motor, or communication skills, tests shall be selected and administered to ensure that the results accurately reflect the child's aptitude or achievement level, rather than reflecting the child's impaired sensory, motor or communication skills, except where those skills are the factors which the test purports to measure.

8. No single procedure is used as the sole criterion for determining an appropriate education program for a child.

9. The evaluation is made by a multidisciplinary team.

10. The child is assessed in all areas related to the suspected disability (Batschke 1986a, 18).

Hearing and Visual Acuity and Functional Use

One of the first kinds of assessment information a teacher needs is the acuity with which students can see and hear. Yet though commonly called for, accurate acuity measures are often difficult to obtain—particularly for students with severe and multiple disabilities. Often the assessments are only "best guesses," and assessment results can be misleading. Two students can have a similar medically oriented diagnosis and yet function quite differently. For example, two students can have the same cause of vision problem and even the same numerical description of the vision loss, but one may be able to read print and the other may not. Information gathered over time on each student's functional vision and hearing by trained personnel tops any list of assessments on a student.

Reliability of Response

Information about the student's abilities in terms of response modes in different situations is among the first kind of information to acquire. "Until a functional and reliable response mode (means to indicate an answer) is identified, or if necessary, trained, there is no way to know the type and amount of sensory information the child is receiving" (McCormick and Shane 1984, 329).

Young, severely handicapped students or those with retardation or language disorders may not even be able to make the simplest responses in assessment situations. In such situations, imitation is a good choice as a modality for assessment. The examiner first instructs the students to "do this," and then the student imitates what the instructor does. Another strategy is pointing to or otherwise indicating choices. Use of a *yes* or *no* response format is a third popular option. But before using this, the examiner must determine the reliability of a child's use of these responses.

The best approach to generalizing simplified assessments is to repeat them in the same format but in different contexts to give the students broader assessment experience. Teachers might also first have to do a task analysis to teach students the procedures they need to know in assessment situations.

Using Assessment to Guide Curriculum and Instruction

The results of student assessments is what guides the special education teacher toward appropriate curriculum choices. Good assessments lead to the development of goals and objectives that "fit" the student. For planning what to assess in students in special education, educational histories, mental-health histories, and medical histories help "zero in" on specific assessment areas and strategies. Interviews with parents or surrogate parents, current and former teachers, and, when appropriate, the students themselves, can also give pertinent information about assessment needs.

Informal observation, anecdotal reporting, and teacher-made tests are probably the most helpful kinds of information to collect once the teacher has determined what to assess and what assessment strategies to use. For a review of this valuable source of information, see Guerin and Maier (1983) *Informal Assessment in Education*.

Disability-specific assessment information is invaluable to the total picture in attempting to link assessment, curriculum, and instruction. Assessment strategies and tools designed particularly for persons with specific disabilities add to the information pool. Disability-specific assessment procedures are generally highly specialized and require expertise for selection, administration, and interpretation. Persons preparing to teach students with one or more of the recognized disabilities will undoubtedly be prepared with highly specialized competencies, which are not covered here. Advanced specialized training is generally needed as well to link these assessment results with curriculum and instruction choices.

Once a teacher knows what areas to assess, the next challenge is to find assessment tools that render the desired information. The final step is to use the assessment results to make effective curriculum and instruction choices for the student. Below is a list of some assessment groupings:

1. Standardized measures
2. Criterion-referenced measures
3. Grade level proficiency assessment
4. Ecological and student repertoire inventories

Becoming familiar with what each type of assessment measures and how it can be linked to the curriculum enables the teacher to make the best use of the assessment process for the student's well-being.

Standardized Measures

Standardized academic achievement tests, tests of intelligence, and many diagnostic tests answer questions about a particular student's performance compared to what is considered average or typical for that age group. Such tests are called norm-referenced. The reasons for using formal, or standardized, academic testing to develop curriculum include (1) they indicate the skill level for instruction and instructional materials, and (2) they compare the student's achievement and ability to that of similar-aged children.

Achievement Tests.   Achievement tests generally measure performance and progress in "the basics." These tests provide global grade level, age level, or percentile scores in the traditional academic competencies of reading, writing, and mathematics. Achievement tests are not appropriate for students with severe retardation or those presenting some disability that precludes their performance in the area of assessment. Instead, such students would be assessed to find competencies and problem areas in practical basic skills and life management skills, which would not necessarily be related to grade-level achievement (Gronlund 1982).

Diagnostic Tests.   Diagnostic tests pinpoint the specific kinds of difficulties students are experiencing within each basic academic skill assessed. Assessments for diagnostic analysis of problems with academics are often very similar to achievement tests. Reasons for using such assessments are to answer questions such as, To what extent are the student's problems in math caused by particular kinds of difficulties?

The subtests within diagnostic tests stress skills and subskills for particular subject areas, but they also include grade or age equivalencies. They can be criterion referenced as well. Diagnostic reading tests, for example, frequently include sections on (1) word reading, (2) phonic skills or uses of consonants and vowels, (3) structural analysis such as reading root words, prefixes, and suffixes, and (4) comprehension.

Intelligence Tests. Intelligence tests usually cover general information, and they can be significant for curriculum choices. Most intelligence tests render an intelligence quotient, or IQ. Depending upon local policy, this information may or may not be used in making decisions about:

1. Eligibility for special services of which special education is one kind.
2. Classification by kind of handicap, for example, communication handicap (CH), learning disability (LD), or mental retardation (MR).
3. Curriculum and instruction choices. For example, students with low IQs are commonly taught with slower pacing and lower or different kinds of curriculum expectations. Those with average to high IQs receive a more accelerated curriculum with more academically oriented challenges.

Tests Measuring General Information. Students weak in the basics and other curricular areas can still interact with others purposefully and interestingly by sharing general information they have accumulated. Such students may perform well on intelligence tests yet do poorly on content assessment. The reverse can also occur.

A good example is a twenty-one-year-old student named Al who had been treated as severely retarded throughout his entire schooling. Al was indeed severely *handicapped,* but in a test of general information administered with modifications to circumvent his inability to talk and write, he revealed knowledge of general information greater than that of the university student observing the testing situation and unofficially attempting the same items. Everyone present was astounded by his ability to select correct choices one after the other without hesitation. In retrospect, the people who knew him realized he must have been learning from what he watched day after day on television and listened to and understood in conversations around him.

Assessing the student's level of general information can be done using a variety of sources: tests of general information, general-information sections on achievement tests, intelligence tests, parent interviews, and direct observation of the student. The ability to take in general information is a measure of the ability to learn, which in turn can positively influence motivation. Thus the level of general information has tremendous implications for curriculum choices. General information can be a valuable clue particularly if students are given some means other than the customary ones to learn and express what they know, if necessary—as in the case of Al. The more students have learned, the more they are motivated to learn. Input and interest in different subjects breed more information and greater interest. These are important assets when considering curriculum options and topics that motivate individual learners.

Speech and Language Assessment.   Certain speech and language tests are specific to particular disabilities; others are designed for general use. General-use formal language tests detail a student's problems and help professionals decide whether additional in-depth testing is needed (Ruder, Bunce, and Ruder 1984). Speech and language tests designed for this purpose with young children include those that assess articulation, auditory comprehension of language, language development, the "language of learning" (as in, "find all the . . .), and basic concepts.

Formal tests of written language are often included in tests of academic achievement. Standardized assessment tools, designed to test oral language, can be either comprehensive or limited to one domain. Comprehensive measures of *oral* language access both reception and expression in different dimensions of oral language: picture vocabulary, grammatic understanding and grammatic completion, word articulation or speech sounds, sentence structure, word and concept meaning, recall and retrieval. A few formal measures test for pragmatics, using language for communication in communicative contexts. Most that test this area are informal assessments though. Formal special education assessment measures to gauge the language proficiency of students whose first language is not English are few for languages other than Spanish (McLoughlin and Lewis 1986).

Adaptive Behavior and Social Skills.   Taylor (1985) broadly describes assessing an individual's adaptive behavior as measuring the person's ability to cope or deal effectively with personal and social demands. He concludes that although it is a difficult construct, it can be measured. He provides helpful summaries and profiles of the adaptive behavior scales.

In using assessment instruments, it is important to recognize their limitations as well as their validity. Both the strengths and limitations of tests used for special education students are covered in the following texts: Compton's, *Guide to 75 Tests for Special Education* (1984), Gronlund's *Measurement and Evaluation in Teaching* (1985), and Salvia and Ysseldyke's *Assessment in Special and Remedial Education* (1985). These references help a teacher make intelligent decisions based on specific assessment information. In addition, there are specialty books on assessment of students with particular physical, sensory, behavioral, or cognitive disabilities.

Link to Curriculum and Instruction.   Much of the assessment information standardized measures generate is only indirectly related to the actual content of what is taught in the classroom. Standardized assessments can, however, give information about cognitive skills such as memory, and they can also provide information on student learning styles. They are probably most helpful when used to indicate gaps in the student's understanding of concepts basic to curriculum material. Diagnostic assessment, in particular, might detail what kinds of errors the student is making, thus suggesting which aspects of the curriculum are problematic.

Traditionally the emphasis has been on the use of standardized tests to assess student performance and to impact curriculum choice. Now, however, professionals question how directly standardized tests relate to the courses of study. The tests are not always seen as providing useful information for instructional planning. They do not bridge the gap between assessment and instruction satisfactorily (Tucker 1985, Gickling and Thompson 1985). Gickling and Havertape (1981) represent the growing numbers of professionals who question the contribution of standardized tests to curriculum and instruction. They state: "When test results do not agree with student performance on classroom curriculum, as is true of many of them, then there is serious question about the convertibility of standard achievement test information for making instructional decisions" (Gickling and Havertape 1981, 11).

Criterion-Referenced Measures

Criterion-referenced tests are self-referenced. They differ from norm-referenced assessments in that the student is measured against her or his own progress either on material or tasks taught or in terms of self-competency. In criterion-referenced assessments, students are not compared to a group or to other students. This type of assessment is made up of a specified set of skills or activities called *criterion behaviors*. It is also called domain-referenced and objective-referenced assessment. They provide answers to specific questions about a student; for example, can Anna button her coat? Can Joan make a jelly sandwich? Can Peter identify all parts of a computer and demonstrate its proper use?

The terms *norm-reference* and *criterion-reference* refer only to the method of *interpreting* test results, according to Gronlund (1982). Gronlund states that in some cases either interpretation could be applied to the same test: "Joan surpassed 90 percent of the students" (norm-referenced criterion) "by correctly completing twenty of the twenty-five chemical equations" (criterion-referenced interpretation). (Gronlund 1982, 14). In criterion-referenced assessment, the items *describe* student performance on specific learning tasks. In norm-referenced assessment, the items *discriminate* among students. Criterion-referenced testing is synonymous with mastery testing; the emphasis is on describing tasks the student can perform. But the level of performance is commonly determined by absolute standards (i.e., demonstrates mastery by defining 90 percent of the listed computer terms).

Items on criterion-referenced tests are easily linked to instructional objectives. Criterion-referenced assessments can be used effectively for any component of curriculum—basic academic skills, basic academic subjects, and life skills including vocational skills. Some criterion-referenced assessments are commercially available; some are developed by educators and published for wider distribution; still others are designed by individual teachers.

The Brigance Diagnostic Inventories (Brigance 1987) are mentioned here as examples of five criterion-referenced batteries:

1. Diagnostic Inventory of Basic Skills, 1976
2. Diagnostic Inventory of Essential Skills, 1981
3. Diagnostic Comprehensive Inventory of Basic Skills, 1983
4. Diagnostic Inventory of Early Development, 1978
5. Diagnostic Assessment of Basic Skills, Spanish Edition, 1983.

In one or more of the batteries, teachers can find something helpful for students from early childhood to the adult. These assessments are best for basic academic skills and for life management or essential skills.

Commercially available criterion-referenced skill lists or inventories have been developed for general use with special education students. These assess basic academic competencies and life management skills. When criterion behaviors are presented in sequential order, the sequence has not always been standardized. Rather sequences are often determined eclectically. They do provide information about what a student does and does not do on specific tasks. They provide no information about comparisons to previous performances by others.

Link to Curriculum and Instruction.   Curriculum for special education students is often represented by a listing of criterion-referenced statements of student outcomes in a particular domain of tasks. Such statements are used throughout the instructional process to identify outcomes against which student performance is measured. Steps of progress toward desired outcomes are described in terms of student accomplishment of subtasks for each stated outcome. One tool that links a criterion-referenced assessment to the curriculum and instruction is task analysis. Item analysis or task analysis is useful in identifying student learning errors and problems in accomplishing curriculum tasks. Task analysis is defined as "the process of isolating, describing, and sequencing (as necessary) all necessary subtasks which, when the child has mastered them, will enable him or her perform the objective" (Bateman, 1971, 33). Thus, task analysis determines the rudiments of certain skills and knowledge areas. "Test items sample sequential skills, enabling a teacher not only to know the specific point at which to begin instruction but also to plan those instructional aspects that follow directly in the curricular sequence" (Salvia and Ysseldyke 1985, 30).

Teachers working from a criterion-referenced curriculum answer questions with, "Yes, a student can demonstrate a particular curriculum skill, knowledge or activity" or "No, a student cannot demonstrate a particular curriculum skill, knowledge, or activity." In addition, they can report whether the student has or has not met a certain standard for mastery or acceptable performance (85 percent correct; eight out of ten times, complete all subtasks of the activity: _____). The specificity of criterion-referenced curriculum-related activities allows teachers and others to obtain a clear description of an individual's performance.

To avoid pressuring a group of similar special education students into trying to meet the same curriculum standards regardless of their individual differences, it is helpful to use such self-referenced phrases as: "three more than accomplished on the pretest," and "half as many more than completed on the pretest." This approach provides for individual learning rates. Many times students can help set their own standards and as a result will be more highly motivated to achieve them.

Criterion-referenced evaluation is not the only way to arrive at individual achievement standards. Whatever approach is used, students should feel they are being judged or are judging themselves in terms of improving their own performance rather than against some arbitrary and external set of standards. A self- or criterion-referenced way of phrasing the objective means the objective is only stating a minimum expectancy. There is always hope that the student will exceed the criteria.

Proficiency Assessment

Grade-level and graduation proficiencies define minimum proficiencies expected from regular students within a school system. The teacher can use assessments linked to these proficiencies. To use them so they fit the assessment needs of individual special education students, regular or differential proficiency standards are established. Proficiency assessments can be altered using an appropriate strategy among those introduced in the previous chapter.

1. same objective—same complexity
2. same objective—reduced complexity
3. lower grade competency
4. different objective
5. unique differential standards

Grade-Level Proficiency. To explore how a teacher might change a proficiency assessment to make it more appropriate for the student, let's look at an example from a list of specific mathematics competencies pupils in one school district are expected to attain at the second-grade level. The competency, or objective, statement is: Write from 1 to 50.

Approach 1: Same objective, same level of complexity (alternative methods).
a. Type from 1 to 50 on a typewriter or a hand-held computer.

b. Sequence flash cards with numerals printed on each to form a series of numbers in order from 1 to 50. (This may be done in smaller groupings, from 1 to 10, 11 to 20, and so on, for practical handling.)

c. Use a printer's stamps, stamp out numbers from 1 to 50.

Approach 2: Same objective, reduced complexity.

a. Write from 1 to 30

b. Write from 1 to 20

c. Write from 1 to 10

d. Write from 1 to 5

Approach 3: Lower grade-level competency.

a. Recognize numerals 1 through 5 (kindergarten competency)

b. Write to 20 by ones (first-grade competency)

Approach 4: Different objectives, enroute skill(s) to regular objectives.

a. Write numerals 1 to 9 when dictated.

b. Copy written numerals 1 to 5.

Approach 5: Unique differential standards.

a. Put one cup on the table at snack time for each place setting.

b. Write own phone number upon request.

c. Pick up 1, 2, or 3 sack lunches at the cafeteria—whichever number is written on a paper.

Graduation Requirements. In most school districts, the elementary proficiencies relate directly to the secondary school proficiencies and so lead to graduation competencies. Graduation requirements are often used as a focus for overall curriculum planning. Let's consider a graduation requirement in the same school district.[2] The first requirement under mathematics competencies necessary for graduation reads: Demonstrate the ability to add, subtract, multiply, and divide whole numbers, decimals, and fractions.

Approach 1: Same objective, same level of complexity (alternative methods).

a. Allow student to demonstrate abilities using a typewriter or computer.

b. Allow student to demonstrate abilities by answering questions orally.

Approach 2: Same objective, reduced complexity.

a. Student may demonstrate ability to perform operations using problems that assess all the operations but with simpler formulations involving fewer digits.

Approach 3: Lower grade level competency.

a. Pass the fifth-grade math proficiencies:

> Multiply two two-digit numbers.
>
> Divide a three-digit number by a one-digit number with no remainder.
>
> Add and subtract like fractions with sums less than one.
>
> Multiply two proper fractions.

Add and subtract decimals to hundredths.

Solve written word problems.

Approach 4: Different objectives, enroute skill(s) to regular objectives.

a. Change the proficiency statement to read: Demonstrate ability to add, subtract, multiply, and divide whole numbers. (These are skills enroute to the original objective; decimals and fractions have been removed from the original proficiency statement.)

Approach 5: Unique differential standards.

a. Demonstrate the ability to count change accurately and to know when proper change is received.

b. Demonstrate ability to set tables with the same number of plates as there are chairs (not a school objective for a regular education similar-aged student; not closely related to original objective).

Link to Curriculum and Instruction. As stated, linkage or the congruency among what is assessed, taught, and described in a curriculum, is essential. A teacher cannot expect a student, especially one with learning problems, to pass a proficiency test in an area not taught as part of a curriculum. But a special education teacher needs to do more than merely look at the district proficiency tests and teach students to pass as many items as possible by rote. The assessment items and the structure of assessments do not in themselves formulate the curriculum. A perceptive teacher can, however, use proficiency assessment to help create a well-devised and articulated curriculum. For while teachers do not teach the specific items in the proficiency tests, they are responsible for including in their curriculum objectives assessed by the proficiency-level tests. In short, they need to teach the skills that lead to proficiencies. Teachers also need to incorporate opportunities for students to show the competencies measured in the proficiency standards (1) in the same or similar way those competencies would be assessed in examinations and (2) in actual or simulated situations in which they would be used naturally and functionally. This should take place in the day-to-day classroom experience and outside the classroom when appropriate.

Because information from these tests is used to choose curricular options in particular competency or subject areas for students, guidelines are needed for appropriate determinations. For example, if students perform on age-appropriate grade-level competencies with average or above scores, they should probably be expected to meet the same objectives at the same levels of complexity as their age peers in the regular grades. If students perform in the lower quarter of age-appropriate grade-level competencies or at average or above on the next lower grade-level proficiency, there are three good choices: have the student meet the same objectives at the same level of complexity, use a lower grade-level curriculum, or have the student meet the same objectives at a reduced level of complexity. Whenever students have trouble meeting assessment objectives at a lower level of complexity, the teacher should consider different, more practical competencies.

Ecological and Student Repertoire Inventories

Ecological inventory assessments are used to determine what students should learn. Unlike learning diagnostic and other tests that solicit information to suggest remediation needs, this category does not seek information on what students *cannot* do. This type of assessment asks questions and then derives goals and curriculum objectives from the answers. Typical questions might include the following (adopted from Wilcox 1986, 2):

What do parents want student to learn?
What would increase the student's contribution to his or her household?
What would increase participation in integrated school and community settings?
What are the preferences of the student him/herself?
What activities are typical of nonhandicapped age-mates?
What are the demands and opportunities of the local communities?

The responses to these questions dictate curriculum content and strategies for program implementation.

Ecological and student repertoire inventory stragegies are community-referenced rather that norm-referenced or criterion-referenced. Ecological inventory strategies are essentially processes or action sequences through which a teacher progresses in an attempt to determine the skills needed by severely handicapped students to function in a variety of current and subsequent natural environments (Falvey et al. 1980). Student repertoire inventories are a method of measuring existing performance against the skills identified in the ecological inventories.

Ecological assessment and subsequent instruction and curriculum do not follow the traditional educational approaches organized along academic sequences such as writing, reading, and math. Instead, the focus is on the basic demands of adult life such as employment, leisure, and community participation (Rusch and Chadsey-Rusch 1985). The curriculum is divided into "domains." Ecological and student inventories are most commonly used with students requiring a life management curriculum.

Brown et al. (1980) suggest organizing assessment and corresponding curricula for severely handicapped students into five nonmutually exclusive curricular domains.

1. The domestic domain—homes, group homes, boarding homes.
2. The vocational domain—job or livelihood preparation.
3. The recreational/leisure domain—skills for broader enjoyment and participation.

4. The general-community-functioning domain—public transportation, shopping, restaurants, public facilities, hospitals, agencies.
5. The interaction-with-nonhandicapped-persons domain—mainstreaming, increased experience, and interaction.

Ecological Inventories. The goal of ecological inventories is to reduce the discrepancies between skill sequences persons without disabilities perform in normal life environments and those people with disabilities perform. Falvey (1986) enumerates the steps for conducting ecological inventories and student repertoire inventories—both necessary to achieve this goal. "Items are identified from an extensive inventory of the skills performed by nonhandicapped age peers in a variety of community environments (ecological inventories). The student is assessed in terms of performance of those skills identified (student repertoire inventories)" (Falvey 1986, 21). The steps for conducting ecological inventories are:

     a. Dividing the curriculum into the following curricular domains: domestic, vocational, recreation, and community [and perhaps an interaction with nonhandicapped persons domain];
     b. Delineating the environments within each domain that are available to nonhandicapped age peers;
     c. Delineating the subenvironments within each environment;
     d. Delineating the activities that occur within each subenvironment; and
     e. Delineating the specific skills required or expected in order to participate in each activity.

Figure 2.1 is an example of an ecological inventory completed within a hospital coffee shop (Falvey 1986, 23).

Student Repertoire Inventories. Figure 2.2 is an example of a student repertoire inventory. It was conducted for a student in the same coffee shop at the work place where the ecological inventory was made. The steps for conducting student repertoire inventories are:

a. Delineating the skills performed by nonhandicapped age peers for a given activity (i.e., the previously listed step e of the ecological inventory);
b. Observing and recording whether the student is able to perform the skills performed by nonhandicapped age peers for a given activity.
c. Conducting a discrepancy analysis of the student's against his or her nonhandicapped peers' performance. Specifically, if a student is unable to perform a skill, educators would observe and analyze the characteristics of that skill (e.g., natural cues and correction procedures, materials, performance criteria). A determination is then made of the specific aspect(s) of the skill with which the student had difficulty. For example, a student may be able to perform the motor components of crossing the street. That stu-

Figure 2.1   Sample abbreviated ecological inventory.

Domain: Community
Environment: Torrance Hospital
Subenvironment: Coffe shop

Activity: Locating a seat
   Skills: Enter doorway
         Scan area for empty table/chair
         Go to empty table/chair
         Sit down in empty chair

Activity: Looking at menu
   Skills: Scan selections
         Determine desired food and beverage
         Replace menu in menu holder

Activity: Ordering desired food and beverage
   Skills: State or point of choice
         Answer waitress/waiter's questions
         Wait for order

Source: Falvey 1986, 22.

dent presumably is unable to respond to the natural cues provided in that environment. Specific knowledge of this inability provides educators with critical information concerning what and how the student will be taught.

d. Utilizing one of the following three options (if the student is unable to perform any of the skills): Teach the student to perform the skill; or develop an adaptation that the student can use to assist in the performance of the skill; then teach the student to perform the skill utilizing the adaptation; or teach the student to perform a different but related skill. (Adapted from Falvey 1986, 22–23.)

Once teachers have developed specific information about a student's skill repertoire, the assessment process continues. Teachers create an assessment plan using the inventories and any other relevant information. For example, as soon as a discrepancy is identified, teachers move to assess the details of that discrepancy. They also need to detail specific aspects of the skill that troubled the student.

Briefly, developing and implementing an assessment plan involves determining the most appropriate and relevant instruments and procedures for assessing individual skill repertoires, learning strengths and styles, and concept development. Falvey (1986) covers this in depth.

When looking at discrepancies and planning to assess them in more detail, certain considerations are significant:

Figure 2.2 Sample student repertoire inventory.

Student: Kraig Rosenburg
Date: 8/23

Domain: Community
Environment: Torrace Hospital

Subenvironment: Coffee Shop
Teacher: Shellie Coots

Nonhandicapped person inventory	Student inventory	Discrepancy analysis	What-to-do options
Activity: Locating a seat			
Skills: Enter doorway	+		
Scan area for empty table/chair	−	No strategy for scanning	Teach scanning skills
Go to empty table/chair	−	Result of no scanning strategy	Teach scanning skills
Sit down in empty chair	+		
Activity: Looking at menu			
Skills: Scan selections	−	No strategy for scanning	Teach scanning skills
Determine desired food and beverage	−	Not able to read	Develop pictorial menu
Replace menu in menu holder	+		and teach
Activity: Ordering desired food and beverage			
Skills: State or point to choice	−	Unable to communicate	Develop and teach an alternative communicative system
Answer waitress/waiter's questions	−	Unable to communicate	Develop and teach an alternative communicative system
Wait for order	+		

Code: + = correct response; − = incorrect response.

Source: Falvey 1986, 23.

53

1. The age-appropriateness of the materials,
2. The naturalness of the environment and context in which skill is assessed,
3. The provision of necessary adaptations such as large print material,
4. The student's culture and native language.

It is also essential for the teacher to develop effective data-collection procedures. These cover student performance and are ways of measuring if student is making progress in learning the skill or activity and is reducing the discrepancy.

Link to Curriculum and Instruction. After carrying out an assessment plan, the teacher does a summary to indicate areas for instruction. According to Falvey, summaries should include three categories of information. The first is *result of the assessments* written as lists of the actual skills and activities assessed and the student's ability to perform those skills and activities. Life management curriculum content and instructional strategies are the outcome this type of assessment seeks to produce. The second is the *observation and determination of learning strengths and weaknesses.* This, for example, would include increased student response when pictorial rather than verbal directions are given. Such observations can guide effective teaching strategies. The third category of information is the *student's entry-level skill repertoire,* or the abilities and inabilities within each activity with attention to use of what natural cues and other skills need to be taught. The process of moving from assessment to instruction is continuous, particularly with students who are at high risk for learning to participate partially or fully in their natural environments.

Instructional strategies that accompany inventory assessments include finding effective reinforcement choices to motivate the student and using reinforcement procedures. Reinforcement strategies are generally used with natural consequences in various real-life environments particularly salient to the student. A good example would be the everyday act of smiling and saying, "Hi." The positive natural consequence would be a greeting and smile in return. The teacher also develops specialized instructional strategies to teach new behaviors and decrease undesirable behaviors. The best teachers also place particular emphasis on finding and using approaches that result in maintaining what the student has learned and generalizing that learning to a variety of circumstances.

Curriculum-Based Assessment

Curriculum-based assessment (CBA) directly links assessment, instruction, and curriculum. "*Curriculum-based assessment* (CBA) is a new term for an assessment and teaching practice that is as old as education itself: using the material to be learned as the basis for assessing the degree to which it has been learned" (Tucker 1985, 199). This is in place of using standardized tests. CBA was originally defined as "a procedure for determining the instructional needs of a student based upon the student's ongoing performance within existing course content (Gickling and Havertape 1981, CBA R4)." Another definition says that "curriculum-based assessment properly includes any procedure that directly assesses student performance within the course content for the purpose of determining that student's instructional needs (Gickling and Havertape 1981). Thus, curriculum-based assessment—whatever form it takes—provides a direct way of linking assessment to curriculum and instruction.

Given the expected outcomes of a board-adopted regular education curriculum, or course of study, CBA measures each student's achievement within this course of study. To do this kind of evaluation requires a course of study that is specified, measureable, and supported by a system of ongoing assessment of student progress in terms of expected outcomes. The availability of a printed curriculum with clearly identified materials and student assignments is imperative to this assessment approach. Curriculum-based assessment measures the direct effects of daily or frequent task-related activities. Traditional assessment has relied more on long-term test scores (Gickling and Thompson 1985). The focus of CBA is twofold: (1) to establish a task-by-task success format for instructional success (Gickling and Havertape 1981) and (2) to measure the performance of students for acceptance into special education and throughout their involvement in the special education program.

Curriculum-based assessment focuses equally on assessment and instruction. The overall emphasis is on how to collect, interpret, and apply data to monitor student achievement frequently and then use this information to form effective instructional decisions. A locally adopted regular education course of study, or curriculum, is the constant standard against which measurements are taken and instruction is directed. Teachers take diagnostic clues about a student's strengths and problems from the child's response to the curriculum as studied rather than from standardized tests.

A model of special education developed and described by Germann and Tindal (1985) based on initial work of Deno and Mirkin (1977) illustrates ways to apply CBA. This model zeroes in on the discrepancies between the student's performance and specific environmental demands in academic, social, communication, physical, independent living, mainstream and vocational tasks. The goal of this approach is to plan, implement, evaluate, and adjust programs to reduce discrepancies so that students are no longer dysfunctional due to these gaps in knowledge or performance.

Once specified areas of difficulty with the school curriculum and environment have been described as part of a referral process for a particular student, assessment verifies the nature and intensity of the problem (Germann and Tindal 1985). The process is started by providing actual performances and discrepancies.

Academic Discrepancies. Within the academically oriented curriculum, assessment consists primarily of determining the child's current level of proficiency on academic components of the curriculum and then comparing his or her skills to those of classmates. Expected levels of performance are synonymous with "district norms for both progress (through the curriculum) and/or performance (within the curriculum) in the areas of reading, math, spelling, and written expression" (Germann and Tindal 1985, 246).

This extract shows one such index to a skill proficiency:

> Reading. The measures in reading involves the student reading aloud for 1 minute from passages (randomly selected or in succession) from the basal curriculum and/or reading aloud for 1 minute from a list of vocabulary words selected at random from the basal curriculum. A count is made of the number of words read correctly and incorrectly (Germann and Tindal 1985, 246).

Any discovered discrepancies between the student's performance and students in regular education serve two basic purposes. First they represent a criteria set by particular districts for admittance to special education, and so they function as a screening device. Second, they indicate how much change is needed in order to approach peer performance levels, with the understanding that, of course, peer performances are also improving during the same time as the special education student's performance is improving. This is an essential factor when interpreting the discrepancy.

Behavioral Discrepancies. To determine the child's current level of proficiency in the area of social behaviors, the teacher investigates where and how the child presents a problem: for example, creating excessive noise, being frequently off task, often in negative physical contact in regular class or elsewhere (Germann and Tindal 1985, 245). It helps to compare the student's behavior to that of classmates and to collect data defining the functioning level of the child's peers on these social behaviors in school or elsewhere. The teacher can establish expected performance standards by directly observing peers in the same situations and documenting any discrepancies between that observation and the special education student's behaviors.

In order to observe students considered to have behavior problems and their peers to collect data, observers first must know what behaviors they are observing and measuring. Problems with social behavior are difficult to define and operationalize in order to measure them. Identity of *social behavior problems* is described as "a statement of the actual behavior, the environmental demands and expectations, and the discrepancy that exists between the two. The problem is not something the child has; rather, it is something the child does or does not do that is discrepant from expectations" (Germann and Tindal 1985, 258).

Four kinds of behavior problems that a teacher can readily observe and help the student work on are: distracting noise, out-of-place movements, unacceptable physical contact, and off-task behavior (Germann and Tindal 1985). These represent departures from the expectations most regular education students meet.

Noise. Any sounds created by the child that distract either another student or the teacher from the current work/activity. The noise may be generated vocally (including "talk outs" or unintelligible sounds) or nonvocally ("tapping a pencil" or "snapping fingers").

Out of place. Any movement beyond either the explicitly or implicitly defined borders in which the child is allowed movement. If a child is seated at a desk, then movement of any sort out of the seat is "out of place."

Physical contact. Any contact with another person or that person's property that is unacceptable to that person. Kicking, hitting, pushing, tearing, breaking, and taking are categorized as physical contact or destruction.

Off task. Any movement off of a prescribed activity that does not fall into one of the three previously defined categories. "Looking around," "staring into space," "doodling," or any observable movement off the current task/activity at hand is included (Germann and Tindal 1985, 259).

Another category of problem behavior is the lack of appropriate social behavior. This can manifest in such behaviors as withdrawal and social isolation. Inappropriate social behaviors also require remedial attention.

Link to Curriculum and Instruction. Deno and Fuchs (1987) note that in the CBA approach, assessment centers on problems that led the student to special education referral. Student progress in the curriculum of the local school is the source of measurement. Instructional-level manipulation and other interventions are direct outcomes of curriculum-based assessment data and subsequent problem solving. Data is collected to provide evidence on whether or not the chosen solutions appear to be effective, thus giving credence to the chosen solution or suggested revision.

Research indicates that task-oriented success on a day-to-day basis is related to academic achievement. Interventions, therefore, include selecting levels of difficulty in curriculum materials, keeping in mind the goal of continually reducing the performance discrepancies between the special education student and regular students. Goals and procedures for measuring progress on the specific goals are directed at the rate the identified discrepancy between actual and desired behavior is to be reduced. The teaching strategies for meeting the goals and objectives are treated as hypotheses that will be tried, or operationalized, in efforts to reduce identified discrepancies. The goals and objectives relate to curriculum-based stimulus materials. The goals, objectives, and measurements relate to local norms. The focus of data collection processes are on "functional discrepancies, as opposed to the more traditional process of identifying 'test' discrepancies unrelated to the referring problem, expectations, and school environment (curriculum)" (Germann and Tindal 1985, 246).

The key determinant in CBA is the *rate* of attaining the objectives through meeting very specific mastery criteria. Program effectiveness is determined by a student's progress documented as trends toward estimated progress, or performance. Graphs are typically used to display ongoing assessment information and to record progress in reducing discrepancies on curriculum-based tasks. "The rate at which goals are achieved determines whether or not alterations or adjustments in the student's program must be made" (Germann and Tindal 1985, 246). Germann and Tindal (1985) is a good resource for the processes of determining, describing, and comparing discrepancies.

By taking time samples and graphing programs, teachers can see if progress is occurring. The challenge becomes one of changing to or maintaining a program that results in desired progress. Decisions to change a program rest on a set of predetermined decision rules. One decision rule relates to *rate* (change the instructional strategy to move the student forward as rapidly as possible from the rate at which he or she is currently progressing). Decisions such as the *timing* (change program when student performance falls below a certain point for a certain length of time) becomes a focus of program evaluation. *Content* of program modifications (start with simple program and systematically embellish it) becomes another.

The curriculum of the local school is the source of assessment stimulus materials rather than items from other sources including those created by commercial test developers. Regular education curriculum and regular education student performance in that curriculum are used as an index. Regular education curriculum thus becomes the common standard against which student performance is tracked for decision-making purposes (Deno and Fuchs 1987).

Assessment Concerns and Goals

It is important to pursue the challenge of finding effective assessment strategies for educational planning. Rotatori, Fox, Sexton, and Miller (1988) describe the procedures and concerns of most assessment approaches used with special education students. Tindal and Marston (1986) provide a comprehensive analysis of issues surrounding the assessment of special education students. They conclude that problems and inconsistencies in psychoeducational assessments and decision-making practices are frequent, and they propose "rather than obtaining a view of student functioning at one point in time (and in one environment) through the use of a diverse array of procedures and instruments, the focus of assessment should be on documented student functioning in several diverse environments over time, utilizing a consistent measurement procedure" (Tindal and Marston 1986, 58). They encourage efforts to find systems for providing "an empirical basis for developing and evaluating educational programs" (p. 79).

Because curriculum design and modification is one of the primary responsibilities of special education professionals, what happens day to day in the education of their students can only be effective when teachers use appropriate concern and skill in planning what should happen over the years in their educations. This planning has to be based on the best assessment information available.

Summary and Conclusion

The ability to choose appropriate curriculum depends on knowing what questions to ask, performing the appropriate assessments to gain that information, and linking assessment results to specific curricular goals and objectives. The IEP forms the basis of the student's special education curriculum and learning experience. The IEP ties information about each student's present level of performance with curriculum objectives for the student's achievement in areas of suspected school problems. In addition, it describes the special education and related services the student will receive. Preparing for and formulating the IEP requires a collaborative effort in which special education teachers play a major role.

Students with disabilities can be assessed using different assessment measures adapted to their needs by means of different access strategies: modifications in student response methods, modifications in instructional modalities, and uses of special conditions. Additional special considerations in assessing these students include the possibilities of misinterpretation after modification, assessment bias, limited hearing and visual acuity and use, unreliable responses, and student ignorance of test conventions.

Five categories of formal assessment can aid in determining and monitoring student curriculum and instruction: standardized measures, criterion-referenced measures, proficiency assessments, curriculum-based assessments, and ecological and student repertoire inventories. The approach selected depends on the question being asked—the reason for the assessment. Questions about a student's academic achievement may be addressed through one combination of assessment approaches, and questions about student involvement in life management curriculum can be addressed using one or more different approaches.

This chapter emphasized the roles and considerations involved in assessing actual or suspected school performance problems related to student disabilities. Assessment information guides a teacher's choice of new or modified curriculum and instruction. Appropriate assessments, intelligently interpreted, provide the basis for a sound and powerful curriculum.

Notes

1. The section of information on IEPs is adapted from and used with permission: Michigan State Board of Education (1984), *A Resource Guide to Developing Annual Goals, Short-term Instructional Objectives and Performance Objectives,* pp. 9, 13, 14 complete; segments from pp. 1, 3, 5, 10, 15.
2. Math competency examples are adapted from the work of Susan Boyd, teacher.

References

Bateman, B. D. 1971. *Essentials of teaching.* San Rafael, Calif.: Dimensions.

Batschke, G. 1986a. Assessment issues: Non-biased assessment. *Counterpoint,* 6(3): 18. (Publication of portion of an address to School Service Personnel Internship Program, Hammit School, Normal, Ill., Nov., 1985.)

Batschke, G. 1986b. *Non-biased assessment: An implementation manual for school personnel.* Springfield, Ill.: Illinois State Board of Education.

Bennett, R. E., and Ragosta, M. 1984. *A research context for studying admissions tests and handicapped populations* (Research Report No. 84-31). Princeton, N.J.: Educational Testing Service.

Bennett, R. E., Ragosta, M., and Stricker, L. J. 1984. *The test performance of handicapped people.* Princeton, N.J.: Educational Testing Service.

Brigance, A. H. 1987. *Diagnostic inventories.* North Billerica, Mass.: Curriculum Associates, Inc.

Brown, L., Falvey, M., Vincent, L., and Kaye, N. 1980. Strategies for generating comprehensive, longitudinal, and chronological-age appropriate individualized education programs for adolescent and young-adult severely handicapped students. *Journal of Special Education* 14(2): 199–215.

California State Department of Education. 1978. Developing proficiency standards for pupils in special education programs. Sacramento, Calif.: Department of Education.

Compton, C. 1984. *A guide to 75 tests for special education.* Belmont, Calif.: Fearon Education, a Division of Pitman Learning, Inc.

Deno, S. 1985. Curriculum-based measurement: The emerging alternative. *Exceptional Children,* 52(3): 219–32.

Deno, S. L., and Fuchs, L. 1987. Developing curriculum-based measurement systems for data-based special education problem solving. *Focus on Exceptional Children* 19(8): 1–16.

Deno, S., and Mirkin, P. 1977. *Data-based program modification: A manual.* Minneapolis, Minn.: University of Minnesota, Leadership Training Institute in Special Education.

Deno, S., Mirkin, P., Lowry, L., and Kuehne, K. 1980. *Relationships among simple measures of spelling and performing on standardized achievement tests: Research Report No. 21.* Minneapolis, Minn.: University of Minnesota Institute for Research on Learning Disabilities. (ERIC Document No. ED197, 508.)

Falvey, M. 1986. *Community-based curriculum: Instructional strategies for students with severe handicaps.* Baltimore, Md.: Paul Brookes.

Falvey, M., Brown, L., Lyon, S., Baumgart, D., and Shroeder, J. 1980. Curricular strategies for teaching severely handicapped students to acquire and perform chronological age appropriate functional skills in response to naturally occurring cues and correction procedures. In *Instructional design for the severely handicapped,* edited by W. Sailor, B. Wilcox, and L. Brown. Baltimore, Md.: Paul Brookes.

Germann, G., and Tindal, G. 1985. An application of curriculum-based assessment: The use of direct and repeated measurement. *Exceptional Children,* 52(3): 244–65.

Gickling, E., and Thompson, W. 1985. A personal view of curriculum-based assessment. *Exceptional Children,* 52(3): 205–18.

Gickling, E. E., and Havertape, J. 1981. *Curriculum-based assessment (A training module).* Minneapolis, Minn.: National School Psychology, Inservice Training Network, University of Minnesota.

Gronlund, N. 1985. *Measurement and evaluation in teaching.* 5th ed. New York: Macmillan Publishing Co., pp. 2–23.

Gronlund, N. 1982. *Constructing achievement tests.* 3d ed. Engelwood Cliffs, N.J.: Prentice-Hall.

Guerin, G., and Maier, A. 1983. *Informal assessment in education.* Palo Alto, Calif.: Mayfield Publishing Co.

Lyon, S., and Lyon, G. 1980. Team functioning and staff development: A role release approach to providing integrated educational services for socially handicapped students. *Journal of the Association for the Severely Handicapped* 5(3): 250–63.

Mager, R. F. 1975. *Preparing instructional objectives.* 2d ed. Belmont, Calif.: Fearon.

McCormick, L., and Shane, H. 1984. Augmentative communication. In *Early language intervention,* edited by L. McCormick and R. L. Schiefelbusch. Columbus, Ohio: Charles E. Merrill, pp. 325–56.

McLoughlin, J. A., and Lewis, R. 1981. *Assessing special students.* Columbus, Ohio: Charles E. Merrill.

McLoughlin, J. A., and Lewis, R. 1986. *Assessing special students.* 2d ed. Columbus, Ohio: Charles E. Merrill.

Michigan State Board of Education. 1984. *Resource guide to developing annual goals, short-term instructional objectives and performance objectives.* Lansing, Michigan: Michigan State Board of Education.

Ragosta, M., and Kaplan, B. A. 1986. *A survey of handicapped students taking special test administrations of the SAT and GRE.* Princeton, N.J.: Educational Testing Service.

Roberts, W. K. 1982. Preparing instructional objectives: Usefulness revisited. *Educational Technology* 22(7): 15–19.

Rotatori, A. F., and Fox, R. A. In press. Comprehensive assessment in special education. Mountain View, Calif.: Mayfield Publishing Co.

Rusch, F. R., and Chadsey-Rusch, J. 1985. Employment for persons with severe handicaps: Curriculum development and coordination of services. *Focus on Exceptional Children,* 17(9): 1–8.

Ruder, K. F., Bunce, B. H., and Ruder, C. 1984. Language intervention in a preschool/classroom setting. In *Early Language Intervention,* edited by L. McCormick and R. L. Schiefelbusch. Columbus, Ohio: Charles E. Merrill, pp. 267–98.

Sailor, W., Wilcox, B., and Brown, L. 1980. *Methods of instruction for severely handicapped students.* Baltimore, Md.: Paul Brookes.

Salvia, J., and Ysseldyke, J. 1985. *Assessment in special and remedial education.* 3d ed. Boston, Mass.: Houghton Mifflin Company.

Taylor, R. 1985. Measuring adaptive behavior: Issues and instruments. *Focus on Exceptional Children* 18(2): 1–8.

Tindal, G., and Marston, D. 1986. Approaches to assessment. In *Psychological and educational perspectives on learning disabilities,* edited by J. K. Torgesen and B. Y. L. Wong. Boston: Academic Press, pp. 55–84.

Tucker, J. 1985. Curriculum-based assessment: An introduction. *Exceptional Children,* 52(3): 199–204.

Varnhagen, S., and Gerbe, M. 1984. Use of microcomputers for spelling assessment: Reasons to be cautious. *Learning Disability Quarterly* 7(3): 266–70.

Wilcox, B. 1986. Still struggling with assessment. *TASH Newsletter* 12(6): 2–3.

CHAPTER

3

Modifying Student Response Methods

Special education teachers find themselves dealing with questions about *student response and performance methods*. How do teachers anticipate a student's need for response modifications? What are some considerations for selecting modified response and performance methods? What adaptations and alternatives to the usual response and performance methods can students with disabilities or impairments use?

To gain access to the curriculum, students must become involved in the same kinds of curriculum activities regular education students do. Special education students must be able to take in information and respond or perform curricular learning activities. Curriculum access is a major goal whether student education takes place primarily within identical and parallel curriculum components, practical academic curriculum components, or life management components. For any curricular activities, increasing the quality and amount of student participation is a baseline goal.

A teacher can conceive of an impairment or disability as adversely affecting educational performance so that specialized instruction is needed to *counteract* any negative effects. A more fruitful way of viewing the situation is to see the same specialized instruction as finding and teaching modifications that enable the student to participate as fully as possible in curriculum. The teacher is thus not helping the student compensate but rather reach her highest level of functioning.

In most regular-education curriculum components, teaching-learning activities and even the student's performance methods are guided by the curriculum content, instructions to teachers in the curriculum guides, teacher manuals, and subject textbooks. But teachers retain the prerogative for making changes, and teachers can carefully select alternatives that help students gain access to the curriculum.

Traditionally teachers adapt the present curriculum to the needs of their special students, but this can lead to a piecemeal curriculum with gaps in the student's skills and understanding. This text emphasizes addressing not only immediate student response and needs but also a continuum of related *future* situations that may also require modifications to the usual access. Information about long-term needs can positively influence two basic decisions: (1) choice of method to meet immediate and anticipated needs while studying different subjects and (2) identification of what response or performance methods individual students need to learn. For example, students might need modifications for *responding* in academic tasks such as writing lessons, telling ideas, taking quizzes and in *performing* other curricular activities such as building models in social studies, using science equipment, and traveling around the community. Both modifications for responding and for performing tasks in curriculum activities are referred to as response methods.

The following list includes the skills and steps needed to help special education students gain the best possible access to the curriculum:

1. Identifying the usual student response and performance methods the curriculum requires.
2. Listing present response methods and delineating likely student needs for modification.
3. Making considerations relevant to choosing modified response and performance methods.
4. Reviewing possible adapted student response and performance methods.
5. Surveying alternatives to the usual student response and performance methods.

Identifying the Usual Response and Performance Methods

Despite what seems a vast array of subjects, certain skills one can look at are basic to learning and participating in educational activities. To detail what these are, the best approach is to seek out curriculum guides, teachers' manuals, instructional materials, and note the most commonly required or recommended activities. (Try using small gummed slips of paper called 3M Post-it notes.) Write one activity on each, such as seeing, pointing, telling, listening, making marks. Later the slips can easily be grouped and reworded for tighter organization. At this point, no organization is necessary; just record in a few words the activities most commonly asked for from students. Let's look at how to do this culling of essential activities within several curricula: a preacademic course of study, an academic course of study with sample subject areas such as reading, language, math, science, social science, and vocational-technical, and an extracurricular activities area.

Preacademic Discipline and Response Methods

The preacademic discipline is difficult to define in terms of separate subjects. Generally the preacademic curriculum includes the areas of *language arts,* both *oral and receptive language, reading readiness, beginning mathematics, art, music, science,* and *motor activities,* including overall mobility and manipulative activities. Developing such abilities as perceptual and cognitive awareness skills, discrimination, memory, figure-ground discrimination, and sequencing ability are also common parts of the preacademic curricula as well. Students use auditory, visual, tactile-kinesthetic, smell, and taste modalities to learn different awarenesses, figure-ground discriminations, sequencing, and memory skills.

The following list represents some of the most common preacademic activities found in *kindergarten* curriculum guides. Though not exhaustive, it does begin to give teachers a sense of what similar-age students do at this level. It helps to think of student response needs as the ways in which students express their ideas, show what they know, study new skills, and participate in preacademic, or early childhood, learning activities. From notes about commonly required or recommended activities, some similarities may emerge. Grouping the activities into similar or duplicate student response activities is one way to start the synthesizing process. Such a grouping might look like this.

Color—within lines.

Mark—the picture that's different.
Show—pictures that _____ , or point to the _____ .

Point—to the symbol that goes with each picture.

Tell—about oneself, about things brought to school, and answers to questions.

Play—with toys and other materials.
Cut—for example, pictures of objects and shapes.
Manipulate—puzzle parts, toys, clothing.
Prepare—materials for work.

Listen to—environmental sounds, reading aloud, stories, songs, tapes.

Use different response methods appropriate in different settings.

Students perform certain activities regularly to prepare for, participate in, and get benefits from lessons and other learning situations in the preacademic discipline. These are the customary methods students use to interact with or react to learning situations. Though these are the customary methods, they are not the only possible or desirable ones.

The preliminary challenge for the special education teacher, before considering modifications is to identify the customary student response methods or access activities. From such an analysis, teachers can plan needed and helpful interventions. Paying particular attention to student responses, teachers can identify which activities, if any, might present problems to students with handicaps. For example, a teacher who realizes that cutting paper is an often-requested activity can come up with a helpful modification for a student who is blind, such as glueing yarn along the cutting line as a guide. Ultimately teachers are challenged to become well versed in a wide variety of possible modifications. Then the teacher can draw from these to accommodate particular students in the early childhood curriculum.

Academic Disciplines and Response Methods

The academic discipline generally includes reading, language (written and spoken), mathematics, science, social science, fine arts, and vocational-technical education. Special education students study the same basics as regular education students do, though some may learn them at a reduced level of complexity or in a functional context.

Reading. Reading is a large heterogeneous subject area that includes reading readiness exercises and learning, word analysis, word-attack skills, and word recognition as well as vocabulary development, comprehension, and literature study. Even functional reading, or the ability to recognize public information signs and simple instructions, is a possible special education subject under the rubric of reading.

Because of its complexity and inclusiveness, reading can be difficult to analyze. The best approach to this diversity is to include as many reading activities as possible in the list rather than to select and exclude any.

Analyzing reading activities shows that some parallel activities in the preacademic discipline. In the following grouping of reading-related activities, those involving *pointing* or *indicating* are placed first because this activity is one of the first young children and students with severe disabilities learn.

Indicates the picture the story described, the picture that shows what happens next.

Tells the phonetic sounds of letters.

Orally tells and interprets what was read silently.
Answers questions verbally about what happened first, second, and last.
Reads aloud so teacher can analyze reading skills and problem areas.
Describes out loud what was read silently.
Answers questions about what happened in a story.
Reads to others for their enjoyment.

Matches printed words to their opposite, same, and so on.

Marks choices—underlines, checks, circles.
Reads story or sentence and writes letters *a, b,* or *c* or numerals *1, 2,* and *3* representing clues to what happened in the story.
Outlines important points, the story line.

Writes answers to comprehension questions.
Reads—literature, recreation, study for data.
Reads—basal readers.
Identifies literary techniques used by authors, for example, the use of metaphor.
Reads at the functional level: street signs, danger signs, simple recipes.
Reads an index.
Reads maps and charts and obtains information from legends or keys.

Listens to others read with comprehension, to teacher reading story, to lessons.

Holds book and turns pages.
Prepares materials for school work and study.
Dramatizes a story or a play.

Language: Written and Spoken.   Individual curricula describe the reading and writing aspects of the curriculum in different ways. To clarify customary student response methods, reading is separated from language skills here. Within the general discipline of language are such specific subjects as spelling, vocabulary, communication, grammar, literature, composition, and debate.

Because the discipline of language includes reading in some districts, the special education teacher should research the local curriculum to identify disciplines and subject areas locally considered part of "the basics." The process outlined here applies within and across disciplines. First the teacher seeks out the basic resource materials—teacher guides, curriculum guides, classroom materials—in the areas of language teaching for the entire school curriculum, either K–6, K–9, or K–12.

Once assembled, survey these materials for representative activities commonly required of students in the area of language teaching. It is fine to collect activities that cross subject matters so long as they are within the discipline of language or language arts. For example, some activities will represent spelling study, some writing reports, others answering questions about a book read aloud in class.

Teachers can then start to group student response skills that are similar. An analysis of activities required of students studying one or another subject within the discipline of language might look something like this:

Points or otherwise gestures to indicate a choice

Traces letters and shapes
Writes spelling
Writes in workbook
Writes ideas
Writes short stories and descriptions
Practices handwriting skills

Asks questions
Makes verbal requests
Answers questions in class
Spells orally in drills and contests

Uses dictionary and other books
Reads language-arts books; exercises on dittos, in workbook, on blackboard, literature texts

Visits libraries

Uses oral language in a variety of situations and with a variety of people

Mathematics.   The discipline of mathematics ranges from simple counting and recognition of counting behavior to numeration, computing, algebra, geometry, trigonometry, and calculus. The activities below, culled from curriculum courses and classroom resources on mathematics, are organized by primary response methods:

Indicates—which is the named number, which pile contains the most, and so on.

Looks at—the piles of counters, the numbers on the board, the pictures in the workbook.

Answers—the teacher's questions of how many.
Tells—how one finds the answer, how many there are.
Asks—for help solving problems.

Reads—problems in text.
Reads—questions on test.

Fills out—the blanks in the workbook.
Circles—the correct answers.

Writes—the answers to the problems.
Writes—computations and solutions.

Draws—a triangle, square, rectangle, circle.

Reads—problems in workbooks, in textbooks, on blackboards.

Moves—counters into piles of tens.
Manipulates—a compass, ruler, straightedge.
Uses—a calculator, computer, slide rule.
Prepares—materials for work or study.

Listens—to lessons.

Applies mathematical understanding in natural settings—helps do measurements at home, estimates cost of groceries, measures ingredients for a cake.

Science. Activities in the list below characterize those commonly required in the science area whether in specific high school science classes such as biology, chemistry, physics or in the general science curricula of elementary school. It saves time later to group similar activities:

Indicates—identifies visual details.
Points to—correct symbol, object named, mineral.

Observes—chemistry experiment, an animal in its natural environment or in a cage.
Looks at—the defining characteristics of trees, flowers, plants, minerals; color, consistency, changes in character.

Answers—questions asked in class.
Asks—for help with problems, why something is so, the correct procedure.
Tells—the results of a course of study or experiment, what went wrong, how something was approached, what one saw.

Writes—lab reports, answers in workbooks.
Records—notes on experiments, observations, collections, class lectures, field trips.

Draws—pictures of experiments, natural phenomena such as plants, flowers, trees, animals, insects.
Marks—correct answer in workbook.
Colors—pictures of natural phenomena.

Reads—textbook, special subject book, instructions, descriptions of experiments, descriptions of natural phenomena.

Listens—to lectures, other students' reports, teacher's instructions.

Prepares—materials or experiments, textbook, tools for dissecting, parts of a plant collected.
Collects—rocks, flowers, common minerals, seeds.
Uses—microscope, magnifying glass, watering can, fish or butterfly net, bunsen burner.
Manipulates—specimens, plants, animals, parts of experiment, study tools, equipment.
Performs—experiments.

Social Sciences. The social sciences form part of the curriculum in elementary schools. They prepare students for full citizenship. Several subjects are included in the general social science discipline: geography, state history, United States history, world history, environmental studies, government.

Below is a grouped listing of common activities within the general discipline of the social sciences:

Finds and indicates—intersections of latitude and longitude, mountain ranges, lakes, rivers, seas, cities, countries.
Watches—movies, live presentations.
Looks at—models of a Greek city, a river system, a mountain range, the U.S. Senate building, famous cathedrals, Chinese junks.

Comments—in class discussions.
Asks—questions, for directions and clarification, why something occurred when it did.
Tells—observations, ideas about history, thoughts.
Answers—teacher's questions, another student's point or question.

Writes—reports, papers, book reports, analyses of lectures or ideas expressed in class.
Records—notes on lectures, answers to questions, test responses.

Draws—maps, graphs, time lines, charts.

Reads—textbooks, outside reading for reports, encyclopedias.
Reads—newspapers, magazines at home.

Listens—to teacher, guest lecturers, recordings, conversations in and out of school on relevant issues.

Creates—models, relief maps, other three-dimensional replicas.
Prepares for—research, study, schoolwork.
Collects—materials for class study and discussion, articles on a particular subject, samples, or examples.

Uses newly learned skills in natural settings.

Fine Arts. The fine arts curricula are broad and varied, including such subject areas as music, art, and drama from the perspectives of audience appreciation and performance as well as painting, sculpture, architecture, music appreciation, art appreciation, ceramics, and the performance of music and drama. A listing of representative fine arts activities includes the following:

Indicates—favorite parts, a called-for example, where to place something.

Looks at—paintings, sculptures, drawings, art books, librettos.

Tells—impressions, interpretations, likes, dislikes, ideas, analyses.
Expresses—feelings, responses, questions.
Tells answers to questions.

Draws—pictures, sketches for scenery.

Writes short answers.
Writes—reports, notes on field trips, book reviews, plays, stories.

Reads—plays, books on art, musical scores, articles about fine arts, signs in museum displays, words to songs.

Listens—to docent talks, lectures, teacher's lessons on perspective drawing, musical records, the radio, concerts.

Prepares—materials for drawing or ceramics.
Prepares to perform music activity in class or a performance in orchestra or a play.
Holds instruments, art tools, musical scores.
Performs—with tools, musical instruments, or voice.

Vocational-Technical Education. This discipline area covers a range of possible activities from typing to woodworking, from using computers and other technological equipment to practices of accounting, inventory taking, business communication, and so on. Many subject areas with little in common could fall under this heading, and so activities could range well beyond the following list. This list represents only a sample. A teacher working in vocational-technical education would need to make up a list of activities from available resources grouped under career or vocational-education headings in the local school curriculum.

Indicates—the proper signs, symbols, machines to use in a specific circumstance.

Looks at—instructions, charts of the typewriter, machine diagrams, signs.

Asks—for needed instruction, questions about procedures, personal questions of why or how.

Tells—how something is or was done, areas of confidence or lack of confidence, reports.
Expresses—frustrations, pleasures.
Answers—teacher's questions.
Tells—parts of machine, steps in process.

Writes—notes on procedures, lectures, visiting guest information, field trips; reports and logs of progress.

Colors—reports, maps, charts, machine diagrams.
Marks—activity sheets, answer sheet on tests.

Reads—instructions, recipes, books.

Listens—to teacher's lessons, guest speakers, tape recordings of technical information.

Prepares—materials to work with.
Manipulates—machine parts, books, papers.

Extraacademic Activities.   Though not a discipline as defined earlier in the chapter, this is a part of most schooling. Under this heading are such extracurricular activities as social clubs, sports, and tournaments. Because these activities are often important to students, they can serve best to motivate them. An astute teacher can then channel this motivated energy into concentrated learning for the students. In this way, the extraacademic areas can have a positive carry-over to the academic disciplines, and they merit teacher consideration. Below are some of the many activities that might come under the heading of extraacademic activities:

Indicates—where to go, the correct direction, the play to be used, the score.

Looks at a physical setup—a social gathering, a gameboard, a playing field.
Looks at—directions, markers, scoreboards.

Tells—the rules, the score, how to play, the plans for the meeting.
Asks—for help, for directions, where something is located, why something is done a particular way, where to find something.
Answers—questions from friends, teachers, others.

Writes—on forms or scorepads; takes notes on how to play a certain game; takes minutes for a meeting; writes letters to friends, pen pals, former teachers; sends for information, tickets, special equipment.

Reads—game rules, game directions, club bylaws, street signs, ballots, voter registration forms, applications for service such as phone, utility, or mail.

Listens—to conversations, directions, referees, lectures, music.

Manipulates games and equipment.
Moves—physically to play a game, from house to town using public transportation, from home to school meetings.
Prepares for extracurricular activities—buys tickets, takes needed materials, makes reservations.

This completes a review of customary activities in standard disciplines for most school curricula.

Inventory of Present Student Response Methods

As soon as teachers have identified the kinds of responses and performances usually required of students *within disciplines*, they can begin to identify response and performance activities in which students with disabilities might run into difficulties. To do this well requires one more analysis. This next step involves looking for response and performance requirements that are the same or similar *across disciplines*. Then these must be categorized in some way. Note from the material on identifying usual response methods that certain common activities are expected of students. Examples include writing or speaking. Society assumes these abilities, and so they are built into almost all curricular activities.

To transform a welter of curricular activities for many age levels to useful information, teachers can categorize and group similar kinds of student responses and performance methods. Take, for example, an activity cluster crossing disciplines and subject areas that involves *pointing to, indicating, looking at,* and *finding*. All these activities could be classified as "*indicating activities.*" (*Look at* is often assumed rather than identified, but the curriculum depends on this skill.) The activities classified as *indication* call for the student to look at, study, or point to something. This general activity is required of students in many disciplines and at all ages.

Teachers can apply this classifying process to other activity clusters. Figure 3.1, the STRAP inventory, shows one attempt at classifying student response and performance activities and making an inventory of them. Specific activities are listed under each group heading. No single classification is better than any other. Such an inventory list functions to help teachers identify student needs for interventions. Using such an inventory, teachers can discover which activities students can participate in fully and which will present difficulty for the students.

Teachers can use the STRAP inventory in several ways. The first is to antici-

Student: _____

Kinds of Response and Performance Activities:	Date	Status	Comments (Current Methods; Recommendations)
Indicating			
1. Points to, finds, shows, looks at colors, symbols, words, pictures			
Speaking (and Conversing)			
2. Replies yes, no, I don't know, etc.			
3. Names personal needs and wants, people, places, and things in simple words or phrases			
4. Reads aloud			
5. Says short answers and gives other short responses to school-work			
6. Expresses thoughts, questions, feelings, etc. in discussions			
7. Privately expresses thoughts, opinions, requests, and feelings			
8. Makes formal presentations, reports, debates			
Handwriting			
9. Draws			
10. Colors			
11. Paints			
12. Marks choices			
13. Draws indicator lines to connect, to underline, etc.			
14. Writes short exercises: answers, stories, reports, note taking			
15. Writes long exercises: formal reports, compositions, letters			
16. Writes numerals, math problems, calculations, and answers			
Performing/Environmental Control			
17. Holds things			
18. Manipulates instructional aids, tools, toys, supplies, lab equipment, on-the-job tasks, computer, etc.			
19. Maneuvers self: moves self to where supposed to be			
20. Maneuvers things: carry, push, lift, turn, use tools/items/utensils			
21. Operates machinery, equipment, appliances in environments			

Status: 4 = present method satisfactory; 3 = needs training in present method; 2 = may need modification; 1 = no method used.

Figure 3.1 Student Response and Performance Inventory (STRAP Inventory)

pate the intervention needs for students with particular disabilities or impairments. The second is to screen the student's actual ability to use each response and performance method and so identify specific intervention needs. The third is to build a cumulative record document a variety of professionals working with student over time can use.

Each student is unique and should be considered a special case whenever possible. But it is not always possible for teachers-to-be to observe student attempts to access curriculum while studying the topic. Yet teachers can anticipate access problems students with certain disabilities are likely to face. Teachers can also apply their knowledge of working with students who have specific handicaps and then expand to general conclusions. For example, a teacher might generalize from a particular disability or impairment to how it might negatively affect student response and performance participation in a range of curricular and extracurricular activities.

When impairments might interfere with a student's present or potential participation in curriculum, that student's special education goals and objectives should address the response and performance methods. The kinds of modifications in student response include making adaptations to the *usual method of response* (e.g., writing with a dark pen so visually impaired students can see their own writing) or using *alternative methods* of response (e.g., using a microcomputer instead of handwriting when a disability apparently causes handwriting to be illegible). Sometimes the usual response methods are augmented, using aided-response modes (e.g., use of a wallet-sized letter board augments communication when speech is not always clear). Certain augmentations are considered adaptations to usual response methods; others are considered alternative methods.

For instance, students with severe speech or language impairment most often need alternative methods of *speaking* or else augmented speaking. They may need to aid spoken communication using communication systems or devices (e.g., a letter board to spell out words whenever someone cannot understand their speech). Or they might require a complete alternative method of communicating. If so, systems and devices allowing alternatives to speaking will serve them more efficiently. Students with *visual impairment* frequently need alternative methods of looking, indicating, handwriting, and possibly handling and experiencing. Students who are mentally retarded may benefit by using customary response methods plus alternatives in all the areas of indicating, looking, speaking, handwriting, handling, and experiencing. This approach also holds for students with *movement disorders*, though here the emphasis in modifications is on methods of handling and experiencing. Students with *learning disabilities* involving perceptual problems will need adaptations to, alternative methods of, or special training in the skill areas of looking, handwriting, handling, and experiencing. Students with *behavior disorders* may technically be able to learn and work in certain methods, but other methods might provide them a needed element of reduced stimulation or more motivation. Students with *hearing impairments* may need alternatives or augmentations such as sign language and finger spelling.

Many students will learn better if they can use the usual response methods with augmentations in the educational process. Alternative methods traditionally associated with certain disabilities merit consideration for uses with different disabilities. Be cautious about narrowing the uses of possible alternatives to certain disability groups. For example, the VOIS, a portable speech synthesizer, has traditionally been associated with physically disabled, speech-impaired persons, yet deaf persons who do not have intelligible speech have used it effectively.

When teachers can observe individual students, the STRAP Inventory serves as a screening tool, offering teachers a systematic process for studying student response needs compared to the lesson requirements. A student's status in using the different response and performance methods has to be recorded in some way. Codes such as these can prove helpful in identifying the student's abilities:

4 = Present method is satisfactory.
3 = Needs training in present method (usual or modified).
2 = May need modification.
1 = No method used.

Teachers can use a "comments" column to write other helpful information and identify the current method used. This is essential. Additionally including any information about adaptations and alternatives being considered is helpful. From this inventory of response information, teachers and others can identify student need for intervention and can start processes toward determining what interventions and training the student needs.

The other use of such an inventory, to document student activity from year to year, lends consistency to a student's program. It facilitates transition from one teaching/learning situation to another, and this is particularly important for students with special education needs.

Certain students cannot demonstrate their true abilities if asked to respond and perform in the customary ways. Until students gain facility either in the customary response methods or in some modification, they may not be able to show what they know, are learning, or can do.

Student response or performance methods can include the customary mode, some adaptation or augmentation to it, or an alternative method. It is a challenge to special education and related services personnel to help students who have learning, motor, behavioral, or sensory disabilities reduce the discrepancies between what they know and can do and what they are able to show others they know and can do. The more this kind of discrepancy is reduced, the greater chance special education students have for success.

Considerations for Modifications in Student Response Methods

The special education teacher can take the leadership in determining if students are working with the response or performance methods that benefit them most. Seldom does a teacher make these decisions alone, though. A team collaboration in problem solving and program implementation is desirable. Any altered response methods must be assessed, explored, implemented, given fair trial by the student, and then it must be evaluated and recommended for continuation or reconsideration.

Considerations for selecting student response methods are many. The most important ones are presented here with the caveat that this information provides only an introduction to an area rich with creative and assessment-based possibilities. The able teacher will want to develop an indepth knowledge and experiential background. The most important consideration in making changes in student response relates to situational needs. The teacher needs to ask, In what natural environments, in what kinds of situations, with what other persons, and for what purposes are response methods needed? Other considerations include (1) ease of student use, (2) potential for independent use, (3) ease of understanding by others, (4) speed of transmission of ideas, and (5) anticipated future needs.

Situational Needs

Although this chapter focuses on preparation for working and participating as fully as possible in the school environment, other environments such as those in the home and community also merit consideration. Students will need different response methods depending on different situations. A teacher might even best serve students by teaching more than one response and performance method within any one situation so the student has a backup.

The student's interaction community, including peers, family, and neighbors, all influence the choice of response methods. Cultural influences, for example, can determine how a family feels about certain modifications, such as electronic devices with "computer speech." It helps to at least recognize family preferences. The family can also influence whether a student uses the same response methods at home as at school. A student could be well understood at home yet need a special adaptation to express herself clearly at school. Therefore, the teacher could chose a certain response method for use in specific situations with certain people, and then chose another response method as more appropriate in other environments with other people. The goal is to chose and teach response methods that are the most broadly and effectively useful after considering all the student's needs and circumstances.

Ease and Independent Student Use

The potential for easy and independent use is a bedrock consideration. Competent use and independence or the potential for independence result from careful and intensive training by qualified persons. Students do not wake up one morning knowing how to do cursive writing. Likewise students do not suddenly understand that those pretty spots on their trays are actually pictures representing ideas, and they can use those pictures to communicate what they want. A student with hearing impairments does not wake up knowing how to speak more clearly or to use signs. Learning effective response methods and how to use them well comes as a result of systematic instruction teachers build into the curriculum for students with special needs. Any intensive instruction the student needs to master new response methods comes from special education or related service providers.

Ease of Understanding by Others

Being understood by others is the foundation of all interactions. This is true particularly of interactions with persons who do not know the student intimately as the family does. It seems valid to assume that people are not always sure if and how a handicapped person talks and writes. Because of their own unsureness, nonhandicapped people may shy away from any interactions with a disabled person. This can often happen in regular classes where teachers there primarily want to be reassured that the student has a way of showing what he knows and can do. Regular teachers also want to be sure they understand students. The special education teacher who is aware of this is prepared to help students. The special education teacher needs to consider possible student response methods in terms of how readily the average person can understand them. To be effective, student responses and performances have to be clear enough to be understood by many persons in a variety of situations.

Speed of Transmission

The speed with which ideas can be transmitted is a universal factor to consider for any response method. One standard reference is the time it takes to accomplish a particular task with each different response method compared to the time peers take to accomplish the same or similar tasks. For example, most people can decode spoken English at a rate of two hundred words per minute. Not all students with disabilities will approximate this speed even with adapted responses. Nevertheless it is important to keep working at increasing their output rate so they can become more functional. The same holds true for speech. For some, this may mean increasing the speed of their natural speech from two to four words per minute. The potential for approximating a functional speed of transmitting communications is a definite consideration. Picture or word boards to help student's transmit ideas is one possibility. Another option is to augment natural speech with a microprocessor-based communication aid. Using such a device, different messages of several words each are sent by activating different locations on the unit for each specific message. Speech output (synthetic speech) is increased significantly with these units, and students can transmit many more ideas. Working on the mechanics of making responses in curriculum activities to develop speed is often included among the special education objectives.

Anticipated Future Needs

By looking at a student's long-range education curriculum, the special education teacher may want to start instruction in a method that has only limited immediate usefulness. The value of looking ahead and acting on that vision is that the student will master a response method so that when needed, the new response will be in place. An example would be Benjamin, a first-grader for whom drawing, coloring, and handwriting are severe problems. Yet in later grades Benjamin will be expected to write compositions and reports. Ben's teacher can start teaching him an alternative method for communicating written language in the first grade even though Ben doesn't need to write often yet. He could teach Ben to use a small electric typewriter so that by the time Ben is in third grade, he will have mastered the alternative mode and can participate fully in any assignments and learning that require extensive writing.

Added Considerations

Other considerations for selecting student response methods include the following when they are appropriate to the user and the situations:

1. Portability
2. Availability
3. Durability
4. Reliability
5. Cost

6. Maintenance
7. Replaceable if necessary
7. Speed of setting up
8. Age appropriateness
9. Accuracy of user output
10. Possibility for automonitoring, or self-correcting
11. Functionality and generalizability to a variety of situations and persons.

One final and perhaps most important consideration is the availability of needed training and ongoing instruction in how to use the modification.

Special education personnel can give intensive direct instruction in whatever method the student is already using or learning to use. Or teachers might provide direct instruction and role playing to teach self-advocacy. A sixth-grader had received this kind of attention from a perceptive teacher when she was in the second grade. The teacher helped Julie understand her unique needs with respect to participating in regular classroom activities. Julie, who is visually impaired but not totally blind, can not *tell* her new teachers each year what kinds of changes and adaptations she requires so she can participate fully in the regular classroom activities. She does this by requesting time with the teacher early in the school year. Together they go over the modifications Julie needs. Julie's teachers have been so impressed by her responsible approach to adaptations that they have all been eager to help. As an added benefit, each teacher seems to come up with a few new ideas that further improve Julie's chance for classroom learning and success, and Julie passes these onto each new teacher. Her special education teacher could just have taught Julie the grade two curriculum. Instead he taught her a constellation of communicating skills for dealing with her own special circumstances that will help her throughout her entire life. This insightful teacher understood the parable about the wisdom of teaching a starving man to fish instead of just giving him a fish for dinner.

Adapted Student Response Methods

Making *adaptations* to the customary student response and performance methods means retaining the customary method, such as speaking, writing, or physically manipulating, and then altering it in some way. An adaptation is one choice when a student cannot use the customary method in the customary manner to transmit efficiently what he knows and can do. Adaptations are often simple, inexpensive, and easy to implement. Modifications or adaptations of the customary methods are the appropriate choice in two types of circumstances:

1. When students cannot use the customary response and performance methods at all without adaptations.
2. When students use the customary response and performance methods but are more efficient with an adaptation.

Examples of the first circumstance would be altering pencils, using keyguards for typewriter and computer activities, or adding knobs to puzzle pieces. Such simple adaptations make it possible for students with physical disabilities to participate in classroom activities using the standard methods. Student could use the regular pencils, typewriter or computer keyboards, and puzzle pieces only because of effective adaptations.

Examples of the second circumstance (making adaptations to improve efficiency) would be to encourage certain students with visual impairments to use a dark felt-tip pen instead of a pencil to write math so they can see their own work with greater ease. In other examples, students could use highlight pens to accentuate certain passages for ease of scanning or use a baseball with a beeper so they can track it if they cannot see well. Or a student with a hearing impairment might do well in a regular classroom with a body-type hearing aid to amplify sound. Small adaptations can make a remarkably big difference in how a student with disabilities learns.

Adaptations to Activity Clusters

Indicating is the first student response cluster noted in Figure 3.1. This customarily involves pointing to something with a finger (e.g., point to the word that says _____), finding something with a finger (e.g., find one like this one), or showing something (e.g., on this map, show the route from school to home). Indicating is customarily done with arm, hand, and finger gestures. Adaptations for students who cannot use the customary modes to indicating might include:

POSSIBLE ADAPTATIONS TO INDICATING

1. Ask a teacher to "Please help guide my pencil" when student's movements are too uncoordinated to point alone.
2. Use colored stickers on the fingernail of the pointing finger to cue a child which finger to use in pointing and to focus the child's attention to a pointing activity.

POSSIBLE ADAPTATIONS TO SPEAKING

1. Use an artificial larynx after an laryngectomy.
2. Use an amplifier to augment a weak or quiet voice.

3. Speak in phrases rather than sentences to avoid trouble with breath supply.
4. Use specialized techniques to avoid or reduce problem areas in speech.
5. Augment speech with signing or writing.

POSSIBLE ADAPTATIONS TO HANDWRITING

1. Add grips to pencils.
2. Add weights to pencils to provide kinesthetic feedback from the process of holding a writing utensil and moving it in certain ways on paper.
3. Tape paper to desk to prevent slippage.
4. Used raised-line paper when lines on paper cannot serve as referents.
5. Use a signature guide when student cannot see where to sign papers and documents.
6. Use color codes on paper to cue where to start and stop in writing.

SAMPLE POSSIBLE ADAPTATIONS FOR ENVIRONMENTAL CONTROL

1. Reinforce toys to prevent breakage.
2. Use extension to usual appendages on items to improve access (e.g., use extensions to keys on a tape recorder).
3. Add handles or knobs to pieces for easier manipulation.
4. Use larger and otherwise adapted versions of equipment, games, and learning aids.
5. Use items designed as adaptations for persons with disabilities (e.g., one-handed can openers or specially designed scissors for students with coordination problems).
6. Use sports equipment with adaptations (e.g., beeper balls for students who cannot see)
7. Use additions to clothing that allow wearers to manipulate clothing (e.g., larger buttons or extensions on zipper handles).
8. Use extended handles on keys to locks of house.
9. Use jigs to operate tools, machinery, equipment, and appliances used on a job. (Jigs mechanically maintain the correct positional relationship of a piece of work and the tool or between parts of work during an assembly process.)

Alternative Student Response Methods

Teaching *alternative* student response methods is usually a more radical intervention than adapting customary response methods. Changing the response method entirely can involve a major technological project. But students requiring alternatives commonly do not already use the usual response methods. This means that learning the most appropriate response method is not a matter of relearning; rather it is one of initial learning.

Three teaching-learning circumstances call for alternative student response and performance methods. Alternative methods are used when:

1. Students absolutely cannot use the customary response and performance methods due to a disability.
2. Students spend so much time and/or energy using the customary response methods that it becomes functionally impractical or educationally detrimental to use it.
3. Students can perform in the customary methods, but these are not, for some reason, the best methods for them to do so.

The first circumstance is the most obvious. The child without sight must find some other way than handwriting to respond in school work. The student who cannot use his hands must find an alternative to writing and drawing for communicating and participating in classroom activities. Examples of such alternative methods are when students use gross gestures instead of words, sign instead of speak, use picture boards in place of talking, type instead of writing by hand, or use a microprocessor-based communication aid in place of writing or talking.

An example of the second circumstance would be a student who takes so much time and effort to communicate in speech that others lose interest or patience, and the student becomes too frustrated to keep trying. An alternative solution here would give the student a way to augment her limited speech capacity. For instance, a communication board using graphic symbols representing words and ideas may give her a facility that she lacks with speech. Alternative methods do not always replace the usual methods; they may augment or supplement them.

The third circumstance—when the customary method can be used but it is not the most effective method—arises with students who can speak with partial intelligibility due to severe hearing impairment. In certain situations, they may need to switch to signing through an interpreter in order to express everything they have to say at the appropriate level of sophistication. Another example would be a student with a severe language disorder who is physically able to express some words and ideas but can communicate more complex ideas and answers when he uses another means of "speaking," (e.g., typing information into a computer and using the computer's voice output capabilities).

A unique combination of both adaptations and alternatives to the customary student response methods may be the best solution. Also, if a radical change in the student's method of communicating and participating seems necessary, he will probably require intense instruction when first using the new method to make it practical and workable. These are two important points for the special education teacher to keep in mind.

Sample Alternatives to Indicating

Alternatives for Pointing to, Finding, Showing. If the student cannot physically indicate selections and choices or show paths using customary methods with or without adaptations, then alternatives are needed. A simple alternative to the customary method of indicating with hands is to develop a signaling system (e.g., kicks, eye blinks, claps, switch activation, or other appropriate voluntary movements). Others include:

1. Make one predetermined movement to indicate a choice of answers from a series someone else reads or writes. For example, the teacher may present a problem and possible choices: "Two times four equals, (pause): "three" (pause), "five" (pause), "eight" (pause), or "nine (pause)?" Always give all the choices once so the student knows all available choices. Then repeat them one by one, pausing to allow time for the student to make the predetermined movement after her choice.

2. Make a predetermined movement to indicate choice as someone scans the choices, pointing to each selection and saying, "This one? This one? This one?"

3. Use a switch-controlled remote lamp feature such as that on the Versascan. (The Versascan[1] (Fig. 3.2) is a set of from two to sixteen remote lamps resembling yellow reflectors that illuminate one at a time in conjunction with pressing a single switch. In the instance of object identification, each lamp can be placed beside the object of choice, such as the choice of a toy, food, or utensil; the user then scans to the item of choice, using a control switch to stop on the choice. The lamps can also be placed beside pictures on communication boards or pictures or numerals in concept lessons. Students with and without physical impairment can use the Versascan to indicate their choice of options on tests such as the Peabody Picture Vocabulary Test or Columbia Mental Maturity Scale.

4. Write, draw, or gesture. Hearing-impaired students and others who do not speak use these alternatives to indicate (verbal) choices.

5. Describe, instead of pointing to, persons, places, or things. Students who can talk but cannot see or cannot physically point can use this alternative.

6. Use a light beam. A beam comes from a light-beam pointer attached to a lightweight visor or headband. By moving her head, the wearer can point out symbols, people, places, or things. The light beam can also be used with published communication boards or boards made up for specific students in a particular subject area.

7. Use a mouth or head wand. Students who cannot point with their hands sometimes use a rod extending from a mouthpiece or a rod mounted on a helmet to point, draw, mark, or trace.

Figure 3.2 A control switch illuminates lamps one at a time and students enjoy stopping the light on their choice.

Sample Alternatives for Speaking

The *speaking* cluster (including conversing) is the next educational access cluster of concern for many students with disabilities. The many specific access activities listed under the classification of "speaking" in Figure 3.1 demonstrates how heavily schools rely on this response method for communicating and participating.

Alternatives for Simple Replies. The primary skill under speaking (#2 on Figure 3.1) is the ability to reply yes, no, I don't know, perhaps, maybe. Students who cannot speak or speak unintelligibly or too slowly, must have an alternative method to serve them. Here are some simple ways to convey these basic ideas:

1. Use eyes to signal
   a. Look at printed yes or no
      (1) on arms of wheelchair
      (2) in opposite corners of chalkboard (the further apart they are, the less confusion as to which was signaled)
   b. Use eye-signal system
      (1) eyes held still may mean
         I don't know
         no opinion
         no decision
      (2) eyes up may mean
         yes
         good
         agree
      (3) eyes down may mean
         no
         not good
         disagree
2. Use signing to relay the communications.
3. Use a consistent though unintelligible vocalization to signal the communications.
4. Point to alphabet letters, words, or pictorial symbols to communicate basic replies.

Alternatives for Naming. The second skill area under speaking and conversing (#3) is oral naming: personal needs or wants, people, places, things in simple words or phrases. The following alternatives enable a student to perform this skill without relying on speaking.

1. Handwrite instead of speak the names of people, places, and things.
2. Point to a related picture on a picture board or spell by pointing to alphabet letters (see Fig. 3.3).[2]
3. Finger spell (and speak as much as possible). (See Fig. 4.2, Chapter 4).
4. Carry words and pictures such as Talking Pictures. Talking Pictures[3] is a series of pocket-sized pictures on cards with the appropriate words on the backs. The pictures are put in plastic holders that are bound by a ring and held by a cord. The student who cannot speak carries these around and uses them to name and otherwise communicate by pointing to the pictures that name a need. There are three kits: survival-living needs, community-living needs, and daily-living needs.

Alternatives for Reading Aloud.   The third category under speaking (#4) is reading aloud. Reading aloud is a skill used to determine mastery in several areas. The teacher's goal in having the student read aloud includes (1) decoding ability and (2) comprehension. For the student who cannot speak, the teacher must find other ways of assessing mastery in these areas:

1. Decode three teacher-made sentences that are nearly the same and indicate which one says what the teacher asks for. (The student would use the indicating skills described earlier.)
2. Read a paragraph or story and indicate the one of three to five teacher-written sentences that most clearly summarizes the paragraph or story.

Alternatives for Saying Short Answers.   The fourth category under speaking (#5) is saying short answers and other short responses to schoolwork. This would include briefly telling ideas. Many of the alternatives for the naming skill area will work for this. Here, however, the skill of making short responses in the classroom setting is stressed.

1. Use gestures—to indicate yes, no, I don't know, or more sophisticated communications.
2. Use nods or kicks to demonstrate numbers: for example, the number of a sentence in which a particular grammatical construction occurs, the paragraph that describes an asked about activity. An extension of this technique is for the student to nod when the teacher touches "something that begins with a *d*" or "says words that rhyme with *time*" and so on.
3. Focus eyes on widely placed choice designates.
4. Point to pictures in situation-related notebooks (e.g., food requests in "cafeteria" notebook, different-sized items in language-arts notebook, characteristics of dinosaurs in a social studies notebook, pictures and names of literary characters and symbols for feelings in an English notebook (see Fig. 3.4).[2]
5. Write on paper or tablet carried at all times.

Figure 3.3 Students without intelligible speech can point to graphics, letters, or numerals on general purpose communication boards.

I CAN HEAR PERFECTLY	PLEASE REPEAT AS I TALK (THIS IS HOW I TALK BY SPELLING OUT THE WORDS)	WOULD YOU PLEASE CALL
A AN HE	AM ARE ASK BE BEEN BRING CAN	ABOUT ALL
HER I IT ME	COME COULD DID DO DOES DON'T	AND ALWAYS
MY HIM SHE	DRINK GET GIVE GO HAD HAS HAVE	ALMOST AS
THAT THE THESE	IS KEEP KNOW LET LIKE MAKE MAY	AT BECAUSE
THEY THIS WHOSE	PUT SAY SAID SEE SEEN SEND SHOULD	BUT FOR FROM
WHAT WHEN WHERE	TAKE TELL THINK THOUGHT WANT	HOW IF IN
WHICH WHO WHY	WAS WERE WILL WISH WON'T WOULD -ED	OF ON OR
YOU WE YOUR	-ER -EST -ING -LY -N'T -'S -TION	TO UP WITH

A	B	C	D	E	F	G	AFTER AGAIN
	H		I	J	K	L	M		ANY EVEN
N		O	P		Qu	R	S	T	EVERY HERE
	U		V	W	X	Y	Z		JUST MORE
1		2	3	4	5	6	7	ONLY SO
	8		9	10	11	12	30		SOME SOON
								THERE VERY

SUN. MON. TUES. WED. THUR. FRI. SAT. BATHROOM	PLEASE THANK YOU MR. MRS. MISS MOTHER DAD DOCTOR	GOING OUT START OVER END OF WORD	$¢½(SHHH!!)?

IS MY NAME

PRODUCED BY GHORA KHAN GROTTO 952 WHITE BEAR AVENUE, ST. PAUL, MN. 55106

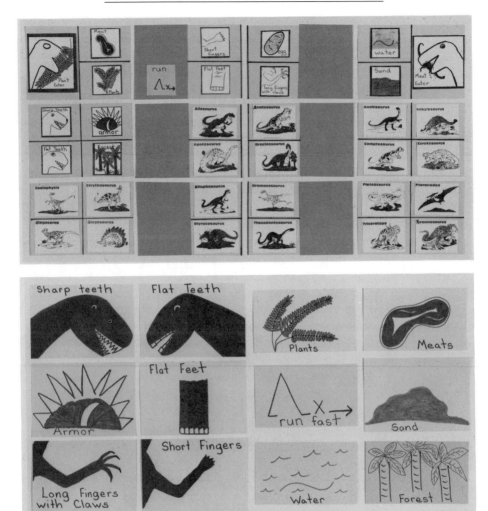

Figure 3.4 Individualized lesson materials at different levels of difficulty allow students with speech and language problems to show what they know in content subjects.

6. Point to a numeral that corresponds to the numeral (including those the teacher has written) beside the correct answers.
7. Use a student or adult transcriber. A person who understands the student's speech or other means of expression writes what the student expresses. The transcriber must be careful to write the student's responses without hinting or suggesting they be changed because teachers need to see and analyze student mistakes.
8. Use electronic education toys (e.g., Speak & Spell, Speak & Read, Speak

& Math[4]). These are readily available educational toys that students who do not speak can use at school. They have a series of learning modules, including early reading, developmental learning, reading, math, and levels of spelling.

9. Use a hand-held computer such as those sold by Radio Shack.
10. Use an inexpensive, portable, beginner's communication aid with synthesized speech output such as the Sonoma Voice. The Sonoma Voice[5] (Fig. 3.5) is about the size of a portable typewriter and weighs less than five pounds. The keys are 1½ inches in diameter and only require light pressure. The easily removed keyguard holds the user-supplied graphic overlays which are easily changed. This allows the use of graphics ranging from written text to drawings and photographs. When one of the sixteen phrase keys is pressed, an entire phrase is spoken. Up to sixteen levels are available, yielding a capacity of 256 phrases. Vocabularies are custom programmed for each user by the manufacturer.

Alternatives for Expressing Questions, Thoughts, Opinions, Requests, and Feelings in a Group. The fifth category under the heading of speaking (Fig. 3.1, #6) is expressing questions, thoughts, opinions, requests, and feelings. This applies in groups as well as to conversing with

Figure 3.5 A beginning speech output aid. Pictures are placed on large spaces, and when touched, synthesized speech relays basic requests and comments.

individuals. The main difference between this response and previous ones are length, complexity, and the unpredictability of the content to be expressed. Again the alternatives just described above might meet these needs, particularly the various communication boards. One of the simplest and easiest strategies to implement is to have the student with disabilities answer yes or no to questions for example, "Are you thinking that ———?"). This permits only minimum effectiveness, however, because the handicapped student is dependent on the sensitivity of others to express what she may be thinking. It is almost impossible for one person to anticipate closely what another would like to say.

Other approaches specifically for communicating in a group and to groups include:

1. Use typewriters and other keyboard-activated machines.
2. Use microprocessor-based speech output communication aids (e.g., Light Talker[6], Fig. 3.6). These communication aids have both computerized speech and print output. They can be easily preprogrammed to say anything a child or adult would want to say. In addition, they "say" anything the user types in. They can also serve as the keyboard for several brands of computers. Students need not be able to read to use them. Pictures, or icons, are used in combinations with each other. They can be accessed by touching, by switch, or by light beam. The student in Figure 3.6 wears a light sensor that activates the multipurpose keys on the keyboard.
3. Carry a notebook computer with speech synthesis added (e.g., Speech PAC[7]).
4. Use sign language and finger spelling with and without an interpreter.

Alternatives for Privately Expressing Thoughts in Conversation with Individuals. Conversing with someone else without making the conversation public to others nearby is a pleasure some persons with disabilities seldom experience (see #7 on Fig. 3.1). Here are a few ideas, but a creative teacher will no doubt think of others:

1. Indicate the symbol(s) on a word or picture board that communicates you have something to "say" in private. Then the communicating partner (receiver) will at least know to talk quietly or whisper when trying to decipher the student's message(s) and participate in a conversation.
2. Hand write or type a message.
3. Use traveler's picture dictionary. To use this type of dictionary, point to pictures or words to express thoughts, needs, or answers to questions. Travelers dictionaries cover a variety of common and unusual situations.
4. Preconstruct messages in the memories of computers and microprocessor-based communication aids. Using speech output aids, turn off or turn down the volume on the speech output option, leaving only the lighted message on the display panel, which can be erased after use.

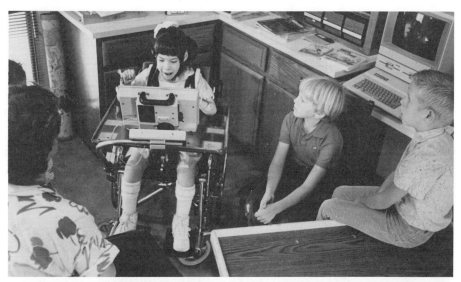

Figure 3.6   Vanessa uses her light talker to take several turns in group discussions.

Alternatives for Formal Oral Presentations.   In Figure 3.1 the category under speaking (#8) is formal presentations, reports, debates. Many of the strategies and devices already described above apply here, especially the microprocessor-based communication aids with voice output. Additional strategies for alternatives to making formal oral presentations include:

1. Type out presentation and ask someone else to read it into a tape recorder. Play the recording at the time the report is due.
2. Use audiovisual aids *"narrated"* by descriptions and captions presented on overheads.
3. Write a simple computer program and use a speech synthesizer.
4. Use the previously listed letter/word/picture communication tools (e.g., communication board) to deliver a talk to someone else who then acts as interpreter and gives or records it for the student on a tape recorder for later presentation.
5. Make tape recordings of presentation composed on microprocessor-based communication aid. Providing a print synopsis will assist persons unaccustomed to the characteristics of the speech output.
6. Use interpreters for person signing their presentation.
7. Use interpreters for individuals with unintelligible speech who are speaking.

Alternatives for Handwriting

　　　　The next general category of modes affecting student access to teaching/learning situations is handwriting. One purpose of writing is to produce hard copy that the writer or someone else, such as a regular-class teacher can refer to later. In each section we include alternatives that will result in hard copy.

　　　　Alternatives for Drawing, Coloring, and Painting.　The first two skill areas in the handwriting category are drawing and coloring. Some of the most effective alternatives for drawing, coloring, and painting include computer technology. Students with handicaps that affect drawing and coloring can:

1. Use the computer programming language, LOGO[8]. In LOGO the computer can perform like a drawing tool, and students can accomplish their goals using turtle graphics.
2. Use commercial hardware and software such as Koala Pad[9] and software for computer. Students can use finger or stylus to draw and color. This enables students with learning disabilities to feel successful. Vivid colors on the monitor allow students with low vision to enjoy the results. The drawings can also be printed.
3. Use commercial computer software that lets students draw and color (e.g., Delta Drawing by Spinnaker)[10].
4. Use custom software that allows students who can access computer only by single switch to draw (e.g., Drawing Program or Motor Training Games[11]).
5. Use raised lines on paper created by trails of Wilhold glue. When lines dry, blind student can detect lines of drawing, diagrams, and areas in which to color.

6. Use a raised-line drawing board designed for people with visual impairment.[12] It facilitates writing script or drawing graphs. It is also helpful to students with perceptual problems. This board is covered with rubber. As the student draws or writes with a pen or similarly pointed object on sheets of special plastic paper, he can feel the lines lift up as they are made. The lines are easily traced tactually or followed by sight (Corn and Martinez 1977).

Alternatives for Marking Choices. Alternatives of the third skill, marking choices (as in multiple-choice exercise) are listed below:

1. Scribbling on choice with crayon (when coordination prohibits marking with predesignated marks).
2. Using paintbrush, crayon, or pencil attached to headpointer.
3. Tracing over the one choice of several options with a pencil.
4. Type (on computer or typewriter) the problem number and the answer (e.g., "1. man").
5. Place block on choice of card among other cards representing choices.
6. Respond to a question and choices read aloud by someone.
7. Press braille dots down on numeral beside choice.

Alternatives for Drawing Indicator Lines. Alternatives to the fifth skill in the handwriting category, drawing indicator lines, are listed below:

1. Use a headlight to connect correct components, to mark choices, or to underline.
2. Use yarn to make indicator line (put yarn between two choices, under a choice, etc.).

Alternatives for Writing Short Exercises. The sixth skill under handwriting involves writing short answers, stories, reports, outlines, short paragraphs, notes from library research. Review earlier writing options to speaking in the alternatives to *indicating*. Consider these additional alternatives that include options from students who do and do not talk and who do not write what they know because of dexterity, perceptual, or spelling problems.

1. "Dictate" to others using some communication symbol system and have them write the words.
2. Use eye gaze to indicate choice or indicate that someone should write it. Choices can be placed apart from each other along a chalk board tray, on a chalkboard, or on the corners of some frame such as a flannel board or desk top.
3. Use computer with word-processing software (i.e., Magic Slate,[13] Bank Street Writer,[14] Multiscribe[15]).

4. Access a computer through some means other than standard keyboard. Use the Adaptive Firmware Card[16] (Adaptive Peripherals). A nontechnical person can install this card into Apple II computers. It has an option to slow programs down for students with learning problems or slow reaction times. It also allows users with physical disabilities to run off-the-shelf software by pressing on a single switch or by using an expanded keyboard. The expanded keyboard (large, rectangular, thin) has membrane-sensitive keys. These keys, activated by touch, can be combined through simple programming to form even larger keys. This alternative keyboard is particularly helpful to students with visual and/or physical disabilities. Wilson (1984) describes in more detail how this card adds flexibility to software and computer uses by persons with disabilities. Use of switch or expanded keyboard with the card does not disrupt use of the computer in the usual way. The Adaptive Firmware Card works with Apple computers. A similar card, the P.C. Serial A.I.D.,[17] works with IBM personal computers.

5. Use print function on a microprocessor-based communication aid such as those already mentioned.

6. Use large-bead abacus as a substitute for writing basic math computations.

7. Use magnet board or flannel board for answers.

8. Spell short answers using some spelling system other than handwriting (e.g., typewriter, communication board, Speak & Spell).

9. Purchase self-carbon notetaking pads or carbonless paper. It is helpful if students invite another student to take notes on carbonless paper and then give the copy to a student who, because of some disability, has trouble taking notes.

10. Use a cordless electronic typewriter or hand-held computer. Some have enough memory so student can store about one page of work. Others have no memory. Unlike printouts on hand-held computers, the printouts are on standard-sized paper.

11. Use Braillewriter or a slate and stylus (see Fig. 3.7). "A Braillewriter is a manually operated, six-key machine like a portable typewriter, which, as its name indicates, types braille (the Perkins Brailler[18]). The slate is a metal frame with openings through which braille dots are embossed with the aid of a pointed stylus. The slate and stylus,[19] used to take notes, are easily carried in a pocket or on a clipboard" (Corn and Martinez 1977, 9).

Alternatives for Writing Long Exercises. The final skill under handwriting is writing formal reports, compositions, and letters. This is obviously an extension of the previous skill, which also involved handwriting but less of it. Any of the systems mentioned above that can extend to allow for more complex communication would suffice here, particularly the electronic communication aids. Some other alternatives for teaching and learning include:

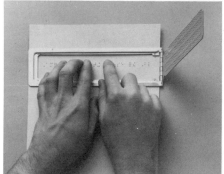 

Figure 3.7 Perkins Brailler, Slate, and Stylus.

1. Use tape recorders to audiotape lessons and notes for later review for persons with hand-use problems. Some recorders have a one-button access to the record function. For listeners who can listen to increased speeds of playback and therefore shorten the time it takes to review a tape, some recorders have speed/time compressors. Minicassette recorders are handy for students with no dexterity problems. Uses of single-switch attachments in remote control outlets allow students with moderate to severe dexterity problems to use them.

Figure 3.8 This student with learning disabilities uses Prompt-Writer word processing software because she needs to hear what she writes and what computer commands to use.

2. Use a voice output word processing microcomputer software such as Prompt-Writer,[20] Talking AppleWorks,[21] and Language Experience Recorder Plus[22] (Figure 3.8). Users can rely on voice feedback of what they type. Students with learning disabilities can rely on the voice output to assist with word recognition in material generated on the screen. Material can be reviewed letter by letter, word by word, and line by line. Voice feedback assists students who have visual impairments or learning disabilities with editing functions such as delete, copy, and block move.

3. Use portable communication tool with speech output such as the Keynote (Fig. 3.9). The Keynote[23] is a communications tool with speech output specifically designed for people who are blind. It provides a powerful information-handling device. For those learning typing or word processing, it is easy to use yet is also quickly responsive, a complete word processor, and a full scientific calculator.

4. Use braille or a paperless braille machine such as the *VersaBraille* Word Processor[24] (Figure 3.10). This device records and stores braille from a braille keyboard onto magnetic disks. Then the braille is played back

Figure 3.9 Two students participate in identical activities using different response methods.

through a paperless display panel (on a panel, readers feel the ends of different patterns of six pins, which represent the dots in the six-dot braille cells). The VersaBraille allows students to write braille and—through an interface to the computer—send print output to a computer screen or directly to an ink-print printer or a braille printer.

Alternatives for Writing Numerals. Many of the alternatives for writing text are appropriate for writing math. Some additional suggestions include:

1. Use talking and larger print display calculator computer software programs such as "CALC-TALK."[25]
2. Use special software that allows a student to use the computer as paper and pencil. Examples are Trace-Math-Aid[26] and University of Washington Math.[27]

Figure 3.10 This student proofreads what she has written on a VersaBrailler before printing it in ink-print for her teacher.

Alternatives for Performing and Environmental Control

The last general category (see Fig. 3.1), encompasses all the participating activities of handling, manipulating, and manuevering. To understand the grouping, first think in the broadest sense of all school tasks and education, then think again about life management roles in the family, home, and community.

The suggestions offered here cannot encompass every possible option or alternative. They are, however, a good place for the teacher with little or no hands-on experience to start generating ideas. Some of the suggested alternatives are simple, easily obtained or made. Others are complex, technological, and so expensive. Their application and appropriateness for the special education student is something the teacher will have to assess based on observations, research, and common sense.

Some of the strategies and equipment suggested below are specific to a particular activity. Others the student can use to do a variety of things. They all, however, enable students who are movement disabled, whether from motor delay, impairment, or sensory impairment, to enter more fully into activities related to schooling. Below is a list of alternatives for in school and out of school experiences.

1. Activate switch-operated toys. Battery-run toys such as musical games and cassette players can be turned into accessible playthings for children with motor disabilities. Special pressure and head-control switches or toy adaptors can be added to toys. See the ABLENET Switch[28] in Figure 3.11.
2. Use environmental indicators such as lights that turn on when the tele-

Figure 3.11 Switch-operated toys.

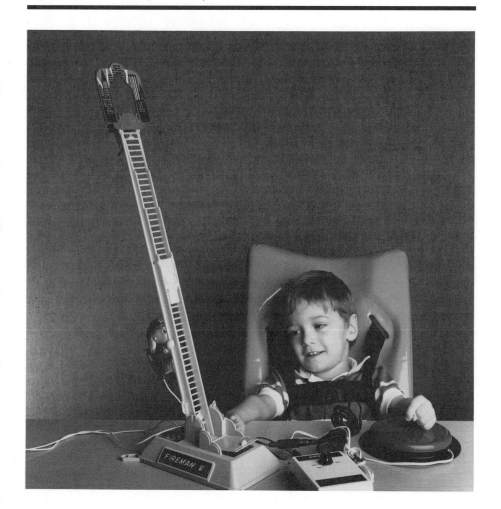

phone rings for persons who do not hear and sound keyed to street-light changes for people who do not see.

3. Drive electric wheelchairs—as an alternative to independent mobility.
4. Activate environmental controls so persons without hand use can turn on lights, radio, and appliances (see Fig. 3.12).[29]
5. Use an electric page turner.

These and other alternatives give students environmental-control skills that enable them to prepare for schoolwork or a job, move about the community, and in general provide maximum self-sufficiency. Many homemade and manufac-

Figure 3.12 Participation is enjoyed by all.

tured alternatives offer environmental control, but the most empowering skill the special education teacher can give in this area is consumer savvy. This will enable older students with disabilities to begin learning how to search out items they can operate to make their lives more manageable. A good example is a standard item from some department stores, a lamp that lights when part of its base is touched. Many environmental controls have been developed for persons with handicaps. These are primarily for use in the home or outside the school, but students can learn about their availability and how to operate them in classes on self-help or daily living skills.

Summary and Conclusion

This chapter stressed the value and importance of finding the customary educational enabling activities as a precursor to determining student response methods in current and future curriculum. The process of listing the commonly required educational activities in all grades within a particular curriculum discipline was explained. Then these were organized across disciplines into like-mode activities with a simple verb or verb phrase name such as speaking, handwriting, indicating. Specific subskills were articulated and listed below the general category of the primary enabling skill.

The chapter also described possible changes to accommodate special education students, including adaptations or alternatives to the customary response methods. Alternatives means replacing the customary response with another that is more serviceable to the student. The importance of making modifications so that the student with disabilities has the best chance to transmit and receive information using a congenial method or modality was stressed.

Teachers were encouraged to use teacher-made and low-technology solutions and to seek and be open to learning about high-technology modifications that might be appropriate.

At a time of rapid technological change, it is important to know sources of the latest information. Several resources list information on updated and current equipment. These include (1) references in books, articles, monographs; (2) directories (e.g., *International Directory of Recreation-Oriented Assistive Device Sources*); (3) disability-oriented social service agencies; (4) community relations organizations (e.g., Telephone Pioneers of America made up of retired telephone engineers who will advise on telephone access by persons with hearing and other disabilities); (5) vendors of equipment and devices; (6) local assistive device centers; (7) local higher education special education faculty; and (8) preservice and inservice teachers.

Information services are perhaps the least known about sources. Some of these are:

1. ABLEDATA System, National Rehabilitation Information Center (NARIC), 4407 Eighth Street, N.E., Washington, D.C. (ABLEDATA is a product describing equipment. NARIC can provide information searches upon request.)
2. AT&T Special Needs Center, 1-800-233-1222, TDD/TTY 1-800-833-3232.
3. Assistive Devices Resource Center, Missouri LINC-University of Missouri, 609 Maryland Avenue, (publication, hotline, assistance).

This chapter on modifying student response methods for curriculum access closes with a letter from a special education teacher, which shows the common frustrations and insecurities about working with technology. In contrast it also illustrates how appropriate modifications can have a powerful positive impact on students with disabilities.

Dear June,

This is the first time I have tried to use the Bank Street Writer (children's wordprocessing program for a microcomputer). I'm not sure if I can get it on the paper or not. Actually, I am not sure of anything.

We got the computer just after Christmas and the Paul Schwejda Adaptive Firmware Card you told me about in February. I borrowed the Bank Street Writer for the weekend to try it out. Since the only computer literacy education I have had came from you in about 30 minutes time last May (believe me it was not enough to prepare me for this ``time-saving'' device), I feel you deserve to be my guinea pig.

Do you remember Angie, the nonspeaking kid in my class who uses her eyes to focus on symbols in a communication book? Well, I bought the Adaptive Firmware Card for her. She figured it out while her guardian, the lady who runs the computer store, and I were arguing about which page to turn to in the manual. She kept kicking away at her foot switch while we patted her on the shoulder and told her to relax — that we would figure it all out for her soon. She kept kicking, and when I finally turned around she had her name and APPLE written on the screen. I took the firmware card home and learned to install it in the computer and to connect the printer over the weekend. On Monday, Angie wanted to write her spelling words on the computer.

Naturally she got *syntax error* everytime she pushed return. She did not like that on her paper, and indicated I had until spelling test on Friday to get rid of it. I told her I needed to buy a word processor or learn how to program to get rid of it, and I just didn't have the money or the skill at this time. She gave me a face like a rabbit at war, and I knew I had until Friday to learn how to program.

I read everything I could find, did not know what any of it meant, but put it on a free disk I had gotten at a conference two years ago anyway. By Thursday night 10:00 P.M. I had a program that would write twelve spelling words without saying syntax error. We got through Friday morning with a 100 percent perfectly typed spelling paper and no tears. I thought I was safe, but at recess she did not want to play. She wanted her communication album, and she wanted to talk — to me. What she said was she wanted to enter the county science fair this year, and she wanted to type her project. I told her she would have to come up with a good topic on her own to enter and that it was a big job and that I did not know how to make the computer do paragraphs. She glared at me, and we went back in the classroom.

I tried to ignore her efforts to talk to me for three days, hoping she would forget about the project. On the third day she was hopping mad and would have nothing of anything at recess until I sat down and listened to her. As I feared she wanted to talk about her science project. When I finally did listen, I found out she had a fairly well thought out question, hypothesis, and procedure. There was really nothing more I could do but turn her entry form into the county and figure out how to write paragraphs neatly on the computer.

It was cut and paste all the way, but we did it. The fair was last week. Three kids from my class entered. All three competed with regular ed. third graders. (Over fifteen hundred kids competed from all over the county — two hundred some odd ribbons were awarded). My kids got two blue ribbons and one red ribbon. Angie's project was one of the blue ribbon winners.

Sincerely

Jane

Jane

Notes

1. Versascan
   Prentke Romich Co.
   1022 Heyl Road
   Wooster, Ohio 44691
2. Situation Boards
   Courtesy: Jane Kelly, Teacher
   Stockton Unified Schools
   Stockton, CA 95204
3. Talking Pictures
      Kit 1 Survival Living Needs
      Kit II Community Living Needs
      Kit III Daily Living Needs
   Crestwood Company
   P.O. Box 94513
   Milwaukee, WI 53204
   (414) 351-0311
4. Speak & Spell
   Speak & Read
   Speak & Math
   Texas Instruments
   P.O. Box 53
   Lubbock, TX 79408
5. Sonoma Voice
   Communications Engineering
   Sonoma Developmental Control
   P.O. Box 1493
   Eldridge, CA 95431
   (707) 938-6306
6. Light Talker
   Prentke Romich Company
   1022 Heyl Road
   Wooster, Ohio 44691
7. Speech PAC/Epson
   Adaptive Communication Systems, Inc.
   Box 12440
   Pittsburgh, PA 15231
8. LOGO (LCSI LOGO)
   555 West 57th Street, Ste. 1236
   New York, N.Y. 10019

9. Koala Pad
   Koala Technologies
   269 Mount Herman Road
   Scotts Valley, CA 95066
10. Delta Drawing Computer Software
    Spinnaker Software
    215 First Street
    Cambridge, MA 02142
11. Motor Training Games
    Don Johnston Developmental Equipment, Inc.
    900 Winnetka Terrace
    Lake Zurich, IL 60047
12. Sewell Raised-Line Drawing Board
    American Printing House for the Blind
    P.O. Box 6085
    Louisville, KY 40205
13. Magic Slate
    Sunburst Communications
    39 Washington Avenue
    Pleasantville, NY 10570-9971
14. Bank Street Writer Plus
    Scholastic Inc.
    730 Broadway
    New York, NY 10003
15. Multiscribe
    Styleware, Inc.
    5250 Gulfton, Suite 2E
    Houston, TX 77081
16. Adaptive Firmware Card
    Adaptive Peripherals
    4529 Bagley Avenue N.
    Seattle, WA 98103
17. PC Serial A.I.D.
    Designing Aids for Disabled Adults
    1024 Dupont Street
    Toronto, Canada M6H2A2
18. Standard Perkins Brailler
    American Printing House for the Blind
    P.O. Box 6085
    Louisville, KY 40206
19. Slate & Stylus
    American Printing House for the Blind
    P.O. Box 6085
    Louisville, KY 40206

20. Prompt-Writer
    Syn-talk Systems and Services
    70 Estero Avenue
    San Francisco, CA 94127
21. Talking AppleWorks 2.0
    (needs Slot-Buster II Speech Synthesizer)
    Access Unlimited—SPEECHEnterprises
    9039 Katy Freeway, Suite 414
    Houston, TX 77024
22. Language Experience Recorder Plus
    Talking Large Print Word Processor
    Special Needs Source:
    Access Unlimited—SPEECHEnterprises
    9039 Katy Freeway, Suite 414
    Houston, TX 77024
23. Keynote
    Sensory Aids Corporation
    205 West Grand Avenue, Suite 122
    Bensenville, IL 60106
24. VersaBraille
    Telesensory Systems
    455 North Bernardo Ave.
    Mountain View, CA 94039
25. CALC-TALK
    Computer Aids
    124 West Washington
    Fort Wayne, IN 46802
26. Trace Math Aid
    Computers to Help People
    1221 West Johnston Street
    Madison, WI 53715
27. University of Washington Math
    Washington Research Foundation
    1107 N.E. 45th St.
    Seattle, WA 98105
28. ABLENET Switch 100
    AccessAbility, Inc.
    360 Hoover St. N.E.
    Minneapolis, MN 55413
29. ABLENET Control Unit and Switch 100
    AccessAbility, Inc.
    360 Hoover St. N.E.
    Minneapolis, MN 55413

References

Corn, A., and Martinez, I. 1977. *When you have a visually handicapped child in your classroom: Suggestions for teachers*. New York: American Foundation for the Blind.

McCormick, L., and Shane, H. 1984. Augmentative communication. In *Early language intervention*. Edited by L. McCormick and R. L. Schiefelbusch. Columbus, Ohio: Charles E. Merrill, pp. 325–56.

Scadden, L. In press. Implications of the research and development of modern technology on the education of blind and visually handicapped students. In *The handbook of special education: Research and practice* by M. C. Wang, M. C. Reynolds, and H. J. Walberg. Vol. 1. Oxford, England: Pergamon Press.

U.S. Office of Education, Department of Health, Education and Welfare. 1977, Pt. II. Education of handicapped children, implementation of Part B of the Education of the Handicapped Act. *Federal Register* 42(163): 42474–518.

Wilson, P. (1984). Adaptive firmware card: Hardware that adds flexibility to your software. *Cognitive Rehabilitation* 2(5): 38–41.

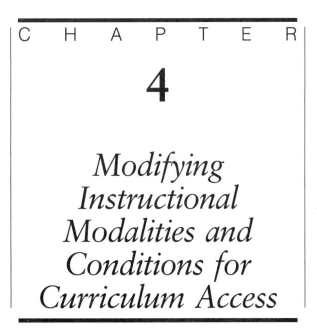

CHAPTER 4

Modifying Instructional Modalities and Conditions for Curriculum Access

VICKI CASELLA AND JUNE BIGGE

Special education teachers use and recommend to others modifications in how they teach and in teaching conditions to accommodate individual students with disabilities. In what situations would teachers need to use, or provide students with an opportunity to use, adaptations or alternatives to usual ways of curriculum presentation? What are some modifications in the conditions or structure of instruction and learning that provide the disabled student access to curriculum. How can microcomputers support teacher efforts to provide students access to curriculum-related activities?

Special educators are particularly concerned with accessibility to the curriculum. This is because certain special education students will not be able to participate fully in the regular-education curriculum or benefit from special-education curricular options until someone makes the curriculum accessible to them. The educational performance of these students is affected because their impairments or disabilities control the way information is transmitted to and received by them. It is possible to analyze and synthesize instructional modalities just as we did customary student response methods. By doing this, teachers can gain insights into making the appropriate changes.

Teachers instruct through various presentation activities including *presenting, stating, gesturing,* or *writing* the content being taught. Then students use different response methods to demonstrate that they understand (or have learned) using the same modalities of stating, indicating, gesturing, writing, manipulating, and demonstrating.

Some of the modifications presented here can be implemented by teachers who are not specialized in teaching students with disabilities. For many of these changes, however, specialized course work and experience are needed to prepare teachers to make knowledgeable and skill-based recommendations. For example, the complex task of evaluating a student's ability to access the curriculum can be based on an increase in student participation, increase in accuracy, increase in independence, and opportunities to benefit from similar modifications in other situations.

Modifications in Instructional and Learning Modalities

Adapting the usual presentation methods can be quite simple, including auditory amplification of what the teacher says. Adaptations to the customary modality for communicating and teaching students with special needs may be nothing more complicated than writing larger on the blackboard, moving the student closer and speaking louder, offering printed material in larger formats with more space and larger letters, and color-cueing written material. *Alternatives* are more radical and include such presentation methods as using contour globes (globes with raised surfaces for continents and elevations on continents) instead of regular classroom globes or a classroom globe with countries labeled in braille. Here the modality is *changed* from visual to tactile. An *augmented* modality might be used when a teacher writes the content of the verbal instruction on the board for people who do not hear well. In this case, the usual auditory modality is augmented with another one.

Adaptations for the Visually Impaired

Reading, writing, and visual transmission modes are not equally accessible to all students. Print enlargement is a common adaptation for certain students with low vision. Persons with some functional vision can read print if the characters are large enough. Normal print is 8- to 10-point type; 18-point or larger is considered large print. If the student is using a computer, she may need a larger than 18-point character on the computer screen. Sources of large-print materials include (1) reproduction (duplicating) machines with enlargement capabilities, (2) local education unit large-print libraries, (3) community libraries, (4) state Clearinghouse Depository for Handicapped Students, (5) certain trade book publishers; (6) American Printing House for the Blind;[1] and (7) the Library of Congress.[2]

Selecting the relevant adaptations and then teaching students the effective use of such adaptations as nonoptical aids and devices are two of the primary responsibilities special education specialists carry. Professionals such as those in local low-vision clinics, can prescribe optical aids. Then special education teachers are responsible for training students to become proficient in using the aids. A goal is to maximally reduce barriers between the students and their educational use of nonoptical and optical aids or devices.

Nonoptical Aids.   Corn and Martinez (1977) describe some of the most important teacher-initiated adaptations that provide student access to the usual learning modalities. Some students may need only a few adaptive materials, while others require a combination of several devices. These devices are generally categorized as *nonoptical* and *optical:*

Nonoptical aids are devices that are not individually prescribed, and they may or may not be designed specifically for the visually handicapped. Below is a partial list of visual aids:

1. Bookstands—these help reduce postural fatigue by bringing the work closer to the reader's eyes. When a bookstand is not available, one can be improvised by placing other books beneath the book being read.
2. Acetate—usually preferred in yellow, though available in various colors. Acetate placed over the printed page will tend to darken the print as well as heighten the contrast of the background paper.
3. Lamps with rheostats—with variable intensities and positioning, lamps can provide the additional or dimmed illumination that a visually handicapped student may need.
4. Bold-line paper—for children who find it difficult to see the lines on regular writing paper. Bold-line papers are available in various formats, for example, graph paper or large-print staves for music notation.
5. Page markers and reading windows—these may be especially helpful to a child who finds it difficult to focus on a word or line of print.
6. Sun visors and other shields—children with light sensitivity (photophobia) may need to block out some of the light and glare in the environment (adapted from Corn and Martinez 1977, 8–9).

Optical Aids.   Optical aids are devices that are individually prescribed and designed specifically for a person with a visual impairment. They provide certain students access to usual lesson materials. Corn and Martinez name three kinds of optical aids: glasses with special prescriptions, magnifiers, and telescopic aids:

A. Glasses with special prescriptions
   1. Bifocals, prisms, contact lenses, or other lens combinations may be prescribed for use at all times or during specified tasks.
   2. Tinted lenses—the light-sensitive student may need to wear dark glasses indoors as well as out.
B. Magnifiers—either hand held or in spectacles, magnifiers increase the size of the image reaching the eye. (For some eye disorders, though, magnification can hinder rather than assist visual abilities.)
C. Telescopic aids—children use small telescopes (hand held or placed in spectacle frames) to view the chalkboard and class demonstrations (Corn and Martinez 1977, 12).

Recent technological approaches such as closed-circuit television (CCTV) magnification devices, large-character computer displays, and large-print ink printers can now be added to this list. "A closed-circuit television camera is focused upon a printed page, computer screen, drawing, or other informational display of interest. The output of the camera is displayed on a television screen in an enlarged form" (Scadden in press).

Using a computer, students with low vision may be able to read something being typed which they could not do with a standard typewriter. Large-character computer displays can be generated in any of three ways. One, the capability of generating large-character displays can be built into the memory of the computer terminal (hardware). Two, specially developed software can generate large characters that appear on the computer monitor. (Macintosh software, in LARGE,[3] is one example.) Three, specialized hardware can be attached to a computer. A screen window pans the monitor display, and it enlarges the print and allows users to scan the full screen with a user-control panel or special joystick.

Also now available are portable electronic enlargers such as the Viewscan from Sensory Aids,[4] small enough to fit in a briefcase. By scanning a pocket-sized camera across any page of school work or a book, the reader can see a bright magnified image of the text on the display screen (Fig. 4.1).

Alternatives for the Visually Impaired

It is sometimes critical to the learning experience of some students that teachers change the modality they use in teaching, that is, use an *alternative* modality in presenting stimulus material. Information typically presented to students through one sensory modality must be presented so it can be secured by students requiring another modality. This occurs when students have disabilities in one or more of the basic sense modalities, such as sight or hearing. Students

Figure 4.1   Viewscan, a portable electronic print enlarger.

who do not see clearly enough to focus on pictures or read print may not be able to learn from gestures, drawings, blackboard information, color cues in books. Or when students have a hearing impairment, they may not be able to learn from the teacher's lectures, lessons, or other auditory input. In such instances, the special education teacher can use the alternative modality for instruction but also prepare others to use alternative modalities of presenting information and lesson in ways these students find accessible.

Examples of presentation alternatives for students with visual impairment include presenting a student's work in braille, books recorded on discs and cassettes, or simple computer programs with voice output for students who cannot see. Teachers who specialize in teaching students with visual impairment will have specific training for providing instruction in different modalities, in determining alternative modalities, and in transposing materials from one modality to another for easier student reception. They will also learn about the effect loss of vision has on learning and will develop sensitivities to the emotional needs of this student population (Hatlen and Curry 1987). After all, visual and experiential deprivation can have major impact on the ways students learn from instruction.

Readers and transcribers are another alternative for the visually handicapped student. They transpose materials from one modality to another to make information more accessible to students. *Readers* are peers, volunteers, or paid workers who read printed material in person or onto audiotapes. *Transcribers* are certified braille specialists, volunteers, and teachers. The certified braille specialists hold Library of Congress certification for preparing braille, large type, and aural media.

Auditory Modality. Human readers, disc recordings, open-reel and audiocassette recordings are several human-generated speech systems that function as alternatives to visual modalities for instruction (Scadden in press). Synthetic speech such as that coming from speech synthesizers on computers allows nearly all students (except those with severe hearing impairment) to benefit from the alternative modality of voice output on computers and on special instruments such as calculators, measuring devices, and clocks.

Sources of material recorded on discs and tapes are Recordings for the Blind (RFB),[5] local community-based volunteer agencies, school district storage, local libraries, and the state librarian. The National Library Service for the Blind and Physically Handicapped, a branch of the Library of Congress,[2] and its regional centers are major sources of information about library materials and services for visually and physically handicapped children and adults.

Tactile Modality. Scadden (in press) notes that braille is the primary tactile means for displaying information to blind students. Teaching students who are blind or need aids to access visually presented material is likely to include such orientation aids as three-dimensional maps and scaled models. These tools provide the students with many kinds of information. (They are also valuable to other students who can benefit from tactile sources of information.) These alternative modalities for teaching can enhance understanding about concepts in school subjects such as geography and about information in a work setting. Most importantly, they can orient students to basic layouts of buildings or areas. For travel in unfamiliar places in their own school and community center, educators can provide a tactile map.

Models, Graphic Aids, and Verbal Aids. Bentzen (1977) states that decisions about the type of instructional aids to use and even their design and construction should be based on the type of information to be presented. He describes three categories of instructional material aids that can be used individually or combined:

> *Models* are three dimensional representations of objects found in the environment.
> When models are made to high standards of scale, texture, and color, they are closer to "the real thing" than graphic or verbal aids. They are particularly useful for

conveying spatial concepts and their relationships between different components of the environment, such as the buildings on a campus.

Graphic aids are diagrams or maps having information perceptible to touch, vision, or both.

Graphic aids excel at representing environmental configurations such as intersections, floor plans of a building, city street patterns, and the relationship between public transportation systems and the area they serve. Graphic aids can be tactile, visual, or both. If the aid is tactile-visual, persons with low vision will be able to benefit from it, and it will allow the blind traveler to seek assistance from sighted pedestrians.

Verbal aids are specific types of spoken or written descriptions of the environment (area maps) and/or ways to travel within the environment (route maps).

Verbal aids can be recorded in tape, braille, or print. They can be used en route and do not require the blind individual to learn new perceptual skills. Information included in the verbal aids can be as detailed and specific as the travel route requires (Bentzen 1977, 453).

Information Storage. Information storage and retrieval are important tools for students because they deal with large amounts of information. Sophisticated alternatives to writing notes and filing them involve electronic braille. Electronic braille (i.e., VersaBraille[6]) is paperless braille used with computers that can store several hundred pages of information on an audiocassette or a computer disc. Many have braille keyboards so users can enter and retrieve data and information for their own use. The device can send information to output devices as such print or braille printers or a computer monitor for later retrieval. Earlier the VersaBraille served as an alternative student response method. Taunnie (see Fig. 4.2) uses the same device for information retrieval.

Orientation and Mobility Aids. "The sighted pedestrian or driver uses visual information for the identification of familiar landmarks which serve for orientation to the environment and for detection of obstacles, stairs, and other changes in the traveled surface which may prove to be hazardous. Alternative modalities are utilized by blind students to significantly reduce the effects of visual impairment by providing the user with information regarding the environments and objects contained within it, information normally obtained visually" (Scadden, in press). Canes and guide dogs can present information about obstacles in a pathway and the spatial layout of one's environment in another sensory modality than the usual one of vision.

Certain precautions are in order. Scadden (in press) reports research on a large proportion of blind students who relied on aural media t acquire information to the detriment of their reading skills development. It is a responsibility of specialist teachers to assure that alternatives to the usual modalities support, *but do not supplant,* the development of needed skills.

Figure 4.2 Taunnie uses her VersaBraille to retrieve information about the tape inventory in a music studio where she works.

Adaptations for Students with Hearing Impairments

The most common adaptation for students with hearing impairments are amplification devices including auditory training units and hearing aids. "*Auditory training units* are designed for use in classrooms where group and individual amplification is needed. Many systems are designed so that children are able to hear the teachers voice at a level slightly above classroom sounds" (Bigge 1982a, 58). *Hearing aids* are small, personalized units that amplify sound. They are designed to meet the needs of each user. Special education needs specialists can accurately evaluate functional hearing use and train students not only to use the amplification devices but also to learn how to attach meaning to the sounds.

These specialists must also teach students to get cues from sound, gaining as much information as possible from whatever sounds they do hear.

Children with hearing impairments frequently do not understand verbal communication at first. If the teacher simply repeats what was said, this adaptation can clarify the communication for some children. For others, though, it will be necessary to change or simplify either the language or language structures used. For example, the teacher may initially say, "When you have completed this assignment, get your social studies lesson and start work on it." If the child does not respond, the teacher might then alter this instruction and say, "Finish this work. Take out your history book. Do the lesson on page twenty-one."

Alternatives for Students with Hearing Impairment

Many students with hearing impairments need alternatives to the use of the auditory teaching modality. Teachers trained in working with students who have hearing impairments develop specialized skills in transmitting the same information using different modalities so they can teach students directly (see Fig. 4.3). But they do more, teaching students the skills it takes to benefit from interpreters who serve as intermediaries between the instructors or other speakers and themselves.

Interpreters translate verbatim from spoken to manual English and manually, orally, or in writing render messages to hearing-impaired students. Sometimes they translate to the "exact English" language system, sometimes to American Sign Language. *Signing Exact English* (SEE) was developed for teachers and parents to provide children with a visual system that corresponded with spoken English. It is a verbatim translation of English into sign and is used primarily for instructional purposes. In SEE, signs are used according to the rules of English. Signing Exact English is based more on themes than concepts. The same sign for a word is used consistently, regardless of meaning, to encourage consistent use of meaning through context, as with spoken English (Bigge 1982a, 60).

American Sign Language (ASL) is a language system based on concepts with a grammatical structure and symbol system different from that of English. National societies of the deaf and deafened recommend ASL. It is often taught to students preparing to make transitions from public school to postschool endeavors. Makaton is a simplified sign system for persons who may not be able to learn the previously mentioned, more complicated systems.

When introducing any universally used system, Smith (1980) suggests that when there is no sign for an idea, the word can be spelled out using the American manual alphabet (see Fig. 4.4). It is also used for titles, proper names, and convenience. The manual alphabet is one tool that hearing persons can use to communicate with hearing-impaired people if they do not know how to use the more complex systems.

Figure 4.3 A teacher uses both speech and sign in class.

Variations in Uses of Interpreters. "The presentation of information in the mainstreamed classroom setting to profoundly hearing-impaired children is frequently based on the translation of *auditory* information into word-for-word visual representation (speech read/sign language) through the services of an interpreter." (Waldron, Diebold, and Rose 1985, 39). These authors propose a model based on their premise that visual and conceptual delivery of information in the classroom is more important than mere verbal transliteration of the spoken material. They suggest changes and procedures so that (1) the symbols used for communication are made available for review by the students at a later time, and (2) new concepts taught to students can be made available in graphic-pictorial form as deemed necessary. They base parts of their thesis on Reynolds and Booher (1980), who found that the best instructional format with deaf students was predominantly pictorial with some ancillary verbal information.

This approach requires that "the person adapting the material into a visual form is familiar with the art of conveying conceptual meaning through signs, graphics, words, or any other medium available to the deaf student" (Waldron, Diebold, and Rose 1985, 40). Using this approach implies that the personnel assisting deaf students should know the material to be covered ahead of time so that they can make appropriate aids or interpretations of concepts. These authors present several examples of their approach. This one is from science:

American Manual Alphabet

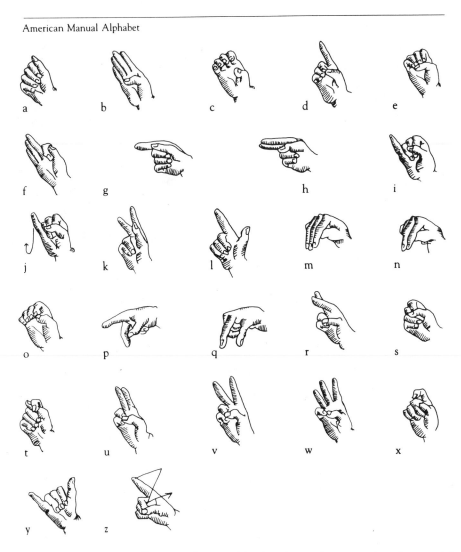

Figure 4.4 Finger spelling can be used by teachers who are not well versed in signing to clarify something a student with hearing impairment did not understand.

The activity is one in which the science teacher describes a scientific experiment with plants. The students are expected to use the scientific method to compare three specimens while changing only one variable. The example by the teacher compares the growth rate of three plants with different wattages of light, keeping all other variables constant. With a traditional interpreter, the interpreter signs, then rephrases, the teacher's lecture. Yet the scientific process probably is not understood by the hearing-impaired student because of words with multiple meanings and new vocabulary which was presented in a transient delivery mode. The student remains frustrated even after asking the teacher for clarification.

In the proposed delivery mode, a set of pictures [see Fig. 4.5] is prepared to explain the meaning of the teacher's statement. The use of visuals with the combined sign and speech delivery provides a consistent visual definition of abstract concepts and vocabulary, available for reexamination at home. (Waldron, Diebold, and Rose 1985, 41).

Another variation for interpreters is when they sit beside and slightly in front of hearing-impaired students but do not obstruct the students' vision of the teachers or the chalkboard. This is in contrast to the usual condition in which a regular interpreter would translate nearly word-for-word from the instructor while standing so that the student must look away from the activity. With the

Set of Pictures Illustrating Experiment Using One Variable

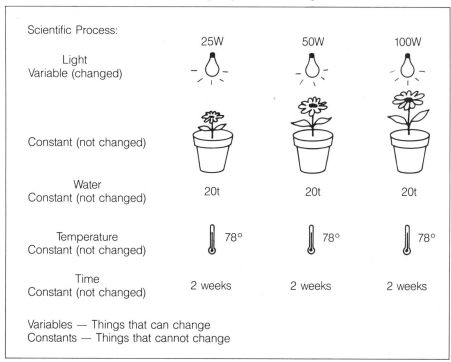

Figure 4.5 Use of visuals with sign and speech presentation.

traditional way, the student falls behind the pace of the class and becomes frustrated from missing questions as well as the responses of peers.

Waldron, Diebold, and Rose (1985) present an example of this from mathematics. The activity involves the teacher randomly selecting problems from textbooks for oral exercises. Students with hearing follow the teacher's instructions auditorally while visually following in their books and volunteering responses. In the change-of-conditions model these authors propose, interpreters can move around, but generally they sit beside a student and point to each problem as the teacher announces it, allowing the student to focus on the book only. "Responses of other students are communicated by the interpreter with one hand, close to the other hand pointing to the problem. Thus the student can visually follow without the lag of refocusing. Also, the student is synchronized in timing so that he or she is able to volunteer responses." (Waldron, Diebold, and Rose 1985, 41)

In addition to manual interpretation, some hearing-impaired students use oral interpreters to receive information. These interpreters sit close to the child and present the same information the teacher gives. The close proximity to the child helps insure clear understanding of the verbal message. The trained oral interpreter will also modify the language when necessary to facilitate the child's understanding.

Augmenting Modalities

Some alternative modalities are used in place of customary modalities. These are usually referred to as augmentations. Other alternative modalities are used *in addition to* the customary modality. When this is the case, augmentations are commonly described in one of two ways: (1) the customary and stronger modality is augmented by an alternative modality or (2) an alternative and stronger modality is augmented by the customary modality.

Teachers use augmentative modalities when students receive the customary modalities but with difficulty until they have been augmented. Augmentative modalities are also an aid when students use them when they are trying to learn the customary modality. For a while students might need to rely on both in order to get the most from their schooling. Manual signing by interpreters while the hearing-impaired student attempts to gain as many clues as possible from the orally presented material would be considered an augmentation.

Changes in Instruction to Affect Curriculum Access

Teachers often discover that certain students benefit from teaching and learn more effectively with changes in the conditions under which the student operates. Such changes are usually not difficult to make; the difficulty lies in knowing which possible change in condition will be most effective. To deter-mine this, the teacher needs to observe the student's characteristic problem and habits. A process of careful experimentation and collection of relevant data can suggest modifications that could work best for groups of students with special needs as well as for individual students. The teacher can evaluate the results of this process using the goals of increased student participation, increased accuracy, and increased independence.

Examples of changes in conditions in the instructional process include (1) spatial changes, (2) temporal changes, (3) using high-preference reinforcers, (4) modifying the rules, (5) modifying the abstraction level of the lessons, (6) modify-ing perceptual organization, (7) changing the instructional formats, (8) changing the location of instruction, (9) modifying for life management activities, and (10) modifying through new technologies.

Spatial and Temporal Modifications

Modifying the physical layout of stimulus materials for students includes format changes in written materials such as those suggested in Chapter 2. The discussion there focuses on assessment. Information gathered prior to, dur-ing, and as an outcome of assessments needs to have a direct relationship with methods used in instruction on a daily or weekly basis.

A teacher can consider special factors when a student is characteristically unable to complete worksheets that offer practice of what is learned in different subjects. Experimenting with spatial changes to improve performance might in-volve reducing the amount of material on each page. A teacher could find that the student completes more worksheet exercises, for example, when every other problem is blocked out with some form of removable correction or cover-up tape or gummed notes. This reduces the amount of stimulus presented simultaneously per page.

Teachers wanting to experiment with changing temporal factors to meet the unique needs of special education students can start by giving extra time. This may enable students to finish and do well without undue strain. A particular student, due to health problems, might need breaks in the time spent on a task in order to see it through to the end. The information on changing test conditions for assessments can also be applied to making modifications in instructional activities.

Using High-Preference Reinforcers

Certain students need special conditions to increase performance on some tasks. In respect to changing teaching or learning conditions to enhance learning by adding reinforcers, Snell and Renzaglia (1986) state that "the identification of objects, foods, and activities arranged in order of the student's preference (a hierarchy of reinforcers) assists the teacher in developing the most effective instructional program. In most cases the use of items and activities to reward appropriate behavior facilitates learning in students with severe handicaps" (p. 282).

Modifying the Rules

Changes in conditions to increase educational effectiveness could include modifying rules in games. Let's look at how that might apply to physical education. One skilled physical education teacher uses such activity modifications but cautions that activities should not be modified any more than necessary for students to participate safely and successfully.[7] Recommendations for modifying the rules in special education start with the regular rules, which are to be followed as much as possible, and include:

1. Limit the amount time each specific student participates.
2. Rotate players.
3. Add or subtract players on teams.
4. Allow rest time if needed.
5. Allow the less-mobile students to play in less-active positions.
6. Build a safety zone for higher risk students (so other students are not allowed within a certain physical range of students with behavior problems or students with physical stability, or balance, problems.
7. Make individual requirements for students according to their skill levels.

Modifying the Abstraction Levels of Lessons

Changing the level of abstraction in the instructional methods and materials used can include teaching with actual objects prior to introducing pictorial representations and symbols for the objects. (See Chapter 5 for a highly systematic way of looking at the complexity level of learning conditions.) Other modifications are changes in learning-teaching equipment paralleling that used in natural situations. An example would be color coding the needed oven and burner dials on a stove and covering extraneous dials to facilitate match to sample activities using color-coded graphic instructions. Another example would be using red-tape strips to mark appropriate calibrations on kitchen timer (Wehman and Hill 1980).

Modifying Perceptual Organization[8]

Part of the teaching-learning process that has received attention constantly is the need to respond to student problems with certain *perceptual processes*. Perception, defined as an activity of the mind intermediate between sensation (input) and throught, is the organizing, integrating, associational process that gives meaning to input. Visual perception then is how people organize visually presented material and relate it to their past experience. Auditory perception is the mechanism for organizing input through the auditory channel.

Reduced Information. Experiencing a perceptual problem may mean a reduction in the information gained from the sense involved. The student may, for example, actually see or hear the information with adequate acuity, but she does not discern it the way most people do. And, clearly, the student who is not integrating information from what she sees and hears is getting less information than the child who does. The child with poor visual perception gets less than usual information from the words and pictures in a story and from the diagrams in a math book. The child with poor auditory perception gets less information than usual from a story read aloud and from class discussion. Reduced information is a problem that compounds quickly. Just as the child who does not read gets further behind due to not reading, so the same child with reduced information processing has fewer concepts with which to think.

If a student experiences reduced information from one sensory channel, the teacher must direct some instruction toward increasing information received through another channel. If a student does not gain information well auditorially, for instance, the teacher can help him gain it visually by making sure that he is where he can see the pictures in a read-aloud book, putting the directions on the chalkboard for him, or having another child help him find the correct page.

Students with visual perception difficulties need to be taught reading with an emphasis on sounds and phonics (an auditory approach). The same students can be taught arithmetic, which is so often presented visually, through verbal directions and manipulation skills. Letter and numeral formation can be taught using verbal cues.

A challenging way to develop changes in conditions is to take a specific skill and plan how to teach it, using each sensory modality. For example:

SKILL	CHANNEL	METHODS
2 + 3 = 5	visually	objects and symbols
	auditorially	taps, taped lessons
	motor	number line, ball bouncing

In general, whenever a teacher is working on a child who has weaknesses in a particular sensory channel, it is helpful to be sure he or she has an alternate way of gaining information.

Inconsistent Information. Perceptual problems result not only in reduced information but also in *inconsistent* information. A major characteristic of distorted perception is in fact its inconsistency. A visual perceptual problem is like an optical illusion—sometimes you see it one way, sometimes another. An auditory perceptual problem, for example with a student who has a hearing loss due to nerve damage, is like a suddenly garbled input. This distorted and inconsistent quality is what makes auditory and visual perceptual problems so handicapping in school. At least a partially sighted child can make an easier adjustment because his condition is constant.

When students appear to receive information that is inconsistent and distorted, teachers need to structure the input, that is, do the organizing for the child. Let's take as a specific example problems with *figure-ground discrimination*. This means that the child is unable to focus on one set of stimuli while screening out others. Thus everything is equally important. Such a child is not inattentive but overly attentive so that, auditorially, all noise in room is of equal value. In effect this means the teacher's voice is no more important than a neighbor's scissors. Visually, a child having trouble with figure-ground discrimination can't attend to one letter or one word. She looses place in reading, can't copy from a blackboard, is more concerned with a ditto splotch than the worksheet problems, and is overly attentive to a classmate's pretty ribbon.

Teachers can structure learning situations to help such students organize information so they can attend to the most important parts of it. Three general rules apply: (1) Reduce the input, (2) emphasize what the child is to learn, and (3) teach specific lessons.

RULES	APPLICATIONS
AUDITORY PERCEPTUAL PROBLEMS	
Rule 1: Reduce the (auditory) input	1. Put towels or mats under manipulative toys; have students use ear plugs; reduce teacher talk; set standards for noise level from all students.
Rule 2: Emphasize what the student is to learn	2. Tape lessons so sound is focused through earphones; stand near student when saying important information.
Rule 3: Teach specific lessons on dealing with (auditory) presentation material	3. Make audiotapes of numeral names and other kinds of information; play tape against music and speech on radio and have child write or tell information from tape.

4. Make audiotape of accentuated usual classroom noises (reading groups, etc.); play tapes while students try to do some schoolwork.

VISUAL PERCEPTUAL PROBLEMS

Rule 1: Reduce the (visual) input

1. Cover pictures in books to encourage child to focus on the print; put window slots in book markers so students see only one row of words at a time; use commercial removable cover-up tape to remove distractions on a visually busy page.

Rule 2: Emphasize what the student is to learn

2. Add color cues to accentuate; use yellow highlighter to emphasize; use enlargements of key pieces of information (plus and minus signs in math).

Rule 3: Teach specific lessons on dealing with (visual) presentation material

3. Encourage hidden-figure activities (i.e., from childrens' magazines, newspapers, etc.); go back over paper and mark certain details (i.e., all *b*'s in red, and *p*'s in green and so on).

Form Constancy. The inability to see form constancy prevents children from making instructional input more consistent. Form constancy is the ability to recognize that symbols have certain properties that make them the same despite variations in size, position, color, texture. This means that form constancy is a generalization skill, which leads to conceptual thinking. Form constancy involves categorizing and organizing associations and perceptions. Auditorially, form constancy is the ability to realize that *m* is still *m* no matter where you hear it in a word. An example of teaching form constancy and auditorially would be a lesson such as: Raise your hand if you hear *m* in this word: milk, ham, summer.

Visually, form constancy is important. A student with problems in form constancy might recognize words on flash cards but not in book. This student might also not see that problems written on different planes are the same.

$$\begin{array}{c} 2 \\ +3 \\ \hline 5 \end{array} \qquad 2 + 3 = 5$$

The teacher can present specific lessons in form constancy that will help the child improve his distorted perceptions. To do this within the visual modality teach through: sorting (size, shape, color), sorting alphabet cards (a b, A B), finding same words written differently in natural situations, making scrapbooks of the same words cut from different magazines and newspapers.

Perceptual disabilities are not strange ailments occurring only rarely. They appear in varying degrees in most children at some time. It is the persistence of the ability that negatively impacts learning. Modality-based techniques like the ones presented in this section apply to many students in each classroom. Certain students in special education, however, may need more than the usual practice with these generalization skills.

Changing the Instructional Format

Instructional formats are the different organizational patterns available for instructional purposes. They can have a significant impact on learning. Changing from one to another can be the teaching-initiated change that makes a difference to certain students. Wallace and Kauffman (1986) describe typical instructional formats, including: "(a) total group(s), (b) small group(s), (c) one-to-one instruction, (d) triads, (e) peer tutoring, and (f) independent seatwork" (p. 91).

Changing the Location of Instruction

The *location* in which students are taught is a condition of instructional strategy. For students with problems in generalization, nonschool environments for educational instruction is an emerging option (Brown et al. 1983, Sailor et al. 1985). Brown et al. describe four instructional location strategies: school instruction only, consecutive instruction, concurrent instruction, and nonschool instruction only.

School instruction only locations are presently the most common. Severely handicapped and most other disabled students receive all their more than twenty-one years of education only on school property. *Consecutive instruction* requires demonstrations of skills at predetermined criteria levels at school before allowing students to try skills in nonschool environments. *Concurrent instruction* refers to "providing systematic, direct and individualized instruction, in both school and nonschool environments within daily or weekly time intervals" (Brown et al. 1983, 9). *Nonschool instruction only* is direct instruction in appropriate nonschool environments where students currently function or are likely to function soon.

To picture concurrent and nonschool instruction, think of an analysis of a job in a local theatre. Potential activities in a subenvironment, such as the lobby condiment counter, are identified. It would be almost impossible to teach students to do such a job using only school or consecutive instruction. Imagine how the various activities there group into logical skill clusters. These can be taught using concurrent instruction.

Sailor et al. (1985) discuss the logistics of implementing a community-intensive curriculum. Community-intensive curriculum primarily involves nonschool instruction. Instruction of students takes place primarily in the community—away from the school building. They note that the newness of a community-intensive curriculum means many practical and logistical problems remain to be solved to bring such a program into being. So far, no problem has proved insurmountable, and different school districts have evolved their own solutions. The most important first step in setting up such a program is the support and backing of the school board and administration. This is essential to any community-intensive program.

Attendant potential problem areas include liability and insurance, teachers unions, transportation to the community, adequate staff ratios, and money for community-based activities. Legal advice may be needed to work out liability issues. Involving unions from the beginning in the liability, job description, and curriculum-planning process can help reduce problems in these areas. Resolutions to transportation problems can include using public transportation, teachers' and aides' vehicles, and district vans and buses. In some districts, students earned bus passes and teachers used driver-education vehicles; one district purchased a vehicle for the program using grant funds.

The funds needed to implement a community-intensive program can be modest at the beginning. The program can then win funding support as the curriculum proves its value. Funds can also be transferred to the program from other areas of the school budget, including money budgeted for instructional supplies, federal per-student funds, career education money, grants, PTA funds, earnings from a school-run cafeteria or restaurant with disabled students who work and are trained there, and parent-funded activities (such as meals eaten off campus).

Modifications for Life Management Activities

In order for the student to participate as fully as possible in different kinds of life management activities, teachers and others might need to modify some modalities and conditions. For example, adaptations to personal self-help buttoning tasks might include adding colored threads to indicate which holes match which buttons. Adapted clothing that meets individual needs for gaining personal independence can be purchased or made. Wristwatches with enlarged numerals can be bought. Adaptations to school tasks might include extending parts to hold or parts to move, such as the buttons on a tape recorder. Adaptations for a work site might include a teacher- or employer-made coded dial attached to the face of a scale on which a student is to weigh cooked foods at a local fast food restaurant. A hand-made aid that accentuates the visual arrow designating the desired weight can be used by a student who is intellectually impaired and cannot interpret the figures on the scale but can perform the physical movements. Modification of instructional procedures is needed when a student can see but is unable to read instructions on a school task or at a job site. Someone can interpret the instructions to the student through a sequence of photos, or other pictures.

For certain students, using alternative modalities increases the amount and quality of their participation in life management activities. Alternative modalities for communicating with others are probably some of the most important modifications. For certain disabilities, gesturing and modeling are alternatives to verbal or written communications. Deaf persons, for example, are assisted when a light signals a doorbell ring or some other sound-based device is activated.

Changing conditions might also involve altering the sequence of an activity, changing the time constraints for completing a task, or restructuring the task. Working with a nondisabled peer rather than alone may be a condition change that makes a great difference in productivity to a student with disabilities. Restructuring a school or job site to accommodate individual posturing or mobility needs are other examples of changes in conditions. Using some technique to reduce noise level is still another.

Modifying Through New Technology

Modifications in instructional modalities and conditions—and in student response modes—can be instituted through the new information technologies. These technologies offer many instructional presentation options that teachers can use successfully with any student and especially students who have difficulty learning the usual material in the usual ways. Microcomputers, with carefully selected software, offer diverse opportunities. Some software allows for setting different parameters (speed of action or size of print on monitor) and for changes in the conditions for or structure of presenting material (choice of vertically or horizontally presented math problems). Standard software also offers multiple options for student response methods (whole keyboard, single key, joystick). Custom software and alternative input devices (see Chapter 3) offer even greater variety of access (single switch, expanded keyboard). Computer software and hardware programs can be matched to the individual needs, the demands of the established curriculum, and the working style of the teacher. Because of the positive impact of carefully selected software on modifying instructional modalities and conditions, more extensive information follows in the next section of this chapter.

Educational videotapes and videodiscs can bring real-life situations and environments to the classroom. Videotapes add realistic pictures, action, and sound to enliven curriculum teaching and learning situations. With the increased ease of use of videocameras, the greater portability of the cameras, and the reduction in videotape cost, this media is becoming more available to teachers. Hofmeister and Thorkildsen (1987), two pioneers in interactive technology, clarify a major difference between videodisc and videotape technology: Videodisc systems allow "both a massive storage capacity and fast random-access facility to combined instructional functions of videotape players and film and slide projectors" (p. 191). Students can interact with instruction in this format in many ways. So far this new media has only begun to penetrate educational programs. Specific applications of this technology pertaining to persons with disabilities has included assessment, academics, and social skills (Hofmeister and Thorkildsen 1987).

Accommodations Through Microcomputer Software

When computer technology and its potential for classroom instruction first came to the attention of educators, the major concern was on selecting the computer equipment—or hardware—itself. Once the equipment was in place, though, classroom teachers realized that the real promise of the new technology lay not in the machinery, but in its integration with the educational curriculum. Educators also understood that in order to realize the potential of computer technology, they had to actively address its interface with the various aspects of the educational program. To be effective, computers had to be considered in relation to (1) the individual needs of the students, (2) the established curriculum, and (3) the teaching style of the teacher. At this point, concern shifted from equipment to questions about using computers to accomplish educational goals and objectives. The answer to these questions invariably centered on evaluating and using computer software.

The formidable task educators face is to implement standard curriculum goals and objectives in a diverse student population. Diversity is a characteristic of all classrooms, but with students needing special education and related services, this characteristic is intensified so that the task becomes even more challenging. But the appropriate educational software can alleviate certain problems inherent in dealing with diverse individual needs.

For example, learning the alphabetical sequence of letters is a reading-readiness skill emphasized in the preschool/primary curriculum. One popular way to teach this skill is to have children complete a picture by connecting dots that form the letters of the alphabet and then to color the finished product. Naturally this task is a major obstacle for children who cannot hold a pencil, who have severe motor problems, or whose hand-eye coordination is limited. Software programs such as Dot-to-Dot from Springboard Software's Easy as ABC can help children with these special circumstances master this curriculum objective by providing exactly the same practice other children can get using conventional materials. The computer monitor becomes an electronic worksheet, displaying dots labeled with letters of the alphabet. To connect the dots, the student uses only the arrow keys and the space bar on the computer. When the task is completed, the computer displays the finished picture in full color, labeled with the name of the object. The computer, in this example, provides the teacher with an alternative delivery system.

This alternative delivery system model can meet many other needs of special learners. It helps to use the students' learning requirements as a basis for selecting software.

Need: Repetition of Material.   The most common use of computers in education is to provide additional drill and practice on content the classroom teacher has already taught. Drill-and-practice software programs can very effectively meet the needs of students who require extensive repetition before they can master a particular concept or skill. Research indicates that students will spend twice as much time on a repetitive drill if presented on the computer as opposed to through pencil and paper tasks. Critics of drill-and-practice programs frequently refer to them as nothing more than electronic flash cards, but for students who cannot access standard writing tools, such programs can make the difference between simply being exposed to educational concepts and actually mastering them.

Need: Sequential Presentation of Material.   Once a curriculum goal has been set, it is the teacher's responsibility to break that goal into its smallest units before presenting it to a class of students. But the size of these units may or may not match the learning needs of each student in the class. Some may be able to master the material when it is presented in large conceptual units, but others may need minute, step-by-step instructions. Excellent software tools are available in some curriculum areas to accommodate these individual differences in learning. The value these programs can have is illustrated in the situation where a child consistently makes computational errors in math whenever regrouping to the next column or columns is required. In this case, the teacher often bases an instructional intervention on the assumption that the child has not mastered basic math facts, which is not accurate. This cycle will persist until the specific errors the child is making are analyzed, and this can take up significant time for the teacher. Programs such as Math Assistant I (Addition and Substraction) and Math Assistant II (Multiplication and Division), from Scholastic Incorporated, provide detailed information on the errors the student makes so that the teaching intervention can be focused on the specific problem area rather than on the entire process of "basic math facts."

Need: Varying Rates of Presenting Material.   To maintain student motivation and increase performance, it is critical that the teacher realize when the student has mastered a given concept and then moves quickly on to the next level. Programs such as the Basic Skills in Math series from Love Publishing Company make this easy for both student and teacher. The program administers an entry-level assessment to the student; branches to the instructional level determined by the assessment; provides practice, not only in getting the correct answer, but also in working through the process as well; tests for level mastery; and advances the student to the next level as appropriate. In addition, the program's record-keeping feature offers the teacher progress data on each student. Students can work at this program independently and constantly be challenged at their individual skill level. Unlike many math software programs that merely present a problem and expect the student to work the problem on paper and then type in the correct answer, Basic Skills in Math allows students to work through the entire problem on the screen. This means students who cannot transfer information from one format to another or who cannot use standard writing equipment can still successfully complete the regular curriculum objective. The large numerals and few visual distractors make this program appropriate for many visually handicapped children and for learning-disabled children who find too many graphics distract them from the learning process.

Need: Development of Problem-Solving Strategies.   Often once children have been identified as special learners, educators focus their instructional program on the mastery of academic information through such teaching strategies as repetition, using alternative teaching materials, and reducing the level of expectation. Doing this to the exclusion of other aspects of the child's cognitive development, can mean missing tremendous learning potential. Software programs that allow a student to explore different approaches to solving a problem, analyze the strategies being used to reach the solution, and promote the attitude of risk-taking are especially important to a total curriculum. A popular software program, used in elementary through high school grades, that encourages these skills is The Factory from Sunburst Communications. Students design factories, create products, and issue challenges to their friends while learning to solve problems by thinking ahead, using visual planning strategies, and learning to break problems down into parts. Little keyboard use is required so that concept mastery is the program's focus rather than keyboarding skills. The new version of the program works with the Personal Touch Window (TM), which further reduces distractors and allows special learners to touch the options on the screen to make choices.

Need: Productive Interaction with Others. The isolation special learners often experience is not an effective teaching and/or learning environment. Here the computer can provide an avenue for integrating special learners with the larger student population. Perhaps the most exciting learning with computers is not reflected in increased academic performance, but rather in the quality of interactions resulting from computer use with groups of children. The standard configuration for computers in classes to date is one computer per classroom rather than one computer per child. At the elementary level, especially, this is an advantage because the situation fosters improved communication skills and increased strategies for establishing social interaction. In addition, such problem-solving and/or simulation software such as Swiss Family Robinson from Windham Classics and Estimation from Lawrence Hall of Science lend themselves to group situations more readily than ditto sheets and workbook assignments do. Providing a role for each participant in the group can allow the special learner to make use of his strengths and as a result can develop self-esteem for the student and new respect from other group members.

Evaluating Software for Curriculum Disciplines

A second major consideration in using computer technology is how the teacher can enhance instruction in each curriculum area through the careful selection of educational software. Excellent programs are available for the different curriculum areas. Skillfully applied, they become valuable assets for the classroom teacher. When evaluating educational software programs, teachers need to remember the diversity of their students' needs and select programs that will aid in meeting those needs while implementing the students' individual instructional plans.

Written Language Skills. One of the most promising uses for computers in the curriculum for special learners is in language arts. Every major educational journal has published research and descriptive articles on using word processing programs to improve students' reading and writing skills, including students who have been identified for special education services. This application of computer technology may well be the most important reason to have computers in the schools. Teachers are enthusiastically reporting that students approach the task of writing with a more positive attitude. They are willing, and in some instances eager, to edit what they have written. They write more, and they express themselves more clearly than with pencil and paper. The three most popular word processing programs used extensively in elementary school programs are Bank Street Writer from Broderbund Software, Magic Slate from Sunburst Communications, and Milliken Word Processor from Milliken Publishing

Company. All three have extensive supportive materials for classroom use and are easy to use. Magic Slate is really three word processing programs in one with a 20-column, 40-column, and 80-column display option. The large, easy-to-read letters in the 20-column display make this an excellent program for use with preschool or primary level children and with visually limited students. The 40-column display is perfectly suited to elementary level students, and the 80-column version is a highly powerful word processing program suitable for high school students and adult use. Many middle and high school programs have chosen to use the word processing feature of AppleWorks from Apple because it is not only a powerful word processing program but also a data management and spreadsheet program as part of an integrated package. An exciting program recently developed by Logo Computer Systems has the potential to become *the* word processing program of choice. LogoWriter combines the programming language LOGO and word processing. This allows students the flexibility of writing a story, illustrating it, and even augmenting the illustrations with text.

A new word processing program, MultiScribe from Styleware has incorporated many features that facilitate use by students with special needs. Some of the problems encountered in many word processing programs include: (1) having to remember the various commands, (2) needing to change to different modes to edit or insert data, (3) the size of the print on the screen and in the printout imposed on the choice of fonts, including style (underline, bold, superscript, etc.), size, flexibility for change, and printout format.

The makers of MultiScribe have taken most of these problems into consideration in developing their program. All the commands available to the user are at the top of the screen, and the student only sees a particular category label. When the student selects that category, all the choices available under the category are displayed. For example, the word for the category SIZE is displayed at the top of the screen. When SIZE is selected, a "window" with the various options opens. The window contains the choices 1.0, 1.5, 2.0, 2.5, 3.0 for the different sizes of characters on the screen and in print.

Offering the option of different character sizes increases the potential for using this program with visually impaired persons needing large-print display. Minimizing the commands that must be remembered increases its effectiveness with learning-handicapped students who might have difficulty recalling specific commands. Maximizing easy use of this program increases the speed with which users can access the program and use it for personal productivity activities.

Readiness Skills. Computers are being used successfully with very young children to assist in developing reading and math readiness skills and to encourage the use of critical thinking skills. Discovery-based programs such as Gertrude's Secrets from The Learning Company and Odd One Out by Sunburst Communications allow children to explore possibilities, learn classification principles, and develop expertise in following directions. It is important for all learners to experience success and be encouraged to take risks to test out a hypothesis they might have. Problem solving and discovery programs facilitate these curriculum objectives.

Most young children have difficulty using the standard computer keyboard, especially when they are trying to learn the letter sequence of the alphabet. Sunburst Communications markets the Muppet Learning Keys, a keyboard specially designed for young children with the letters and numbers in sequential order. This is excellent for young children, visually limited students, and students with motor problems, and it comes with software that helps develop reading and counting skills. Sunburst and other software companies have also developed a variety of programs that will operate with the Muppet Learning Keys and make it an excellent addition to the supply of classroom teaching materials. Learning the alphabet becomes child's play with Easy as ABC from Springboard Software and Alphabet Circus from Developmental Learning Materials.

Science. Due to physical limitations, problems with hand-eye coordination, or a visual handicap, many youngsters are excluded from science classes or projects involving gathering data or conducting experiments. The Science Toolkit from Broderbund has made many scientific experiments and observations accessible to special learners. The Science Toolkit includes the software, a user's manual and experiment guide, an interface box for the computer, a temperature probe, and a light probe. Students from elementary through high school can take part in scientific experiments while using the computer in much the same way scientists use it to collect and interpret data. Grolier Publishing Company combined the use of a textbook with a computer program in The Secrets of Science Island, which has generated excitement among elementary school special learners. In this program the user is stranded on an island and must gather stones together to build a shelter before an impending hurricane strikes. To play the game, one must drive a car around the island and answer questions that appear on the various road signs. The answers to the questions are found in the accompanying book, and students must use the table of contents or the index to find the information. The format and requirements of The Secrets of Science Island make the program an excellent group activity; one student can be responsible for moving the car around the screen from one road sign to the next; another could take the responsibility for reading the textbook to find answers to questions; a third could be the "spell master" and make sure that answers are typed correctly; and a fourth child, the "resource guide," could look up additional information in another source if necessary. Carefully selecting the group and assigning tasks could result in the special learner taking a major role in playing this educational adventure. As an example, one second-grade student with severe learning problems was the very best "driver" in the class and was always chosen for teamwork when Secrets of Science Island was the program of the day. He was able to maneuver the car around the screen without a single accident or loss of time due to a wrong turn, which made him a valuable asset as a team member. His skill earned him respect from the group and resulted in his being chosen for other team efforts as well.

Social Studies and Geography.   One curriculum goal in geography requires students to know the names and capitals of all the states as well as their location on a map of the United States. Learning this information takes abundant repetition using a variety of teaching strategies and materials. Learning-disabled students might have difficulty remembering how to spell the names of the states; physically limited students might have a problem when it comes to labeling the map with the state names; other special learners might need an extraordinary amount of drill and practice before mastering this information. At least two programs add some excitement and motivation to this otherwise routine memorization task. States and Traits by DesignWare allows students to "move" the outline of a state into its proper location on an outline map, "point" an arrow to the capital of each state when requested, or find a state from a clue provided in the program or added by the classroom teacher. States and Traits requires only the arrow keys, the return key, and the space bar to operate, making it an excellent choice for children with limited typing skills.

Where in the U.S.A. is Carmen SanDiego? from Broderbund has done more to encourage the memorization of information about the states than any other single educational material. Students become detectives and must chase an elusive thief throughout the fifty states and Washington, D.C. based on clues provided about each possible hideout location. No typing is required so students can pay full attention to the program content. "Carmen SanDiego" comes with a Fodor's Travel Guide of the United States, and students can confirm clues using the guide as a source of information. This program not only teaches geography, it also includes some historical information.

A number of local, state, and national resources and media and materials centers focus on reviewing and evaluating software and hardware for special education use. Knowing about these sources and how to access use of them enables teachers to appropriately select and recommend the most useful material and equipment for special education students. Some examples are:

- Access Unlimited-SPEECHenterprises
  9039 Katy Freeway, Suite 414
  Houston, TX 77024
- Trace Center International Software/Hardware Registry
  Trace Research and Development Center for the Severely
  Communicatively Handicapped
  University of Wisconsin
  314 Waisman Center
  1500 Highland Ave.
  Madison, WI 53706
- Closing the Gap
  P.O. Box 68
  Henderson, MN 56044

- Apple Computer
  Office of Special Education
  20525 Mariani Ave., Mail Stop 36M
  Cupertino, CA 95014
- The Center for Special Education Technology
  The Council for Exceptional Children (CEC)
  11920 Association Drive
  Reston, VA 22091

Summary and Conclusion

Special education teachers use and recommend to others modifications in instructional modalities and conditions to accommodate the curriculum access needs of students with disabilities. In situations related to student disabilities, teachers may need to use, or provide students with chances to use, adaptations or alternatives to the usual ways the curriculum is presented. Teachers may also have chances to share how microcomputers, videodiscs, and educational videotapes can be used to support improved access to curriculum related activities for the disabled student.

Consultation and leadership about modifying instructional modalities and conditions come primarily from special education teachers and related service providers who have expertise in serving students with a particular disability. When students have more than one disability, these professionals collaborate. When appropriate, they can also confer with the individual student, parents, and others concerned with a particular student. At times, regular teachers, students themselves, peers, and paraprofessionals can find novel and effective solutions to problems of student access to curriculum. Any and all approaches strive to provide students who have disabilities with access to the curriculum that equals the amount and quality nondisabled peers experience.

Notes

1. American Printing House for the Blind
   P.O. Box 6085
   Louisville, KY 40206
2. National Library Service for the Blind and Physically Handicapped
   The Library of Congress
   Washington, D.C. 20542

3. inLARGE
   Berkeley System Design
   1708 Shattuck Avenue
   Berkeley, CA 94709
4. Viewscan
   Sensory Aids Corporation
   White Pines Office Center, Suite 122
   205 West Grand Avenue
   Bensenville, IL 60106
5. Recording for the Blind, Inc.
   20 Rozel Road
   Princeton, NJ 08540
6. VersaBraille
   Telesensory Systems, Inc.
   455 N. Bernardo Ave.
   P.O. Box 7455
   Mountain View, CA 94039
7. Material contributed by Leslie Anido, teacher
8. Material contributed by Carolyn Compton, educational consultant,
   Palo Alto, CA 94039

References

Bentzen, B. 1977. Orientation aids for visually impaired persons. *Environmental modifications for the visually impaired: A handbook.* New York: American Foundation for the Blind (teacher made), p. 4–11.

Bentzen, B. 1984. Orientation aids for visually impaired persons. *Environmental modifications for the visually impaired: A handbook.* New York: American Foundation for the Blind (teacher made).

Bigge, J. 1982a. *Teaching individuals with physical and multiple disabilities.* Columbus, Ohio: Charles E. Merrill.

Bigge, M. 1982b. *Learning theories for teachers.* 4th ed. New York: Harper & Row.

Brown, L., Nisbet, J., Ford, A., Sweet, M., Shiraga, B., York, J., and Loomis, R. 1983. The critical need for nonschool instruction in educational programs for severely handicapped students. In *Educational programs for severely handicapped students,* Vol. XII, by L. Brown, J. Nisbet, A. Ford, M. Sweet, B. Shiraga and L. Gruenwald. Madison, WI: Department of Studies in Behavioral Disabilities, University of Wisconsin, pp. 1–11.

Corn, A. and Martinez, I. 1977. *When you have a visually handicapped child in your classroom: Suggestions for teachers.* New York: American Foundation for the Blind.

Hatlen, P. H., and Curry, S. A. 1987. In support of specialized programs for blind and visually impaired children. *Journal of Visual Impairment of Blindness* 81(1): 7–13.

Hofmeister, A., and Thorkildsen, R. 1987. Interactive videodisc and exceptional individuals. In *Computers and exceptional individuals,* by J. Lindsey, ed. Columbus, Ohio: Charles E. Merrill, pp. 189–205.

Mangold, S., and Mangold, P. 1986. *Mangold math #1: Read and write braille numerals.* Castro Valley, Calif.: Exceptional Teaching Aids. (Manual in both braille and ink print. Student material in Braille.)

Reynolds, H. N., and Booher, H. R. 1980. The effects of pictorial and verbal instructional materials on the operational performance of deaf subjects. *Journal of Special Education* 14: 175–87.

Sailor, W., Halvorsan, A., Anderson, J., Goetz, L., Gee, K., Doering, K., and Hunt, P. 1985. Community intensive instruction. In *Education of learners with severe handicaps,* edited by R. Horner, L. Meyer, and B. Fredericks. Baltimore, Md.: Paul Brookes.

Scadden, L. In press. Implications of the research and development of modern technology on the education of blind and visually handicapped students. In *The handbook of special education: Research and practice,* Vol. 1, edited by M. C. Wang, M. C. Reynolds, and H. J. Walberg. Oxford, England: Pergamon Press.

Smith, L. 1980. *The college student with a disability: A faculty handbook.* Sacramento, Calif.: California Governor's Committee for Employment of the Handicapped.

Snell, M. E., and Renzaglia, A. M. 1986. Moderate, severe, and profound handicaps. In *Exceptional children and youth,* 4th ed., edited by N. Haring and L. McCormick. Columbus, Ohio: Charles E. Merrill, pp. 271–312.

Waldron, M., Diebold, T., and Rose, S. 1985. Hearing impaired students in regular classrooms: A cognitive model for educational services. *Exceptional Children* 52(1): 39–43.

Wallace, G., and Kauffman, J. M. 1986. *Teaching students with learning and behavior problems.* 3d ed. Columbus, Ohio: Charles E. Merrill.

Wehman, P. and Hill, J. W., eds. 1980. *Instructional programming for severely handicapped youth: A community integration approach.* Richmond, Va.: Richmond Secondary Project, School of Education, Virginia Commonwealth University.

C H A P T E R

5

Effective Strategies for Instruction

It is through the technology of teaching, called instruction, that students experience the school curriculum. Students with problems in learning both the academic and nonacademic curriculum present special challenges to teachers. What instructional strategies work with students who are having problems in academic achievement? What strategies are effective for students who have problems learning nonacademic behaviors important to their age group and to community living? How do the strategies relate to curriculum and instruction of students? What are the major instructional techniques used within each general strategy?

Special education teachers learn particular bodies of knowledge and skills for meeting the unique needs of individuals and groups of students who have specific impairments. Certain developmental and educational needs are, for instance, unique to blind and visually impaired students. These are a direct result of their limited or lack of ability to observe the environment and respond according (Hatlen and Curry 1987). The developmental and educational needs of students with other disabilities are just as disability specific. The specialized preparation they receive enables teachers to make appropriate decisions about curriculum and instruction and to understand how the nature of the disability influences these areas. Teachers learn how to help students overcome potential deficits related to specific disabilities, and they also learn what students with specific disabilities need to be taught that other students do not. Students with visual impairments, for example, need to learn independent safe travel and access to printed information in ways that are unnecessary for other students.

In many cases, the content of the instruction is as specialized as the instructional processes. Again consider the example of educating students with visual impairments. It is unique to their needs to learn how to move independently around the community and to learn how to gain access to printed information either without sight or with limited sight. Often both content and strategies of instruction have to be special due to the past impact of impairments, the current influence of impairments, the nature of the tasks to be learned, and combinations of all these and other factors. Yet even while teaching unique content and incorporating specialized instructional processes, clearly articulated instructional strategies are important.

Certain instructional strategies have been found helpful and productive with special education students but are not necessarily limited to use with them. Some of these are:

1. Traditional instruction
2. Task analysis
3. Content and application-centered instruction
4. Direct instruction
5. Academic learning time modification
6. Curriculum-based assessment (and instruction)
7. Community intensive instruction
8. Transitional instructional strategies

Traditional instruction is the group of instructional strategies that are common to the practice of most teachers. *Task analysis* helps determine the content and sequence of skills, behaviors, and activities to be taught through instruction. *Application-centered instruction of content* of a subject helps determine rudiments of a subject for instructing students unable to study the subject as deeply as most students can. *Direct instruction* is the process of using highly systematic, explicit, and sequenced instruction. *Academic learning time modification* controls variables that result in increased amounts of time students spend in high-success performance in school subjects. *Curriculum-based assessment* (and instruction) incorporates strategies for determining optimal levels of student performance and then controls curriculum to maintain academic success. *Community-intensive instruction* is a process that uses the community as the classroom and teaches the kinds of skills students need to function as fully as possible in their communities. *Transitional instructional strategies* focus on training the student to move from one school-influenced crossroad of life to another (e.g., from school to work).

The reasons a teacher has for choosing one instructional strategy model over another vary. Some teachers select models consistent with their chosen learning theory (which is a systematic integrated outlook on human nature and how people learn). Then daily feedback on student achievement is used to determine whether to continue or change the strategy. Teachers also apply research findings and specialized practices pertaining to individuals with disabilities learned in professional preparation programs. Teachers can select teaching methods that are compatible with their personalities and personal abilities. Some teachers use instructional methodologies that result in students spending certain amounts of time doing content they can perform with high success. Teachers often use strategies that prepare students for mainstreaming, and this facilitates the students' social and academic integration into regular classrooms.

Instructional strategies are selected because they teach students with different physical, learning, and behavioral disabilities to learn among other things which strategies work best for them in different situations. Certain instructional strategies are chosen because of their effectiveness in teaching students who have difficulty generalizing training undertaken at school to other school and non-school situations. Still other strategies are chosen because they prepare students for transition from school to postschool environments.

Traditional Instruction

Knowing the instructional methodologies commonly used in regular education is important information for specialist teachers. Familiarity with a variety of practices is valuable for several reasons. First, many students receiving special education and related services will be participating in regular classes where traditional instructional models are used. They may need special education support for doing this. Second, students could need to be taught skills and given experiences for transition into regular classes where teachers are using certain traditional models of instruction. Transition into regular classes will be enhanced if students have been taught some of the routines the teachers of these classes use. Third, these traditional instructional models represent proven, effective teaching practices; special education teachers can use them with and without modifications for students with disabilities. Now let's identify some of these usual instructional models and briefly review the newer ones.

Joyce and Weil (1980) identify and describe the instructional models used in teaching. Teacher educational programs for preparation of regular teachers include:

1. Demonstration, explanation, telling, and showing
2. Small-group projects
3. Concept attainment
4. Guided practice
5. Role play or creative dramatics
6. Games or simulations
7. Inquiry
8. Field trip or outdoor education
9. Television/movie/filmstrip
10. Learning centers
11. Guided imagery
12. Problem solving
13. Contingency management
14. Computer-assisted instruction

To these we add cooperative learning and megacognitive strategy instruction. These strategies are typically taught in regular education and have implications for students in special education. These are among the newest approaches to instruction and both regular and special education teachers can use them effectively.

Cooperative Learning. Using cooperative learning strategies, teachers and students engage in problem solving and work toward mutually held objectives. Cooperative learning strategies are taught and employed in a variety of situations. Groups of students together might study information the teacher provides. Students might work together on such activities as tournaments and games to reach common ends. Students could discuss and cooperatively report on a topic (Slavin, Madden, and Leavey 1984, Paris and Oka 1986). These are all examples of cooperative learning.

Cooperative learning situations require students to develop and use the kinds of social skills necessary for building and maintaining a stable family, a successful career, and a circle of friends. Though not traditional curriculum material, these skills have to be taught just as purposefully and precisely as reading and math skills. One advantage of cooperative learning situations is that social skills with long-term value are required, used, reinforced, and mastered within a task situation. Basic elements of cooperative learning are (1) individual accountability, (2) face-to-face interaction, (3) positive interdependence, and (4) cooperative skills.

Metacognitive Strategy Instruction. Palincsar (1986) defines and describes metacognitive strategy instruction as being based on teaching students knowledge about themselves as learners. This in turn leads to student regulation of learning activities.

Palincsar states that "the purpose of metacognitive strategy instruction is to influence how the learner interacts with the learning situation" (p. 118). In metacognitive strategy instruction, the teacher's goals are to teach students to plan, implement, and evaluate strategic approaches to learning and problem solving. Students gradually take over control of their own learning. Teachers start by providing "explicit instruction regarding efficient strategies and gradually relinquish control for the application of these strategies to learners who are informed regarding the purpose and consequences of their activity" (Palincsar 1986, 123–24).

With metacognitive strategy instruction, students are taught about themselves as learners, taught about strategies that could enhance their learning, and taught to discern for themselves which strategies are best for them under what circumstances. A simple example of a metacognitive skill occurs when a student realizes that it is necessary to prepare differently for a multiple-choice test than for an essay test. Eventually students have to monitor and regulate their own use of these strategies, noting the utility and consequences of the strategies in particular situations and changing strategies to better accomplish their goals.

Task Analysis

Task analysis is both a process and a product (Bailey and Wolery 1984) that involves breaking a complex skill or series of behaviors into teachable units. As a process, task analysis is a way to break complex skills or behaviors into smaller steps. As a product, task analysis generates a written series of steps for the student to learn. It allows teachers to determine the content and sequence of instruction, the points where instructional strategy needs to intervene, and the next skill or behavior in the series to be taught.

According to Mank and Horner (1988), the purpose of task analysis is to "facilitate training by focusing the instructor's attention on the specific demands of a task and by providing a method for gathering data during training about the acquisition of the task by the student", See Table 5.1 for a sample task analysis.

Mank and Horner (1988) identify nine points or guidelines for building a task analysis:

1. The specific objective for the task should be identified and recorded.
2. The person who will be doing the training should perform the task several times before constructing a task analysis. [This is not always possible; for example, the trainer may not be able to sit in a wheelchair and manipulate the controls.]
3. The person who will be doing the training should analyze the task and construct the task analysis.
4. The task should be broken down into response units which are small enough for successful instruction to the student.
5. The steps in the task should be sequenced in exactly the order in which they will be performed.
6. The discriminative stimuli or the antecedent condition for each step should be identified.
7. The criterion for successful completion of each step should be identified.
8. Use the sequence of steps to construct a data collection format for use during training.
9. Ensure that the sequence of steps results in completion of the task.

Job analysis is a good example of one use for task analysis. In job analysis, the tasks comprising the job duties are identified and sequenced. Mank and Horner (1988) use the work of Buckley, Sandow, and Smock (in press) to differentiate job analysis from task analysis. Job analysis tends to focus on the decision rules for determining which tasks come next and on the sequence of task performance. In contrast, task analysis focuses on the specifics of "what to do," detailing each step comprising the job duties. The purpose of conducting a job analysis, according to

Table 5.1   Sample Task Analysis

DISCRIMINATIVE STIMULI	RESPONSE (SUBSKILLS)
1. Ready to clean floor.	1. Procure broom, dust pan, mop and mop bucket.
2. Materials ready.	2. Go to dining room.
3. In dining room.	3. Put chairs on tables.
4. Chairs on tables.	4. Go to far corner with push broom.
5. In far corner.	5. Sweep under tables.
6. Under tables swept (entire area).	6. Go to far corner.
7. In far corner.	7. Sweep aisles toward door.
8. Aisles swept.	8. Sweep debris into single pile.
9. Debris in single pile.	9. Pick up dustpan.
10. Dustpan in hand.	10. Sweep debris into dustpan.
11. Debris in dustpan.	11. Empty dustpan in trash receptacle.
12. Dustpan emptied.	12. Return broom and dustpan to door.
13. Broom and dustpan at door.	13. Get and fill mop bucket.
14. Mop bucket filled.	I4. Take mop and bucket to far corner.
15. Mop and bucket in far corner.	15. Mop under all tables.
16. Mopping under tables completed.	16. Go to far corner.
17. In far corner.	17. Mop aisles from corner toward door.
18. Aisles mopped.	18. Empty mop bucket.
19. Mop bucket emptied.	19. Gather all implements.
20. Implements gathered.	20. Return implements to custodial closet.
21. Implements in closet.	21. Go to next task.

Source: Modified and used with permission from D. Mank and R. Horner. 1988. "Instructional Programming in Vocational Education" in *Vocational Education of Persons with Handicaps,* edited by R. Gaylord-Ross (Mountain View, Calif.: Mayfield Publishing Co.).

Mank and Horner, is to ensure that the student meets the requirements of the employment position. "In other words, the tasks must be performed at the proper time and in an acceptable way to result in completion of the entire job" (Buckley, Sandow, and Smock in press). See Figure 5.1.

The types of task analyses people are most familiar with are those that are *sequential,* or *serial,* in nature. Each step (also referred to in the literature as *subtask, substep, link, subskill,* or *enroute skill*) is taught independently of the others. Each step in a serial task analysis leads to the next step as in a ladder, and each must be mastered before moving on to the next.

Logical ordering and *instructional* ordering are two task analysis concepts

Figure 5.1 Job Analysis Summary

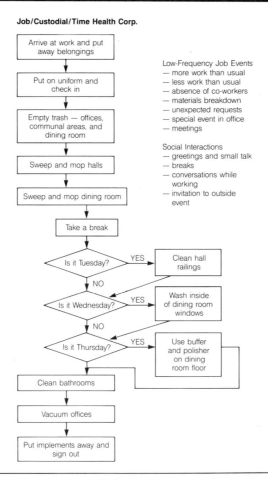

Used with permission from Mank and Horner (1988).

described by Sailor and Guess (1983). Logical ordering is a task analysis that starts at the first step (step or subskill #1) and progresses in logical sequence to the last step. Instructional ordering comes in three varieties depending on the order the steps in a task analysis are taught: *forward* chains, *backward* chains, and *mixed* chains.

In forward chains, *instructional* ordering and *logical* ordering are the same. Both start with step one and move step by step to the end of the sequence. A sample forward chain for the single skill objective, "maneuver own electric wheelchair," is as follows:

1. Put on seat belt.
2. Turn power on to low.
3. Identify a path to travel.
4. Keep hand on control.
5. Apply even pressure to controls.
6. Move in the identified path.
7. Stop before nearing obstructions (furniture or people).
8. And so on . . .

In reverse chaining, information is conveyed that the "logical (forward) chain of steps is not to be followed in instruction" (Sailor and Guess 1983, 139). Rather the order of instruction occurs from the bottom of the chain, teaching the last step of the logical order first and then moving sequentially to the first step. Sailor and Guess give this example of a reverse chain of instruction with an objective for a child to remove a slipover shirt and place it on a table:

9. Grasp bottom of shirt with both hands.
8. Raise shirt to underarms.
7. Grasp shirt at back of neck over head with both hands.
6. Pull shirt over head.
5. Grasp shirt at left shoulder with right arm.
4. Pull shirt off of left arm.
3. Grasp shirt with left hand.
2. Pull shirt off of right arm.
1. Place shirt on table.
    (Sailor and Guess 1983, 136)

In mixed chaining, the order is neither forward or reverse chaining. Instruction would not proceed systematically in logical order. Nor would it proceed systematically from the last to the first step in a reverse order. Rather, instruction would result in mastery of steps in mixed order.

"Instructional ordering is always conveyed by the numbering system to the left of the steps in the chain" (Sailor and Guess 1983, 139). Sailor and Guess (1983, 141–149) describe principles of using student motivation, cue analysis, and other rationales for different ordering of instruction. Since each step is a discrete behavior, accomplishment of each can be measured independently of the others. Criteria for listing steps, or subskills, in serial order can vary for each step: "Percent, frequency, rate, duration, and length typify measurement schemes applicable to serial chains in task-analyzed objectives." (Sailor and Guess 1983, 159).

Sometimes students learn much more quickly and easily than expected. This could change the process from a serial strategy to a more concurrent strategy. Instead of learning one thing at a time forward, backward, or mixed in sequence, students might learn several subskills at once. This is fine if teachers recognize what is happening and change from a serial teaching-learning strategy to one that facilitates learning several subskills simultaneously.

The initial identification of skills and subskills need not always result in the serial ordering of subtasks. Task analysis can also result in skills grouped in clusters that can be taught concurrently. Sailor and Guess clarify that in the case of concurrent chains the objective is to teach all steps concurrently. Criterion statements then would not relate to accomplishing individual subskills but to completing all subskills or at least completing a designated percentage of the subskills. To denote mastery, teachers often require students to meet the standard a certain number of consecutive times or to complete all or a designated part of the subtasks a set number of times, repetitively.

An example of cluster skills for concurrent instruction is as follows:

Disciplines: Life management: orientation (O); mobility (M); communications (C)

Competence Goal: Enter any room, manuever to the people in the room, look someone in the eye, and ask permission to join the conversation

1. Locate entrances to room.
2. Ask persons to open closed doors.
3. Thank persons for assisting.
4. Maneuver through doors.
5. Wheel to a person or group of people.
6. When the first person acknowledges presence, look them in the eye and say "Hi."
7. And so on . . .

Still another way to organize skills, according to Sailor and Guess, is to order them "in a manner that is natural to the various environments in which the student is expected to perform" (1983, 184). For maximal generalization—which is the desired outcome—the standard would include demonstrating the skill or cluster of skills "across material, persons, settings, tasks, and contents" (Sailor and Guess 1983, 189).

Content- and Application-Centered Instruction

Special education teachers frequently find themselves responsible for instructing the rudiments of content and application in different school subjects. These teachers then institute certain strategies so that their students will have opportunities to learn the core subjects and elective subjects even though they cannot learn them with the same breadth and depth as nonhandicapped students.

The first step in this process occurs when a gifted special education teacher asks, "How can I deny these special education students the right to study, understand, and appreciate the variety of subjects other students study just because they can't keep up with the others?" Such teachers then find themselves dissecting one or more school subjects to find the rudiments, or most important ideas and concepts, and the applications. In doing this, the teachers' goals to help students learn as much as they can and keep up to the best degree possible. Special education teachers can either teach the subjects themselves or provide assistance to regular teachers. Teacher strategies include determining which of the usual teaching-learning experiences should be included, which augmented, and which excluded. Concurrently, teachers strive to find reading and other materials to which they can direct students for studying the topics.

In working on choosing and analyzing tasks, special education teachers find themselves responsible for sorting out the rudiments of a variety of different subjects at many different grade levels. At the elementary level, teachers are generally familiar with most subjects. At the middle and high school levels, though, knowing most subject matter can become a major challenge because collectively students are involved in a wide variety of core and elective subjects. It would be unusual for any one teacher to have a working knowledge of the various subjects studied—art, literature, biological science, European history, and so forth. At this level, the job becomes more formidable.

To prepare for teaching content rudiments a teacher needs to know where to start and how to find the rudiments of a subject or discipline. There is no simple or single approach, but here are some time-tested tactics:

1. Find patterns of emphasis in different resources.
2. Find longitudinal progressions.
3. Note key vocabularies.
4. Analyze concepts.
5. Use appropriate complexity levels in methods.
6. Select and use appropriate student materials.

The first tactic is to *find patterns of emphasis in different resources*. First, look for patterns of repetitions in the information emphasized in different resources. Whether a person is a young or older student or adult learning about field sports, certain patterns are present: teams, scoring, rules, penalties for rule infractions, time limits, equipment, boundaries, and so on. Whether a person is a young or older student, students likewise learn similar topics. For example, many topics appear in all levels of science study. Life science patterns include the study of human systems, green plants, animals, the five senses; earth science patterns include the changing earth, weather, solar system, and natural resources. Patterns appearing repeatedly in physical science are energy, electricity, machines, and sound. When studying about economics at all levels, people learn about scarcity, consumers, producers, money and its value, the marketplace, profits, competition, wages, and income. To discover patterns in any subject, look for repetitions, or overlaps, of the same information stressed in curriculum guides, courses of study, teachers' manuals, and student textbook editions. Tables of content and focus-of-skill lists are good places to start. Dictionaries, special topic encyclopedias written for children and youth, specialty books written as reference books, district resource centers and resource persons with expertise on the topic are other sources for finding patterns and extracting the rudiments of a subject or field of study. Notice any same or similar skills and knowledge fields that appear as important teaching objectives or student outcomes, and jot these down. (Post-it Notes work well because they can easily be rearranged as more definite patterns emerge.)

The second tactic is to *find longitudinal progressions.* The sequenced steps in developing proficiency in all phases of language is one illustration of a longitudinal progression. In academic subjects, teachers use scope and sequence charts to see which subskills in subjects are taught prior to others. These charts show the whole longitudinal progression of skills from the very simple ones to the more complex ones within one subject. (See Chapter 9 for an example of a life management curriculum built on a longitudinal listing of age-appropriate and functional activities.) Look for increasingly complex progressions within each pattern. Once you have noticed that there seems to be a pattern in all the resources for teaching certain concepts, knowledges, or skills, trace that development either from more complex to reduced complexity, or start with the most basic concepts, knowledges, and skills and notice how they gradually become more complex. This suggests an instructional progression, even though not all students in special education will progress at the same speed. It also suggests ways to reduce the complexity of the same concepts, knowledges, or skills for students who cannot accomplish them at the same level of complexity as their peers do.

The third tactic is to *note key vocabularies.* Terms and definitions are extremely important. Teachers may choose not to teach students the definitions and terms by rote, but they might want to do so by example. Sometimes it is helpful to note the more familiar terminology in a subject area in order to teach the technical terminology. Notice how the terminology for the basic ideas changes or remains the same from early childhood curriculum in music to those for teaching the same information to older students (i.e., the word *fast* in describing tempo, or speed for young students, when *allegro* and *vivaci,* more technical terms, are used to describe those same concepts to high school music students.)

The fourth tactic is to *analyze concepts.* Based on content analysis and the student's need to apply the concepts in daily life and problem solving, extract critical enroute concepts. "In teaching concepts, we are teaching *meaning,* not words." (Rowntree 1981, 70). Similar to the process of defining enroute skills critical to performing higher-order skills, define the concepts that are critical to learning higher order knowledges and skills. Note the attributes, or characteristics, that make persons, places, things, or ideas examples or instances of what is to be taught and perhaps applied in an appropriate context. This process of analyzing concepts is perhaps one of the most important steps. The tactic of identifying attributes or characteristics not only helps teachers understand rudiments of a subject or discipline, but it also provides one or more basic teaching strategies that can be of great help to the students.

To analyze a concept, Rowntree (1981, 73) suggests these basic techniques of analysis:

1. Isolate the concept.
2. Define the concept.
3. List model examples.
4. List counterexamples.
5. Examine related examples.
6. Identify borderline examples.
7. Invent examples.
8. Compare social contexts.
9. Explore personal contexts.

A first step is to isolate or sort out the concepts from facts, examples, and exercises. For example, "Has rock music imposed danger to listeners?" is a question of concept, not fact. Defining the concept as a dictionary or textbook would is the next step. Then define the concept, listing model examples and counterexamples and examining related examples and identifying borderline examples.

Rowntree (1981, 74–76) discusses these and the remaining techniques of analysis: inventing examples, comparing social contexts, and exploring personal contexts. Teachers can help students test concepts by inventing imaginary cases ("Let us look at this situation as it might be seen by a visitor from outer space"). Comparing social contexts gives teachers and students an opportunity to recognize that people from different places, times, and cultures might not agree with our culture's examples and nonexamples of concepts. Exploring personal contexts allows people to heed what concepts mean, personally, to different individuals. Different experiences, values, anxieties, knowledge, and so forth will have insured that the concept has acquired different connotations.

Teachers do not stop by conducting concept analyses of materials they are to teach. A next step involves relating these concepts to other concepts and evolving principles, or generalizations.

The fifth tactic is to *use appropriate complexity levels in methods and materials*. In teacher's editions of textbooks note how one level of difficulty or complexity is different from another. This can suggest strategies for reducing or increasing the complexity level. Some can be direct resources for teachers, suggesting strategies teachers can use to transmit the essence of the material.

Charts of curriculum "scope and sequences" can be another place to start. These are generally not presented in enough detail, but they might show similarities and differences of objective complexities to be taught at different grade levels. Teachers might be able to use lessons designed for younger students by modifying the materials, problems, and discussions to make them appropriate for older special education students. Teachers can also find clues to reduced complexity levels by studying the "review" sections in the usual grade-level materials.

Complexity change strategies often parallel those suggested in upcoming chapters on reducing levels of complexities and teaching basic thinking skills to students with learning problems. This includes moving back from abstract to concrete (from more to less complexity) and moving ahead from recognition or discrimination to identification (from less to greater complexity).

Good special education teachers must know how to analyze and change commercial and teacher-made materials to the best format for their particular students. Such teachers need to learn how to acquire reading and other learning resources that provide the necessary information and skills for extracting the rudiments, or fundamentals, of curricular topic or skills to be taught.

A final tactic described here is to *select and use appropriate student materials*. Choosing student-use materials and aids is part of facilitating instruction of important rudiments in content areas and their related applications. Gickling and Havertape (1981) discuss factors to consider in selecting materials. Materials, like instructional methods, are selected according to their theoretical approach, their organization, and the sequencing of the concepts. Important specific factors are the amount of material presented, the rate of introduction of new concepts, the amount of time devoted to teaching new concepts, the amount of repetition and practice, and the types and flexibility of the students' response requirements.

Actual objects and firsthand activities provide concrete experience and chances to gain perceptions for students who need a more concrete introduction to concepts. Films, videotapes, and other audiovisual materials can accompany or be substituted for information usually acquired through reading. And teacher-made and commercially produced reading materials are additional sources of student learning.

Teachers may have to write or rewrite student-use reading matter. For example, students with hearing impairment are one group requiring materials written to meet their particular needs. Subject matter in standard commercially available materials (e.g., social studies, science, and reading) "is usually presented through linguistic structures too complex for most hearing-impaired students. Thus, teachers must rewrite materials or work with students on specific language skills prior to introducing what is supposed to be the content of the course" (Lowenbraun and Thompson 1986, 387).

The reason teachers write student-use materials is to meet the individual needs of special students. Teachers who write their own materials not only have to determine the rudiments of a subject, but they also have to have some idea of the readability and other characteristics of the material they write for groups and individuals.

Several different types of commercial high-interest, low-reading-level reading materials (high/low) are available for student reading and reference. High/low student materials are available on many school subjects (e.g., economics, history of America), basic academic skills (spelling), research and study skills (outlining), practical academic skills (banking), literary classics (*Treasure Island*), and special interests (country music stars).

Computer software is also available for students with reading problems. Chan (1985) identifies computer software for students with reading problems, suggesting a core collection of high/low computer programs. Sometimes teachers can be even more creative in finding ways to use microcomputers to enhance student learning.

To make intelligent selections about student-use materials for students to read and gain information for their school work, teachers need to determine the readability of the materials. To avoid presenting reading matter too hard for students, teachers must use a guideline for determining difficulty levels.

Several factors influence the degree of reading difficulty. One way to measure reading difficulty is to use normative data. Perritt (1985) explains readability factors and methods for determining reading levels. She states that some of these factors "are inherent in the language: vocabulary and its levels of meaning, sentence length, sentence structure, complexity of concepts and levels of abstraction, and variations in format and organization. Other factors are unique to the reader: interest, motivation, language competence, and experiential background" (p. 86). Readability can be determined as it relates to difficulty of materials read by most children in a certain grade.

According to Perritt, readability formulas typically rely on word length, word frequency, and sentence length because researchers have found that these are the most important quantitative measures to use in predicting readability. Readability formulas as applied are expressed as grade levels with a margin of plus or minus one full grade level. For many students with learning problems, this will not be a fine enough discrimination, and teachers will still need to use what they know about each individual to select the appropriate lessons material.

Take for example, the three-level reading materials by Upton et al. (1955). Under similar book covers, titled the same and coded subtly to indicate reading levels, the same basic information is presented to students. *Tom's America* fits into a study of the westward movement. Upton (1955, 4–5) gives illustrations from three versions of the book (See Fig. 5.2).

Tom's America (Upton et al. 1953) was a social studies book for grade five published on three reading levels. Different groups of users enjoyed the same reading experience with material suited to their reading levels. The authors used then-current information about readability factors. The lower level was written for children whose reading grade level was from 2.8 to 4.0. The middle level was for children reading between grade level 4.5 and 5.5. The upper level was for children whose ability was grade level 6.0 or above.

The narrative and information presented the same meaning in the three books

---

LOWER LEVEL

The man looked at Tom. He could tell what the boy was thinking. "You may need to give up going to California," the man said.

Tom did not want to give up. "I don't think I will give up," he said. "Other people go past the jumping off place. People do go to California. If they can, I can!"

MIDDLE LEVEL

The man's sharp eyes were watching Tom. He seemed to be reading Tom's thoughts. "You may have to give up the idea of going to California."

The words "give up" made Tom want to go on more than ever. He did not like the idea of giving up. "I don't think I will give up going to California," he said. "Other people go past the jumping off place and get to California. If they can, I can!"

UPPER LEVEL

The man's shrewd eyes were watching Tom as though he were reading the boys thoughts. You may find it necessary to give up the idea of going to California," Mr. Travis suggested.

The words "give up" were like a challenge to Tom. He did not come from the kind of people who gave up easily.

"I'm not so sure about that," he said with spirit. "Other people go past the jumping off place and get to California. If they can, I can!"

Figure 5.2 A social studies book is published in three versions, each with a different reading level.

---

and was even found on the same page in each book. Information on the lower level was presented with the use of very simple words limited to a universally identified list of beginning reading words. The sentences were short. The same meaning was presented in more complex sentences and interesting words as the difficulty level increased. A teacher's manual of suggestions on the use of three-level reading materials was also provided.

Presently, student texts with these features are nearly nonexistent. This does not mean that the situation cannot be changed. Teachers have responsibility and power to influence publishers to provide the types of materials students need. Letters, calls, and conferences can inform publishers of potential markets for products with desirable features.

Direct Instruction

Direct instruction, and components of it, are probably the most frequently used strategies with special education students. According to Gersten, Woodward, and Darch (1986), direct instruction is the "systematic, explicit teaching of academic strategies to students" (p. 17). Direct instruction depends on explicit instruction on each step in a sequence of problem solving strategies and design of instructional delivery systems including carefully constructed curriculum materials. Direct Instruction is also referred to as *direct teaching* and *directive teaching*. Direct and daily measurement are characteristics of direct-instruction methodologies. Other instructional strategies that are considered direct instruction and have these characteristics are behavior modification, applied behavior analysis, precision teaching, and responsive teaching (Lovitt, 1982).

The work of Carl Bereiter and Siegfried Engelmann (1966) formed the basis of this strategy. The original materials to accompany the direct instructional delivery system were the DISTAR programs to teach the rudiments of reading, math, and language. Remedial programs comprising "The Corrective Reading Series" (Engelmann et al. 1978) were developed later.

Instructional Format

Gersten et al. (1986) state that the key principle in the design of direct instruction programs is that in order for all students to learn, both the materials and teacher presentation of these materials must be clear and unambiguous. With direct instruction, teacher instruction and the curriculum are both detailed and precisely crafted. The definitions, concepts, and relationships to be taught are clearly articulated. Instructional steps in lessons become precisely described strategies for students to learn and later apply on their own. For a strategy to be effective, according to Gersten et al. (1986), it must have certain features. Features appear some place in strategy instruction "from the highly teacher-directed introduction of a strategy to the point where students can perform complex operations or problem-solving routines with minimal prompting" (p. 19). For any one strategy, these features of instruction should all appear at some place in the format of instruction:

1. Teach an *explicit* step-by-step strategy.
   (When this is not possible or necessary, model effective performance.)
2. Develop mastery at each step in the process.
3. Develop strategy (or progress) correction for student errors.
4. Gradually fade from teacher-directed activities toward independent work.
5. Use adequate, systematic practice with a range of examples.
6. Use cumulative review.

An example might be a direct instruction program for students who are poor readers—ones who do not analyze letters in words or analyze the word endings when they read. This instruction incorporates the strategy of teaching how to decode words with long vowels. The source of the explicit step-by-step strategy, "The Corrective Reading Decoding B Program" (Engelmann et al. 1978) is a set of instructional materials in which the materials and teacher presentations are clear and unambiguous.

One task illustrates these features. The task is to read these words in isolation within 30 days of instruction: *shaded, conning, traded, cones, maker, conned, blade, and conner.* (Remember the objective is learning to analyze the letters in words, not necessarily to comprehend the word meanings.)

Students are first taught to identify the long and short sounds of the vowels: *o* and *a* and *e.* Pointing to the letters in lessons on sound introductions, teachers may prompt students by pointing to one letter, for example, *o* and saying:

> **One sound you learned for this letter is the same as the letter name. Everybody, what's that sound?"** Signal: *ooo*
> "Yes, ooo."
> "What's the other sound?" Signal: ŏ
> "Yes, ŏ."

Once all students can identify the long and short sounds of vowels, the teacher gives them a strategy for decoding the words. Students "are given six words written on the board (r<u>o</u>de, r<u>o</u>d, f<u>i</u>n, f<u>i</u>ne, r<u>o</u>be, r<u>o</u>b) and the following rule: **"If the last letter is *e,* you'll hear a letter name in the word. You'll hear the name of the letter that is underlined"** (Gersten et al. 1986, 19). The strategy taught to the students is explicit and highly prompted (that is, the letter in question is underlined) in order to increase chances for success.

Once students develop mastery of this step in the process, the teacher teaches use of the strategies in slightly expanded contexts. In the previous decoding example, students are presented with five other words on the board (r<u>o</u>bes, r<u>o</u>bs, n<u>o</u>ted, l<u>a</u>ter, l<u>a</u>tter) and given the following rule: **"If the last letter of that under-lined part is *e,* you'll hear a letter name in that part."**

Once students develop mastery of this step, they are no longer given the rules. Instead they are asked about rules through examples. From this point on in this instructional sequence, students are asked, not told, about the rules. When presented with the word, *t<u>a</u>les* (with an underline prompt), the students are asked,

"Are you going to hear a letter name?" Students respond yes or no and then read the word.

Eventually prompts are faded or deleted, and the teacher-directed activities regarding rules are faded from direct naming of rules, asked but not told about the rule, reminded about a possible rule until finally all reminders of the appropriate rules are dropped from teacher presentations, and students do the tasks with no prompts. In the explicit step-by-step sequence of decoding tasks, the same kinds of words are presented with prompts deleted and with teachers using only reminders such as, **"You will hear a letter name in the first part of some of these words, but the first part is not underlined, so be careful."** Eventually all prompts and reminders are dropped, and students again perform the strategies with no help.

In the initial demonstration phase, teachers provide clear, controlled presentations of new material. Guided practice follows demonstrations and allows teachers to ask questions of students, check for understanding, and give feedback. This is only done with highly structured routines.

Teacher Techniques

Research (Rosenshine and Stevens 1984) has shown that low-performing students repeatedly show higher academic achievement when their teachers follow a consistent practice of organizing lessons around (1) demonstration, (2) guided practice, (3) feedback, and (4) providing opportunities for student independent practice. To do this, teachers use recognized techniques to manage the students and present the tasks. These techniques are specified by some of the direct instruction founders (Engelmann et al. 1978, 16–19). They describe specified techniques including (1) scripted presentations, (2) formatted exercises, (3) correction procedures, (4) lesson set-ups, (5) pacing, (6) signal use, (7) teaching to low performers, and (8) positive reinforcement.

Scripted Presentations. Scripted presentations specify within a lesson what the teacher says for each activity and how the teacher corrects student mistakes. Scripted presentations are used to guide and control the wide range of details that are essential in successful teaching. Such details include the sequence of tasks that make up a lesson, the instructions given to students, the number and type of examples that are practiced, and the precise steps in the development of each skill. In the presentation books and other curriculum materials specially designed for direct instruction, one typeface indicates what the teacher says, a second typeface indicates what the teacher does, and a third typeface shows the students' responses.

Recognizing initial teacher reservations about such a firm structure, Engelmann et al. (1978) describe that in addition to controlling program sequences, scripted presentations have other advantages:

- Scripted directions allow teachers to present a number of examples quickly. Some teachers might present wordy explanations that do not permit the time to present many examples.
- Scripted directions standardize the wording from example to example, so that students will not be confused by varying instruction.
- Teacher training is simplified because trainers can work on common presentation problems.
- Scripts provide efficient correction procedures that contain few words and build on what the students have already been taught.
- The time spent on each activity is controlled; therefore, a more effective development of a range of skills is guaranteed (Engelmann et al. 1978, 17).

Formatted Exercises. Exercises are structured so that the same format can be used to accommodate similar tasks. The advantage is that the clarity of presentations through consistent format assists both students and teachers. Teacher behavior remains basically the same for all examples of a format, simplifying the presentation of similar activities. Formats also help students understand what is being presented because the directions and wording are the same for similar kinds of material. Thus the format can serve as a prompt for applying a newly learned strategy to new examples and in a variety of contexts.

Correction Procedures. The teacher's procedures for correcting students are essential to effective teaching in the direct instruction approach. Student mistakes provide teachers with important information about the kinds of difficulties students are having. These difficulties might be general in nature. For example, students can fail to answer when a signal is given for them to respond or they respond at the wrong time. The error was in knowing when to respond, not in the content of the response. General correction procedures are used in these cases, such as repeating the segment and saying, "I have to hear everybody!" This give students in error another chance without identifying them by name. The difficulties can relate to specific content. Students could, for example, identify letters by the wrong name. Then specific correction procedures are necessary, and these are often scripted into materials designed for direct instruction use. Specific corrections include steps of following the error with (1) modeling, or demonstrating the response students are to make; (2) testing, or presenting the task again to give the teacher feedback about whether the correction worked; and then (3) retesting, or going back to earlier steps and presenting the full task again embedded in the context of other responses.

Lesson Setups. In direct instruction, recommendations for lesson setups are specific. Students should all be seated so they can see what the teacher points to in presentation books or writes on chalkboards. Placement directly in front of the teacher so the teacher can monitor responses and behavior is specified for lower-performing students and those whose behaviors pose problems. Worksheet exercises that follow boardwork are organized so they can be passed out quickly.

Pacing.   The pacing of exercises is a commonly used factor in direct instruction. Teachers are to move quickly but not to rush students so much that they make mistakes. Teachers review exercises ahead of lessons so they can present them smoothly and without having to look at the script. "Lines should be said quickly, and instruction should be concise" (Engelmann et al. 1978, 18).

Signals.   Different signals are used to keep a group of students together and to prevent some from copying what others say. A point-touch signal is used when pointing to words or symbols in a presentation book. Audible signals such as finger snapping and clapping are used when students are attending to materials on worksheets and not looking at teachers ("**Everybody touch part B on your worksheet!**" Fingersnap.) Sound-out signals provide timing for students to respond and move together as they sound out and blend parts of words. Finally, sequential-response signals are used in orally presented tasks that require students to give different responses in a specific sequence. An example of signal use is an exercise showing basic evidence using facts (Engelmann et al. 1978, 23), illustrated below.

EXERCISE 1. BASIC EVIDENCE: USING FACTS

The first Thinking Operations today is Basic Evidence.

1. *You're going to use two facts to explain things that happened. They are the only facts you can use. Hold up one finger. First fact.*

   The man was very strong. Say it. Signal.
   The man was very strong. Repeat until firm.
   Hold up two fingers. *Second fact.*
   The plane had a broken engine. Say it. Signal.
   The plane had a broken engine. Repeat until firm.

2. *Everybody, say those facts again.*

   Hold up one finger. *First fact.*
   The man was very strong.
   Hold up two fingers. *Second fact.*
   The plane had a broken engine.
   Repeat until the students say the facts in order.

Teaching to Low Performers.   This exercise and the related teaching techniques involve the process of repeating tasks. Teachers use the low-performing students in a group as a gauge of whether the group is "firm." Rapidly paced repetitions take little time and assure that all students can do the tasks. When all students can perform the tasks, the teacher moves on to the next tasks.

Positive Reinforcement. Positive reinforcement is used to increase the likelihood that the students will practice the skills taught. Positive reinforcement is particularly important for students who have histories of low performance for one reason or another. Many have acquired negative attitudes about even trying academic tasks. Teachers need to use programs designed so that the sequences of tasks are readily learnable. "Without achievable tasks, students will continue to make many mistakes and, therefore, their negative attitude will not change. The program must provide students with the evidence that they are improving to counter their tendency to interpret every mistake as proof of failure. The sequence must be planned so that students conclude that there is indeed a purpose, a direction, a development in their reading [or other] performance" (Engelmann et al. 1978, 19).

Teachers institute reinforcement systems so that students earn points for their success rates, and then they summarize weekly progress on charts. For young children, the points can be as simple as strips of colored construction paper. Positive reinforcement is an important technique for encouraging students to improve their performances.

Applications Beyond Academics

Davis, Uhler, and Kelly (1986) describe direct instruction strategies that are used to help students with behavior disorders gain self control. One approach using direct instruction strategies teaches individual students to emit self-directive verbal statements and guide their behavior accordingly. The content of these self-instructions are selected based on the unique needs of individuals. A distractible student, for instance, may be trained to emit self-directive verbal statements such as, "I'll keep my eyes on my work." An impulsive student might be trained to say, "I'll slow down, relax, take my time." Other instructional strategies, consistent with direct instruction, include modeling and prompting by the teacher and a fading of student self-prompts from aloud verbal self-instructions to silent self-instructions. Direct instruction can also be applied to functional activities such as learning to cross the street. Teachers help students learn to cross streets by being very direct about teaching them and measuring progress— in this case, in natural situations. If a student has a problem such as not knowing how to ask for directions at a street corner, then teachers are forthright in teaching that part of the process.

Direct-instruction techniques are also used to teach independent living skills and competent work skills and behaviors. General case or general use strategy is the main technique (Engelmann and Carnine 1982, Horner and McDonald 1982, and Mank and Horner 1988). According to Mank and Horner (1988), this process "emphasized the role of selecting and sequencing teaching examples so students who complete training perform new behaviors across all appropriate stimulus conditions and do not perform these new behaviors in inappropriate stimulus conditions. The focus of general case instruction is on understanding the range of conditions under which a behavior needs to occur as well as similar but inappropriate situations in which the behavior should not occur."

The explicit strategies in these instructions help teachers define a range of stimulus conditions across which behaviors should be performed. Another aspect of preparing for instruction and the actual instruction is carefully selecting a small number of examples that adequately sample the range of relevant stimulus variations an individual might normally encounter. Once teaching and testing examples are selected, the teacher follows carefully structured teaching routines.

Sprague and Horner (1984) used direct-instruction principles to research how effective different methods of teaching use of vending machines were to students with severe learning problems. The vending machines used in this hands-on instruction consisted of examples that adequately represented the class types of vending machines individuals might normally encounter. Research focused on finding the training conditions that lead to the highest correct performance on machines other than the ones used to train the students. Training on a *set* of vending machines that sampled the range (adequately represented a class that individuals might encounter) resulted in greater correct performance than did training on just one vending machine and training only on machines highly similar to each other.

Teachers using direct instruction, or the directive teaching methodologies, are straightforward in telling students what it is students are being taught. (So often teachers do not think to do this and inadvertently keep their expectations for students a big secret from those students.) At times we take it for granted that students will automatically see how and when to use specific skills appropriately in other situations, but generalizing in this way can be difficult for some students with learning and other disabilities. Students need to be taught to use the skills at other times and in different situations. Lovitt (1982) uses as an example the special education student who is integrated into a regular class and attends to lessons only when he is approached as an individual. Due to many years of one-to-one instruction, this student has to be directly instructed to attend to group instructions as well. The student simply did not seem to see that the group lessons pertained to him. Teaching particular skills must be accompanied by teaching of principles or rules about when to use those skills in the future. When we fail to do this, our students are not as successful when it comes to maintaining and generalizing the things they learned (Lovitt 1982).

Direct teaching or direct-instruction techniques are most frequently used in task-related learning. It is used most often to teach skill acquisition whether it be an academic skill or a skill of participating at home, in school, or in community situations. This approach can also be a method for teaching such higher cognitive tasks as problem solving, critical thinking, and creativity (Lewis 1983). Similarly, it is a viable option for teaching metacognitive strategies such as self-monitoring.

Academic Learning Time Modification

Academic learning time (ALT) is defined as "the amount of time a student spends in relevant content [academic tasks] that he or she can perform with high success" (Denham and Lieberman 1980, 8). High ALT (compared to medium and low ALT) is an optimal learning performance condition assumed to be a prerequisite to optimal academic achievement. Thus academic learning time is used as an instrument for measuring daily task success and becomes a variable to control during instruction for increasing student achievement. Different behavioral dimensions compose components of ALT and are manipulated as variables in order to affect change.

Wilson (1987) describes the three observable components of ALT: "student engagement rate (time on task), amount of instructional time [time spent in learning], and student success rate (percentage of correct responses)" (p. 13). Applied classroom research has demonstrated a significant positive relationship between each of the ALT components and student achievement (Wilson 1987). Wilson also provides guidelines for integrating research findings into instructional practices.

Information Collection

In using ALT, the first step is to gather information about student performance through direct observation of academic learning time (ALT). Direct observation is preferable to using formal tests (Wilson 1987). Information gathered using direct observation of students is objective because it can be openly observed. It is also relevant because it relates directly to daily student performances on tasks that individual teachers feel are important parts of the program. Furthermore it is immediate because the results tell how each of the students is doing on the day observed rather than waiting for formal test results.

But direct observation has disadvantages as well. Teachers are not always free to do the observations, and observations do not provide information about students' thoughts and feelings. Still this kind of information is only one aspect of the broader information on students, and if the lack is kept in proper perspective, direct observation can be used productively.

Components of Academic
Learning Time

Student engagement rate, according to Wilson (1987), is "the time a student spends actively looking at some appropriate instructional object or person" (p. 15). Teachers are encouraged to observe the most important instruction. This may be math for some students and speech training for others.

The teacher gathers on-task information by using a momentary time sampling procedure: The observer, using a watch, looks up at the target student every 10 seconds for three to fifteen minutes. At each 10-second interval, the student's behavior is rated. A plus (+) is recorded for on-task behavior; a minus (−) for off-task behavior. Looking at the board, looking at the teacher, looking at the book or worksheet are the types of behaviors considered on-task if at the time these were considered appropriate targets for student attention.

Keeping eyes closed or looking toward a window, door, and nonparticipating classmate are considered off-task behaviors. (Errors in rating can occur because students may be looking toward the appropriate target but not be attending, or they can be attending but looking out a window. Such errors tend to cancel each other.)

On-task behavior is usually reported in percentages using these steps: (Wilson 1987, 15):

1. Total the number of +'s.
2. Total the number of −'s.
3. Divide the +'s by the sum of the total number of both +'s and −'s.
4. Multiply the result by 100.

The totals represent the time on-task and are arrived at by the following formula:

$$\frac{+\text{'s}}{+\text{'s} + -\text{'s}} \times 100$$

The results can be used for averaging the time on-task over several days or weeks, comparing information with peer averages and noticing the presence or absence of time on-task for one student.

Instructional time is the time students spend learning. Commonly there is a difference between the time teachers allocate in their plan books to teaching and the time they actually spend teaching. Wilson (1987) notes that of the two, "actual instructional time (which is typically about 80 percent of allocated time) is more closely related to student achievement and is, therefore, more appropriately observed in the classroom . . . Only teacher-directed and seatwork activities should be included as actual instructional time for purposes of observation" (p. 14). Noninstructional activities such as passing out paper, disciplinary action, and socialization are not included.

Instructional time is measured by timing the length of all teacher-directed and seatwork activities presented in the classroom for target students over one or more whole days. Observers (aides, volunteers) record the beginning time of each school activity (e.g., reading, math, lunch). During each activity, observers also record the major instructional format the teacher used. These formats are generally teacher-directed instruction (TD), seatwork (SW), or noninstructional activity (NA). (The activity designation changes when the format changes, and then the timing starts again.) Next observers record the number of minutes of activity (including NA) and briefly describe major student tasks (e.g., TD for math instruction; SW for checking own math problems; NA for putting away math homework and moving into reading group).

Total instructional time is represented by the totals of teacher-directed instruction and seatwork time. This formula is used to calculate the percentage of the day that is instruction (Wilson 1987, 14):

$$\frac{\text{TD time} + \text{SW time}}{\text{TD time} + \text{SW time} + \text{NA time}} \times 100 = \% \text{ of day that is instruction}$$

In addition, teachers can calculate the percentage of time that is teacher directed or seatwork.

The *student success rate* is the percentage of correct answers individual students give to problems or questions the teacher assigns. Student answers can be given during oral or written work, either orally or in writing. The success rate is divided into the categories based on the percentage of correct student answers. Wilson uses categories research by Silbert, Carnine, and Stein (1981) and Stephens (1977). These are (1) mastery, or independent, level performance, (2) instructional level performance, and (3) frustration level performance. Levels are corresponding percentages of student success rates are:

LEVEL	SUCCESS RATE
Independent or mastery level	90% or higher
Instructional level	60 to 85% or higher correct
Frustration level	less than 70% correct

It is assumed that students who show high success profit most from materials and instruction presented on their instructional level and least from materials on a frustration level (Wilson 1987, Gickling and Thompson 1985).

Student success-rate information is more difficult to gather. Oral and written responses are recorded separately. A plus (+) indicates a correct student answer; a zero (0) indicates an incorrect answer. Teachers can calculate success rates for each category, activity, and entire day. Teachers and observers might want to establish their own guidelines for handling different kinds of situations that arise (e.g., variations in scoring in which students correct themselves or give correct answers after teachers have provided more information; variations in scoring that can arise if an error is counted for each digit rather than one error for an entire math problem). Mastery, instructional, and frustration levels also change for different student activities. For oral reading, as an example, the success rate percentage for each level is higher than those stated earlier.

Patterns in the data have important implications for students in special education. The information gathered from handicapped and nonhandicapped classmates can be compared. It might help the teacher to ask these questions: When nonhandicapped and mildly handicapped students are in the same classroom, do special education students spend much less time than their classmates working on high-success or mastery-level tasks and much more on low or frustration-level tasks? Relative to their current skills, are students in special education assigned much harder tasks than their regular education classmates?

Suggestions for Increasing Student Achievement. All of the behavioral dimensions measured are potentially within teacher control. Thus the teacher can treat each as a classroom variable related to student achievement, and she or he can make changes to increase the percentages of rates and amounts of student on-task behaviors, instructional time, and success rates. Actions to try improving the instructional program come after interpreting and synthesizing the information-gathering systems and comparing these to regular and special class averages.

When on-task rates are low, the teacher can introduce ways to increase on-task behavior with intent to improve academic performance. After doing a literature review Wilson (1987, 16) named the following strategies to increasing on-task behavior: rewarding academic performance, building study cubicles for independent work, imposing a small penalty for each descriptive act (loss of 2 minutes recess), giving the entire class a small reward when the student works hard (extra recess), and using self-recording of on-task or off-task behavior.

When teachers observe below-average amounts of total instructional time or excessively high percentages of seatwork (over 80 percent), they can institute plans to modify how classroom time is allocated (Wilson 1987). Research on academic learning time offers suggestions for increasing instructional time, including:

1. reducing transition time, recess, or free time and
2. making organizational activities more efficient (Stallings 1980).

Additional ideas to increase teacher directed instruction include:

3. using parents and/or volunteers to assist with organizational chores (e.g., passing out papers, setting up learning centers).
4. creating more instructional groups with more teachers (e.g., use student teachers, peer tutors, and volunteers) (adapted from Wilson 1987).

When low success rates are recorded for individual students, teachers can act on this information to improve student performance by attending to the type of task assigned (reading, drill, seatwork) and the difficulty level of each relative to mastery, instruction, and frustration student performance levels. Using guidelines to establish placement levels through use of criterion-referenced assessments is one way to maintain student success rates at desirable levels. Standards for levels and corresponding success rate percentages for various subjects have been defined in various places in the literature. In math, for instance, see Silbert, Carnine, and Stein (1981).

An example of a math standard is if a student can compute only zero to nineteen digits correctly per minute and/or makes eight or more errors per minute, his success rate is less than 60 percent. The student performance level is thus at frustration level, and the problems should be made easier for him. If a student computes twenty to thirty-nine digits correctly per minute and/or makes three to seven errors per minute, then his success rate is 60–85 percent. This is at the instructional level, and instruction can take place here with recommendations that material to be used from the mastery, or independent, level to insure success. Finally, if a student can compute forty to one hundred digits correctly per minute and makes two or fewer errors per minute, then his success rate is 85 percent or more.

Teachers are urged to teach at students instructional levels and independence levels regardless of the task or subject. If student performances do not conform to these levels repeatedly, then the difficulty of the assignment should be readjusted (Gickling and Havertape 1981). As stated, the classroom variables associated with academic learning time are positively related to student achievements (Wilson 1987). Therefore, using information on the ALT components—percentage of time on-task and in learning and percentage of correct response in student success rates—is one means of achieving better instruction for student who have handicaps in learning.

Curriculum-Based Assessment

Curriculum-based assessment (CBA) is a procedure for determining the instructional needs of students using their course content and daily lessons as the basis. CBA uses student responses to curriculum assignments as diagnostic tools, and it capitalizes on the known skills each student has (Gickling and Thompson 1985).

For a variety of reasons, many students in special education fall behind, picking up only fragmented skills. Then as they proceed to the next instructional grade or level, all they have is an incomplete and fragmented education. Yet they are expected to learn the new curriculum objectives as if they had the same solid foundation and prerequisites as their nonhandicapped peers do. It is likely that many students try their best, but since even their best efforts result in poor performance compared to their peers, they themselves and others make harsh judgments about their poor performance. These judgments tend to focus on their deficits rather than how well they are doing despite the gaps in their previous preparation.

CBA includes a focus on the positive aspects of what the student *has learned* within a particular course or term. A major goal in curriculum-based assessment is to eliminate, or significantly reduce, the instructional mismatch between the skills of students with academic problems and the inordinate demands their curriculum assignments put on them (Gickling and Thompson 1985). In curriculum-based instruction, the degree of instructional match or mismatch relates to the degree of the interface between the student's skills and the learning demands of the instructional task (Gickling and Havertape 1981). "When the task is sufficiently familiar, yet still provides some measure of challenge to bring about optimal learning for the student, the task is said to be on an instructional level. When performance indicates too little challenge or too great a challenge, the student is said to be on an independent level or a frustrational level, respectively" (Gickling and Havertape 1982, 2). The goal is to maintain the match at the instructional level and thus achieve better overall performance over time. Curriculum-based assessment and academic learning time (discussed earlier in this chapter) are often companion practices.

According to Gickling and Armstrong (1978), research suggests that making appropriate curriculum choices for a student can result in high success in daily tasks, and such success can in turn be the antecedents to long-term achievement. The same study indicated that daily task success is an antecedent to appropriate classroom conduct.

Assessment Data and Instruction

As stated, curriculum-based assessment focuses equally on assessment and instruction. The direct and immediate relationship between assessment data and instructional decisions was described in Chapter 2. To further emphasize the curriculum-based orientation to assessment and the assessment-based orientation to instruction, Gickling and Havertape (1981) use the term *convertible data*. Thinking of "convertible" as the ability to change or transform, they apply this concept to CBA. They conclude that "if assessment information is not immediately convertible, then it is of limited instructional use" (p. 11).

Measuring Student Performance

To measure student performance using the CBA concept, teachers use direct and repeated measurements. They assess student performances frequently—even daily—in relation to the course of study. They also determine how well the student performs on a daily task-by-task basis. Increasing academic learning time (ALT), or the time spent on relevant tasks performed with high success, is a way to move each student toward her or his optimal level of performance. Using CBA to measure student performance also means *planning* instruction so students have high academic learning time (high ALT). Teachers need to determine if students achieve high, medium (average), or low ALTs and then use instructional strategies to attain high ALT ratios.

Think of ALT as an instrument for measuring daily task success. Then think of CBA as a way to increase ALT on the general performance level of poorer functioning students. Two basic processes for measuring student performances are to: (1) assess student performances frequently—even daily—in relation to the course of study and (2) plan instruction so students have high academic learning time (high ALT).

Does this mean that in using special methods to allow low-achieving students to experience a high ratio of daily-task success teachers eliminate instructional mismatches between the students' skills and the demands of their curriculum? Not necessarily. Or does this mean that these students will be able to "catch up" to their peers? Not necessarily! Regular students are moving ahead as well, perhaps much faster, and thus keeping the gap open. Special education students may not be able to keep up with the routine pace, because instruction moves too fast, and the demands are too great.

Application of CBA (aligning assessment practices with what is taught in the classroom) and ALT (practices of measuring student progress) provide special education students with similar types of learning conditions (high ALT) their more successful peers enjoy (Gickling and Thompson 1981). "This statement is not to imply that they will be able to function at the same ability levels as their average and above average peers, but that they will have similar opportunities for task success in relationship to their own entry skills and that they will begin to make more systematic progress in school" (Gickling and Thompson 1985, 217).

Instructional Delivery Model

A CBA model for delivering instruction has been created to focus on selecting materials and methods based on the variables of task difficulty and student performance. In an instructional decision-making process, what to teach and how to teach it are to be considered simultaneously. Usually within the technology of teaching, it is easier to determine what to teach than to plan how the material should be presented. The process of teaching varies among teachers.

Proponents (Gickling and Thompson 1985) describe one CBA instructional delivery model. This and other CBA instructional delivery models can provide a structure for limiting the difficulties teachers run into in deciding what to teach and how to present the instruction. This model is based on the CBA assumption that maintaining an optimal level of individual student performance is the criterion for establishing whether a teacher has successfully individualized the instruction.

The Gickling-Thompson model is based on the observation that every instructional task contains three essentials: task types, task items, and performance levels. These three essentials then constitute the major areas of the delivery model. Combined information from these components provides information that enables teachers to measure instructional decision making, make instructional changes on a daily basis, and deliver instruction systematically.

Task types are the classifications of activities into which proponents of CBA divide instruction. For the purpose of this discussion, school tasks for students fall into two basic activity groups: reading and drill. These two task types were identified because of the emphasis teachers give to these tasks in their instruction. Reading refers to obtaining meaning from print (e.g., reading a story). Thus, reading is *from* context and *for* meaning. Drill represents the practice stages of acquiring any new information. Thus drill includes all other kinds of assignments; that is, everything that is not reading (e.g., all forms of computational skill, writing and spelling, social studies, response to teacher questions, and reading-related activities including phonics instruction and word attack skills).

Task items are the particulars of school tasks to which students respond in attempting to do the task. They are classified according to student performance on them. Task items are categorized as *known, hesitant,* and *unknown.* Gickling and Havertape (1981) describe these as follows:

> A known response is a high emission response, which means that it is emitted rapidly and correctly all the time.

> A hesitant response represents a delay in providing a correct response or a "sometimes" [response]; it is correct at times and incorrect at other times.

> An unknown response is a definite error. (Adapted from Gickling and Havertape 1981, 5.)

Instructional delivery is based on the idea that instruction is a ratio problem. The ratio Gickling and Havertape use is the ratio of *known* information to *challenge* information (unknown and hesitant responses). This means that each assignment, regardless of its difficulty for a particular student, will contain a percentage of known-to-challenging information. These percentages become critical criteria for judging the suitability of instructional tasks.

The teacher can change the ratios of known to challenge material in several ways. One is to "sandwich" just the recommended percent of challenge material into the known material. Another is to take the known material, such as words in a story, and rewrite the story using known words and eliminate all but 3 to 7 percent of the hesitant and unknown words.

Known responses are not in the area of challenge. Hesitant and unknown responses are described as areas of unknown or challenge information. During initial instruction, hesitant responses are characteristically correct some times and uncertain, slow, or mistaken at other times. After being introduced and practiced, these responses that were unknown or hesitant hopefully become high-emitting (or known) responses.

In the literature, certain ratios are identified as criteria for judging the suitability of instructional tasks. Assignments may be far too challenging for a student (ratio approaches known to unknown of 0/100). Or they can be much too easy (known to unknown: 100/0) or lie on a continuum between these extremes. If student performances do not conform repeatedly to acceptable ratios, then their assignment difficulty needs to be adjusted.

Reading accuracy tasks work best for students when their instruction results in a range of approximately 93 to 97 percent known items with a 3–7 percent margin of challenge items (that is, 3–7 percent from hesitant and unknown task items). Comprehension should be 75 percent or higher. For drill types of tasks, the instructional ratio of known to unknown items should be 70 to 85 percent known to 15 to 30 percent challenge.

These percentages are entry-level values. The intent is that students start at these levels, not start with lower levels of known information and build up to these recommended percentages. Teachers are encouraged to strive conscientiously to build this amount of known information into every new task before presenting the task to students.

Performance Levels. Identifying performance levels means determining the degree of instructional match or mismatch between the skills of the students and the learning demands of the instructional tasks (as discussed in the previous section on ALT). The goal of such assessments is to examine the student's performance on each regular daily task. Then the teacher can make any necessary modifications to maintain a match at an *instructional* level. Proponents of CBA encourage teachers to teach to students at the instructional and independent levels (and not at the frustration level) whether the task type be drill or reading. It is even wise to start students on new assignments slightly below their functional levels to guard against failure.

Awareness of task difficulty versus student performance is a feature of CBA (Gickling and Havertape 1981, Gickling and Thompson 1985). Student performance on tasks is designated as student success rates, which is the percentage of correct answers the student gives to problems or questions the teacher assigns.

Tasks that are familiar or comfortable for students yet provide some measure of challenge are considered to be on an instructional level. They foster optimal learning. If a student's success rate during drill activities, for instance, is 70 to 85 percent correct or higher, this student is working on an instructional level—that is, the best level for instruction. When student performances indicate little challenge exists—with a success rate of 90 percent or more—students are said to perform on an independent, or mastery, level. When the tasks are too great a challenge—with less than 70 percent correct—students are said to be performing on a frustration level.

Application of the Model. Certain rules are recommended to facilitate application of this approach. These instructional considerations (see Gickling and Havertape 1981) need to be taken into account when applying the model.

Keep the Percentage of Known Items High

It is important to determine what are the smallest meaningful items of a task, and to control the number of new items introduced so that the ratio of known to challenging items is within an instructional level for the student. Maintaining high percentages of known items provides built-in reinforcement for the student.

Confine New Material to the Margins of Challenge

Exceeding the recommended percentages of challenge increases the probability of the pupil facing a frustrational task, and also creates an unmanageable sequence of instruction. As mentioned before, the margin of challenge includes both unknown and hesitant responses.

Items of Undetermined Status Are Treated as Unknowns

The probability of jeopardizing an appropriate instructional ratio is increased if there are items of undetermined status within the task. Therefore, to be reasonably sure that success can occur, this type of item should be treated as an unknown response when calculating the ratio. It is especially important to do this for the student of very limited ability.

Prepare Content Before Drill

Too many times, teachers drill students on items which are unrelated to the next instructional task. By examining planned content and then designing drill work to conform to the content, the two tasks become coordinated and enhance the learning situations.

Present Drill Before Content

Drill activities are presented to the student in order to prepare him for the next task. If drill goes well, and drill and content have been coordinated, then the student should be able to perform on an instructional or independent level when the next task is presented.

All Tasks Are Carried to Their Logical Conclusion

No task should be left at a subskill level at the end of the day. The goal should be to take every task to its logical conclusion, which requires both independent performance and comprehension on the part of the student. Naturally, there is a concerted effort to make every task as contextural as possible (from Gickling and Havertape 1981, 6).

Using these rules as guidelines has resulted in effective instruction. This model was validated by some studies comparing *on-task* and *task-completing* behaviors of students with different instructional treatment procedures (Borg 1980). Other studies (Gickling and Armstrong 1978, Thompson, Gickling, and Havertape 1983) added *task comprehension* to the variables used to measure the effectiveness of this model. Other research findings supported the relationship between effective learning and levels of instructional difficulty (Gickling and Havertape 1981). As the levels of difficulty changed within assignments, the percentages of on-task behavior, task-completing behavior, and comprehension also changed. When assignments were within the established ratios enabling students to function on an instructional level (compared to independent or frustration level), the percentages of all three variables were consistently high (the condition of high ALT was being maintained at this level). For assignments that were too difficult, the percentages of these three behaviors were respectively low. When assignments were too easy, percentages of comprehension and task completion were high, but time on-task was low because of unused time.

Teachers have options when it comes to determining the instructional needs of their students. Based on assessment and other information, teachers decide what to teach, where to teach, and what materials are needed. They can also develop teaching styles they are most comfortable with and that suit their students needs as well.

Within this area are other decisions about the learning environment and the structure for learning. One of the most difficult variables to control every day across the curriculum is task difficulty. Yet controlling the difficulty level is critical for students whose performances have been inadequate. Research studies are beginning to show cause and effect relationships between task-oriented success (high ALT) and overall academic achievement.

Community-Intensive Instruction

Community-intensive instruction teaches students the kinds of skills that enable them to function at some level of competence in their communities. Much of the instruction is carried out "on location" at various places in the community such as the bus station, grocery store, post office, drug store, library, and city parks. This is in contrast to more traditional classroom-based curriculum. A community-based curriculum in differing amounts has great value for most with disabilities. Students severely disabled with retardation require an intensive life-skill management curriculum and can benefit from community-*intensive* instruction.

The information here on community-intensive curriculum and instruction draws heavily from "Community Intensive Instruction" a chapter in *Education of Learners with Severe Handicaps* by Sailor et al. (1986). To begin with, Sailor et al. (1986) report research showing that severely disabled students do not readily generalize a skill learned in one environment to another, even though the second environment may be a more natural for that skill. What this means is that the best place for a student to learn how to cross a street properly is at an actual intersection. Students with severe disabilities are best prepared for a functional life by learning everyday skills in their ordinary settings, where they are needed and where the student can accomplish something real. A second advantage to teaching age-appropriate and normative functional skills on location is that the disabled student will be among nondisabled people who can serve as role models and can motivate and encourage the student.

Characteristics of a Community-Intensive Curriculum

The community-intensive curriculum is implemented in three areas: (1) the classroom in a regular public school, (2) nonclassroom areas of the school such as restrooms, cafeteria, playgrounds, library, and so on, and (3) the community itself including stores, restaurants, housing areas, pools, parks, streets, and employment areas. The last two are what make this curriculum different from a classroom-based curriculum. Young students in the community-intensive curriculum start by spending most of their time in the classroom, but this changes as they grow.

Students three to six are in the classroom 65 percent of their school day, spending another 25 percent outside the classroom but in school, and 10 percent in the community. The student aged six to nine is in the classroom 40 percent of the time, in the school but not the classroom 35 percent of the time, and in the community for 25 percent. From ages nine to twelve, the percentages are 25, 25, and 50 for classroom, nonclassroom-school, and community respectively. Ages twelve to sixteen, the percentages are 10, 15, and 75. Then from ages sixteen to twenty-one, the percentages are 0, 15, and 85.

During the elementary years, a main focus of both classroom and nonclassroom instruction is teaching the disabled child to interact with nondisabled costudents appropriately in a variety of settings. Students also learn how to perform chores around the school building that are prevocational skills. In the community, students practice basic skills as a part of such normal community activities as buying a snack from a vending machine or purchasing an item for school snacks at a grocery store.

By high school, most learning/teaching is not in the classroom; it is either in the school or in the community where students practice functional and work-related vocational skills. They work at skills in the areas of social interaction, eating, prevocational training, domestic chores, self-care and grooming in non-classroom settings (the home economics rooms, hallways, gyms, yards, bathrooms, cafeteria) and in school work areas (maintenance yards, offices, school kitchen, first aid room, grounds, library, and faculty lounge). Participating in extracurricular activities also offers disabled students occasions to practice their normative social skills.

Community sites for this age include any public transit systems, recreational facilities, stores, parks, banks, and any public service centers. Students in such programs have been successfully trained in a variety of jobs, including unpacking and hanging clothes in retail stores, doing basic landscape maintenance, washing vehicles, setting and clearing tables, performing assembly-line work, and doing simple shopping.

Of necessity, a community-intensive curriculum requires a low student-to-teacher ratio: four to one is necessary for effective nonclassroom or community instruction. Resources other than classroom teachers include student teachers and college students, aides, trained parents, nondisabled student peers as well as speech, occupation, and physical therapists when appropriate. For example, a speech therapist could be integrated into the program to help design a communication system that allows the student to interact in all settings (or different systems could be developed for different uses). Then the therapist could work with the student out in the community to insure that the system is in fact workable.

One strategy that supports the on-site teaching process while it reduces the demand of a low ratio is heterogeneous grouping. This means mixing students from different disability groups and differing levels of disability. In mixed groupings, the moderately disabled can be effective in giving the severely disabled not only more attention but also the consistent attention they need, and they can also serve as role models, too.

Goals and Objectives

Teachers and anyone else who is part of the disabled student's support team work together to define objectives for the student and to determine community sites appropriate for teaching specific skills. To begin with, they list the objectives in terms of priority with age-appropriateness as a relevant factor. Their overall goal is to prepare the student with disabilities to function as fully as possible in normal community environments. They establish priorities for skills in terms of several factors: the number of school years remaining for the student; the student's current level of participation at school, at home, and in a work or prevocational environment; the basic skills the student has already mastered; additional skills the student needs or can learn.

The team lists objectives as a skill or series of skills. For the disabled elementary student, objectives may start as classroom instruction in (1) reaching for an object and (2) holding onto an object. Then this is transferred to a community-based skill such as (1) serving oneself in a public cafeteria or (2) buying a soda in a deli. Objectives can focus on areas such as eating, movement, communication, social interaction, paying for goods and services, choosing purchases, or navigating city terrain.

Implementation

Several specific implementation strategies further the success of a community-intensive curriculum. Using a nondisabled student of the same age as a role model in the classroom is one of the techniques Sailor et al. (1986) identify. The nondisabled student can also function effectively as a tutor and aide. Using a low student-teacher ratio (of 4 : 1) in settings that are natural and realistic and thus have implicit rewards for learning are other effective implementation strategies. A disabled student who learns to negotiate a shopping transaction winds up with a double reward, a purchased item as well as having mastered an important everyday function.

Implementation gets a big boost when parents are told about the value and practicality of the curriculum early in the process, and they form parent support groups to aid the school effort. Such groups can form a parent network, providing information, mutual support, and interaction with other community groups. They can also train others in awareness and better attitudes toward students with disabilities.

Transitional Instructional Strategy

Transitions from one life crossroad to another are a challenge for everyone at any age. To move across environments (or domains) or within environments is the kind of transition students with handicaps can find particularly difficult. Teachers can develop and teach specialized preparations for important transitions. Instruction for transition already occurs but is not limited to that provided adolescents and young adults leaving school. Parents as well as children need to be prepared for transitions as early as the first big transition to preschool (Hanline, in press). Robinson, Braxdale, and Colson (1985) present guidelines for what to teach and how to teach as transitional curriculum to dysfunctional students before entry into the junior high school environment. Transition preparation is also needed as part of the curriculum for elementary to middle or junior high school environments, from middle school to high school environments, and into "mainstream" environments.

The literature stresses current and potential situations likely to be available to each handicapped student as an adolescent and adult. Environments (or domains), described variously in the literature (Wehman, Moon, and McCarthy 1986, Brown, Neitupski, and Hamre-Nietupski 1976, and Wehman, Renzaglia, and Bates 1985), represent vocational, home, community, and leisure environments and the subenvironments within each. Here we add the school, which is assumed as an environment but is not always designated as such.

Transitions to Work

Vocational transition is a major life change focused on in special education. Wehman, Kregel, and Barcus (1985) define vocational transition as "a carefully planned process, which may be initiated either by school personnel or by adult service providers, to establish and implement a plan for either employment or additional vocational training of a handicapped student who will graduate or leave school in three to five years; such a process must involve special educators, vocational educators, parents and/or the student, an adult service system representative, and possibly an employer" (p. 26).

Teachers conduct ecological analyses to determine ways of improving the transition from school to working life for students with disabilities. The more specifically the teacher can describe the environment in terms of (1) activities that occur within each environment and (2) the behaviors necessary to function within it, the better subsequent instruction can be. The analyst gauges behaviors using those exhibited by nonhandicapped adults considered to be successful as a standard. It will only be possible to hypothesize about some environments and behaviors, but others can be described specifically.

At certain times during schooling, teachers speculate about potential vocational environments based on screening local resources (Wehman and Moon 1985) and cataloging local opportunities (Wilcox and Bellamy 1982). To accomplish this, Wehman and Moon suggest reading newspaper classified ads, interviewing personnel in local employment agencies, and talking with vocational rehabilitation professionals who have placed others successfully. Such screening and questioning will develop information about the kinds of job skills particular positions require.

Currently, the transition to employment begins by placing students on jobs three or more years before they leave their school program. This means employer needs and expectations can be clearly identified rather than merely hypothesized in ecological inventories. Teachers can assess student performance against the *actual* jobs rather than in relation to the kinds of jobs a student might be able to get. The teacher can observe and assess work-related social skills such as meeting people and engaging in "small talk." The teacher can also observe such nonproduction yet job-related skills as completing necessary information forms and the ability to keep busy.

Supported work or supportive competitive employment (a regular job at standard pay) exemplifies one transitional instructional strategy in which students learn competitive work from *job coaches* while on the job. Supported work emphasizes structured assistance in job placement and job site training (Wehman, Moon, and McCarthy 1986, 5). During the school years, education personnel become the supported-employment educators or job educators or job coaches. This entails working the job with the handicapped employee from the beginning to the end of the day. As implied by the title, the supported-employment educator helps the student seek and acquire the job and then does a detailed on-the-job task analysis of the steps necessary to complete the job competitively. These task analyses involve such variables as speed and accuracy at tasks as well as completing the job tasks themselves. As the employee learns the job from the supported-employment educator and perhaps other employees, the supported-employment educator does less and less of the job, and the employee does more and more. Having the coach fade from the work site is a key aspect of supported training and one objective of transition instructional strategy.

An ongoing network of assessment and instruction or training is, of course, the crux of this process. While the student is still enrolled in the schools, the vocational component of her curriculum takes place in the community or wherever the job exists. When the handicapped person is no longer a student, adult service agencies continue the assessment process as necessary to assist the person with employment challenges and problems.

Holding onto the job is also heavily linked to assessment and consequent instruction. Besides making spot checks back at the job site to verify that the worker is maintaining or improving performance, job coaches fill other roles in helping individuals maintain jobs. One ironic possibility is that some employees are so successful and become so confident that they prematurely decide to leave the current job to try for a different one. The person has little concept of what it took to prepare him, manage any necessary accommodations, and even to attain the job placement in the beginning. It might be necessary for the job coach to caution the student against too hasty a change. Job coaches also do counseling and help handicapped workers do assessments of their own skills against those required by the current job and possible future jobs. The multifaceted role of the educator is to prepare students for vocational transition, train them in desirable social and work habits, find initial employment, train and provide regular follow-up support, and take action to assure job retention.

Information and data from an ecological analysis of current and possible future student vocational activities form the basis of the "individualized transitional plan (ITP)." According to Wehman et al. (1986), the individualized transition plan may either be part of the IEP or addressed separately. They suggest that ITPs be developed by the time students are sixteen years old. As with the individualized educational programs for students, the parents' and students' continuous involvement in the entire process is vital. The ITP is the key to successful transition of students into work and community living options by the time they leave school (Wehman et al. 1986). The vocational portion of the ITP contains specific objectives that lead to employment goals and have projected completion dates. Wehman et al. (1986, 10–11) illustrate a sample ITP (see Fig. 5.3).

When individuals leave school and begin receiving services from state rehabilitation agencies, similar written plans are required by federal law. These statements, called individual habilitation plans (IHPs) or individual written rehabilitation plans (IWRP) describe individual employment goals and training. It is important that individualized transition and individual habilitation plans work together to provide good bridging from school to work. To do this, joint involvement of school personnel responsible for training and job procurement and appropriate representatives of vocational rehabilitation and other adult service agencies is necessary.

Many educators are concerned that the focus on the transition from school to adult and working life overemphasizes work. Reports from the National Association of Directors of Special Education address this concern, reminding schools of the need to include other, perhaps equally important, goals. They state that this high emphasis on the transition to working life should not ignore the importance of transition plans that include recreation, leisure, and community living and that greater emphasis should be placed on these areas (Halloran et al. 1986).

The challenge of teaching individuals in special education does not end with using professional expertise to assist students with access to curriculum. The way to learning from that curriculum comes from the competence teachers develop in using instructional strategies effectively. Teachers owe it to their students to be as clear and efficient as possible in instructing those students.

Summary and Conclusion

Eight representative strategies for instructing students in special education were introduced in this chapter. Strategies were chosen for their generalized applications to students with different disabilities. They were also chosen because they represent strategies that are effective for different kinds of curricular problems. Some strategies, for instance, are more appropriate to teaching academic material to individuals for whom learning academic subjects is not easy. These are the traditional approaches, content and application-centered instruc-

Figure 5.3 Individualized Transition Plan

FOCUS ON EXCEPTIONAL CHILDREN   JANUARY 1990

FIGURE

INDIVIDUALIZED TRANSITION PLAN

Name: Bob   Age: 16   Date: April 20, 1990

A. Employment Goal:
To become employed in an enclave by May, 1995 (age 20).
Educational Objectives:
1. To receive training in a production job enclave within a local industry with minimal supervision on a daily basis by December, 1985.

Activities	*Person(s) Respnsible*
– Locate a job site	Voc. Ed. teacher, Rehab. counselor
– Provide job site training	Sp. Ed. teacher, Voc. Ed. teacher
– Provide transportation training	Sp. Ed. teacher
– Assess skills as part of vocational assessment	Voc. Ed. teacher, Sp. Ed. teacher
– Develop behaviorial interventions as necessary	School psychologist, Sp. Ed. teacher

2. To receive training in a food service enclave with minimal supervision on a daily basis by May, 1990.

Activities	*Person(s) Responsible*
Same as #1	Same as #1

3. To receive training in a technological job such as micrographics or data entry with minimal supervision on a daily basis by December, 1991.

Activities	*Person(s) Responsible*
Same as #1	Same as #1

4. To receive training in a janitorial and/or grounds maintenance enclave for an office building with minimal supervision by a job coach by May, 1991.

Activities	*Person(s) Responsible*
Same as #1	Same as #1

5. To receive a completed vocational assessment and job identification on skills and interests by September, 1991.

Activities	*Person(s) Responsible*
– Collect and analyze vocational assessment data during job training	Voc. Ed. teacher, Sp. Ed. teacher, Rehab. counselor
– Determine appropriate job for Bob based on skills and interests demonstrated through job site training	All ITP team members

6. To receive intensive job site training within the enclave type identified in #5 by December, 1993.

Activities	*Person(s) Responsible*
Same as #1	Same as #1

Administrative Objectives:
1. To assure the development of a nonprofit organization receiving state, federal, and/or local funds to provide enclave supervison by May, 1994.

Activities	*Person(s) Responsible*
-- Meet with community service boards and local rehabilitation agency to discuss the need for enclaves	Sp. Ed. coordinator
– Lobby for funds to be allocated for an enclave	Parent

2. To develop personnel policies to accommodate job site trainers by September, 1990.

Activities	*Person(s) Responsible*
– Develop overtime pay or compensation	School superintendent
– Develop policy to allow teachers to have flexible hours based on enclave hours	School superintendent

Used with permission as modified (dates on figures were changed). From Wehman et al. (1986).

B. **Community Living Goal:**
   To move into a semi-independent apartment with not more than two other residents with disabilities and one staff resident by May, 2000.
   Educational Objectives:
   1. To perform the following domestic tasks with periodic checks by staff: housecleaning, grocery shopping, clothing list development, meal preparation, grooming, yard maintenance, and make necessary phone calls (doctor, MH/MR case manager, family) by May, 1994.

Activities	*Person(s) Responsible*
– Train skills in home	Sp. Ed. teacher
– Locate apartment for training	MH/MR case manager
– Develop nesessary adaptations	Sp. Ed. teacher, O.T., Speech therapist

   2. To initiate the performance of all routine home activities through use of a picture schedule for each day by May, 1994.

Activities	*Person(s) Responsible*
– Train independence in following sequence of tasks	Sp. Ed. teacher
– Develop daily schedules	Sp. Ed. teacher

   3. To respond to unusual situations in the manner outlined in the safety manual with no assistance from staff by May, 1994.

Activities	*Person(s) Reponsible*
– Identify situations to be dealt with	MH/MR case manager, apartment staff member
– Develop safety procedures manual	Sp. Ed. teacher, apartment staff member
– Train skills to deal with situations	Sp. Ed. teacher

   4. To use the city bus with another student to go to the shopping mall, park, and medical clinic by May, 1993.

Activities	*Person(s) Responsible*
--Transportation training	Sp. Ed teacher

   5. To locate appropriate store and shop for groceries or supplies with another student by May, 1993.

Activities	*Person(s) Responsible*
– Set upchecking account	Parent, Bob
– Locate appropriate mall	Sp. Ed. teacher
– Train community skills	Sp. Ed. teacher, Parent

   6. To initiate and independently perform at least one leisure skill in each of the following areas by May, 1994: solo activity such as needlework solo outdoor activity such as bike riding; outdoor activity with another person such as frisbee, and a community activity such as skating.

Activities	*Person(s) Responsible*
– Select activity in each category	Bob
– Train leisure skills	Sp. Ed. teacher

   Administrative Objectives
   1. To complete referral process to appropriate adult services by May, 1991.

Activities	*Person(s) Responsible*
– Make referral to VR	Rehab. counselor
– Make referral for SSI and Medicaid	Sp. Ed. coordinator

   2. To obtain insurance coverage for students and staff during training in the apartment by September, 1990.

Activities	*Person(s) Responsible*
– Obtain insurance coverage	School superintendent

   3. To assure the availability of semi-independent homes in the community to accommodate students leaving schools by May, 1993.

Activities	*Person(s) Responsible*
– Meet with local agency officials	Sp. Ed coordinator

tion academic learning time modification, and curriculum-based instruction. Other strategies have proven particularly effective for teaching functional life management skills and activities for students who must have more preparation than usual in these areas. Illustrative strategies included curriculum-intensive instruction and transitional instructional strategy. Then there are strategies that are considered multipurpose. Task analysis and direct instruction are two of these. They assist teachers in identifying exactly what it is they want to teach and then lead teachers into obvious, clear-cut steps in instruction. Instruction could be directed at either content areas, processes, or major life activities.

In a survey book such as this, it is impossible to cover instruction of students in special education thoroughly. Here teachers can review many recognized strategies used with students in special education (and often in regular education as well). The information provides the major parameters of each strategy and cites key resources of information on each strategy. More in-depth study on each strategy is recommended before attempting to implement the strategies. In addition teachers should not be limited by the information in the chapter; rather they can use it as an introduction to further personal and professional exploration.

Wise (1984) urges teachers to take advantage of research articles. To do this the special education teacher needs basic knowledge of research methodology, design, and statistics, enough to be cautious about embracing research findings unquestioningly. Also when reading about a technique for teaching a certain thing, Wise cautions teachers not to expect it to work for all students or to work immediately for any student.

Teachers can use two basic approaches for drawing on research findings to design and improve instruction. They can study and, when appropriate, apply other research, or they can conduct their own research and design and improve instruction based on the results.

In attempting to reduce teacher anxiety about the idea of research, Wise clarifies that research is merely a work that describes the process involved in answering questions. She starts teachers thinking about their own situations by pointing out that educators ask themselves these questions that research studies can answer:

How might _____ learn better?
What can I do to motivate _____ ?
Am I really doing any good?

Quantitative research and *qualitative research* are two kinds of research teachers conduct to answer special education-related questions. Stainback and Stainback (1984) compare the two approaches. Briefly, quantitative researchers focus primarily on the results (i.e., did the program work or not). Qualitative researchers focus on the process as well as the product (i.e., exploring why a program did or did not work as well as people's perceptions of its effectiveness). With quantitative research, "The emphasis is on searching for the facts and causes of human behavior through objective, observable, and quantifiable data." (Stainback and Stainback 1984, 40). With qualitative research, data are gathered by people engaging in natural behavior: talking, visiting, looking, listening, and so on (Bogdan and Biklen 1982, 3). Such researchers gather information where the events of interest occur naturally.

Though these two approaches have different purposes and aims, they are sometimes used in conjunction with each other. Knowing the differences in approaches assists teachers in studying or conducting research that answers relevant questions. Drawing on research findings can help teachers answer questions that could have a positive impact on their instructional practices. Such information can verify that teachers are using the best practices or can indicate the need for changes.

References

Bailey, D. B., and Wolery, M. 1984. *Teaching infants and preschoolers with handicaps.* Columbus, Ohio: Charles E. Merrill.

Bereiter, C., and Engelmann, S. 1966. *Teaching disadvantaged children in the preschool.* Engelwood Cliffs, N.J.: Prentice-Hall.

Bigge, M. 1982. Learning Theories for teachers. 4th ed. New York: Harper & Row.

Bogdan, R., and Biklen, S. 1982. *Qualitative research for education: An introduction to theory and methods.* Boston, Mass.: Allyn & Bacon.

Borg, W. R. 1980. Time and school learning. In *Time to learn,* edited by C. Denham and A. Lieberman. Washington, D.C.: U.S. Department of Education, National Institute of Education.

Brown, L., Nietupski, J., and Hamre-Nietupski, S. 1976. The criterion of ultimate functioning and public school services for severely handicapped children. In *Hey, don't forget about me!* edited by M. A. Thomas. Reston, Va.: Council for Exceptional Children, pp. 2–15.

Buckley, J., Sandaw, D., and Smock, K. In preparation. *Job analysis for supported employment.* Eugene, Oreg.: University of Oregon.

Chan, J. M. 1985. The promise of computers for reluctant readers. In *High/ Low handbook: Books, materials and services for the problem reader,* 2d ed., edited by E. LiBretto. New York: R. R. Bowker, Co.

Davis, R. W., Uhler, R., and Kelly, L. J. 1986. Strategies and self-instructions for behaviorally disordered students: A direct instruction approach. *Directive Teacher* 8(1): 18–19.

Denham, C., and Lieberman, A., eds. 1980. *Time to learn.* Washington, D.C.: U.S. Department of Education, National Institute of Health.

Dishon, D., and O'Leary, P. W. 1985. *A guide book for cooperative learning: A technique for creating more effective schools.* Kalamazoo, Mich.: Learning Publications, Inc.

Engelmann, S., Becker, W., Hanner, S., and Johnson, G. 1978. *Corrective reading: Series guide.* Chicago, Ill.: Science Research Associates.

Engelmann, S., and Carnine, D. W. 1982. *Theory of instruction.* New York: Irvington.

Gersten, R., Woodward, J., Darch, C. 1986. Direct instruction: A research-based approach to curriculum design and teaching. *Exceptional Children* 53(1): 17–31.

Gickling, E., and Armstrong, D. L. 1978. Levels of instructional difficulty as related to on-task behavior, task completion and comprehension. *Journal of Learning Disabilities* 11: 559–66.

Gickling, E., and Havertape, J. 1981. *Curriculum-based assessment* (CBA) (A workshop manual). Minneapolis, Minn.: The National School Psychology Inservice Network, University of Minnesota.

Gickling, E. (1977). Controlling academic and social performance using an instructional delivery model. *Programs for the emotionally handicapped: Administrative considerations.* Washington, D.C.: Coordination Office of Regional Resource Centers.

Gickling, E., and Thompson, W. 1985. A personal view of curriculum-based assessment. *Exceptional Children.* 52(3): 205–18.

Halloran, W., Engelke, S., Donekey, A., Lewis, L., and Walsh, S. 1986. *Severely handicapped youth exiting public education: Issues and concerns.* Washington, D.C.: National Association of State Directors of Special Education (NASDSE), p. 5.

Hanline, M. F. (In press). Making the transition to preschool: Identification of parent needs. *Journal of the Division of Early Childhood Education.*

Hatlen, P. H., and Curry, S. A. 1987. In support of specialized programs for blind and visually impaired children: The impact of vision loss on learning. *Journal of Visual Impairments & Blindness* 81(1): 7–13.

Horner, R. H., and McDonald, R. S. 1982. A comparison of single instance and general case instruction in teaching a generalized vocational skill. *Journal of the Association for the Severely Handicapped* 7: 7–20.

Johnson, D. W., and Johnson, R. T. 1986. Mainstreaming and cooperative learning strategies. *Exceptional Children,* 52(6): 553–61.

Joyce, B., and Weil, M. 1980. *Models of teaching.* 2d ed. Englewood Cliffs, N.J.: Prentice-Hall.

Lewis, R. B. 1983. Learning disabilities and reading: Instructional recommendations from current research. *Exceptional Children* 50(3): 230–40.

Lovitt, T. 1982. What does the direct in directive teacher mean? *The Directive Teacher* 4(1): 24–25, 27.

Lowenbraun, S., and Thompson, M. 1986. Hearing impairments. In *Exceptional Children and Youth,* 4th ed. edited by N. Haring and L. McCormick. Columbus, Ohio: Charles E. Merrill.

Mank, D. M., and Horner, R. H. 1988. Instructional programming in vocational education. In *Vocational education for persons with handicaps,* edited by R. Gaylord-Ross. Palo Alto, Calif.: Mayfield Publishing.

Palincsar, A. S. 1986. Metacognitive strategy instruction. *Exceptional Children* 53(2): 118–24.

Paris, S., and Oka, E. R. 1986. Self-regulated learning among exceptional children. *Exceptional Children* 53(2): 103–8.

Perritt, P. 1985. Readability factors and methods for determining reading levels. In *High/Low handbook: Books, materials, and services for the problem reader,* 2d ed., by E. LiBretto. New York: R. R. Bowker Co., pp. 85–96.

Robinson, S. M., Braxdale, C. T., and Colson, S. E. 1985. Preparing dysfunctional learners to enter junior high school: A transition curriculum. *Focus on Exceptional Children* 18(4): 1–12.

Rosenshine, B., and Stevens, R. 1984. Classroom instruction in reading. In *Handbook of research on teaching,* edited by D. Pearson. New York: Longman Publishers.

Rowntree, D. 1981. *Developing courses for students.* London: McGraw-Hill.

Sailor, W., and Guess, D. 1983. *Severely handicapped students: An instructional design.* Boston, Mass.: Houghton Mifflin.

Sailor, W., Halvorsan, A., Anderson, J., Goetz, L., Gee, K., Doering, K., and Hunt, P. 1986. In *Education of learners with severe handicaps: Exemplary service strategies.* Edited by R. Horner, L. Meyer, and B. Fredericks. Baltimore, Md.: Paul Brookes.

Silbert, J., Carnine, D., and Stein, M. 1981. *Direct instruction mathematics.* Columbus, Ohio: Charles E. Merrill.

Slavin, R., Madden, N. A., and Leavey, M. 1984. Effects of cooperative learning and individualized instruction on mainstreamed students. *Exceptional Children* 50(5): 434–43.

Sprague, J. R., and Horner, R. H. 1984. The effects of single instance, multiple instance, and general case training on generalized vending machine use by moderately and severely handicapped students. *Journal of Applied Behavioral Analysis* 17(2): 273–78.

Stainback, S., and Stainback, W. 1984. Broadening the research perspective in special education. *Exceptional Children,* 50(5): 400–8.

Stallings, J. 1980. Allocated academic learning time revisited or beyond time on-task. *Educational Researcher.* 9(1): 11–16.

Stephens, T. 1977. *Teaching skills to children with learning and behavior disorders.* Columbus, Ohio: Charles E. Merrill.

Thompson, V. P., Gickling, E. E., and Havertape, J. F. 1983. The effects of medication and curriculum on task-related behaviors of attention deficit disordered and low achieving peers. *Monographs in behavioral disorders: Severe behavior disorders of children and youth,* Council for Children with Behavioral Disorders, Arizona State University, Series 6.

Upton, R. 1955. Some suggestions for the use of three-level reading materials. (Out of print.) Seattle: Cascade Pacific Books.

Upton, R., Durfee, B., Tucker, E. B., Doak, H., and Bennett, M. 1953. *Tom's America.* (Out of print.) Seattle: Cascade Pacific Books.

Wehman, P., Renzaglia, A., and Bates, A. 1985. *Functional living skills for moderately and severely handicapped individuals.* Austin, Tex.: Pro Ed.

Wehman, P., Kregel, J., and Barcus, J. 1985. From school to work: A vocational transition model for handicapped students. *Exceptional Children* 52(1): 25–37.

Wehman, P., and Moon, S. 1985. Critical values in employment programs for persons with developmental disabilities. In *Competitive employment for persons with mental retardation: From research to practice,* edited by P. Wehman and J. Hill. Richmond, Va.: Virginia Commonwealth University.

Wehman, P., Moon, S., and McCarthy, P. 1986. Transition from school to adulthood for youth with severe handicaps. *Focus on Exceptional Children* 18(5): 1–12.

Wilcox, B., and Bellamy, G. T. 1982. *Design of high school programs for severely handicapped students.* Baltimore, Md.: Paul Brookes.

Wilson, R. 1987. Direct observation of academic learning time. *Teaching Exceptional Children* 19(2): 13–17.

Wise, P. S. 1984. You need to do research. *The Directive Teacher* Winter/Spring: 22–25.

6

Teaching Basic Thinking Skills

JOSEPHINE CARPIGNANO and JUNE BIGGE

Teachers inevitably use constructs about thinking and learning as they plan curriculum and develop lesson plans. What are some useful theories of learning? How do students develop thinking skills? What are the prerequisites to such higher order skills as problem solving? How can teachers analyze advanced skills and teach their components directly to younger students and older students with learning problems? How do teachers instruct in basic thinking skills?

As students begin to learn new skills or develop skill with unfamiliar tasks, we assume that they rely heavily on previously learned skills for much of their current learning. Stated simply, we all build upon what we already know whenever we approach something new. For example, in order to learn to do the complex task of long division, a student must first have mastered addition, subtraction, and multiplication. Each of these skills also has prerequisites such as enumeration, grouping, and number recognition. Even more basic are the abilities to distinguish one numeral from another and to match numerically equivalent sets. A similar process applies when students learn about integrating complex scores written for different instruments of the orchestra. Before managing the subtle interactions of sound, students must first be able to associate specific sounds with specific instruments, recognize similarities and differences among groups of instruments, and—even more basic—distinguish one musical sound from another. Once these prerequisite skills have been acquired, learning about orchestration becomes more manageable.

Certain basic mental skills form the prerequisites for a range of learning activities but unlike motor skills, basic thinking skills (also referred to as learning or cognitive skills) are "invisible." They are not easily observed or measured. This chapter offers a hierarchical model of thinking skills that helps teachers assess at what level or with which aspects of thinking a student currently operates. Teachers can use this model for students with learning problems to gauge reducing complexities in assessment and instruction and develop alternative methods and materials for advancement to the next higher level. Similar to a task-analysis model, the thinking hierarchy allows movement across as well as up and down. If a "ladder of learning" analogy were used, one might visualize a very wide ladder so that lateral steps (sideways allowing a wider variety of examples at each level) can occur as well as progress up.

From a teacher's perspective, a hierarchy of thinking skills is useful in three major areas. _First_ a need exists for a general structure that provides progressive steps for cognitive skills, just as step-wise structures are already established for most curriculum areas. For example, arithmetic and reading stages are currently well defined, but to date no one has paid enough attention to levels of thinking and the basic cognitive skills learning requires. A hierarchy of thinking skills addresses this need.

Second, considerable confusion and a general absence of consistency characterizes the literature about sequences of learning and thinking skills. Various interpretations are applied to many of the basic concepts associated with thinking skills. When this occurs, as it commonly does, these concepts become confusing to teachers. Certain terms are used interchangeably at times but as different and distinct at other times. Good examples are the terms used about students' _understanding, thinking, reasoning, conceptualizing,_ and _problem solving._ These are all closely related to one another—yet different authors use them in different ways. We intend to define the terms we use and be consistent in our application of these terms. The hierarchy of thinking skills presented here is clear and consistent. The terms _thinking skills, cognitive abilities_, and _learning skills_, used interchangeably, all refer to the intellectual processes needed to acquire academic skills.

A _third_ use of a thinking hierarchy, already mentioned, is that it helps the teacher assess the student's current strengths and weaknesses. Teachers of students with learning problems need to know about (1) discrepancies in achievement across subject areas (arithmetic versus reading versus spelling versus science, and so on), (2) discrepancies in cognitive abilities (problem solving, rule learning, etc.) and (3) discrepancies between overall cognitive ability and overall achievement. Many times a student's thinking abilities are well above her ability to write what she knows or her ability to express thoughts verbally. Similarly, reading and comprehension skills may be far in advance of arithmetic and science competencies. A deep knowledge of rock bands may exceed familiarity with individual musical instruments, their sound characteristics, or how each contributes uniquely to the total musical effect. Or students can show surprising ability to solve problems of judgment and reasoning using high levels of abstraction while at the same time demonstrating minimal proficiency with simple word analysis in reading.

As these examples show, the purpose of the hierarchy is to provide a model that clearly indicates the sequences of learning, that furnishes clarity and consistency in its use of terms, and that is flexible enough to meet students' needs at any point in their learning process. The hierarchy of thinking skills begins with simple discriminations and evolves through several levels to higher-order, complex, problem-solving abilities, all in relation to various academic, intellectual, and life management areas. Teachers can use this model to diagnose where in the progression students are currently proficient. Teachers can also use the model to ascertain which cognitive skills the student is and is not currently using. Additionally, the hierarchical form of the model helps teachers determine what methods and materials are needed to temporarily simplify and structure instruction for particular students and help them progress toward more advanced levels or go to "lower" not yet attained levels.

Review of Recent Literature

During the past ten years, experimental programs addressing the teaching and learning of thinking skills have proliferated across the country (Wang and Resnick 1978, Blank, Rose, and Berlin 1978, Feuerstein, Rand and Hoffman 1979, Feuerstein, Rand, Hoffman, and Miller 1980, Lipman, Sharp, and Oscanyan 1980, Jones 1982, Blank 1983, de Bono 1982 and 1983, Falkof and Moss 1984, Sternberg 1984). Some researchers have addressed specific, well-defined age groups (e.g., Wang and Resnick 1978, Blank 1983); others have focused mostly on gifted and creative students, emphasizing higher-order thinking abilities and metacognitive skills (e.g., de Bono 1982 and 1983, Sternberg 1984). Some models find developmental considerations essential (Wang and Resnick 1978, Blank 1983); others find developmental changes inconsequential (e.g., Feuerstein et al, 1979, 1980).

In Feuerstein et al. (1980), the emphasis is on the interactive aspects of learning and the essential interventions educators provide students through "mediated learning experiences." "Mediation" here is defined as the process by which an adult selects and organizes stimuli for a child. Feuerstein's initial work was done with learning disabled adolescent immigrants to Israel. He proposes that regardless of what causes a learning difficulty, structuring the learning experiences of low-functioning students will change their thinking in a positive direction. For example, a student with "blurred and sweeping perception" (difficulty focusing on the task at hand) can learn with the appropriate intervention, to attend and become a successful learner. While Feuerstein's theory has gained significant status and is effective in treating specific cognitive deficits, it applies to a limited age range, has not yet demonstrated transferability to general curriculum areas, and tends to ignore developmental stages. Feuerstein (1980) refers to the thinking abilities contained in our hierarchy of thinking skills as *cognitive operations*. His list includes recognition, identification, classification, seriation, logic, and reasoning, and he does acknowledge the importance of identifying the necessary prerequisites for each operation (p. 106). The greatest value of Feuerstein's theory is its emphasis on the teacher-student interaction and the carefully structured questions and interventions (mediated learning experiences) that lead students to become independent problem solvers.

According to Falkof and Moss (1984) the very questions teachers ask during instruction can be hierarchically arranged and will coincide with developmental changes in children's thinking. Their model of instruction for elementary and secondary school students in Illinois is fairly consistent with our hierarchy of thinking skills and includes the ability to list attributes, to observe similarities and differences, to categorize, to compare and contrast, and to make analogies. Falkof and Moss propose that these skills emerge sequentially and are closely related to cognitive development.

A similar sequential model was developed by Blank, Rose, and Berlin (1978) and Blank (1983) who worked extensively with preschool children. Blank, who focused on the relationship between language and thinking in the early years, emphasized the powerful interaction between language development and cognitive development in preschool children. In the hierarchy that they developed, Blank et al. (1978) explained that at the first level of abstraction, called *matching perceptions,* children use words to refer to objects as a whole—usually with nouns or verbs. In their responses to questions or directives (e.g., "What is this?" "Find me a _____." "What do you see?"), young children match words with perceived objects or actions (e.g., while looking at pictures of the objects ball, car, dog, and boy, the child would answer the question, "What is this?" by saying the word *ball;* to the question, "Find me a dog" by pointing to the correct picture; and to "What do you see here?" with the word *car.*) A second level of abstraction, *selective analysis of perception,* evolves when the child learns the specific attributes of a percept in responding to questions such as "What color is this?" or "What shape is that ball?" The third level of abstraction requires that children reject perceptual characteristics and inhibit their predisposing responses. This stage, called *reordering perception,* is associated with use of negative terms: "Where is the car that is not blue?" "Show me the glass that is not empty," and so on. A fourth level of Blank's hierarchy, *reasoning about perception,* is the highest level preschool children usually attain, and it asks that they think about what might, could, or would happen under certain conditons, (e.g., "Why doesn't wood sink when it's in the water?" "What will happen to a seed if you plant it in the ground?" (1978, 15–19). Blank et al. also emphasize the teacher's verbal formulations and their influence on thinking skills that the child develops.

These theorecticians and researchers have focused attention on certain critical aspects of thinking related to the type of instruction adults provide children. All these authors conclude that students learn best (and most efficiently) when adults structure the learning environment for them and structure it in such a way that the child is led to develop independent thinking skills. In other words (for students with learning problems, as well as for nondisabled learners), students' thinking skills develop through mediated learning experiences with teachers and caregivers who intentionally provide an appropriate framework for acquiring cognitive skills. In education, this framework requires both a sequential progression (related to the child's cognitive development) and a hierarchical arrangement (related to progressing task difficulty in content).

The hierarchy of thinking skills uses the developmental model proposed by Jerome Bruner (1966, 1973) and the hierarchical model developed by Robert Gagnè (1974, 1977) to provide a sequential framework for the growth of thinking skills in students with learning problems. It is relevant to all age levels and applicable across any area of instruction that teachers of children who have difficulty learning might encounter. Unless teaching thinking skills is fully integrated with instruction and applied across all ages and to all levels of learning ability, it will have limited value in our schools. The idea of teaching thinking skills is dramatic, but only the intelligent application of this idea can bring about truly dramatic results. The hierarchy here provides a significant framework for those who teach students with learning problems from preschool to high school, and it includes both developmental progressions and instructional content sequences. This model is compatable with most of the current research directed toward thinking skills and should prove useful to teachers striving to offer meaningful and effective instruction for students with learning difficulties. By selectively combining the ideas of Robert Gagnè and Jerome Bruner, the intended purpose of this chapter is to provide a framework of thinking skills that applies across all ages and all proficiency levels as well as to all areas of school curriculum.

Hierarchy of Thinking Skills

This thinking hierarchy, modeled after the theories and learning sequences of Robert Gagnè (1974, 1977) and Jerome Bruner (1966, 1973), includes *selectively* borrowed ideas from conflicting positions. Because Gagnè considers *discrimination* basic to all learning, designating it as the foundation on which all other skills are developed, we begin by studying and analyzing discrimination. Next in order, according to Gagnè, are *concepts* (concrete and abstract generalizations), which then serve as prerequisites to *rules* (predictable relationships). *Higher-order rules* (such as problem solving) are at the top of Gagnè's hierarchy (see Table 6.1).

At present, the basic notion of hierarchical models remains unproved—but in this model we *assume* that the lower steps of the hierarchy must be mastered before the higher steps. Indeed, we agree that ". . . there may well be a kind of cyclical development in learning, in which the various stages must be repeatedly expanded and refined . . ." (Hilgard and Bower 1981, 553). But, as Hilgard and Bower also note, "The main point is that Gagnè has found the hierarchical principle a useful one for moving from learning principles to the sequencing of instruction" (p. 554).

Realizing that there may be exceptions, we present information from a hierarchical frame of reference, while knowing the complexities and individual varia-

Table 6.1 Interdependence of Intellectual Skills

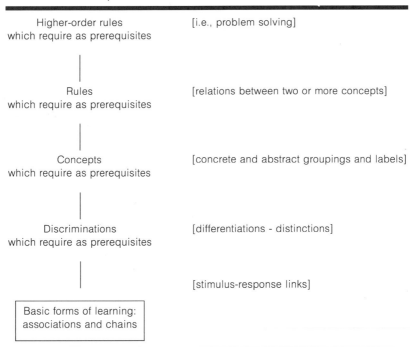

Higher-order rules   [i.e., problem solving]
which require as prerequisites

Rules   [relations between two or more concepts]
which require as prerequisites

Concepts   [concrete and abstract groupings and labels]
which require as prerequisites

Discriminations   [differentiations - distinctions]
which require as prerequisites

[stimulus-response links]

Basic forms of learning:
associations and chains

SOURCE. R. Gagnè. *The Conditions of Learning.* 3d ed. (New York: Holt, Rinehart & Winston, 1977) p. 34, with added notations in brackets.

tion in human beings, we also assume hierarchies are not absolutes. We realize, for instance, that children who are deaf present exceptions. Deaf children seem able to classify before they learn the labels to *identify* the concept, although the hierarchical model suggests that people learn to discriminate and identify before they classify.

Watch deaf children sort pictures of all kinds of cars and trucks. To find out what concepts they are using, note the attributes of a child's sorted groups of pictures. One grouping may indicate the process of a *concept* of "carness" and "truckness" even though students might not yet know the *identifying* terms of *cars* and *trucks*. Other groupings may indicate "sports carness," "standard carness," and "truckness." Such sorting requires skills beyond simple discrimination. But we have to be cautious about interpreting these activities since our knowledge about the thought processes of deaf children is limited.

To help teachers of academically limited students, we expanded portions of Gagnè's basic model, beginning with the skill of making discriminations and working up to presenting a complete model for studying student learning and planning corresponding instruction. The model begins with discrimination learning because, as stated, this thinking skill is considered basic to all learning, and the teacher may have to teach this skill deliberately and directly to some students with learning problems.

In this model, Gagnè's "higher-order rules" (or learning strategies) are termed problem solving because this seemed a more practical way of addressing the highest, most complex level on the learning ladder. *Problem solving* is a process by which the learner discovers a combination of previously learned rules that can be applied to solving a novel situation (Gagnè 1977, 155).

Another modification to Gagnè's basic outline is to add *identification skills* and *classification skills.* We feel these are important to add as separate steps in the ladder, especially for the very young student and for the substantially handicapped. In their simplest form, *identification skills* are labels—the names of things and events. It is important for students to develop this ability to name and to use the names of objects and the qualities of objects, actions, and direction of actions. *Classification skills* include recognizing relationships and commonalities among objects and events. Rather than addressing classification separately, Gagnè puts classification skills under concept learning. Jerome Bruner (1966) talks of classifications as "complexes," "groupings," and "collections." Figure 6.1 shows our hierarchy after making the above changes.

To instruct students with significant learning problems, we focus heavily on the underlying skills of *discrimination* and *identification,* which form the basic foundations for further learning. Keep in mind that discrimination refers to "perceiving a difference" and that identification refers to naming. (These and other terms used in our hierarchy of learning are defined and illustrated in Table 6.2.

The basic skills of discrimination and identification occur in every area of curriculum and instruction for all students, and these skills are taught directly to younger children. Older students who might have significant problems in communication, though, cannot always tell us whether they are able to perceive differences between objects or symbols, or if they do, on what basis they make these distinctions. If a student has problems with either of these basic learning skills, for example, it would be important for the teacher to take this into consid-

Figure 6.1
A Sequence of
Learning Skills
An Integrated Model

Problem-Solving Skills

Rule-Learning Skills

Concept-Learning Skills

Classification Skills

Identification Skills

Discrimination Skills

Table 6.2   Definitions for the Hierarchy of Learning

STEPS IN HIERARCHY	DEFINITION OF TERMS	EXAMPLE
PROBLEM-SOLVING SKILLS	The process by which the student discovers new combinations for previously learned rules. Involves application of previously mastered rules that yield new learnings.	Composes simple symphony after having mastered composition of musical score for various instrument groups.
RULE-LEARNING SKILLS	A defined concept or capability that enables the individual to respond to a class of situations with a class of performances because the stimulus and the performance are predictably related.	Demonstrates knowledge of rule: to make instruments sound, something has to set up and sustain vibrations.
CONCEPT-LEARNING SKILLS	The generalization of a concept across classes. These may be concrete, defined, or thinking complexes that relate one concept to another.	*Beats* in music—regular patterns—rhythm stress in music. May not be able to define it but can demonstrate by application to jazz, waltz, opera, and so on.
CLASSIFICATION SKILLS	Classification by observed physical characteristics or by some common abstract property. These are called "complexes," "groupings," and "collections."	Realistic pictures of musical instruments are sorted or distributed into groups of brass, wind, percussion, and string instruments.
IDENTIFICATION SKILLS	The names of things and events. The labels we apply to objects, classes of objects, actions and kinds of actions.	A *trumpet* is a specific instrument, the *brass* instruments are a group within the orchestra, the *orchestra* names the entire group, and the *symphony* identifies the event (naming).
DISCRIMINATION SKILLS	Making distinctions, perceiving a difference, differentiating between one stimulus and another.	Give a body signal each time student hears rock music as teacher scans FM radio stations (recognition).

eration when planning the instructional program. Progression to higher levels on the thinking hierarchy can be impeded if the basic, lower-level skills continue to present problems to the learner.

Differentiating between discrimination skills and identification skills can be confusing. Because of this confusion, teachers sometimes present lessons in sequences that unnecessarily complicate learning. We will show recommended learning sequences for discrimination and identification skills and later present a "Changing Difficulty Levels" chart (Fig. 6.3) that shows how to increase or decrease difficulty levels when teaching discrimination or identification skills based on students' performance.

Teaching Discrimination Skills

Definition and Description

Discrimination makes it possible for the learner to differentiate among stimuli and to respond differentially to objects or sounds that are different from one another. The word *discriminate* is used synonymously with *differentiate* and *distinguish*. The ability to discriminate is simply the ability to *perceive a difference*. Gagnè (1974) states, "It should be carefully noted . . . that discrimination makes it possible for the learner only to *tell the difference* among stimuli— *not* to name them or use them in some other way." This means children must be able to discriminate *before* they can identify or label. Gagnè concludes: "Thus learning discrimination is important mainly because it is a prerequisite to other learning" (p. 57). For example, one of the tasks that teachers of students with significant learning problems often face is teaching the value of various coins in our monetary system. Before students can learn to name (label, identify) coins, they must first be able to perceive the difference (discriminate, distinguish) between a quarter, a nickel, a dime, and a penny. That is, the student must be able to observe that these coins have distinguishing features which make them distinctly different from each other (differences in color, size, thickness, design, texture, etc.). The student need not verbalize that they are different or even have the inner language to describe the differences; he only needs to be able to distinguish one from the other perceptually. Gagnè (1977) also used coins to illustrate the process of discrimination:

> The learner must be able to *tell the difference* between objects varying in these particular qualities: between a color that is silver and one that is not silver, between a shape that is small and round and one that is not, and so on. Telling the difference between variations in some particular object-property is called a *discrimination*. (p. 33)

In using the word *tell*, Gagnè does *not* mean to name verbally. He refers here to perceptual differentiation and could as easily have said "see" the difference.

(Though the student who is blind would make this discrimination by touch instead of visual distinction.)

The teacher must also bear in mind that differences in appearance between a quarter and a penny are much greater than visual differences between a quarter and a nickel. This means that discrimination skills must be more highly developed for the latter. For some students, these discriminations are obvious. For students with substantial learning problems, discrimination skills do not come so easily.

Perceptual Skills Involved in Discrimination

Discrimination applies to taste and smell distinctions, touching and other kinesthetic differentiations, and emotional discriminations as well as the more commonly mentioned visual and auditory discriminations. Figure 6.2 presents the various perceptual skills in the order in which they may be acquired, though there is no general consensus about this sequence.

Auditory Discrimination. Babies tested minutes after birth are able to localize the direction of sounds coming from different sources. They can also distinguish one sound from another even before birth (Bower 1977). Students demonstrate sound discrimination in many everyday experiences (turning to a familiar voice, recognizing environmental sounds, preferring a particular musical group, etc.)

Tactile Discrimination. Exquisitely sensitive to touch, the newborn shows preferences for soft textures and warm temperatures. In many elementary school classrooms, students are directly taught to distinguish soft, rough, smooth, hard, and so on.

Figure 6.2 A Model of Subskills for Discrimination Learning

Discrimination (Perceptual Differentiation)

Perceptual Skills	Perceptual Progressions	Applications
Emotional discrimination Kinesthetic Proprioceptive Visual discrimination Olfactory Gustatory Tactile discrimination Auditory discrimination	Concrete to abstract Gross to fine Simple to complex Whole to part	Differences Recognition Matching

Olfactory and Gustatory Discrimination. The closely re-
lated senses of smell and taste are also developed at a very early age. Newborn
babies can distinguish sweet-tasting solutions from plain water within a week
after birth. Fine distinctions between different smells also develop quickly. Most
children entering school can discriminate between something cooking and something burning; between the smell of a carnation and the smell of a rose; between
cinnamon and nutmeg, lemons and strawberries, and so on. The popularity of
"scratch and sniff" stickers illustrate this.

Visual Discrimination. Visual discrimination is thought to de-
velop at a slightly later stage than auditory, gustatory, and tactile discriminations.
This may be based on the fact that, physiologically, the visual system develops
more slowly and is not fully mature at birth.

Proprioceptive and Kinesthetic Discrimination. Pro-
prioceptive receptors lie in our joints and respond basically to the angle between
two bones. This sensory system tells us where the mobile parts of our bodies are
in relation to all the rest—where our hands are in relation to one another, to the
head, to the trunk, and so on. *Kinesthetic* sensation is similar but refers more
exclusively to the muscle system and to movement itself. Though the terms are
often used interchangeably, proprioception is more inclusive. It applies to the
sense of position in space and can involve other senses.

Emotional Discrimination. As early as five to six months of
age, infants are able to discriminate between friendly and angry voices (Furuno et
al. 1979), whether the voices are familiar to them or not. Thus, making distinctions among emotional states in others is another skill developed early.

It is interesting to note that at this basic level, the ability to distinguish and
differentiate between one stimulus and another is generally inborn. Bower (1977)
reports that when newborn babies where placed in cribs with devices for recording their movements, they demonstrated the ability to discriminate between a
buzzer and a tone. If the baby turned his head to the right, he received a sweet-
tasting solution at the sound of a tone, but he had to turn to the left to receive the
solution at the sound of a buzzer. Babies no more than a few hours old were able
to accomplish this auditory discrimination task in about ten trials. Another group
of babies learned similar discriminations followed by reversing the conditions, so
that responses appropriate to the tone became appropriate to the buzzer and vice
versa. This means the babies had to unlearn the old task in order to learn the new
task (p. 17).

This kind of learning depends on the existence of certain inborn abilities. In
order to learn these responses, the newborn must already be able to: (1) distinguish between sweet and nonsweet (*gustatory discrimination*), (2) distinguish
between the tone and the buzzer (*auditory discrimination*), (3) differentiate be-

tween a head movement to one side and a head movement to the other (*kinesthetic and proprioceptive discrimination*), (4) make a link between sound, head movement, and sweet taste (*connect* three events separated in time), and (5) *disconnect* events previously linked and make new connections (Bower 1977, 16–17).

These basic perceptual abilities of gustatory, auditory, and kinesthetic discrimination are probably all present before birth. They are the earliest signs of cognitive development and can also be considered a prerequisite for subsequent learning or an integral part of early learning.

Levels of Difficulty in Teaching Discrimination

At this stage, of teaching discrimination, teachers need to develop an awareness of how increasing difficulty in the materials they present affects young children or students with learning problems. Perceptual discrimination is a learning task that gets more difficult and in general follows these patterns: from *whole to part,* from *simple to complex,* from *gross discrimination to fine discrimination,* and from *concrete to abstract.* For consistency and continuity of instruction, teachers can accept a basic premise about learning such as this one of progressions and then approach teaching and solving student problems using the premise as a guideline. There are, however, bound to be variations in this particular premise, or any premise, and in some cases direct contradictions. Figure 6.3 is a visual representation of learning tasks that progress from least to most difficult in our experience.

Figure 6.3   Changing Difficulty Levels

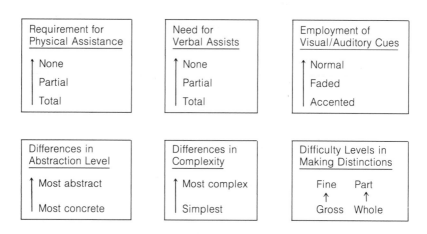

From Whole to Part. Because of the relative immaturity of their visual system at birth, babies first attend to detail as representations of whole objects. Bower (1977) describes research which demonstrates that infants attend to parts of their mothers' faces before they can perceive the full head. Seeing the entire head configuration is achieved by three months of age; then the direction of difficulty changes so that the simpler task is recognizing or discriminating the whole object rather than part of it. In older infants and most children with intact visual acuity, discriminations progress in difficulty from whole to part. In learning to distinguish between a trumpet and trombone, for example, the school-aged child would first attend to the whole configuration, perceiving the difference in shape before discriminating the position of the valves or the shape of the tubing. Similarly, when children begin to distinguish among zoo animals, their first distinction is the shape of the whole animal. They only notice details such as horns, trunk, and ears later.

From Simple to Complex. Consistent with most learning, visual and other perceptual discriminations proceed from simple to complex as well as from whole to part. To illustrate, Lieberman (1982) provided a modern translation for the principles of Jean-Marc-Gaspard Itard who worked at the beginning of the nineteenth century to educate a wild child rescued from the forests of France. According to Lieberman, Itard provided a special education curriculum that has "occasionally been equalled but seldom surpassed." The basic principles Itard used translated into modern terms are still applicable: (1) Attend to the nature of the child and begin with his interests; (2) recognize that attention and sensory discrimination are fundamental to the thinking process; (3) give rewards for activities that you want to be pursued again; (4) teach oral and written language by association and imitation; and (5) provide instruction that proceeds from the *simple to the complex.*

In modern curricula the transition from simplicity to complexity is clearly demonstrated in teaching arithmetic. Before learning to combine and separate sets (addition and subtraction), the child must first be able to discriminate (see the difference between different numbers and different numerals), match (perceive that two numerals are the same and that two sets are the same in number), associate (know that the symbolic numeral represents a specific number), then combine and separate (add and subtract). In other words, to be able to process addition and subtraction problems, the student must have not only *discrimination* skills, but also *identification* skills (representational symbols).

From Gross Discrimination to Fine Discrimination. Gross discriminations occur when differences between stimuli are large (elephant versus mouse, tree versus grass, basketball versus golf ball, quarter versus penny, trumpet versus piano, and so on). Fine discriminations require smaller distinctions and are more difficult to perceive (rat versus mouse, tree versus bush, basketball versus soccer ball, trumpet versus trombone). In the classroom, when a student is required to discriminate between a trumpet and a trombone, the teacher may first need to explore whether the student can discriminate between a trumpet and a piano or a trumpet and a drum which are more gross (and therefore easier) discriminations. Similarly, learning to discriminate between a quarter and a penny is easier than to discriminate between a quarter and a nickel, a more fine (and therefore more difficult) discrimination.

Increasingly finer discriminations between shape, color, texture, and sounds are often emphasized in the education of toddlers and preschool children. Then in the primary grades, the highly selective forms with many similar characteristics of letters and words require skilled differentiation before the child can become an effective reader (*r* from *n* from *h, b* from *d, f* from *t,* and so on). A prerequisite skill to these fine distinctions is that students must be able to discriminate a circle from other circular shapes, a square from other angular shapes, a horizontal line from other directional lines, and so on. When a student demonstrates difficulty with fine discriminations and/or complex discriminations, the teacher needs to go to a less complex (or less fine) level or to one that involves a simpler discrimination. Successful accomplishment of the learning task at a simpler level often boosts the child's motivation to continue learning until she can master finer discriminations. To assist in clarifying a progression from gross to fine discriminations, Table 6.3 suggests an instructional sequence progressing from easiest to more difficult differentiations.

From Concrete to Abstract. The progression from concrete to abstract is an important theme in learning. In learning to read the word *basketball,* the learner is assumed to have had some experience with a real basketball and to know what the spoken word *basketball* refers to. Ferrier and Shane (1980) discuss the progression from concrete to abstract in the representation process. Their detailed outline of various stages of symbolic representation is simplified in the example shown in Table 6.4.

At the earliest stage of development, the child's level of representation is concrete and nonsymbolic. At this point, the object itself, or a three-dimensional

Table 6.3 Scale of Progressions from Gross to Fine Differences among Nonexamples

---

↑ Degree of Difference

3. **Slightly different:** Nonexample belongs to the concept and to the same family at a given level in the hierarchy. However, the object can be discriminated from other members of its family (e.g., violin and cello).

2. **Moderately different:** Nonexample belongs to the concept but does not belong to the same family at a given level in the hierarchy (e.g., string and brass instruments).

1. **Greatly different:** Nonexample does not belong to the concept (e.g., baseball bat and violin).

Table 6.4 Progression from Concrete to Abstract Representations

Most Abstract: ↑	The printed word (*basketball*)
	Iconic symbols (Rebus, Bliss)
	A picture symbol
	A line drawing of a basketball
	A picture of a basketball
	A photograph of a basketball
	A three-dimensional representation: (a plastic toy basketball) optional if not age-appropriate
Most Concrete	A real basketball

toy resembling the object, begins the progression. (For a blind child, touching the object and hearing the sound it made would be even more basic.) The first level of *symbolic* representation on a two-dimensional plane is the photograph of a familiar object or person. As children mature perceptually and cognitively, line drawings—which are more schematic and conventionalized—can be used. With a further advance in cognitive ability, children can process more arbitrary symbols such as Rebus or Bliss that are iconic representations of objects and ideas. Rebus symbols are combinations of pictures and letters that stand for whole words or parts of words. Bliss symbols are pictographic symbols, each standing for a single concept, but they can be combined to code new concepts. Examples of Rebus and Bliss symbols are presented for clarification and comparison in Figure 6.4.

For the child who has developed to the most abstract stage of representation, the goal is reading and writing words. A thorough assessment of a child's reading readiness level is required as a prerequisite to this step. Readiness level combined with an evaluation of the child's visual and auditory perceptual preferences might lead to selecting a sight, phonic, or linguistic reading approach.

Teaching Discrimination Skills from Concrete to Abstract

In learning to discriminate a trumpet from other brass instruments, learning-handicapped students follow the progression shown in Figure 6.5. This specific example illustrates a general teaching strategy for students interested in music who do not learn easily. These students can be taught new things if their teachers use techniques designed to teach discrimination in a step-by-step procedure. Many students, of course, do not require such highly structured methods of instruction. We suggest that teachers use customary teaching procedures whenever the student demonstrates the ability to learn in more tradi-

Figure 6.4 Examples of Symbolic Representations

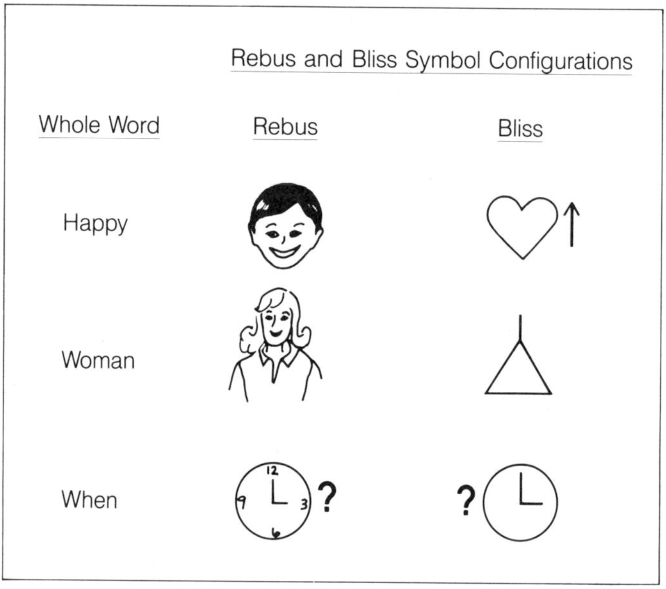

From Ferrier and Shane 1980, 24.

tional ways. Tasks A, B, and C in Figure 6.6 were extracted from the complete list in Figure 6.5 to demonstrate using a screening process. It may or may not be necessary to use this detailed procedure for every step shown in Figure 6.5.

The example in Figures 6.5 and 6.6 shows concrete to abstract progression so we can illustrate possibilities in both directions (toward more abstract or toward more concrete). Teachers can use this illustration to follow the direction the student's current level of functioning, interest level, and rate of success suggest.

Common Ways to Apply Discrimination Skills

The progressions from making simple discriminations to more difficult discriminations in terms of concrete to abstract, gross to fine, simple to complex, and whole to part apply to the various types of discrimination as well. *Matching, recognition,* and *differences* are three subtypes, or "applications," of discrimination most often used in education. Figure 6.6 illustrates how progressions occur in these types of discrimination tasks. This uses a trumpet, but the same process would apply with any instrument or any object (animals, sports equipment, furniture, and so on). After *matching* a real trumpet with an identical

Figure 6.5 Competence: Discriminate Trumpet Picture Symbol from Picture Symbols of Other Musical Instruments (Using both concrete-to-abstract progression and gross-to-fine discrimination)

Select the trumpet picture symbol (which is identical to a sample shown by the teacher) from a *series* of picture symbols   (*C* in Figure 6.6)
- which are slightly different
- which are moderately different
- which are greatly different

> Select the trumpet picture symbol (which is identical to a sample shown by the teacher) from *two* picture symbols
> - which are slightly different
> - which are moderately different
> - which are greatly different

Select the trumpet picture (which is identical to a sample shown by the teacher) from any *series* of pictures   (*B* in Figure 6.6)
- which are slightly different
- which are moderately different
- which are greatly different

> Select the trumpet picture (which is identical to a sample shown by the teacher) from *two* pictures
> - which are slightly different
> - which are moderately different
> - which are greatly different

Select the trumpet photo (identical to a sample shown by the teacher) from a *series* of photos
- which are slightly different
- which are moderately different
- which are greatly different

Select the trumpet photo (which is identical to a sample shown by the teacher) from *two* photos
- which are slightly different
- which are moderately different
- which are greatly different

Select the toy trumpet (which is identical to a sample shown by the teacher) from a *series* of toys
- which are slightly different
- which are moderately different
- which are greatly different

> Select the toy trumpet (which is identical to a sample shown by the teacher) from *two* toys   (use only if age-appropriate)
> - which are slightly different
> - which are moderately different
> - which are greatly different

Select the real trumpet (which is identical to a sample shown by the teacher) from a *series* of objects   (*A* in Figure 6.6)
- which are slightly different
- which are moderately different
- which are greatly different

> Select the real trumpet (which is identical to a sample shown by the teacher) from *two* objects   (use only if age-appropriate)
> - which are slightly different
> - which are moderately different
> - which are greatly different

Start here

203

Figure 6.6 Competence: Discriminate Trumpet Picture Symbols from Picture Symbols of Other Musical Instruments (Using both concrete-to-abstract progression and gross-to-fine discrimination)

C. Select the *trumpet picture symbol* (which is identical to a sample) from any series of picture symbols
   - which are slightly different
   - which are moderately different
   - which are greatly different

Student materials: Four picture symbols of brass instruments (which differ slightly), one of which is a trumpet.

Teacher materials: One picture symbol of a trumpet.

Procedure: Teacher shows picture symbol to student and says, "Show me this."

If student responds successfully, go from discrimination tasks to *identification* tasks.

If student responds unsuccessfully, go to less complex, simpler task (B)

Criteria: Four correct in five consecutive trials.

B. Select the *trumpet picture* (which is identical to a sample) from any series of pictures
   - which are slightly different
   - which are moderately different
   - which are greatly different

Student materials: Four pictures of brass instruments (which differ slightly), one of which is a trumpet.

Teacher materials: One picture of a trumpet.

Procedure: Teacher shows picture to student and says, "Show me this."

If student responds successfully, go to next more abstract task (C)

If student response unsuccessfully, go to more concrete task (A)

Criteria: Four correct in five consecutive trials.

A. Select the *real trumpet* (which is identical to a sample) from any series of objects
   - which are slightly different
   - which are moderately different
   - which are greatly different

Student materials: Four objects (which differ greatly), including a real trumpet and a real chair.

Teacher materials: A real trumpet.

Procedure: Teacher shows real trumpet and says, "Show me this."

If student responds successfully, go to more abstract task (B)

If student responds unsuccessfully with this least-abstract, least-complex, least-difficult task, consider the questions below.

Criteria: Four correct in five consecutive trials.

Prerequisite Considerations:

1. Are there any auditory or visual acuity problems that may be interfering with the student's receptive capabilities?

2. Is the response mode an appropriate one for this particular student? (Will eye glance be more accurate than pointing wth finger or nodding with head?)

3. Is the reinforcer appropriate for this student?

4. Can the student perform more personally relevant discrimination (foods, favorite toy, mother's voice)?

5. Is the student able to attend to the task?

real trumpet, the next step might be to match a toy trumpet with the real trumpet (concrete objects to this point). *Matching* photographs or drawings of trumpets would be more abstract than matching toys or real objects, while matching Rebus characters, Bliss symbols, or written words would be the most abstract. *Differences* would move through the same progression with selecting "the one not the same"—first from the real objects, then from three-dimensional representations, then from photographs and pictures, and finally from verbal or printed symbols. Similarly, *recognition* would begin with most concrete, and most simple items, and progress to most abstract and most complex.

At various times during this progression through discrimination phases, the teacher may give an object a verbal symbol or sign. Though the process of naming (identification) can overlap with the more basic discrimination skills, these two aspects of learning are discussed separately here. This does not mean that mastery of discrimination must occur before identification skills can start, but simply that, given a specific task, discrimination skills *usually begin* before identification skills begin. It is important to keep in mind that though we end our formal discussion of discrimination here, discrimination skills continue to be developed and refined all of our lives. We learn new discriminations with every new task we perform no matter how old we are when we learn it. For example, in wine tasting we see how differentiations and distinctions (discrimination) of very subtle taste differences can be learned later in life.

Remember, in order to discriminate, the student must be able to perceive that one object differs from all unlike objects and that it matches identical objects. Applying discrimination skills to the activities of matching, recognition, and differences forms a large part of the preacademic program in most schools. Preschool and kindergarten children are consistently required to look at shapes and pictures and identify those that are the same and those that are different. Matching colors, shapes, sizes, and numbers are activities most teachers of young children frequently assign.

Matching.   Matching requires the ability to observe a stimulus presented as a model and compare it with a second stimulus. As used here, matching initially refers to the simpler form of learning by direct comparison of two identical objects, two identical pictures, or two identical words. For example, when a teacher is presenting a curriculum in music to an older student whom he wants to develop matching skills, he might show a picture of a trumpet along with several pictures of other instruments. The student would be directed to select the identical matching item. Pointing to the correct one on the teacher's command, "Show me this" would be a matching task. At this point the object has not been named so "identification" or labeling is not involved, and the teacher is still operating at the level of discrimination, a particular *kind* of discrimination called "matching." Matching occurs when the student can recognize that the stimulus and the example are the same. The ability to demonstrate that knowledge is also an essential part of the task (pointing with the finger or other body part, using eye glance, and so on). Prompts as mentioned in Figure 6.5 and Figure 6.6 might be used for students who have difficulty at this stage. Higher levels of matching would include pairing dissimilar visual representations of the same object (an actual trumpet with a photograph of a trumpet, a photograph of a trumpet with a line drawing of a trumpet, or two drawings showing different views of a trumpet). A higher level would be matching individual objects with a class of objects (trumpets with other brass instruments, violin with other string instruments, drum with other percussion instruments, etc.).

Recognition.   Recognition is closely related to matching, but it also involves remembering. Recognition requires the memory to store an image (or set of specifications) for a specific object (or picture or word). Bruner (1973) refers to this internal representation as "mapping" (p. 14). In recognition, the student compares a presented stimulus with a previous stimulus that is no longer present or visible, and she makes a judgment that indicates how close the input comes to fulfilling the specifications required. The student must decide how may attributes the object has in common with the specifications or how far off the mark the input is.

Infants can distinguish between their mother's face and a stranger's face. This implies that infants remember their mother from an internalized image based on previous experience. This match of the immediate percept with a remembered percept is what we call *recognition*.

In learning about musical instruments, a child may become familiar with his brother practicing on a trumpet. At first it may seem to the youngster that his brother, the trumpet, and the music he hears are a single entity since it is a single experience to the baby. Soon he sees his brother as separate from the trumpet that he puts up to his mouth, and the trumpet is also internalized as a distinct and separate percept. At some point, seeing a trumpet on a table, the child matches immediate percept (trumpet) with the remembered image of the trumpet, and he *recognizes* the object. Recognizing the trumpet's sound might be another aspect of this remembered experience.

In another example, a blind adolescent girl might repeatedly search out on a radio band a station that features rock music. She does not see the numbers of the stations or might not be able to name the kind of music she enjoys, but when she finds what she's searching for, there is no question that this is the music she remembers and enjoys. This kind of recognition occurs in a variety of ways every day.

Differences.   In noticing differences, we find a process closely related to matching. Discriminating an item that is *different* from a set of otherwise identical items requires that the student first be able to recognize the *likenesses* within the set (matching). Discriminating differences is more complex than simple one-to-one matching since it requires comparing three or more items. For instance, a student presented with photographs of musical instruments and asked to select the "different" one would require at least two similar (or identical) items so that he could compare the *different* photograph to them. The discrimination of difference is not restricted to individual items; it applies to differentiation of categories as well. For example, given a picture set of musical instruments including a tuba, a trumpet, a drum, and a trombone, the student asked to find the "different one" would be expected to observe that the drum does not share characteristics in common with all the other instruments (the brass instruments). Observing this difference requires making distinctions at a higher level of thinking than the simple perceptual discriminations discussed earlier.

While matching, recognition, and differences are all *discrimination* tasks and considered to precede *identification* in the learning hierarchy, they are also integral to the process of identification. The major distinction between discrimination and identification, then, is whether or not the *name* of the object, action, feeling, and so on is used. Essentially the process of discrimination is one of perceptual differentiation, while the process of identification is one of providing a label. Figure 6.7 shows various aspects and some of the sequences involved in discrimination and identification processes.

Figure 6.7 Some Aspects of Discrimination and Identification

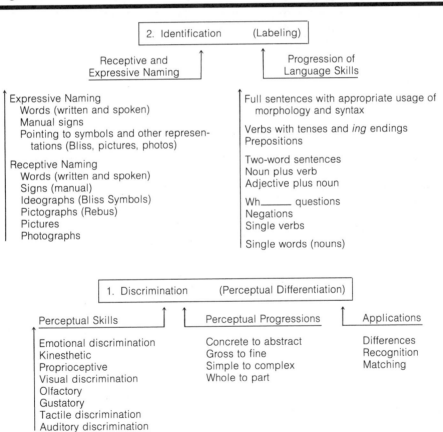

Teaching Identification Skills

The process of identification follows the ability to discriminate since an object is usually perceived and recognized before it can be named. Identification occurs when children learn that objects and events *have* names. Identification actually consists of recognizing that objects and events have *symbolic representation* in *any* form. For example, a house could be represented by a toy, a photograph, a pictorial symbol or icon, a manual sign, a spoken word, or a printed word. All these are symbols that denote the actual object: the real house.

According to Gagnè (1974), "Acquiring a discrimination merely enables the child for example, to *respond differently* to 'd' and 'b'. Of course he must be able to do the first (discriminate) before he can do the second (name). Thus learning discriminations is important mainly because it is a necessary prerequisite to other learning" (p. 57). Similarly, when we reach into a fruit bowl and select an orange instead of a banana, we do not need to know the names of these fruits; we only need to be able to see that they are different to select the one we prefer. This is *discrimination*. Asking for the orange by name, or responding correctly when asked to get an "orange" from the fruit bowl, provides a label for the object. This is *identification*. Additional examples of discrimination and identification are presented for further clarification in Table 6.5.

Levels of Difficulty

Since labeling or identification involves language (and using single words as representational symbols for objects heralds the beginning of language development), we will frequently refer to the stages of language development. However, since we largely concern ourselves with students who have speech problems, language delays, or are nonvocal, some words of caution are in order when we refer to "stages of language development." These stages are based on samples of what children *say;* they do not represent what children *understand.* In other words, what is commonly referred to as "stages of language development" does not reflect *receptive* language since most estimates of language acquisition are based upon *expressive* language, and the two may not be the same.

Menyuk (1974) discusses the early development of receptive language stating that "most observations of language development during these early months have only been concerned with describing the structural utterances produced. Thus, data on the infant's perception of linguistic structural properties and his comprehension of the function of these properties are still largely missing" (p. 213). This absence of data on language comprehension (receptive language) is due to the difficulty of measuring this ability in very young children. Similarly, little is known about the inner language of nonvocal students.

Table 6.5   Learning to Differentiate Between Discrimination Tasks and Identification Tasks

DISCRIMINATION TASKS	IDENTIFICATION TASKS
Turning to the sound of a car while crossing a busy street (this is recognition—no naming is required).	Saying, "That's hot!" after tasting a spoonful of hot soup (labeling the sensation that has been experienced).
Responding to the smell of something burning in the kitchen while people in the room are smoking cigars and pipes (differentiation of one smell from another).	Naming your favorite perfume when a friend wears it (this is both recognition and labeling).
Selecting the picture of a violin to match a sound heard on a tape (matching, no naming required).	Selecting the correct part of a sound track when asked to locate the "violins" (recognition and naming).
Responding to the phone ringing as a child plays with toy that has a bell (distinguishing one sound from another).	Locating the correct toy when asked to "find the one with a bell" (location by naming).
Recognizing a friend's voice when you are blind before he tells you who it is (recognition, no naming required).	Finding a photograph of sister from an array of family photos in response to "Where is sister?" (selection by name).
Selecting a trumpet from an array of pictures when shown a model to match, when asked "Find one like this" (matching—without naming).	Saying "Trumpet" in response to request, "What is this?" (object is named).
Selecting a picture of a drum from an array with a series of trumpets (finding the one that is different).	Selecting the picture of a drum from an array when asked, "Show me drum" (selection by label).
Imitating those behaviors of peers for which peers were rewarded (distinguishing behaviors rewarded from those not rewarded).	Selecting a printed phrase or symbol that tells what was observed on the playground (action is named).
Giving a sympathetic pat on the head to the peer who is crying (recognizing which child is crying).	Signing the feelings exhibited by a peer: "He's *mad!*" (labeling a feeling).
Pulling out imperfect objects in quality-control job (differentiating imperfect from perfect objects).	Repeating to self the (six) steps of a task to be completed (naming steps to self).

Even when researchers assess the *expressive* language of young children, they can only make a few generalities since rates of learning and the onset of specific linguistic forms vary considerably from one child to another. Nevertheless, and with all these shortcomings considered, we have no alternative to using the progressions of language acquisition derived from samples of nonhandicapped expressive children. Currently no other reliable guides exist to the language-acquisition sequence for students with different disabilities that impact on language.

Therefore, the language sequence in Figure 6.7 was derived from assessing the development of expressive language. This represents a grossly simplified outline of the many complex aspects of language development though. The following studies explore this area in greater depth: Bloom (1970), Brown (1973), Greenfield (1976), Bates (1976, 1979), Silverman (1980), and Miller (1981).

In the process of identification, the student uses a word, symbol, or sign to represent the real object. To do this, the student must be able to recognize and/or supply a spoken word, symbol, or sign in addition to being able to distinguish or discriminate one object from another and one word from another word. Varying degrees of abstraction are involved in the identification process. Bliss Symbols and written words form higher levels of abstraction than the spoken word does. Speaking children usually identify first by naming orally and then by labeling with written words. Disabled nonspeaking individuals may first label with manual sign, pictorial symbols, or written words. Table 6.6 presents a simple sequence that illustrates the use of examples and nonexamples within successive levels of difficulty in framing questions for an identification task. This method allows the student to respond according to his own level of proficiency.

Identification Skills Using Direct Teaching

Strategy One.   Once students have learned to discriminate specified items, we can teach them to *name* (or *label*, or *identify*) those items. We teach a specific routine, or set of subtasks, to instruct students to vocalize, use an electronic communication aid, or produce visual symbols of some kind to indicate a label. This structured direct-teaching strategy involves teacher modeling through naming an actual item (or picture of an item) placed before the child. The teacher models by saying the name of the item (or pointing to a word or other visual symbol of the item), then pointing to the actual item (or to the picture of the item) the symbol represents. The student is then encouraged to imitate the procedure just demonstrated by the teacher, either by *saying* the word or *pointing* to the symbol for the object and then pointing to or looking at the object.

To make the task of identification more complex, distracters are added one at a time to see if the student can still match the verbal or written symbol to the item. The routines gradually lead the student to the skill of identifying an item by name or symbol when someone points to it in more natural situations and requests of the student: "Show me what you see" or "What do you want?"

Strategy Two.   For curriculum options and related instructional activities, we offer strategies in which teachers present a variety of different examples of items one at a time. Among the examples is one (or more) item that is not an example: it is a nonexample. Teachers can use this example/nonexample in

Table 6.6 Levels of Difficulty in an Identification Task

	TEACHER SAYS:	STUDENT RESPONDS:
Level 6	Teacher is passive. Does not request or elicit response.	Student initiates: "Look at that basketball!" in a real-world situation.
Level 5	Using an example and a nonexample: "What is this?"	"Basketball"
Level 4	Using an example and a nonexample: "Which is a basketball. This is not a basketball." Points to one: "Is this a basketball?"	Responds yes or no
Level 3	Using an example and a nonexample: "This is a basketball—This is not a basketball—*Where* is the basketball?"	Attends Responds by pointing
Level 2	Using an example and a nonexample: "This is a basketball—This is not a basketball—Show me a basketball."	Attends Responds by pointing
Level 1	Using a positive example only—no distracters. "Basketball" pointing to the item "This is a basketball." Asks: "Show me a basketball."	Attends to task Indicates by non-verbal means (pointing, looking, etc.)

many situations to teach identification of any items or concepts. First the teacher tells students which are examples (Es) and which are not examples (NON-Es): "This is a basketball." "This is not a basketball." Then she demonstrates a routine that she will later expect students to follow. The routines conclude with the students demonstrating their ability to identify a designated item by answering yes or no to questions about the items the teacher just designated as examples and nonexamples (i.e., "Is this a basketball?"). Students will answer yes to examples of the basketball and will respond by indicating no to items that are nonexamples (football, baseball, soccer ball, kickball, etc.).

Structured direct-teaching routines allow students with unintelligible speech to indicate *yes* and *no* in whatever way is available to them. If they do not yet know how to respond, we suggest strategies to teach them. If they do not yet know how to respond with *yes* and when to respond with (or indicate) *no*, we include ideas on how to teach this as well. If students do not have ways to show that they do not know the answer to a specific question, we include ways to teach them how to indicate "I don't know."

Selecting examples is fairly obvious since the process of selection is one of simple matching. If actual objects are not readily available, begin with photographs or colored pictures of the item. Selection of nonexamples is somewhat more complex because we suggest graduating nonexamples from those that are greatly different to those that are only slightly different from the examples. In

Table 6.3 the first example compares a baseball bat and a violin as greatly different items; string instruments and brass instruments as moderately different items; and a violin and a cello as slightly different items. As this indicates, items that are *greatly* different have only one or two attributes in common with the example. The teacher can extend this to a comparison of one item as a nonexample with several items that are examples. When the nonexample is greatly different, it has only one or two attributes in common with the attributes common to all the examples. Those that are *moderately* different have more attributes in common with the example, and those that are only *slightly* different from the example are very much like them. Nonexamples presented last with an array of examples that have most (but not all) attributes in common with the example are the *slightly* different examples. These are the most difficult discriminations for students to make.

This same strategy is useful for teaching discriminations, classifications, and rules. It can be expanded to teach identification not only of items seen, but also of actions seen and sounds heard. This mention of auditory and visual processes brings us to an addendum that provides the physiological and attitudinal foundations for our hierarchy of thinking skills.

Prerequisites to Learning

So far we have assumed that students who participate in the learning process are (1) able to receive the information presented to them and (2) are willing to respond to the instructional program presented to them. Because teachers cannot always assume that students see and hear adequately, or that they are eager to learn, these two prerequisites require attention and evaluation. We mention them here so that teachers will be aware of their importance as basic prerequisites to learning. Table 6.7 represents the minimal consideration that must be given to acuity and motivation before a teacher can expect any kind of learning to occur.

Table 6.7
Physiological and Attitudinal
Prerequisites to Learning

PREREQUISITE SKILLS	
ACUITY	MOTIVATION
Visual	Interest
Tactile	Feelings
Auditory	Attention

Acuity. Sensory acuity includes visual, auditory, and tactile acuity. Traditional methods of instruction require that the student be able to see, hear, and feel. Teachers assume that students are listening to them and hear directions and instructions that are presented vocally. Teachers also expect that visual presentations are received clearly too. Students are also expected to carry out instructions that require them to move through space and perform tactile/ kinesthetic tasks such as writing, sharpening pencils, drawing, walking across the room, and so on.

Visual acuity is related to the functioning of the eye. Nearsightedness, farsightedness, and astigmatism are all problems of the eye mechanism that relate to receiving visual stimuli. Students cannot make even the simplest visual discriminations unless they can *see* what they are looking at.

Deafness or hearing loss will prevent or distort sound reception. A student with auditory acuity problems may not be able to understand directions or perceive instructions given orally since he does not accurately hear what is said.

Tactile acuity involves the sense of touch and the ability to distinguish between textures, temperatures, and consistencies. Proprioceptive functions including kinesthetic acuity refer to movement, direction, and the extent and weight of movement in space. Proprioception is the inner sense of what is happening with the muscles, tendons, and joints of the body in motion. Difficulty with this modality interferes with responses involving the muscular coordination and automatic movements required in activities such as speech, pointing, writing, drawing, walking, running, riding a bicycle, and so on. This includes kinesthetic as well as spatial accuracy.

Knowing the degree and extent of impairment in any of the areas of acuity is critical to the teaching-learning process. This is illustrated forcefully in our experiences with students who had been labeled as having intellectual retardation or severe learning problems when in reality they had visual or auditory impairment. Any learning problem should immediately alert the teaching staff to review the records or interview parents for information about current vision and hearing tests.

Motivation. Most teachers know students who show high potential but appear not to care much about learning. This phenomenon may be due to difficulties with *attention* (attending to activities or interests other than what is presented by the teacher), having a short attention span, or being easily distracted, *feelings* (emotional problems that interfere with the natural desire to learn), and *interest* (an absence of the desire to learn). Other aspects of motivation are also important; sources of motivation, individual differences in motivation, methods of stimulating motivation, and so forth.

Motivation is a highly complex and many faceted process that requires much more intensive and extensive exploration than it has received to date. Though we cannot examine it fully here, we emphasize its importance. Without good student motivation, the most carefully structured and exciting curriculum is slated for failure. The teacher must be aware of the student's level of motivation and understand that it can easily vary from day to day or even from one situation to another.

Figure 6.8 summarizes the learning skills discussed so far. This figure adds the prerequisite skills to discrimination and identification skills shown in Figure 6.7. The hierarchy of learning skills is beginning to take shape here, laying the foundation for the next level of learning, which is classifications.

Figure 6.8   Identification and Discrimination with Prerequisite Skills

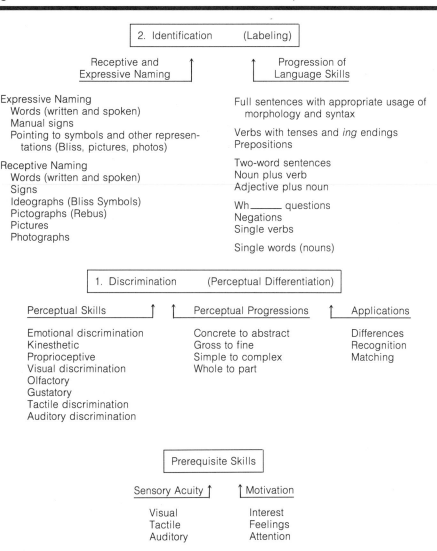

Teaching Classification Skills

Bruner's theory of cognitive development and learning differs somewhat from that of Gagnè. While Gagnè's ideas about learning are closely related to social-learning theory, Bruner's developmental theory more closely resembles Piagetian cognitive development. Bruner, Olver, and Greenfield's *Studies in Cognitive Growth* (1966), a collection of research projects conducted under Bruner's sponsorship at Harvard University, relate systematic investigations of how children learn to represent and classify objects and events in their lives. Bruner's later work, *Beyond the Information Given* (1973) elaborates and refines the results from these studies. Bruner proposed three basic modes of representation:

- Enactive—learning by doing
- Iconic—learning through pictures or images
- Symbolic—learning through language, sign, or written word

The *enactive* mode is the child's first method of representation, which may correspond developmentally to the sensorimotor period Piaget defined. By the time children complete their first year of life, the *iconic* mode can replace the enactive mode (perhaps because of the object permanence aspect that develops at this age). The *symbolic* mode, last to develop with the onset of language, is further divided into *descriptive* language (nouns and adjectives), *prescriptive* language (verbs), and *relations* (prepositions).

Basic Representation Modes

Bruner (1973) sees the enactive, iconic, and symbolic systems as unique and independent and possibly as developing parallel to one another. He asserts that each depends on the previous one for its development; yet all of them remain more or less distinct and intact throughout life (p. 327).

The Enactive Mode. Toward the end of the first year, the child perceives actions and objects as inseparable. The identification of objects depends on the actions the objects evoke rather than upon the nature of the objects themselves. For example, Piaget described his son Laurent at seven months as having lost a cigarette box that he played with by swinging it. In order to recover the box after he accidentally dropped it, Laurent swings his arm again, expecting the box to reappear.

The Iconic Mode. The iconic mode is characterized by visual imagery and pictorial representation of real objects. Vision and visual discrimination develop early in infancy. Even though visual skills mature more slowly than auditory skills, researchers believe that some visual acuity may be present as early as the first day after birth. Coordinating visual focus on an item with the tracking of its movement in space is called visual tracking. Using visual tracking of movement, the child's next task is to make the sequential world of action correspond with the spatial world of vision. This characterizes the learning that occurs in the enactive mode. Later, when using the iconic mode, children learn to free the perceptual world from the control of action.

The Symbolic Mode. Language is the most specialized natural system of symbolic activity. The idea that a name goes with a thing and that the name is arbitrary is generally accepted as the earliest symbolic functioning (referred to in this text as *identification* or *labeling*). When children learn words, they see them as signs (standing for the thing present before them) rather than as symbols. The word is first seen, then, as integral to the object itself. In everyday conversation we continue to say, "This is a violin" rather than, "We call this thing a violin" or, "The name of this is *violin*."

Without training in the symbolic representation of experience, a child could grow into adulthood depending largely upon enactive and iconic modes of representing and organizing her world. As soon as children develop an organization of experience that in some sense can match the structures of language, the state of independence between the two systems recedes (Bruner 1966, 50). In other words, children use language for labeling at first, but when a certain level in the development of mental capacities (cognitive abilities) exists, language can be organized into thinking. The symbolic mode, then, is the highest level of representation. It begins with simple labeling but advances with development to include complex verbal abstractions.

Further discussion of the enactive, iconic, and symbolic modes of thinking may be found in Bruner, Olver, and Greenfield, *Studies in Cognitive Growth* (1966) and in Bruner, *Beyond the Information Given* (1973).

Equivalence Modes

Olver and Hornsby (1966) refer to the process of determining how things are alike and different as the concept of *equivalence*. One of their research projects in *Studies of Cognitive Growth* compared children from six to nineteen years on a series of equivalence tasks to determine *how* they made decisions. Specifically, they wanted to know on what basis children determined that foods (banana, peach, potato, meat, etc.) or objects (bell, horn, telephone, radio, newspaper, book), presented as a series of pairs, were alike and different. They found that six-year-olds used color and shape more often, while sixteen-year-olds used various other categories more often. Several of these studies found that five major modes seemed most characteristic of the responses children in the age ranges examined gave. The five modes, their subclasses, and examples are presented in Table 6.8.

These studies showed that six-year-olds mostly used perceptible cues (directly observable characteristics such as color or shape). From six years on, a steady increase developed in the use of functionality, so that at nineteen years, 73 percent of all responses were related to the object's functional attributes (common uses such as "for eating" or "for playing"). Nine-year-olds most frequently responded in terms of what they could do to the object ("functional" in the egocentric form such as, "You throw them" or "I can make it ring").

As a result of extensive research using these simple techniques, Bruner et al. formulated what they believed was a reliable hierarchy of difficulty in equivalence (see Table 6.9). Dale (1976) supports Bruner's view of the hierarchy, asserting that children's performances on classification tasks illustrate well the quality of their thinking:

> When young children are given a group of pictures to be sorted into categories, they are likely to group on the basis of color, shape, or size. Around the age of six or seven there is a shift from reliance on perceptual or iconic properties to reliance on symbolic representations. Older children are more likely to group using a superordinate word, for example "They are all tools." (p. 260)

Similarly, given a group of musical instruments to categorize, younger children might group them according to size; older children can more readily recognize that *regardless of size* trumpets, trombones, French horns, and tubas consti-

Table 6.8 Five Major Modes of Equivalence
(See Table 6.9 for *order* of acquisition)

1. *Perceptible:* Use of color, size, shape, or position in time and space
   a. Perceptible intrinsic: immediately observable qualities (they're yellow, have dots on them, they're round)
   b. Perceptible extrinsic: qualities observed in general environment (they're in a house, use them in daytime)

2. *Functional:* what they do and/or what can be done to them
   a. Functional intrinsic: immediate specific qualities (they make noise)
   b. Functional extrinsic: observed in more removed settings (you can turn them on)

3. *Affective:* the emotion they arouse (you like them both, they're important to people)

4. *Nominal:* a name that provides a classification (both are fruit, both are toys, both are tools)

5. *Fiat equivalence:* a statement that objects are alike without giving a reason (the same thing, that's all)

SOURCE: R. R. Olver and J. R. Hornsby. "On Equivalence," in *Studies in Cognitive Growth* by J. S. Bruner, R. R. Olver, and P. M. Greenfield. (New York: John Wiley & Sons, 1966), pp. 71–72.

Table 6.9   Hierarchy of Difficulty in Equivalence

Perceptible	1. *Color:* Equivalence using color cues requires fewer transformations. Attention to a single dimension is all that is required.
	2. *Shape:* Even if unidimensional, equivalence by shape requires a finer distinction than color since one must attend to: straight line vs. curve, number of sides, corners, etc.
	3. *Size:* The variation of size is along several dimensions (height, width, curvature, sides, regularity).
Functional	4. *Function:* The use of an object or the purpose to which it is put constitutes a more abstract, less immediately available cue.
Nominal	5. *Class Inclusion:* The nominal mode which provides a name for a class to which an object belongs is the most abstract of the modes used.

SOURCE: R. R. Olver and J. R. Hornsby. "On Equivalence" in *Studies in Cognitive Growth,* by J.S. Bruner, R. R. Olver, and P. M. Greenfield. (New York: John Wiley & Sons, 1966).

tute the brass section of an orchestra. This ability to use the category of class inclusion is a more highly developed level of classification skill.

Teaching Classifications

It is well documented that at earlier levels of development children tend to classify using perceptual information almost exclusively. In our culture the ability to sort objects by color is the earliest perceptible classification that appears. This is followed by predominantly using shape in classification tasks. This shift is usually accomplished by age seven. Next to develop, after sorting by color and shape, is sorting by pattern or design. Following this is classification by size. Much later comes the ability to classify objects according to the materials from which they are made. We also know that, at early levels, children group objects on the basis of a single characteristic or attribute; the ability to use two or more attributes may not develop until around age nine or ten.

Although Olver and Hornsby (1966) report five major modes of classification or equivalence (see Tables 6.8 and 6.9), we have condensed these to four that appear in Figure 6.9 under *classifications:*

- Perceptible (size, shape, pattern, color)
- Functional (to eat with, to work with, to play with)
- Compositional (made of wood, made of metal, made of glass)
- Categorical or nominal (are animals, are fruits, are toys)

Lowery (1981), who along with Bruner et al. adheres closely to Piagetian theory, provides us a further refinement of classification skills. His hierarchy includes most of the major elements Bruner, Olver, and Greenfield (1966) mentioned and supplies greater detail to the structure and concept of levels of classification ability (see Table 6.10).

Lowery used a technique similar to that Olver and Hornsby (1966) used in evaluating children's classification skills. Given groups of objects from the same general class (blocks, leaves, coins, shapes, etc.), the child is asked to put the objects into groups that belong together. For example, if the child is given a set of pictures that depict musical instruments, the child may be directed to arrange the pictures in groupings. Beyond the random "clumping" described by Vygotsky (1962), the child may decide to group all the instruments by color or size. Grouping could be based on other perceptible characteristics as well. Lowery lists the various solutions to the classification task and designates the age levels at which these are usually mastered. Table 6.10 provides a summary of the hierarchy with definitions and examples for each level.

Detailed lessons and specific directions for classification skills are further explored in Lowrey (1981), *Learning about Learning: Classification Abilities*. Though theoretically based on the ideas of Piaget, Lowrey's book also acknowledges the contributions of Bruner and Gagnè. For further exploration of Piagetian contributions to concept development, see Scholnick (1983), Siegler (1986), and Ginsburg and Opper (1979).

We have to this point combined ideas from a theory of instruction (Gagnè) and a theory of cognitive development (Bruner) to provide a sequence of learning processes and thinking skills for teachers to use in planning instruction. Figure 6.9 is the completed organizational model for skills considered essential in acquiring information, as developed from our investigation of these two theorists.

Concepts, Rules, and Problem Solving

Up to this point, each step in the "ladder of thinking skills" has received separate consideration and considerable detailed elaboration. In contrast, as we come to upper levels of the thinking-learning hierarchy, the discussion is less complete, and we combine concepts, rules, and problem solving into a single section. This condensation does not mean that these levels are any less important. *Concepts, rules,* and *problem-solving* skills are just as important as *discrimination, identification,* and *classification* skills for students with learning problems. However, we develop them less fully here and rely on other sources for more detail (Rohwer, Ammon, and Cramer 1974, Gagnè and Briggs 1974, Gagnè 1977, Copeland 1979, Ginsburg and Opper 1979, Feuerstein 1980, Lowrey 1981, de Bono 1982 and 1983, Sternberg 1984, Siegler 1986). In defining and

Table 6.10 Levels of Classification Ability

LEVEL	PRINCIPLE	EXAMPLES
I. Resemblance Sorting Ages 4–6	Two objects can be grouped together because they are alike on the basis of *one* common attribute (color *or* shape).	Color / Shape Shape Only — long, triangular Grouping balls by size:
II. Consistent and Exhaustive Sorting Ages 6–8	*All* objects in a group are grouped on the basis of one attribute: (shape *or* size *or* color).	Shape lobed edge, smooth edge Grouping different shapes of various color by size.
True Classifying Abilities		
III. Multiple Membership Classification Ages 8–10	An object can belong to more than one class or set at the same time (shape *and* color).	Color / Shape shape and edging Grouping balls by color and size.

		Vehicles / Leaves / Kinds of Balls
IV. Inclusive Classifying Ages 10–12	If one class is included in another, then all objects in the smaller class are a part of the larger. Conversely some objects in the larger class includes all of the smaller.	**Vehicles** bus → cars → train sport convertible station wagon **Leaves** smooth edge → lobed edge → toothed edge long, square, triangular → l., sq., tri. → l., sq., tri. **Kinds of Balls** Large: basket, soccer, kick, foot Med.: tennis, hand, billiard Small: golf, ping pong
V. Horizontal Reclassifying Ages 12–14	An array of objects can be classified into groups using one set of attributes and can be reclassified on the basis of another set of attributes.	$24 + 32 = 56$ or $= 7 \times 8$ or $= (3 + 4) \times 8$ or $= (3 \times 8) + 32$ Leaves of { desert trees, forest trees, jungle trees Leaves of { evergreens perennial, deciduous Grouping balls by use, size, color: (basketball, football, soccer ball, kickball, baseball).
VI. Hierarchical Reclassifying Ages 14–16	Objects or events may be arranged and rearranged into useful hierarchies of increasingly more inclusive classes.	A periodic chart of the elements. Evolution of species. Species of trees, shrubs and vines. Classes of extinct plant species Grouping games by number of persons who participate, by complication of rules, etc.

SOURCE: Adapted from Lowery. *Learning About Learning: Classification Abilities.* (Berkeley, Calif.: University of California Press, 1981), pp. 1, 4, 6, 8, 11, 13.

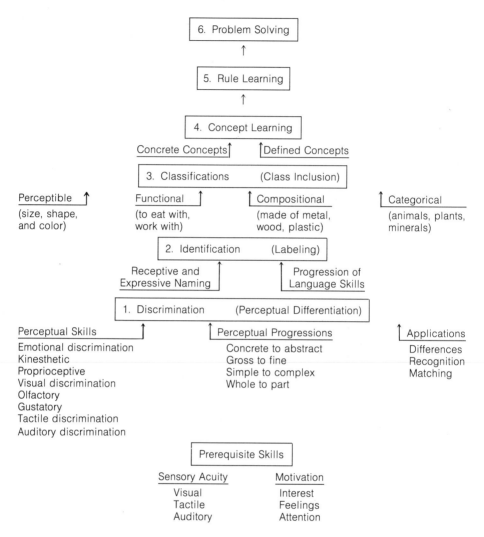

Figure 6.9   The Sequence of Learning Skills: An Integrated Model

describing concepts, rules, and problem solving, we once again rely heavily on the ideas of Robert Gagnè (1974, 1977), but elaborations in some areas are derived from Becker, Engelmann, and Thomas (1975) and others, some previously mentioned in this chapter.

Concept Learning

Becker, Engelmann, and Thomas (1975, 238–305) describe a "concept" as a set of common characteristics unique to one group of objects and so not common to other objects. At the concept level of learning, students demonstrate their ability to know, define, and describe objects, attributes, and activities based on their abstract properties. The major characteristic distinguishing concepts from discriminations and identifications is that generalization is involved. This is what makes it possible for the individual to respond to things or events as a class. For example, the concept of "curved" applies not only to circular and oval shapes but also to a particular kind of line, parts of the body, architecture, roads and streets, and so on. Concept learning thus represents the first true level of conceptualization in thinking. Gagnè (1974, 75) further divides the conceptualization level into "concrete" and "defined" aspects.

Concrete Concepts. These consist of classifications listed in Table 6.10 under "True classifying abilities." They represent a transition between *classifications* and *concept learning* in the *hierarchy of thinking skills* (Fig. 6.9). Included are classification by multiple membership, inclusive classifying, horizontal reclassifying, and hierarchical reclassifying. Concrete concepts depend on direct observation (hence the term *concrete*) and often involve objects, but observable actions and events are also included. Though the observable events can vary widely in appearance, what is important is that the student respond to them in terms of some common abstract property.

To illustrate, consider how a student might develop the concept of "corner." The first step might be to acquire the label itself in relation to a particular object, a table for example. The student might first be led to discriminate and identify the *surface* of the table, the *sides* of the table, the *edges* of the table, and then be introduced to the *corners* of the table. When the concept of "corner" has been integrated and further applied to other objects (box, bed, room, paper, book, street, etc.), then it is generalized. At this point the student has acquired the concrete concept of "corner."

Defined Concepts. These are concepts that have meaning best expressed by definition rather than by example. This means that one must use words and sentences (language) to identify a class of things, events, or actions. Students acquire defined concepts when they can demonstrate how to *use* the definition of a concept (i.e., *knowing* the definition is not enough).

Gagnè (1974) illustrates a defined concept by using the word *obstacle*. Since it would be impossible to identify the entire class belonging to the word *obstacle* by pointing out various instances of the concept, the word's definition is the best way to convey its meaning. Thus the meaning communicated by the sentence "An obstacle is something that stands in the way" is a defined concept (p. 59). The term *musical instruments* is another example. Since it would not be practical to name all possible instruments included in this concept, its definition is the most appropriate way to convey its meaning. Defined as "devices used to produce music," the meaning of the term is clearly conveyed without endless examples or an exhaustive listing. To demonstrate the use of these concepts, a student would be able to correctly apply examples and nonexamples of obstacles and musical instruments or to use the terms in appropriate situations (e.g., "I encountered an *obstacle* when I asked for permission to go on the camping trip.").

Rule Learning

A rule is a learned capability that makes it possible for the individual to *use* concepts. For example, a young child could be told that "round things roll." Before learning the rule in that statement, the child must first grasp the meanings of the two concepts. He must know "round things" as a class of objects with specific characteristics that includes such various things as discs and cylinders as well as spheres. Similarly, the concept "roll" must be understood and distinguished from such actions as tumbling and sliding. With these prerequisites, the learner is prepared to combine the two concepts and use them in relation to one another (Gagnè 1977, 137). This constitutes *rule learning* which is characterized by the capacity to *use* symbols and concepts previously learned in combination with each other. A person who has acquired a rule has learned a new relationship between previously learned concepts.

Another way of saying this is that the *prerequisite* to rule learning is that the concepts, classifications, identifications, and discriminations in the rule must be integrated or combined before learning the rule. Similarly, learning one rule can facilitate learning another rule if both involve one or more of the same components (concepts, labels, etc.). The educational process involves all kinds of rules. Young children learn rules that enable them to decode words in reading, encode words in spelling, perform arithmetic computations, and so on. The following are simple examples of rules that arise in classroom instruction:

- The letters *ph* are pronounced as *f* in most common words (decoding the words photograph, elephant, and telephone)
- When a word ends in *y* change the *y* to *i* before adding an ending (encoding the words *story-stories, reply-replies,* and so on)
- When a set is combined with another set, a new set is formed (two pennies added to two other pennies will equal four pennies)

Older students learn rules that enable them to perform complex tasks in chemistry, physics, biology, statistics, and countless other fields. A college student or adult also learns many rules such as the structure of poetry, the rules of musical composition, and the construction of a foreign language (Gagnè 1974, 61). Such learning is regarded as "rule-governed" behavior.

Rule-governed behavior makes it possible for an individual to respond to a class of things with a class of performances. For example, learning that adding a particular ending to a word will place it in the past tense (*ed*), make a plural of it (*s*), or modify it to make an adverb (*ly*) means that the rule can apply to an entire class of words. Rule learning entails the ability to generalize from an instance to a large class of instances.

Problem Solving

When people combine complex rules to solve new problems, they are engaged in the highest level of learning, *problem solving*. Many kinds of performances can result from problem solving, but they all share one thing: They would not be possible by applying a single rule. Just as rule learning involves combining previously learned concepts, problem solving involves combining previously learned rules. Students need not be able to state the rules used, but they must be able to show that they know the rules they use. The activity of problem solving is a natural extension of rule learning; however, it should be guided by much less teacher direction and little or no direct instruction. In Gagnè's words (1974, 128–29) "Problem-solving tasks are often employed to promote transfer of learned capabilities to novel situations. . . . For example, a problem for a class in social studies might be one of predicting the growth of stores in a local shopping center, based upon the projected pattern of housing in the surrounding area. Reasonably original solutions to such a problem require a number of skills on the part of the students—the construction of graphs, extrapolation of trends, and the concepts of ease of transportation, population density, family income, and others. Students who have indeed attained these intellectual skills will be able to participate in the process of solving the problem in ways that are valuable for their learning." Problem solving is a process by which the student discovers a combination of previously learned rules to apply to solving a new problem.

A simpler example of problem solving already mentioned is the complex task of long division; to do it, students must already know the rules for subtraction, addition, and multiplication. The first mathematician to discover that these rules applied to problems of long division was doing *problem solving*. Gagnè (1977) stresses that true problem solving refers to finding solutions to *novel problems* and should be carefully distinguished from routine learning of new concepts and rules. Thus, in the example above, the student who is *taught* long division is not actually problem solving, but the first person to develop the process of long division *was* problem solving. Problem solving also entails using individual cognitive strategies. It is, for the most part, an "internal" process since it requires applying previously acquired rules newly *combined* to achieve a goal. The only external conditions appropriate to the problem-solving process is the presentation of the problem. All subsequent steps, according to Gagnè's definition (p. 156), must be the responsibility of the learner.

When referrring to "cognitive strategies," Gagnè implies a specific kind of cognitive skill that learners use to guide their learning processes. These strategies influence and govern the processes of attending, learning, remembering, and thinking. For further examinations of cognitive strategies and how they influence the learning process, see Covington, Crutchfield, Davies, and Olton (1972), Gagnè and Briggs (1974), Brown (1978), Feuerstein (1979, 1980), Campione, Brown, and Ferrara (1982), and Sternberg (1982).

As a thinking skill, problem solving requires students to discover a higher-order rule without outside help. In this way students construct new rules using their own cognitive strategies. Rohwer, Ammon, and Cramer (1974) demonstrate the relationship between concepts, rules, and problem solving by an example involving flotation (pp. 76–77). A student is given several objects that vary in size, weight, shape, and material (cork, needle, wood, rock, and so on) and is asked to identify those that will float or sink in water. In order to solve this problem, the student must follow the rule that objects having a density less than water will float and those having a greater density than water will sink. But, this rule is very complex as it combines several simpler rules, each in turn made up of prerequisite concepts. The word *density* itself represents the ratio between weight and volume and is also made up of simpler rules and other concepts. Since the flotation rule involved a comparison of the density of the objects with the density of water, an enormous amount of prerequisite learning is required for the student to be able to solve this problem.

Suppose though that the student had learned the flotation rule and is now presented with the problem of finding a way to float objects that would ordinarily sink. The solution is to combine a sinkable object with one that does not sink so the combined volume is increased more than the sum of the two weights (place the needle on the cork or the rock on the piece of wood). To problem solve, the student must first have learned the rule for flotation and then must generate (independently) a higher-level rule for combining the densities of two objects. Other examples of thinking skills required at the problem-solving level abound in the literature on teaching critical thinking, logico-mathematical reasoning, and metacognitive processes to older children and young students with higher-order skills: Meeker 1969, Covington, Crutchfield, Davis, and Olton 1974, Karplus 1974, Gagnè and Briggs 1974, Rubenstein 1975, Feuerstein et al. 1980, Lipman, Sharp, and Oscanyan 1980, Campione, Brown, and Ferrara 1982, de Bono 1982 and 1983, Weinsten and Underwood 1983, Siegler 1986).

M. Bigge (1982) provides a summary and further clarification to distinguish between concept learning, rule learning, and problem solving:

> Concept learning is making a common response to a class of stimuli. [These are classes or *concepts* that are generalizations from a specific instance of the class.]
>
> Rule learning is forming a chain of two or more concepts so as to enable one to respond to a class of stimulus situations with a class of performances. [These are concepts that are combined to convey information about relationships between concepts.]
>
> In problem solving one applies previously learned rules to achieve a solution of a novel situation so as to achieve a higher order rule. [From a described situation, one is expected to predict the outcome and give the reason for the prediction].
>
> Thus all three types involve gaining explanatory understandings through a behavioristically characterized learning process (p. 301).

To illustrate the application of concepts, rules, and problem solving in a classroom of students with learning problems, let's consider the issue of learning about bird migration.

Concept Learning. At this level, students must master the individual concepts. The teacher assumes that lower-level skills (discrimination, identification, classification) have been mastered. Students now need to learn generalized concepts about *birds,* common characteristics of birds, different species, and so on; about what *migration* means and how it applies across many situations; about *seasons* and how they differ in different parts of the world; about *flying* and how the term applies to kites and planes as well as to birds. (Recall that a concept is a generalization from a specific instance to a class of instances.)

Rule Learning. This level requires a combination of concepts so that a rule may be stated: "Birds fly south in winter." This assumes that the concepts of *bird, flying, south,* and *winter* have all been mastered so that these concepts can now be combined in a meaningful way. The rule includes two or more concepts and conveys information about the relationship between them. Other rules can combine concepts related to bird breeding patterns, habitats, song patterns, or feeding habits.

Problem Solving. For problem solving to occur, the student must generate her own solution when presented with the question, "If ducks and geese fly south in winter, why don't other birds living in the same areas migrate south?" The solution would require that the student apply previously learned rules to achieve a higher-order rule. Combining rules learned about bird breeding patterns, environmental needs, feeding habits, and so forth, the student should solve the problem independently by understanding the meaningful relationship between the previously acquired lower-order rules.

Summary and Conclusion

This chapter presents an integrated model developed from hierarchies proposed by Gagnè and Bruner that can serve the teacher of students with learning problems in all areas of curriculum development. Combined with specific instructional objectives outlined in other sections of this text, these sequences can greatly facilitate the learning process.

The chapter first explored some of Gagnè's many ideas about thinking and instruction, highlighting the concepts and procedures most applicable to developing instruction for substantially disabled learners. Most useful are his conceptualizations of instructional phases and learning sequences.

Next the chapter examined the ideas of Bruner, including his formulations of classification systems children use. These are invaluable for disabled learners. Though his theories of cognitive development differ from Gagnè, they are compatible with a hierarchical model.

Finally the chapter synthesized the ideas of these two educator-researchers to build a hierarchy of thinking skills applicable to learning handicapped students. This synthesis provides a structure of learning that teachers can use to develop competencies in various curriculum areas.

To illustrate how to apply all the hierarchical steps referred to in this chapter, let us look at a substantially handicapped student who has learned independent travel skills. A student who can take public transportation to and from school has probably attained skills at the problem-solving level if the final behaviors in the sequence have been developed independently.

Discrimination Level. Initially the ability to distinguish among various types of vehicles, discriminate between a yellow school bus and whatever color the public transportation bus was, and differentiate between the various numbers on the public transportation buses was required.

Identification Level. The vocabulary necessary to understand, name, define, and describe the various objects, behaviors, and events in waiting for the bus, boarding the bus, and so on occur at this level. Simpler language (naming, pointing, selecting from an array) may be learned simultaneously with discriminations at the previous level though.

Classification Level. The ability to classify vehicles on the basis of their specific qualities (size, shape, function, or category) would assist in the process of learning which was the appropriate vehicle to take to and from school.

Concept Learning. A more advanced level of classification could include *concrete concepts* such as modes of *transportation* (air travel, land travel, water travel), various types subsumed under each of these (land travel equals trains, buses, cars, motorcycles, bicycles), and subclasses within those (buses equal school bus, city bus, Greyhound bus, army bus, etc.). *Concrete concepts* and *defined concepts* require that the student respond to them in terms of some common abstract property (i.e., A bus is a land vehicle with tires that carries more passengers than a car can carry, or a bus is a vehicle that takes me to and from school.).

Rule Learning. This entails combining one or more concepts already learned. Having learned to respond appropriately by boarding Bus #34 when it stops across the street from home, combined with having learned to respond by disembarking at the corner of California and Sacramento Streets (at the school) demonstrates having acquired a rule. At this stage, the student should be able to verbalize or in some other way communicate the concepts—getting *on* the bus across from home and getting *off* the bus at a specific corner. Performing the activity in itself is not enough since it could be learned without understanding the concepts involved.

Problem Solving. Having understood and mastered the rules needed to get from home to school, returning *independently* as a result of developing his own rules might be considered a problem-solving process. For this to qualify as true problem solving, no teacher instruction could be provided at this stage. For students with learning problems, teachers often do not wait for this level of independent thinking to emerge. Especially with students requiring special education, it is vitally important to encourage and support problem-solving skills without providing too much assistance too soon. Table 6.2 presents another example of the full use of the hierarchy of thinking skills as applied to the music curriculum.

Combining the ideas of Robert Gagnè and Jerome Bruner has led to a useful and practical hierarchy of thinking skills that teachers can apply across all ages and proficiency levels, as well as in all areas of the school curriculum. We believe that teachers of students with learning problems will find this a valuable framework providing a much-needed sequential structure for instructional objectives.

References

Bates, E. 1976. *Language and context: The acquisition of pragmatics.* New York: Academic Press.

Bates, E. 1979. *The emergence of symbols.* New York: Academic Press.

Becker, W., Engelmann, S., Thomas, D. 1975. *Teaching 2: Cognitive learning and instruction.* Chicago: Science Research Association.

Bigge, M. 1982. *Learning theories for teachers.* 4th ed. New York: Harper and Row.

Blank, M., Rose, S. A., and Berlin, L. J. 1978. *The language of learning: The preschool years.* Orlando, Fla.: Grune & Stratton.

Blank, M. 1983. *Teaching learning in the preschool: A dialogue approach.* Cambridge, Mass.: Brooklin.

Bloom, L. 1970. *Language development: Form and function in emerging grammars.* Cambridge, Mass.: M.I.T. Press.

Bower, T. G. R. 1977. *A primer of infant development.* San Francisco: W. H. Freeman.

Brown, A. L. 1978. Knowing when, where, and how to remember: A problem of metacognition. In *Advances in instructional psychology,* Vol. I, by R. Glaser. Hillsdale, N.J.: Lawrence Erlbaum.

Brown, R. 1973. *A first language.* Cambridge, Mass.: Harvard University Press.

Bruner, J. S., Olver, R. R., and Greenfield, P. M. 1966. *Studies in cognitive growth.* New York: John Wiley & Sons.

Bruner, J. S. 1966. On cognitive growth (Chaps. I, II). In *Studies in cognitive growth,* by J. S. Bruner, R. R. Olver, and P. M. Greenfield. New York: John Wiley & Sons.

Bruner, J. 1973. *Beyond the information given.* New York: W. W. Norton.

Campione, J. C., Brown, A. L., and Ferrara, R. A. 1982. Mental retardation and intelligence. In *Handbook on human intelligence,* edited by R. J. Sternberg. Cambridge, Eng.: Cambridge University Press.

Copeland, R. W. 1979. *How children learn mathematics.* New York: Macmillan.

Covington, M. V., Crutchfield, R. S., Davies, L. B., and Olton, R. M. 1972. *The productive thinking program.* Columbus, Ohio: Charles E. Merrill.

Covington, M. V., Crutchfield, R. S., Davies, L., and Olton, R. M. 1974. *The productive thinking program: A course in learning to think.* Columbus, Ohio: Charles E. Merrill.

Dale, P. 1976. *Language development: Structures and function.* 2d ed. New York: Holt, Rinehart, & Winston.

de Bono, E. 1982. *de Bono's thinking course.* New York: Facts on File.

de Bono, E. 1983. The cognitive research trust (CORT) thinking program. In *Thinking: The expanding frontier,* edited by W. Maxwell. Philadelphia: Franklin Institute Press.

Falkof, L., and Moss, J. 1984. When teachers tackle thinking skills. *Educational Leadership* 42(3): 4–9.

Ferrier, L., and Shane, H. 1980. Communication Skills In *Educating the severely physically handicapped: Curriculum adaptations,* Vol IV, J. Umbreit and P. Cardullias, eds. Columbus, Ohio: Special Press.

Feuerstein, R., Rand, Y., and Hoffman, M. B. 1979. *The dynamic assessment of retarded performers: The learning potential assessment device, theory, instruments, and techniques.* Baltimore, Md.: University Park Press.

Feuerstein, R., Rand, Y., Hoffman, M. B., and Miller, R. 1980. *Instrumental enrichment: An intervention program for cognitive modifiability.* Baltimore, Md.: University Park Press.

Furuno, S., O'Reilly, K., Hosaka, C., Inatsuka, T., Allman, T., and Zeisloft, B.

1979. *Hawaii learning profile (HELP): Acitivty guide.* Palo Alto, Calif.: Fort Corp.

Gagnè, R. 1974. *Essentials of learning for instruction.* Hinsdale, Ill.: The Dryden Press.

Gagnè, R. 1977. *The conditions of learning.* 3d ed. New York: Holt, Rinehart & Winston.

Gagnè, R., and Briggs, L. 1974. *Principles of instructional design.* New York: Holt, Rinehart & Winston.

Ginsburg, H., and Opper, S. 1979. *Piaget's theory of intellectual development.* 2d ed. Englewood Cliffs, N.J.: Prentice-Hall.

Greenfield, P. M. 1976. *The structure of communication in early language development.* New York: Academic Press.

Hilgard, E. R., and Bower, G. H. 1981. *Theories of learning.* 5th ed. Englewood Cliffs, N.J.: Prentice-Hall.

Jones, B. F. 1982. *Chicago mastery learning reading.* 2d ed. Watertown, Mass.: Mastery Education Corporation.

Karplus, R. 1974. *Science curriculum improvement study: Teachers handbook.* Berkeley, Calif.: University of California.

Lieberman, L. 1982. Itard: The great problem solver. *Journal of Learning Disabilities* 15(9): 566–68.

Lipman, M., Sharp, A. M., and Oscanyan, F. S. 1980. *Philosophy in the classroom.* 2d ed. Philadelphia: Temple University Press.

Lowery, L. 1981. *Learning about learning: Classification abilities.* Berkeley, Calif.: University of California.

Meeker, M. N. 1969. *The structure of intellect: Its interpretation and uses.* Columbus, Ohio: Charles E. Merrill.

Menyuk, P. 1974. Early development of receptive language: From babbling to words, In *Language perspectives—Acquisition, retardation, and intervention,* by R. Schiefelburch and L. Lloyd. Baltimore, Md.: University Park Press.

Miller, J. F. 1981. *Assessing language production in children.* Baltimore, Md.: University Park Press.

Olver, R. R., and Hornsby, J. R. 1966. On equivalence. In *Studies in cognitive growth,* by J. Bruner, R. Olver, and P. Greenfield. New York: John Wiley & Sons.

Rohwer, W., Ammon, P., and Cramer, P. 1974. *Understanding intellectual development.* Hinsdale, Ill.: The Dryden Press.

Rubenstein, M. F. 1975. *Patterns of problem solving.* Englewood Cliffs, N.J.: Prentice-Hall.

Scholnick, E. K., ed. 1983. *New trends in conceptual representation: challenges to Piaget's theory?* Hillsdale, N.J.: Lawrence Erlbaum.

Siegler, R. S. 1986. *Children's thinking.* Englewood Cliffs, N.J.: Prentice-Hall.

Silverman, Franklin H. 1980. *Communication for the speechless.* Englewood Cliffs, N.J.: Prentice-Hall.

Sternberg, R. J., ed. 1982. *Handbook on human intelligence.* Cambridge, Eng.: Cambridge University Press.

Sternberg, R. J. 1984. How can we teach intelligence? *Educational Leadership* 42(1): 38–48.

Wang, M. C., and Resnick, L. B. 1978. *Primary education program: A developmental program for early childhood learning skills.* Johnstown, Pa.: Mafex.

Weinstein, C. E., and Underwood, V. L. 1983. Learning strategies: The how of learning. In *Relating instruction to basic research,* by J. Segal, S. Chipman, and R. Glaser. Hillsdale, N.J.: Lawrence Erlbaum.

Vygotsky, L. 1962. *Thought and language.* New York: The M.I.T. Press and John Wiley.

7

Reducing the Complexity of Objectives

Customizing proficiency standards and curricular objectives for students in special education or helping others do so is a major responsibility of special education teachers. What assessment options are available when special education students have problems in basic academic skills and cannot be expected to meet regular grade-level and graduation proficiency standards? What are differential and alternative standards? How are they derived? How can special education teachers use these approaches to modify difficulty levels in curriculum, instruction, and assessment in basic school subjects? How can special education teachers help other teachers change lessons so special education students can study the same things at the same time as regular students but in less demanding ways?

More than ever before, states and local education agencies are establishing proficiency-standard testing or minimum grade-level and graduation standards for education accomplishment. This kind of testing is fast becoming a part of what is required to measure the success of education programs. These standards or skills do not comprise the total curriculum or instructional program, but teachers must assess and teach these as "core" proficiency skills, though they also assess and teach wider varieties and higher-level skills as well.

It is important for teachers to learn how to recognize—and perhaps change—the complexities of these proficiency standards in order to improve the *technical adequacy* of their teaching practices. Improving technical adequacy here means upgrading curricular and instructional validity—being able to analyze and gain reasonable proof that skills and skill levels tested have in fact been taught (Bracey 1983). The direct relationship between proficiency standards and curriculum and instruction has been stressed throughout this text, but teachers require specific strategies to make movement among these factors systematic and definitive.

This chapter explains in detail one set of steps teachers can use to determine the need for differential proficiency standards when assessing basic academic competencies. It teaches methods for deriving differential standards from regular standards. It also describes how to establish lower grade-level and unique standards for students. These processes are applied to curriculum, instruction, and evaluation in basic school subjects as sample illustrations. The process is also applied to activities within group lessons.

Proficiency Assessment Options for Special Education Students*

When it is not appropriate for students in special education to be assessed using regular education standards, they are sometimes assessed using *differential standards*. Differential proficiency standards diverge from the regular proficiency standards in the degree of complexity required. They are usually less complex.

To review, proficiency standards include statements of a skill or academic competence to be measured and of the level of complexity at which the skill will be measured. Proficiency assessments can be administered as grade-level and graduation proficiency tests or as grade-level and graduation minimum-competency tests. The terms *skill, competence,* and *competency* are commonly used interchangeably even though technically *competence* and *competency* refer more to thought processes. *Competency statements* as used here mean statements of the skills and knowledges to be measured. *Proficiency* means the level(s) of complexity (or standards) at which skills and knowledges—or competencies—will be measured. The competencies measured in grade-level and graduation proficiency assessments are usually "the basics"—the three Rs—and, perhaps in the future, the 3 Cs: computing, calculating, and communicating with technology (Bracey, 1983).

"Other" standards may be loosely or not at all related to regular standards, but *differential standards definitely stem from regular standards*. Those that are not necessarily derived from regular proficiency standards are called *lower grade level* and *unique standards*. As complexities for special education students usually need to be replaced rather than increased (if changed at all) only differential standards resulting in reduced complexities are described and illustrated here. Teachers need only reverse the process to increase difficulty levels.

---

* This section draws freely and makes adaptations from California State Department of Education, workshop outline, "Developing Proficiency Standards in Pupils in Special Education Programs" (1978). Permission granted.

Individual teachers can specify standards for individual use, and local education unit teams can prepare differential standards for district-wide use. Special education teachers are often involved one way or another in the process of revising the regular proficiency standards to make them more appropriate for certain special education students who need other than the regular standards.

Deriving Differential Standards

Two means are available for deriving standards from regular proficiency standards to meet the needs of some students in special education. *Derived differential standards* involve either (1) changing the level of complexity at which the regular skill or competency will be measured, or (2) changing the competency statement of the regular standard to one of its enroute skills or subskills.

Step 1: Task Analysis. Use of task analysis (see Table 7.1) on regular education proficiency assessment items begins with discerning the major skill areas of the academic competencies to be assessed. Doing a task analysis enables teachers to define a list of the major skill components first and then to describe each in more detail.

For the math skill in Table 7.2, "divide decimal fractions without rounding

Table 7.1   Steps in Deriving Differential Standards

STEP 1:	Task analyze regular education proficiency standards.
STEP 2:	Design a skills continuum based on regular education proficiencies.
STEP 3:	Indicate the student's present level of functioning on the skills continuum.
STEP 4:	Identify as critical (or salient) skills those key component subskills without which the student would be unable to perform the competency at any level of complexity.
STEP 5:	Determine if the student probably will or will not be able to attain the regular proficiencies. If **yes,** go to Step 6**a.** If **no,** go to Step 6**b.**
STEP 6**a**:	Derive a new proficiency statement that relates to the regular competency but reflects a reduced level of complexity.
STEP 6**b**:	Select an enroute skill to the regular competency and make the enroute skill the main competency.
STEP 7:	Generate relevant items to assess student proficiency.

Source: Adapted with permission from California State Department of Education. 1978. "Steps in Devising Differential Standards." In *Developing Proficiency Standards for Pupils in Special Education Programs: Workshop Outline and Agenda.* (Sacramento: California State Department of Special Education).

off," a cursory task analysis identifies five primary arithmetic skills students must have some experience with to be able to attain the proficiency level required. These skill areas include: *numbers and enumeration, subtraction, multiplication, division,* and *decimals.*

Initial task analysis also suggests that students have to first understand what is being asked, then know or figure out which operations are needed and in what sequence, and finally perform the operations accurately in that sequence to answer the question. The value of task analysis is that it can guide teachers and even IEP teams to select the most appropriate aims for particular students, whether that aim should be meeting regular standards or differential standards. Analysis of students must, however, extend beyond this list of major skill components to their use of cognitive subskills. These subskills are what give the ability to synthesize independent math skills in ways that will lead to the correct answers.

Step 2: Skills Continuum.   Task analysis is used also to define enroute, or subskills, that make up the major skill components and to organize these enroute skills in some systematic way. For purposes of finding ways to reduce complexities of material, enroute skills are generally organized into a hierarchy. They are organized sequentially by difficulty or in developmental order. Table 7.2 is an example of a skills continuum for the proficiency under scrutiny: "Divide decimal fractions without rounding off."

Table 7.2 takes the five primary skill areas called for in initial task analysis and breaks them into enroute skills. To be able to divide decimal fractions without rounding off, students must have certain enroute skills or subskills. The sequence given in Table 7.2 parallels the way mathematical skill areas are usually listed in a curriculum and taught. This figure represents the second step in devising differential standards: Design a skills continuum for each skill measured on the regular proficiency test.

Step 3: Present Functioning.   A skills continuum is used as a basis for pinpointing student's current proficiency levels by identifying present performances and determining the likelihood of the student learning any remaining enroute skills. Let's look at Ronald, a student who did not make the required scores on several computation proficiencies. One problem area was the math subtest that measured the ability to "divide decimal fractions."

On a continuum of enroute skills or subskills for dividing decimal fractions to the difficulty level on the tests, the IEP team agrees the assessment information on Ronald's current proficiency shows that he knows *A:* numbers and enumeration skills; *B* and *C:* the operations of subtraction and multiplication; and *E:* decimal concepts. He can use the division operation (*D*) but is limited to dividing three digits by a two-digit number (*D-9*).

Step 4: Identify Critical or Salient Skills.   How a student performs on the skills continuum determines which of two types of altered proficiencies she or he will have to attain or whether the student will have an altered

Table 7.2   A Skills Continuum

Enroute or Subskills

A. Numbers and enumeration
   1. Read and write ordinal numbers.
   2. Know place values of: ones, tens, hundreds, thousands.
B. Subtraction operations
   1. Knows basic subtraction facts (0–20).
   2. Subtract two places with no renaming.
   3. Subtract two places with renaming.
   4. Subtract three places with no renaming.
   5. Subtract three places with renaming.
C. Multiplication operations
   1. Know multiplication as repeated addition.
   2. Know multiplication facts through tens.
   3. Multiply two digits by one-digit number.
   4. Multiply three digits by one-digit number.
   5. Estimate products.
D. Division operations
   1. Read division symbol.
   2. Know division as repeated subtraction.
   3. Know division facts.
   4. Check division by multiplication.
   5. Divide two digits by a one-digit number.
   6. Divide three digits by a one-digit number.
   7. Divide four digits by a one-digit number.
   8. Divide two digits by a two-digit number.
   9. Divide three digits by a two-digit number.
   10. Divide four digits by a two-digit number.
   11. Divide five digits by a two-digit number.
   12. Divide six digits by a two-digit number.
   13. Divide three digits by a three-digit number.
   14. Divide four digits by a three-digit number.
   15. Divide five digits by a three-digit number.
   16. Divide six digits by a three-digit number.
   17. Estimate a quotient.
E. Decimals
   1. Read and write decimals.
   2. Know place value of decimals (tenths; hundredths).
   3. Add decimals.
   4. Subtract decimals.
   5. Multiply decimals.
   6. Divide decimals.
   7. Convert mixed numbers to decimal equivalent.

Source: Adapted from California State Department of Education. 1978. "Using Task Analysis for Deriving Differential Standards" in *Developing Proficiency Standards for Pupils in Special Education Programs*. (Sacramento: California State Department of Special Education) p. 60.

proficiency at all. Do teachers choose to maintain the level of complexity, reduce it, or substitute a different competency statement? The moment of truth is here. What informs this important choice of a reasonable expectation for a student?

The student must have or be able to learn the *critical or salient skills,* that is the subskill or subskills absolutely necessary to carry the proficiency through to completion. Some educators refer to crucial or salient skills as *enabling* skills in harmony with Bracey's (1983) use of the term. Bracey (p. 718) defines an enabling skill as "one that allows a child to go on to higher levels." For example, "Extract the main ideas from the paragraph," is seen as an enabling subskill for the skill, "Discern the author's purpose."

Without performing certain critical subskills, the student would be unable to master the proficiency statement at any level of complexity. A skills continuum can suggest critical or salient skills required for accomplishing a certain kind of task or skill *at any level of complexity.* For the skill of dividing decimal fractions, the continuum illustrates that critical, or salient skills are:

1. Use dividing operation: at least divide two digits by a one digit number.
2. Divide decimals.

Item specification is what contributes to identifying of those critical skills. *Item* is used here as a test item (problem students are to solve or statements of performances they are to demonstrate). *Item specification* is a way to identify critical or salient skills.

Table 7.3 illustrates the various components of item specification, or detailed descriptions of item characteristics. Understanding the practice illustrated in the figure is basic to grasping the item-specification process (and generating multiple items with the same characteristics). Table 7.3 shows a detailed item specification describing how one math skill is assessed and how item-stem characteristics and distracter characteristics are used to determine sample items. This figure gives detailed item specifications describing how "dividing decimal fractions" is assessed in a particular proficiency test. Specifications for *content area, subcontent area, skill,* and *performance objective* are not new concepts in this text. The new concepts introduced here include *sample item, item stem characteristics* and *distracter characteristics.*

Sample items are problem samples that, when accomplished, give evidence that students have mastered the skill or competency. For each different problem measuring the same skill, there is one correct answer and several distractors or wrong answers. To obtain consistency among the correct answers for several different problems on each skill, the correct answers will have certain characteristics—that is, *item characteristics.* Even wrong answers, or distracters, may have their own definable *distracter characteristics.*

Information giving specifications of a *sample item* is in two parts: (1) the item stem or test question or challenge itself and (2) the answer, or response choices. *Item stem characteristics* give specifications about the problems itself. Item stem

Table 7.3 Sample Item Specification

Detailed item specification describing how "dividing decimal fractions" is assessed in a particular proficiency test:

CONTENT AREA: Math

SUBCONTENT AREA 1.0:   Arithmetic computation.

SKILL: Divide decimal fractions without rounding off.

PERFORMANCE OBJECTIVE: Given two numbers, one a whole number and the other a deci-
                               mal fraction with a correctly positioned division symbol $\overline{)}$,
                               the student will divide the two numbers and select the correct
                               answer from four options.

SAMPLE ITEM: $19.2\overline{)1248}$
                               a. 6.5
                               b. 65
                               c. 239616
                               d. 6.6

ITEM STEM CHARACTERISTICS:
1. The division symbol will be $\overline{)}$
2. The decimal fraction will be the divisor.
3. The divisor will contain no more than three digits.
4. The decimal in the divisor will indicate a place value of tenths.
5. The dividend will contain no more than four digits with no decimals.

DISTRACTER CHARACTERISTICS:
1. Each Distracter will be the result of:
   • errors made in basic division or multiplication facts
   • failure to interpret the operational signal
   • failure to interpret positional value
2. The distracters will contain no more than two digits to the right of the decimal.

Source: Adapted with permission from: California State Board of Education. 1978. "Definition of Terms," Workshop Outline for *Developing Proficiency Standards for Pupils in Special Education Programs*. Sacramento: California State Department of Special Education), pp. 57–58.

characteristics make it possible to generate varieties of problems that test the exact same skill. Last specified are *distracter characteristics*. Proficiency tests commonly offer choices of one correct answer and several wrong ones. Making distracters challenging and yet clearly incorrect is difficult without some logical way to determine them. Distracter characteristics in Table 7.3 suggest one approach in which persons contructing tests anticipate the kinds of mistakes examinees might make. Then they use the results of these mistakes as distracters. Look for this in the first group of characteristics of distracters (number 1). The characteristics described in statement number 2 determines that the distracters will be uniform in the maximum number of digits to the right of the decimal. Refer again to the sample item and notice the distracter characteristics applied to distracters in choices:

a. 6.5 (failure to interpret positional value)
b. 65 (correct answer)
c. 239616 (failure to interpret the operational signal)
d. 6.6 (errors made in basic division or multiplication facts)

Distracter characteristics are an integral part of the item specification process. They do not however, directly assist with identification of critical or salient skills.

When the same kinds of information are gleaned both as enroute on a skills continuum and as item stem characteristics, teachers are alerted that the duplicated information suggests a critical skill. Regardless of the order in which they were obtained, these pieces of information relate directly to each other. Look at the item stem characteristics described Table 7.3 and the continuum of skills in Table 7.2. Notice those subskills on the continuum that are the same or very similar to some of the item stem characteristics in Table 7.3:

SUBSKILLS IN CONTINUUM (TABLE 7.2)	ITEM CHARACTERISTIC (TABLE 7.3)
#D14: Divide four digits by a three-digit number.	#5: The dividend will contain no more than four digits with no decimals.
	#3: The divisor will contain no more than three digits.
#E6: Divide decimals.	#2: The decimal fraction will be the divisor.

Notice that (1) dividing four digits by a three-digit number and (2) dividing with decimals are two skills students must know in order to attain the competency or demonstrate the skill, even at lowered levels of complexity.

Teachers who understand item-specification techniques can reduce ambivalence about the kinds of skills students are expected to demonstrate. They help clarify what students are being taught and evaluated for as part of their regular lessons and the nature of proficiency standards through which students are evaluated annually or every few years. Similarly, analyzing item specifications can reduce ambiguity about interpreting student performance. Most importantly, item stem specifications point teachers to the critical or salient skills without which students will not be able to master the proficiency at any level of complexity. The time students have left in the educational program and their histories of learning rate influence the determination teachers make of whether or not they have a chance to learn the critical skills.

Step 5: Regular or Differential Proficiency. At this point it becomes necessary to establish that a student in all likelihood will or will not be able to learn critical or salient skills. Maria is one student about whom there was a question in this math proficiency. Maria's teachers, based on the best information available to them, draw a tenable hypothesis that Maria *would* be able to learn and be tested on the skill but at a reduced level of complexity because she possesses the two salient skills required for dividing decimal fractions. She could demonstrate this on simpler problems. Her teachers would then proceed to Step 6a to derive proficiency assessment options for her.

Take for another example the skill of reading a paragraph and identifying the main idea to illustrate the process for determining presence or absence of critical skills. A question arises about a high school student who can read a three-sentence paragraph at the second-grade reading level. He can identify the main idea but is unable to attain the corresponding skill at the high school level. This student possesses the critical skills of being able to pick out the main idea but is not able to read at the ninth-grade level. For this student, the level of complexity would have to be lowered, but the statement of a skill in the proficiency statement could remain the same—the student can read a paragraph and identify the main idea. His teachers would proceed to Step 6a to derive proficiency assessment options for him.

Another student might for some reason be able to decode the ninth-grade material (read the words) but be unable now or possibly even in the future to identify the main idea. This student would require a change in the competency statement. The same test material could be used, but the skill would be changed to "list facts from a designated single sentence in this three-sentence passage." His teachers would proceed to Step 6b to derive a different proficiency assessment competency.

Step 6a: Same Objective at Reduced Level of Complexity. Using the same objective but at reduced complexity is an alternative when teachers determine that students presently possess or probably will be able to learn the critical or salient skills. In the case of Maria and the math objective, for instance, the planning team decided that the level of complexity of the proficiency standard should be lowered for this student in the areas of dividing decimal fractions among other areas. Then, using a skills continuum as a reference, they alter the item specification in a systematic way in order to retain the same objective but reduce the complexity. Compare their derived item stem characteristics to the item stem characteristics for the original proficiency in Table 7.3:

DERIVED ITEM STEM CHARACTERISTICS

1. Same (same as the original example in Table 7.3: The division symbol will be ⌐.)
2. Same (The decimal fraction will be the divisor.)
3. The divisor will have no more than *two* digits. (In original proficiency: *three* digits.)
4. Same (The decimal in the divisor will indicate a place value of tenths.)
5. The dividend will have no more than *two* digits with no decimals. (In original proficiency: *four* digits.)

DISTRACTER CHARACTERISTICS

1. Same (Each distracter will be the result of:)
   - errors made in basic division or multiplication facts
   - errors made in basic subtraction facts
   - failure to interpret the operational sign
   - failure to interpret positional values
2. Distracters will contain *one* digit only to the right of the decimal. (In original proficiency: *two* digits to the right of the decimal.)

An example of problem that falls within these new specifications might be:

$$1.5\overline{)60}$$

This then completes a process of keeping the same objective but reducing the level of the complexity.

Another example is student performance on a competency statement that requires the ability to divide whole numbers with remainders, for example the item $432\overline{)5293}$. One differential option would be to keep the same objective—divide whole numbers with remainders—but to alter the level of complexity by substituting a less difficult item, such as $5\overline{)48}$.

Step 6b: Different Competency Statement. Changing the competency statement of the regular proficiency standards, the second strategy for obtaining differential standards, also requires task analysis. The first four steps in this approach to deriving differential standards are the same as those used for establishing standards with reduced levels of complexity. Step 5 still is a major decision point. (Results of considerations at Step 5 determine whether or not (based on the information available) students have or can learn critical skills lead to Step 6a (same competency, lower level of complexity) or fall back to Step 6b (change in the competency statement). Review information on Steps 5 and 6a and 6b of Table 7.1. "Steps in Devising Differential Standards."

Take as an example another student, Leslie, who (like Ronald and Maria) failed the same parts of the test to divide decimal fractions. Her teacher establishes that on the dividing decimals skills continuum (Table 7.2) Leslie can understand numbers and enumeration and can do the subtraction and multiplication, but cannot do even the simplest operation of dividing two digits by a one digit number. She also cannot accomplish another of the critical or salient skills: She cannot divide with decimals; she can only add them. The assessment, therefore, is that she does not have the two critical skills for the proficiency and in all practicality in the time left in school, Leslie is unlikely to learn them both in order to perform the skill. Consequently the instructional team chooses one enroute skill which would help with money concepts such as subtracting decimals and determines that the student must show her ability to perform it. Leslie's regular and special education teachers locate a subtest of the district's math proficiency test that assesses the ability to subtract decimal fractions, and they use this as a means of assessment and a guide for instruction. The enroute skill then becomes the competency for the differential standard.

In Leslie's case, the proficiency standard was altered by substituting an enroute skill for the grade-level proficiency statement in math. In another case, the IEP teams again derived a different proficiency standard using a skill related to the regular objective because it is one indicater (or enroute) skill of the original skill. Tables 7.4, 7.5, and Figure 7.1 present a different but similar approach of using an enroute subskills, or performance indicaters, for the original competence as the new competency. *Indicaters,* as used here were synonymous with *enroute,* or *subskills.*

Table 7.4 is a format used to indicate the major competency statement and the list of performance indicaters collectively used as evidence of performance of the competency, "Communicate information by letter and telephone." Table 7.5 is a format used to indicate that one of its subskills, or indicaters will be substituted for the original competency. The subskill chosen was #5.2: "Given the necessary information, the student will properly address an envelope." Item specification information here is slightly different than in earlier examples. The presentation mode and performance method as well as item characteristics are listed.

Figure 7.1 is a sample of the actual assessment item used. It is assumed that in the student's curriculum he has had opportunities to demonstrate this competence in this simulated method as well as with actual envelopes.

Step 7: New Items.   Item specification also works as a way to generate new assessment items that have defined, clearly understood characteristics. Item specification is what allows consistency when many people are involved in identifying competency statements or objectives and generating related methods of assessing them. Using item specification here also requires careful analysis

Table 7.4   Writing/Language Arts Competency

Competency 5:   The student communicates information by letter and telephone.

Performance
Indicators/Objectives   5.1 Given distinct parts of a letter and a blank letter form, the student will place the letter parts in their appropriate spaces.
5.2 Given the necessary information, the student will properly address an envelope.
5.3 The student will write a simple personal letter to a friend.
5.4 The student will write a simple business letter to inquire about a product or service.
5.5 The student will make a personal phone call to a friend or relative.
5.6 The student will make a business telephone call to complain or give compliments about a product or service.

Table 7.5　Item Specification for Differential Standards

Competency Number:　___5___

Performance Indicator/Objective:　___5.2___
　　"Given the necessary information,
　　the student will properly address an
　　envelope."

Presentation:　Given the printed names and addresses of the sender and the sendee, and a to-scale drawing of a personal-size envelope with lines to accommodate the information.

Response Method:　The student will write address parts in the correct places.

Stem Characteristics:　The item stem will direct the students to address the envelope using the information given.

Figure 7.1　Sample Assessment Item.

Below is an envelope. Send it to Mr. Tom Mayfield
at 7 Cityview Way in Topeka, Kansas 93726.
The sender is Mrs. Susan Brown. She lives at
1434 Randolph in Miami, Florida 36489. Place her
return address on the envelope as well.

```
 _____                          ┌──────────┐
 _____                          │  PLACE   │
                                           │  STAMP   │
 _____                          │  HERE    │
                                           └──────────┘

                  _____
                  _____
                  _____
```

to assure consistency between specification, or characteristics of the skills assessed, and the skills taught. Thus, this process fosters teacher accountability.

These examples point out that special education teachers and other instructional resource personnel have a leadership responsibility. They would need to explain the context and layout of the standard proficiency tests as well as the individual student's abilities. These are explained to others involved in an individualized educational program (IEP) team making decisions about differential proficiency standards a special education student will be expected to meet.

Competency Tests from Lower Grade Levels

Using lower-grade-level tests is an approach to curriculum development that represents a combination of reducing the complexity and changing the competency statement. This is the case because lower-grade-level minimum competency tests can be the same or nearly the same as higher-level competencies but reduced in complexity. Or lower-grade-level minimum competency tests can be the same or nearly the same as competencies that would result from changing the competency statement as described above. Using lower-grade-level minimum competency tests can only be justified if there is good direct relationship between these lower level tests and the higher level tests. This requires an integrated, well-sequenced curriculum. Teachers also need to consider the appropriateness of item content. Lower-grade-level items can sometimes be too immature or otherwise age-inappropriate. This consideration is of particular importance when choosing competencies and developing proficiency standards.

It is sometimes difficult to know just how far back to go in selecting lower-grade-level material. Marston and Magnusson (1985) describe a process that involves "sampling back" in the school curriculum to determine how many years a particular student is behind. Statistics are usually available that describe scores within which local groups of regular students typically fall at each grade level. Teachers can use this information for screening students. A child's performance level is determined by how his performance compares on materials of a particular grade level. The key question is, Does the performance fall within the "normal" range of peers on that grade level. For example, the typical reading performance of a particular group of fifth graders in one board-adopted reading series during the winter was about 116 word read correctly in one minute. One fifth grader reading 116 words correctly on *fifth-grade* material and another fifth grader reading 70 words correctly on *fourth-grade* material would fall within the typical range. A fifth-grader who read 69 words or less in the *fourth-grade* material would be tried on *third-grade* material. "Sampling back continues until the child falls within the typical range of performance at a given grade level" (Marston and Magnusson 1985, 273). Using this process expedites determination of complexity levels that represent reasonable expectations for students for whom regular standards are inappropriate.

Developing Unique Differential Standards

Neither regular proficiency standards nor differential proficiencies based on regular proficiency standards are appropriate for some students in special education. Assessments of proficiencies in functional skills in such curricular areas as self-help and daily living, prevocational or vocational preparation, and social adaptation are probably more viable options for these students. Rather than demonstrating skill proficiencies in pen-paper mode or in an alternative for it, *unique proficiency standards* are more profitably demonstrated by some activity or a chain of behaviors that produce a functional or useful range of skills. Often natural settings or simulations of these settings are used for teaching these skills.

Unique differential standards frequently have no direct relationship to the regular education proficiencies in reading, writing, or math. They are unique to groups and individuals with disabilities. This does not mean, though, that proficiency in such activities as self-help, vocational preparation, and social adaptations are without value for students who are not in special education. Students without disabilities—and some with disabilities—learn easily what other students cannot learn without intense and specialized interaction. Certain students depend deeply on this instructional focus, which is highly valuable for them.

Standards that are unique yet still incorporate some measure of ability in reading, writing, and computation use the district's proficiency standards only as points of departure. Basic skills in this approach are not taught and assessed as abstracts, but teachers can introduce them in a functional context that relates to their immediate use. For example, basic skills might be incorporated into the life-management skill of counting change, reading signs and simple directions, or signing one's name to a check or document.

Life Management functional activities serve as basis for unique differential standards (see Chapter 9). Publicly identified proficiency standards that guide curriculum in this area, though divergent from regular district standards, assure continuity and focus for the student so that she or he is not allowed to drift through what could become a noneducation.

Applications to School Disciplines

The approaches just presented have merit as means of establishing differential proficiency standards—the purpose for which they were developed.

But their usefulness to teachers does not stop there. Teachers can use these same approaches to change complexity levels not only of the curriculum and instruction relating to basic skills and proficiencies but also to any other areas of curriculum as well. In different areas of curriculum, teachers can use these strategies whenever objectives have been or need to be identified. Skills, competencies, or objectives associated with those assessed at grade level and for promotion and graduation are the most obvious uses. Other uses include daily lessons, lesson objectives for units of study, semester objectives, IEP objectives, and curriculum objectives that take more than one year to accomplish.

It is important for special education teachers to learn to recognize, and change, complexities of curriculum-based activities so they can (1) use and recommend appropriate curriculum, instruction, and evaluation modifications, and, as mentioned, (2) improve the technical adequacy of teaching and evaluation of pupil progress. Teachers also need to learn to identify the specifications that guide their efforts. Finally special education teachers need to be able to describe and give relevant examples of the process so others can learn it. Why is it important for teachers to learn the process for changing complexity levels of curriculum-based objectives? Consider some of these important reasons.

By reducing complexities of skill or competency objectives for special education students, teachers can "eliminate the instructional mismatch between the skills of low-achieving and mainstreamed students and the inordinate demands placed upon them by their curriculum assignments" (Gickling and Thompson 1985, 205). Identifying specifications that result from complexity modification provides control over both task level and characteristics. This means the affected students spend large amounts of time in relevant content that they can perform with high success (Denham and Lieberman, 1980). To master the process also means that special education teachers can assist regular education teachers, job coaches, and employers with adjusting the difficulty levels of both learning and work activities.

Determining Whether to Keep or Change Objectives

Deciding whether or not to use the regular education objectives as expectations for students is a major responsibility of those determining the instructional programs of students with special needs. If they decide that age-appropriate regular education objectives are not appropriate, different but related objectives or unique objectives become options. Studying courses of study, textbooks, or curriculum guides from lower grade levels can sometimes save time and effort in reducing the complexity of objectives. Teachers may find in such lower-grade-level material objectives identical to or at least closely related to the targeted standards.

Using the best information available at the time, the teacher needs to consider whether the student has or can learn the critical or salient skills necessary to accomplish the objectives. Table 7.6 identifies the steps in devising differential curriculum objectives. Because of importance of linking assessment with curriculum and instruction, the steps here for deriving differential curricula are similar to those for deriving differential proficiency assessment items. Note especially the importance of Step 5.

To show applications of how to change the complexity levels of curriculum-based objectives, two samples are presented, one from the *language arts discipline,* the other from the *practical arts discipline.* The procedures used to establish item stem characteristics for formal proficiency assessments work as well to modify school subject curriculum objectives, instruction, activities, and evaluation. Similarly, teachers can use the procedures for establishing distracter characteristics to conduct an error analysis in regard to student performance. This analysis can then be incorporated into the teaching process to help students correct or avoid errors. It can also suggest that expectations are too difficult and should be modified to allow students a greater success rate in school subjects.

Sample applications to the language arts and practical arts disciplines specify the (1) subject or content area, (2) subcontent area, (3) skill or competency, (4) instructional objective, (5) performance objective, (6) skills continuums and (7) activity specifications.

In an even larger view, it is strategic use that differentiates the nature of curriculum and objectives for *identical curriculum, parallel curriculum, practical academic curriculum,* and *life management curriculum.* Five approaches illustrate compare specifications for differential curriculum and instruction:

Approach 1: Same curriculum objectives with same level of complexity: modifications for student access to curriculum are necessary; identical curriculum.
Approach 2: Same curriculum objectives at reduced levels of complexity: parallel curriculum.
Approach 3: Different curriculum competency statements: practical academic curriculum.
Approach 4: Lower-grade-level curriculum: combination of parallel curriculum and practical academic curriculum.
Approach 5: Unique curriculum: life management curriculum.

Language Arts Discipline[1]

Subject/Content Area: Language arts
Subcontent Area: Writing paragraphs
Skill/Competency/Instructional Objective: Organize written information in logical order.

Table 7.6   Steps in Deriving Differential Curriculum Objectives

To change the level of complexity of material being taught/learned/studied/or tested keeping same objective	*To change the objective* but keeping within the same proficiency area
Teachers need to:	Teachers need to:
1. Task analyze the regular material	1. Same
2. Design a skills continuum based on the objectives of regular materials being taught/learned/studied.	2. Same
3. Indicate the students' level of functioning on the skills continuum.	3. Same

Step 4: (Both)

4. Identify as critical or salient skills those key component subskills without which the student would be unable to perform the task or objective at any level of complexity.

5. Determine that the student will probably be able to achieve the objectives.	5. Determine that the student will probably *not* be able to achieve the regular objective.

Main Question:

Does the student possess the critical or salient skills—or is there probability for student to learn these in a reasonable amount of time?

If yes, use same objective but reduce complexity.

If no, substitute one of the enroute or enabling skills to the original objective as the educational objectives.

6a. Derive a new objective that relates to the same competency statement but reflects a reduced level of complexity.	**6b.** Select an enroute skill and make the enroute skill the main objective.
7. Generate the relevant teaching, learning, studying, testing skills.	7. Generate skills that lead to new main objective.
Example: Identify the main idea (critical skill)	Example: Identify the main idea (critical skill)
Unnecessary to change objective: Student may not do skill at level of peers but can do skill. For example, high school student may be able to identify the main idea of a three-sentence passage at a second-grade reading level.	Must change objective: Student may be able to decode anything but doesn't understand and can't get the main idea. So change objective to "identifying details from a single sentence in a passage."

Source: Adapted with permission from California State Department of Education. 1978. "Steps in Devising Differential Standards." In *Developing Proficiency Standards for Pupils in Special Education Programs: Workshop Outline and Agenda.* (Sacramento: California State Department of Special Education).

Performance objective: Given a series of related sentences, the student will firs₁ locate the topic sentence, write it down, then continue to write the detail sen₁ tences in logical order in paragraph form. Students meet criteria when they cor₁ rectly write at least four consecutive sets of sentences in the right order.

Activity 1: (This is an example using the regular objective at the regular complex₁ ity level—fifth-grade lesson.) Students are to locate the topic sentence, write i₁ down, and then continue to write the detail sentences in logical order in para₁ graph form.

- First Larry and Mariann checked the valve.
- Larry's bike had a flat tire everyday.
- Finally the mystery was solved.
- Next they questioned the neighborhood children.
- Then they discovered a box of tacks on the floor.

Using adapted or alternative response methods doing regular curriculum activities at regular levels of complexity students may:

a. Number sentences to designate order.
b. Use word-processing program and move sentences to correct order.
c. Read/dictate sentences in order in which they should be written.
d. Listens to sentences as read aloud by someone else and write them in braille in proper order.

Before moving to *Approach 2* and *Approach 3,* which have to do with differential curriculum, study a skills continuum for this original objective (Table 7.7). This figure illustrates one special education teacher's task analysis of skills enroute to the accomplishment of the skill organizing written information in logical order.

Approach 2: Same objective: reduced level of complexity

Activity 2: (This is an example using the regular objective but reducing the level of complexity for student lessons by substituting a similar but simpler activity.)

- First she looked in the yard.
- Sarah lost her dog.
- Then she looked under the house.
- Finally, she found him under her bed.

In the activity at the regular level of complexity, each sentence series consists of five or more sentences; in the activity at the reduced level of complexity, each sentence series contains no more than four sentences. Students completing these last activities would be meeting the regular objective but at a reduced level of complexity. Students would still have to locate the topic sentence and arrange the

Table 7.7 Task Analysis of Objectives: Organize Written Information in Logical Order

Enroute Skills:	Key: + does do
	− does not do

A. Vocabulary
  1. Understands word meanings. Has adequate vocabulary to meet the objective   +
  2. Ability to derive word meanings from context clues.   +
  3. Uses alternate ways to find word meanings (dictionary).   +

B. Sentences
  1. Reads and writes simple sentences consisting of subject and verb.   +
  2. Reads and writes sentences consisting of subject, verb, and object.   +
  3. Reads and writes more complex sentences including the use of adjectives, adverbs and other parts of speech.   +
  4. Discriminates between a phrase and a sentence.   +
  5. Utilizes punctuation and capitalization rules when writing sentences.   +
  6. Understands that a sentence states a complete idea.   +
  7. Discriminates between related and unrelated sentences.   +

C. Topic Sentence
  1. Summarizes information into a main idea.   +
  2. Identifies the main idea or topic sentence in a group of sentences.   −
  3. Understands that detail sentences support the topic sentence.   −
  4. Discriminates between the topic sentence and detail sentences.   −

D. Paragraphs
  1. Arranges events in logical order.   −
  2. Understands and identifies time-order words such as *first, second, next, finally,* etc.   −
  3. Understands that a paragraph is a group of related sentences, all supporting one main idea.   −
  4. Writes in paragraph form using indentation and proper punctuation.   −
  5. Organizes a group of related sentences into a logical order in paragraph form.   −

remaining sentences in logical order. Notice these other differences in characteristics between the two exercises:

SPECIFICATIONS FOR APPROACH 1: COMPLETING REGULAR LESSON OBJECTIVE AT *REGULAR* LEVEL OF COMPLEXITY

- Each series of sentences consists of five or more sentences
- Not every sentence begins with a time-order word (there is not always a clue)

- Each sentence contains between five and ten words
- Vocabulary is at grade level or above
- Sentence construction is according to fifth-grade reading level

SPECIFICATIONS FOR APPROACH 2: COMPLETING REGULAR LESSON OBJECTIVE AT *REDUCED* LEVEL OF COMPLEXITY

Each series of sentences consists of no more than four sentences

Every sentence (except the topic sentence) begins with a time-order word that student can use as a clue when arranging sentences in logical order

Each sentence contains no more than seven words

Vocabulary is at second-grade reading level

Sentence construction is kept to simple, not compound, sentences

Sample Lessons: Some Comparisons. At the *regular* level of complexity, the *regular* curriculum objective would be met through a written assignment taken directly from the book or a similar lesson from another book. The teacher would have first given similar examples to the students in a group lesson; together they would organize a series of related sentences into logical order. During the lesson, they would be taught to discriminate between a topic sentence and detail sentences. The students would also learn to look for time-order words to use as clues when arranging sentences in logical order.

Some special education students could participate in the same teacher-directed and group activities as their peers. When it came time to order the sentences on their own, the sentences of reduced complexitites could be given to these students. Other students, however, might need more instruction than their regular peers.

Instruction to meet the regular objective at the *reduced* level of complexity would include more examples before allowing students to attempt completing the assignment. The teacher would also use role-playing examples of the logical order of events so the students could get even a better grasp of logical order. The teacher would also give more emphasis to the use of time-order words when arranging events in logical order. Initially, the teacher would write the sentences in logical order without writing them in paragraph form and would omit the topic sentence. Later the topic sentence would be included, and the sentences would be organized in paragraph form. Students would also be working with sentences at a reduced vocabulary level and with a simpler syntactical structure. The students would complete many examples in group lessons before attempting to meet the objective individually. As a result, instruction would be at a much slower pace than usual.

Approach 3: Changed competency statement

When it is questionable whether or not the student can ever learn the critical skills necessary to perform the original objectives or learn them within a reasonable amount of time, the change of competency is one option. While considering this option, teachers may need to review the steps for deriving differential curriculum objectives.

Table 7.6 "Steps in Deriving Differential Curriculum Objectives," provides a step-by-step guide to choosing or devising differential curriculum. It is modeled after steps that are used to assist with choosing or devising differential standards for skill testing. The process is basically the same—merely expanded to influence a variety of curriculum and instruction modifications.

Completing step 4 on Table 7.6, teachers might use a task analysis such as that in Table 7.7 and identify these:

Critical or Salient Skills:

1. Identify main idea or topic sentence from a series of related sentences (C2)
2. Discriminate between topic sentence and detail sentences (C4)
3. Recognize and utilize time-order words (D2)
4. Sequence events in logical order (D1)
5. Organize sentences into logical paragraph form (D5)

One of the critical enabling tasks needed to meet the objective was number C2 under the heading of "Topic Sentence" (Table 7.7). The subskill states that the student will identify the main idea or topic sentence in a group of sentences. This skill is important for students so they can meet the regular objective of organizing sentences into logical order after the topic sentence. If a student cannot identify the main idea of the paragraph (C2), he will have difficulty organizing the supporting details, and a different objective is in order:

Different Objective: Given a series of related sentences, the student will locate and write down the sentence that states the main idea or summarizes all the information given in the other sentences.

Sample Lessons: More Comparisons. Compare evaluation and instruction for the regular objective at the regular level of complexity with evaluation and instruction of this different objective. The same or a similar activity used for the previous exercise would be used for the regular curriculum objective as well as the different objective at a complexity level reduced from the original regular objective.

Instruction and evaluation for the *different* curriculum objective at a reduced level of complexity would *not*, however, be the same as learning activities for the original objective: first, the objective is not the same, and second, the teacher must teach different concepts. In learning activities associated with the original objective, students were expected to already know how to locate the topic sentence. There the emphasis was on teaching the concept of logical order. In this case, the focus is not on arranging sentences into logical order but on finding the main idea in a group of sentences. So instruction here might include ways of teaching students how to identify what all sentences have in common and locating the sentence that generalizes the information given in the other sentences. For example, using the series from a previous example:

- First she looked in the yard.
- Sarah lost her dog.
- Then she looked under the house.
- Finally, she found him under her bed.

The teacher might say, "Sarah is looking for something in the sentences. What is she looking for? Which sentence tells or describes what she is looking for?" (Sarah lost her dog.) This sentence tells the student why Sarah is looking and what she is looking for. Questions like these can help students identify the topic sentence. After the students have accomplished the task or objective of identifying the main idea, hopefully they will then be able to move closer to achieving the regular objective of arranging sentences into logical order under that topic sentence.

Approach 4: Lower grade level

Reduce the level of complexity by using an identical or similar lessons from a lower grade level competence.

Activity 4: Organize pictures in logical order to convey a message.

This lower grade-level competency does relate directly to other competencies in the language arts discipline, but it is not identical. Learning to organize pictures in logical order may help students organize thoughts logically and enable them to relate logically to a new experience. Organizing pictures gives students another way to demonstrate knowledge of the concept. Through the organization of pictures, a student might also learn beginning syntax structure, for example: who is doing the action, what is the action, and what object receives the action.

The lower grade-level competency can also be related to competencies in other disciplines. For example, most disciplines require students to follow directions in logical order when completing tasks. Being able to organize pictures logically will eventually lead to following other logical directions. Another example could be in math, where equations must be set up in logical order to be done.

Using lower grade-level instruction and evaluation relates to the regular objective because it, too, deals with arranging information into logical order. The difference here is the instructional media, pictures instead of words. A student with reading and spelling difficulties is likely to use pictures more easily than words to indicate a topic and to put the details in logical order. For example, in another subject area, the student may be studying the life cycle of the butterfly and has acquired all the necessary information to restate details in logical order. Through a series of pictures (e.g., a caterpillar, building of the cocoon, the butterfly, etc.), the student can show her understanding of the life cycle by organizing the pictures logically. This could be much easier for the student than organizing written descriptions of the life cycle. Instruction again would include a variety of examples and ways of teaching students how to identify specific information from pictures that would give clues as to their order of arrangement. Eventually word descriptions could be added to the pictures to help students make the transition to organizing written information.

Approach 5: Unique curriculum objective

Unique curriculum objectives may or may not relate to regular education objectives. A related objective would be to use a series of graphics that a student looks at one by one in order to complete steps of work tasks in logical order. Picture cards, for instance, can be used to cue students to the next steps in an assembly task. Another objective alternative might be entirely unrelated to the original one. It may be more important, for instance, for a particular student to learn to reduce inappropriate behavior outbursts. Otherwise, a supported work job in which he uses picture cards as clues might never become even an option.

Practical Arts Discipline[2]

These approaches provide modified ways to teach a basic aspect of design to students with disabilities. Here is what a middle school teacher of drafting has to say:

> My objective, using these approaches, is to make it possible for all students to start to become technologically literate. I have reduced the levels of complexity as it pertains to using equipment and strategies similar to those being used in the design field rather than relying heavily on use of alternatives and adaptations that are so customized that they exist only in a classroom. These skills can then be taken out of the classroom and used in actual work settings without any unnecessary adaptations or explanations as they are already an accepted way to accomplish tasks and complete assignments.
>
> To work in any capacity in the industrial world, we need to have imagination, to be able to show others our idea, to make changes and adaptations in a language that is clear and concise. I want to offer all the students the opportunity to learn this process of industrial communication. Some will be able to learn and use all the traditional methods by using basic manipulative hand and machine skills. But for some these traditional skills require physical control and/or mental processing skills that they don't have and cannot acquire even through hours of practice. These students still have the imagination and the desire to work, contribute and be a part of the industrial world.

Subject/Content Area:	Drafting
Subcontent Area 1.0:	Sheet layouts with figure placement
Skill/Competency/Instructional Objectives:	Place a figure (drawn object) in the center of self drawn layouts.

Performance Objective: Given a figure, its size and scale, the student will choose the correct paper size, draw the layout with title block and work space, and mark the figure's outside dimensions centered in the work space correctly. This will be done in the manner prescribed in the textbook and according to current drafting conventions.

ITEM STEM CHARACTERISTICS OF REGULAR OBJECTIVE:
REGULAR LEVEL OF COMPLEXITY

1. Uses scale for measuring work spaces and figures.
2. Measurements will include: whole numbers, mixed fractions, and fractions.
3. Fractions used will be: 1/2s, 1/4s, 1/8s, and 1/16s.
4. Uses subtraction and division of mixed numbers and fractions.
5. All lines will be either vertical or horizontal.

Table 7.8   Enroute or Subskills

A. Numbers and Enumeration
   1. Read and write ordinal numbers.
   2. Know place values of: ones and tens.
   3. Know relationships of fractions to each other and to whole numbers. 1, 1/2, 1/4, 1/8, 1/16. These will not have to be learned all at once but as an accumulation of facts.
   4. Convert numbers from actual size to half size (needed to make layouts).
B. Use of Mechanical Scale
   1. Identify different sizes of scale (1/2, 1/4, 1/8).
   2. Read numbers from left to right or from right to left.
      Example: 111110123456789   987654321011111
   3. Measure from point to point.
   4. Mark point on center figure on a layout.
   5. Mark points and draw a layout.
C. Use of Templates and Guides
   1. Manipulation of various circle and shape templates.
   2. Manipulation of various lettering and line guides.
D. Use of T-Square and Triangle
   1. Align T square with paper.
   2. Align triangle with paper.
   3. Use T square to maintain horizontal accuracy.
   4. Use triangle and T square to maintain vertical accuracy.
E. Use of Teacher-Made Measuring Device
   1. Align paper correctly.
   2. Place device correctly.
   3. Mark points on paper to correspond to lines on edge of device.

6. Border lines will be dark and thick.
7. Guidelines will be thin and light.
8. Construction lines will be very thin and very light.
9. Lines will be placed to within a plus or minus 1/16-inch accuracy.

ERROR ANALYSIS/DISTRACTER CHARACTERISTICS:

Each error/distracter is likely to be the result of:

- Errors made in basic subtraction of mixed fraction facts
- Errors made in basic division of mixed fraction facts
- Improper reading of scale
- Incorrect use of scale
- Poor equipment manipulation

Approach 1: Same objectives with same level of complexity

A student with poor hand use or perceptual problems may use a teacher-made adaptive layout measuring device. An adapted triangle may be patterned after standard triangles used in industry but is made instead out of thick, clear acrylic and has a handle glued to the top side. (Picture the usual tool for completing the activity and the adapted tool for doing so.) T squares and triangles are customarily used in these activities. Students need to use a T square to align the drawing with the edge of a table. Students need to use a triangle to draw various diagonal lines. T squares present no problem because at the T end is a protrusion that hooks over the end of a table and stabilizes the tool. An elbow could hold it in place instead of a hand. The triangle, on the other hand, does present a problem. It is almost impossible to use when, because of a handicap, someone cannot open his hand to grasp, pick up, and manipulate this tool. The teacher explains that designers use many guides and templates to do their work. There are two main reasons for using aids in design work; the work produced is more accurate and uniform, and it is faster to use templates with premade shapes than to draw figures by hand each time one is needed.

After a time, students starting with the guide will be able to do the layout on their own, and the teacher-made guide will be replaced by a scale in most cases. Even if a student continues to use the guide, no stigma is attached as there are already plenty of pieces of equipment on everyone's desks. With this adaptation, the student will be completing the enroute or subskills of the regular objective (See Table 8).

Approach 2: Same curriculum objective: reduced level of complexity

SAMPLE ACTIVITY SPECIFICATIONS: REDUCED LEVEL OF COMPLEXITY

1. Uses scale for measuring figures. (In original objective: Uses scale for measuring work space and figures.)

2. Measurements will include: whole numbers, mixed fractions, and fractions. (Same as original objective.)
3. Fractions used will be: 1/2s, 1/4s, 1/8s, and 1/16s. (Same.)
4. No use of subtraction and division of mixed numbers and fractions. (Uses subtraction and division of mixed numbers and fractions.)
5. All lines will be either vertical or horizontal. (Same.)
6. Border lines will be dark and thick. (Same.)
7. Guidelines will be thin and light. (Same.)
8. Construction lines will be very thin and very light. (Same.)
9. Lines will be placed to within a plus or minus 1/16-inch accuracy. (Same.)

ERROR ANALYSIS/DISTRACTER CHARACTERISTICS:

Each error/distracter is likely to be the result of:

- Incorrect reading of the scale
- Incorrect position of the center point
- Incorrect use of scale
- Poor equipment manipulation

This modification (#4) removes the need for working knowledge of basic subtraction and division of mixed numbers and fractions (see #4 of regular objectives at regular level of complexity). The task remains the same, *to place a figure in the center of a layout that a student has drawn.* For students who find processing mixed numbers and fractions a barrier, this moves them past figure placement to the drawing process, yet they still complete the objective 100 percent.

Approach 3: Changed competency statement

Skill: (Original)	Place a figure (drawn object) in the center of self-drawn layouts.
Critical or Salient Skills:	1. Conversion of numbers from actual size to half size (A4, Table 7.8) 2. Measure from point to point (B3, Table 7.8)

For the immediate future, it did not seem this student would be able to learn the two critical or salient skills needed to make the layouts (see A4 and B3 on continuum of enroute skills). To keep from wasting the student's time, it was important to make the task functional for him. After discarding several possible solutions, we provided him with a photocopied layout on which to place his figure. This led to the different objective.

Different Objective: Place a figure in the center of a photocopied layout.

This change may be permanent or temporary depending on the student's ability to learn to draw layouts. Permanent need for photocopied layouts would not be a tragedy. The teacher has based the use of such layouts on industrial use. Very few designers out in the field make thier own layouts. They usually purchase them with the layout preprinted, and they fill in the title block with the appropriate information. In fact, some large companies have the title block spaces partially filled in with their name and address, which leaves only the job information blank. This means that the hours spent in practice learning to do layouts might more wisely be spent learning vocabulary, equipment manipulation, and measurement in more appropriate ways.

Approach 4: Lower grade level: not applicable

Approach 5: Unique curriculum objective

A life management objective that is somewhat related to the regular objective is to learn to put meal plates in the center of place mats. Time may be too precious to start with regular education objectives in order to develop unique curriculum objectives, and this could be an indirect route. For certain students, it is more worthwhile to conduct ecological inventories or establish unique objectives in some other way. Chapter 9 discusses objectives unique to individuals and objectives for life management curriculum in more depth.

Summary and Conclusion

Proficiency assessments are rapidly becoming an institution in schools. Yet with proper access modifications, certain students in special education can take and meet regular grade-level and proficiency standards. For others, however, these proficiency expectations may not be reasonable, and special education teachers can help determine the need for differential standards and other alternatives.

This first part of this chapter introduced the concept of proficiency assessment options for students in special education. It described seven steps special education teachers can follow to identify specifications of regular and differential assessment standards. From these, teachers can go on to identify present student performance on enroute skills compared to the skills are needed to accomplish the competency even at reduced levels of complexity. The chapter then outlines how to determine which of two options for deriving differential standards are most appropriate and demonstrates using that option to derive the appropriate standard. The two options are (1) to derive new proficiency statements that relate to the same competency but reflect a reduced level of complexity or (2) to select an enroute skill and make this enroute skill the main competency to be assessed. The final step details how to generate new and differential items for proficiency assessments.

Similar kinds of considerations pertain to each school discipline—particularly in those in which students may have difficulty. Proficiency standards only apply to certain parts of curriculum—generally to basic academic skills. Even in these areas, grade-level and graduation proficiency assessments cover only part of the basic skills curriculum. The remaining parts of the basic skills curriculum, and curriculum in basic academic and elective subjects, have objectives that are equally important to address.

The second part of this chapter illustrated the use of the seven-step process for deriving differential curriculum objectives. Instead of stemming from proficiency assessment and standards, the process started with curriculum objectives. Applications to the school disciplines were illustrated using two disciplines: the language arts and practical arts. Specific examples showed five methods teachers can use for customizing curriculum objectives in various school disciplines. The end result is consistent with the different curriculum options discussed throughout this text: identical, parallel, practical academic, lower grade, and life management.

Teachers can use the steps described throughout this chapter to develop expertise in reducing task complexity, choosing appropriate objectives, and individualizing lessons to meet the needs of certain students. Special education teachers can study the model for changing complexities of curriculum-based objectives and its variations presented here to learn the process. Experience and expertise can develop from this beginning.

This chapter presented one model for devising proficiency standards and discussed its place in the school, its relevance to curriculum, and its impact on modifying the complexities of ongoing curriculum and day-to-day lessons for special education students individually and in a varied group. This is a good starting place, and only that. Teachers need to explore how to apply this model and its many possible creative variations to their own unique teaching challenges.

Notes

1. Application to language arts, section by Eileen Vukicevich, teacher.
2. Examples in practical arts application by Tim Main.

References

Bracey, G. W. 1983. On the compelling need to go beyond minimum competency. *Phi Delta Kappan* 64(10): 717–21.

California State Department of Education. 1978. Steps in devising differential standards. In *Developing proficiency standards for pupils in special education programs.* Sacramento, Calif.: California State Department of Education.

Denham, C., and Lieberman, A., eds. 1980. *Time to learn.* Washington, D.C.: U.S. Department of Education, National Institute of Health.

Gickling, E., and Thompson, W. 1985. A personal view of curriculum-based assessment. *Exceptional Children* 52(3): 205–18.

Jefferson Union High School District. "Course of Study: Freshman English— Regular and Advanced (mimeographed copy). Daly City, California 94015.

Marston, D., and Magnusson, D. 1985. Implementation of curriculum-based measurement in the special and regular education setting. *Exceptional Children* 52(3): 266–76.

C H A P T E R

8

Parallel and Practical Academic Curricula

Specially designed courses of study provide the foundation curriculum for many students in special education. To produce these documents, teachers have to modify existing curricula, help other teachers make modifications, and—in the absence of an existing curriculum—develop their own. Where do special education teachers start in this demanding process? How do they proceed when students need specially designed courses of study—parallel curriculum, practical academic curriculum, or life management curriculum? What are characteristics and examples of different kinds of specially designed courses of study? Where are sources for these courses of study? What kinds of information are in curriculum syllabuses and guidelines?

Teachers of special education students will be actively involved in curriculum development activities in a variety of ways. Some local education units provide teachers with comprehensive board-approved curriculum guides and related materials detailing specially designed courses of study. These guides do not appear out of thin air. Teachers who know how to develop specialized curriculum and instruction have to be among the major authors. Existing curricula developed in universities as special projects or in other states and local education agencies are other sources. These, of course, need to be modified to meet local needs.

Curriculum with objectives the same as, or similar to, the regular education course of study is classified as *parallel curriculum*. In a parallel curriculum, students meet all or most regular education course objectives but at reduced levels of complexity. Classroom curriculum with objectives that are in the same discipline but derived from skills enroute to regular objectives (or otherwise selected for their practicality) is called a *practical academic curriculum*. These are taught in the classroom, separate from their use in natural life activities. When basic academic skills and subjects are taught for immediate incorporation into natural situations in which their use is needed—not separated from the activities themselves—they can be described as being part of a *life management* curriculum. Though these are defined as separate curriculum options to attempt to give order to curriculum, in reality overlap is likely. Each local education unit can establish its own parameters.

To maintain consistency with regular education courses of study, parallel and practical academic specialized courses of study for special education students include at least these five factors: (1) a *syllabus,* or summary that outlines the course of study, (2) *guidelines* to assist teachers with instruction, (3) content and intended *outcomes* (objectives) for students, (4) specifications for each *unit,* or subdivision within the course, and (5) specifications for *lessons* within the units or subdivisions.

Excerpts from teacher resource material for parallel and practical academic (applied) curriculum from a local education agency will illustrate these five factors. These curricula demonstrate the kinds of resource material available to support instruction. These examples also illustrate the characteristics of parallel and practical academic curriculum. They show the organizational structures and contents of the resource materials available to teachers. When these are not available in the local curriculum, teachers can use these factors and examples of parallel and practical academic curricula to develop their own local curriculum.

Parallel Courses of Study

Specially designed courses of study provide an adapted curriculum that parallels the regular district curriculum for special education students. The parallel curriculum has objectives that are the same or very similar to those of the regular curriculum in each subject. Simplified, these objectives enable students with learning problems to acquire and apply rudimentary skills, concepts, insights, and values. Teachers and other curriculum developers conduct content analyses and focus on the rudiments they consider most important to simplify and develop the content of a parallel curriculum.

Specialized courses paralleling the district's curriculum can be used with mixed groups of special education and nonspecial education students for whom they are appropriate, with individuals in special education placements, and with individuals who need modifications for studying coursework with peers in regular classes. Parallel components can make up part or all of the curriculum for special education students.

Through specialized courses that parallel regular courses, special education students have the chance to appreciate and learn what their peers who are not special education students do. Through such courses of study, students in special education may be able to learn, study, and discuss along with classmates in regular classes. Often students are given credit for parallel curriculum objectives toward graduation. Thus a parallel curriculum can be an empowering curriculum for the student in special education.

Documents that identify outcomes of *board-adopted regular and parallel curriculum for each grade level* are perhaps the best resources for teachers whose students are possible candidates for a parallel course of study. The challenge then is to determine curriculum and instruction that leads to accomplishing true parallel outcomes. Teacher-developed curriculum and existing parallel curriculum guides provide the basis for making this determination.

Teachers can borrow from existing developed objectives and content for specialized parallel courses of study when none exist. Or they can reduce the complexity of the regular objectives using the existing regular education curriculum guides if this has not already been done systematically. Most regular curriculum guides, if well organized and well-differentiated, can serve as a basis for task analyses. Certain guides even include special information about making adaptations for students with learning and other handicaps. Lower grade-level guides are also helpful.

To illustrate the resources available to teachers, a parallel-course syllabus is presented here as well as other helpful components of a parallel curriculum, including: (1) excerpts from guidelines for teachers, (2) specifications for one study unit, and (3) specifications for one lesson sequence within that unit. These present examples of varying complexity implementations of a curriculum, and they demonstrate the content of the kinds of support materials available to teachers or that teachers can prepare when they aren't available. The section on parallel curriculum illustrates:

1. Course syllabus and introductions to guidelines.
2. Guidelines introducing suggested format for lessons.
3. Guidelines suggesting teaching methods to accompany different lesson formats.
4. Overview of one course in the social studies discipline.
5. Guidelines for teacher preparation of one specific unit of study within that course.
6. Guidelines for teaching a specific lesson within the unit.

These all represent factors that help structure and organize any curriculum. There are many ways to develop a syllabus and curriculum guide materials. The information presented here is meant to be illustrative, one way that parallel course of study teacher-resource materials can be organized. Certainly it is not the only way. To do their best work, teachers can use the same elements adapted from the local curriculum with their own preferred teaching style and methods. It is helpful to recall that the guidelines for the following material are prefaced with statements of study skills, critical-thinking skills, and personal and social development skills that are to be infused throughout the material taught.

Course Syllabus

This syllabus is identified as "Multilevel World History, Geography, and Economics 1, 2"

PARALLEL COURSE: SYLLABUS

Course Description:

Two-semester course, grades 9–12.
Prerequisite: None.
This course provides an adapted program for special education students paralleling district curriculum. Students practice geographic skills by interpreting maps, globes, charts, pictures, tables, and three-dimensional illustrations. Students study the everyday living patterns and heritages of people in the world's major cultural regions. Instruction emphasizes the interdependence among the economies of the world.

Major Outcomes:

The student will:

- Identify four ways the agricultural revolution changed the ways humans live.
- Describe the form of democracy practiced by the ancient Greeks; state one reason why the Greek form of democracy is not practiced by modern nations.
- Identify three areas of culture in the United States that have been influenced by the Roman culture.
- Select any two of the following civilizations and state how religion influenced people's ideas about life: Kush, Egyptian, Chinese, and Mayan.
- Identify at least two of the contributions of the following peoples: Hebrews, Phoenicians, Mayans, Muslims, Japanese, Incas, Ghanans, Indonesians, and Malis.

---

* Used and adapted with permission. From San Diego (1985). *Course of Study, K–12: Special Education Edition.* San Diego: Superintendent of Schools, San Diego Unified School District, pp. 672–73.

- Explain the roles of lords, vassals, knights, freeholders, and serfs in the feudal system.
- Explain how the crusades helped to bring an end to the Middle Ages.
- Define the Renaissance and list three significant changes that took place during this period.
- Locate on a map of the world five areas explored during the Age of Exploration; identify five of the chief explorers and their sponsoring governments.
- Explain how English Common Law has contributed to the political system of the United States.
- Identify four ways the Industrial Revolution changed the ways humans live.
- Identify at least two causes and two effects of both World War I and II.
- Identify at least two causes and two effects of both the American and the French Revolutions.
- Identify two twentieth-century dictators and explain how they influenced modern history.
- Identify and explain the roles of the three worlds of contemporary society.
- Draw conclusions from graphically presented materials (charts, graphs, maps, time lines, etc.).

Basic Texts and Teaching Guides: Wallbank et al., *History and Life: The World and Its People,* Scott, Foresman and Company, 1984. Danzer, *World Atlas,* Scott, Foresman, and Company, 1982. Myers and Wilk, *People, Time, and Change,* Allyn and Bacon, 1983. (San Diego 1985, 672–73)

Introductory materials generally accompany course descriptions and statements of course outcomes. From comprehensive curriculum guides, special education teachers select appropriate topics for use, either to support the regular curriculum or use totally in special education classes.

Teachers can use curriculum guides developed specially to support special education students in different ways. Special education teachers can introduce them to regular teachers, and then the regular teachers can infuse the ideas into their instruction. As with most teacher guides, teachers can generalize the suggestions.

Teachers guidelines often describe formats for instructional lessons and include suggestions for teaching within those formats. Information about pacing, lesson formats, objectives, and materials needed for lessons helps teachers prepare to do their work well.

Parts of one set of teacher guidelines, defined and briefly described below, illustrate their essential features. Parts of lesson formats in this set of teaching guidelines include:*

I. Prereading
II. Vocabulary instruction
III. Study guide instruction
IV. Key questions
V. Reading

VI. Activities
VII. Homework
VIII. Audiovisual and other material use
IX. Review

Guidelines Introducing Suggested Lesson Formats

I. Prereading

This part of the lesson establishes the purpose for the lesson, encourages students to tell what they know about the general subject, and directs them to use information in order to predict the topic. The prereading activities were designed to generate a discussion that encourages a free exchange of information and enables students to become actively involved in the learning process.

II. Vocabulary Instruction

New vocabulary words are identified in the "As You Read" box at the beginning of each lesson. However, additional vocabulary words may be needed.

The vocabulary study sheet contains words presented in the "As You Read" box and other words identified as critical for passage comprehension. In *Direct Instruction Reading* (1979), Anita Archer has addressed vocabulary assistance in the chapter entitled, "Reading Instruction in the Content Area Textbook." Archer (p. 367) stressed that, "Words for vocabulary instruction should be limited to a small number of words that are crucial for passage understanding and beyond the child's experiential background. Children should not be overwhelmed with a large number of difficult words to understand in a single presentation. Critical words should be carefully introduced, practiced, and reviewed in subsequent lessons." Therefore, the words identified as the most critical are listed at the beginning of each vocabulary section

---

* With permission, this section quotes heavily from the *Special Education Guide for World History, Geography, and Economics, 9–12* (San Diego Unified School District, 1983), pp. 3–21. Modifications constitute (1) elimination of some material due to space limitations and (2) reorganization and revision of certain sections to clarify this somewhat abbreviated version.

and included on the vocabulary study sheet. Additional words that may need to be discussed depending upon the vocabulary needs of the class are listed below the instructions for the study sheet.

The vocabulary study sheets list the words and their definitions. Teachers are directed to select the vocabulary instructional procedures appropriate to the performance level of their students from the suggestions detailed in the study skills: vocabulary portion of the management section.

III. Study Guide Instruction

The study guides were developed to improve the reading comprehension of special education students in the content area and to enable students to locate information in the text. Information for the study guides was taken directly from the text and emphasizes the most important points. The study guides are duplicated and given to each student at the beginning of a unit. The study guides are written for the unit and divided into sections that parallel each lesson. A fill-in-the-blank response is required. The page number that identifies the location of information in the text follows each question. The study guides were also designed to provide reinforcement for assigned reading.

Dr. Archer stated, "When presented before reading, the written assignment becomes a study guide that extends the preview of the selection by alerting students to the salient information in the passage and establishing specific purposes for reading" (1979, p. 374). Key questions presented before each reading selection also assist the student in establishing a purpose for reading. Strategies for completing the study guide will be detailed in the study skills: study guide portion of the management section.

IV. Key Questions

The key questions are presented as in the "As You Read" box at the beginning of each lesson. These questions stress the main ideas.

V. Reading

Specific pages from the text are listed. The teacher is directed to select the reading procedures appropriate to the performance level of the students in the class by consulting the "Study Skills: Reading" area in the management section.

VI. Activities

The activities begin with a discussion that gives the teacher an opportunity to check students' comprehension. The concepts and skills developed are discussed, and the teacher is reminded to discuss the key questions with the class.

The skeleton-activities section focuses on a minimum of two worksheets. The first is generally the vocabulary practice exercise. If very few words are presented in the vocabulary study sheet, a separate follow-up worksheet may not be presented until after the next lesson. The vocabulary practice sheet might then include words from both lessons. The second worksheet is the study guide that is geared to review the main ideas presented in the lesson. In some units, a third worksheet may be included. This could be an excerpt from a newspaper or magazine designed to relate information in world history to current events. It is recommended that worksheets be corrected in class to afford students feedback regarding the quality of their work. In addition to worksheets, teachers can generate their own essay questions to compliment information in the lesson. In general, lower-performing students benefit from controlling the linguistic complexity of questions. Question formats might begin with the following words:

1. Name . . .
2. List . . .
3. Who, What, Where, When, Which . . .
4. Describe . . .
5. Do you agree . . .
6. Would you . . .
7. Identify . . . (literal)
8. Why . . . (literal)
9. How . . . (literal)

Higher performing students might find questions using the following leads more challenging:

1. Compare . . .
2. Contrast . . .
3. Why . . . (inferential)
4. How . . . (inferential)
5. Discuss . . .
6. Explain . . .
7. If . . .
8. Determine . . .
9. Identify . . .

VII. Homework
This section was designed to provide reinforcement for information presented in the lesson. Activities that require students to apply new concepts without teacher assistance are not included in homework assignments.

VIII. AudioVisual and Other Material Use
This section at the end of each lesson provides a listing of available films and filmstrips from the Instructional Media Center (IMC). A publication date and the level of material are also listed to aid in selecting the materials. Previewing the audio-visual material is recommended to judge its appropriateness. Previewing will also enable the teacher to develop discussion questions as a follow-up activity to presenting materials. The introduction in the instructional sequence is important to the success of these educational tools and is left to teacher discretion.

IX. Review
Review procedures include teacher-directed instruction to review main ideas, group discussion, and use of study guides.

Instructional Lesson Strategies

SAMPLES OF STRATEGIES FROM GUIDELINES   Specialized instructional strategies are of particular assistance to teachers of students with ranges of problems in (1) learning new vocabulary, (2) reading well enough to read the lesson material, (3) knowing how to use a study guide, and (4) reviewing material in preparation for a unit test. Strategies are identified and illustrations assist teacher using this and other specialized curriculum. Strategies also serve as models for persons learning to teach special education students.

For teaching students with special needs, there are eight specific procedures teachers can choose from to determine the most effective method of vocabulary instruction to insure student success. The particular method of vocabulary instruction chosen will depend on the level of student performance, lesson complexity, time availability, and student interest. Emphasis is on contextual analysis that alerts the student to use skills taught as teachers use different procedures. This demonstrates the selection of vocabulary words that were considered crucial to passage understanding and were unlikely to be in the student's experiential background. Also included is the identification of the teaching strategy suggested with descriptions of different stimuli such as the book and words on the chalkboard, related teacher dialogue or responses, and probable student responses in terms of action and dialogue.

To further assist teachers, instructional procedures suggest different approaches to assigning reading in the content areas to accommodate students with different reading abilities. Decoding-assistance ideas are suggested. Ways to handle assigned readings with higher-performing students, lower-performing, and nonreading students are also given.

The method in which vocabulary, study guide, reading, and review are presented will depend on the academic needs of the class and the range of disabilities within the class. Parts of the lesson format detailed for illustrative purposes are vocabulary instruction (II), study guide instruction (III), reading (V) and review (IX).

II. Vocabulary Instruction

Vocabulary instruction is an important component of this guide. Each lesson is introduced with vocabulary instruction. The particular method is presented in advance by the teacher depending on the level of group performance, lesson complexity, time availability, and student interest. A lesson in the guide begins by referring to the vocabulary study sheet. The teacher can then determine the instructional method by referring to this section. The first procedure is recommended as the core method for the average multilevel social studies student. But teachers should become familiar with all vocabulary methods in order to determine the most effective one to insure success.

PROCEDURE 1:

- Distribute the vocabulary study worksheet. Read the first word and definition. Use the word in several sentences that provide contextual experience for students. Formulate sentences that vary from those in the text. Have students volunteer to use the words in a sentence. Correct wrong usage after student has finished speaking. Reinforce students' correct usage.

PROCEDURE 2:

- Direct students to refer to the vocabulary study worksheet when reading.
- Have the students keep a vocabulary notebook. Ask them to write new sentences using a few words after following Procedure 1.

PROCEDURE 3:

- Provide instruction using Procedure 1 a day before the assigned reading. Assign the first part of the vocabulary review worksheet as seatwork or homework. Direct the students to complete the remaining part of the vocabulary review during the *activities* section (VI). In some cases, a teacher might want to assign the entire vocabulary review in advance. Teachers should preview each exercise to identify the activities that need prior instruction in the lesson's context and direct students to complete them during the *activities* section.

PROCEDURE 4:

- Provide exercises in which students write sentences using the word. Assign during *activities* section as independent seatwork or homework. Give students opportunities to work in pairs and edit each other's sentences.

PROCEDURE 5:

- Direct students to complete all or part of the vocabulary review before vocabulary instruction, using the text's glossary or the dictionary. Correct orally in class or have students check their own work using the accompanying vocabulary study exercise.

PROCEDURE 6:

- Use teacher-directed instruction to facilitate mastery of vocabulary words. In the book, *Direct Reading Instruction,* Archer (1976) discusses a number of vocabulary instruction strategies that apply equally well to content area instruction. These strategies include:

  1. Teaching through examples
  2. Teaching through a synonym
  3. Teaching through definitions
  4. Locating the meaning in the dictionary
  5. Determining the meaning using morphemic analysis
  6. Teaching the use of context clues

Dr. Archer points out that, "though all of these strategies can be used in content materials, emphasis should be placed on developing contextual analysis" (1979, p. 367). Direct instruction in contextual analysis will alert students to the use of these clues and encourage them to hunt for the word's meaning within the discourse.

The following steps should be followed in designing a direct-instruction vocabulary lesson to accompany a content area selection.

1. Examine the text and select vocabulary words that are crucial to passage understanding and unlikely to be in the students' experiential background.
2. Select a teaching strategy for each word using contextual analysis when possible.
3. List the focus words on the board.
4. Present the words to the students using the designed strategy.
5. Test the students on their vocabulary knowledge.

A Sample Lesson for Vocabulary Instruction. The material presented here is a sample lesson for vocabulary instruction. It is a specific example of the teaching strategies outlined in Procedure 6 (Steps 1–5) from the section above on "Instructional Lesson Strategies."

Based on pages 92–95 *People, Time and Change*. Follett Social Studies Program.

SELECTION OF WORDS AND TEACHING STRATEGY

Word	Teaching Strategy
myths	definition paired with context
pyramid	definition paired with picture
mummy	glossary paired with context

STIMULUS	TEACHER RESPONSE	STUDENT RESPONSE
Book and words on board	"Today we are going to read a chapter in social studies to learn about the beliefs of the Egyptians.	
		Opens book
	First we need to learn some of the new words in the book. Open your book to page 92." "The first part of the chapter describes the Egyptians' belief in life after death. Look at the first word on the board. Ready. (pause) "What word?" (signal)	
		Myths
Myths	"Read the first word on the board." (pause) "What are myths?"	
		"Myths"

STIMULUS	TEACHER RESPONSE	STUDENT RESPONSE
	"Find the word myths in the first line of the first paragraph in column 2. Myths are stories about gods. What are myths?"	
		"Stories about gods."
	"The Egyptians believed in life after death and had special ways of burying people. This chapter describes their beliefs. Look at the second word on the board. Ready." (pause) "What word?" (signal)	
		"Pyramids"
Pyramids	"A pyramid is a great tomb built for Egyptian kings. A pyramid is shaped like a triangle. What is a pyramid?	
		"A tomb built for Egyptian kings, shaped like a triangle."
Picture in Text	"Is this a pyramid? (points to a boat) "How do you know?"	"No" It isn't a tomb, and it isn't shaped like a triangle."
	"Is this a pyramid? (points to pyramid) "How do you know?"	"Yes" "It is a triangle, and it is shaped like a great Egyptian tomb."
Mummy	"Find the word *mummy* in your glossary." Read the definition of the word mummy. Ready."	Students look up the word *mummy*.
		"A mummy is a body preserved by embalming, as by the ancient Egyptians."
	"Good. A mummy is a body preserved by the ancient Egyptians. Read the last sentence on page 94. Look for the word *mummy*."	

STIMULUS	TEACHER RESPONSE	STUDENT RESPONSE
		Children read sentence.
	"Listen to me read the sentence with the definition instead of the word, *mummy*. Now the body preserved by embalming by the ancient Egyptians was ready for burial. What do we call the body prepared by embalming by the ancient Egyptians?"	
		"A mummy"
Review and firm up new concepts.		

PROCEDURE 7:

- Provide experience with forms of the vocabulary word. Try to use variations of the word during *pre-reading* and *discussion* dialogue with the students. Prepare worksheets that illustrate changes in the root word using the following examples:

Example 1: Tense
- Say, "As some areas are studied, you will be finding out what has already happened. This will be written in past tense. Many words show past tense by adding 'ed'."
- Prepare a worksheet:
  Root word + ed   = _____
  1. isolate*
  2. evaporate*

- List the root words under the appropriate heading. Have students write the new word. Ask them to say or write it in a sentence. Review spelling rules if appropriate.

Example 2: Plurals
- Say, "When studying regions, we learn about individuals and groups, one thing or many things (i.e., country, countries). Many words show that they refer to more than one thing by adding +s or +ies [or es]."
- Prepare a worksheet:
  Root word + s or *ies*   = _____
  1. nomad
  2. refinery

- List the root words under the appropriate heading. Have students write the new word. Ask them to say or write it in a sentence.

Review spelling rules if appropriate.

Example 3: Affixes
- Teach the meaning of the prefix or suffix.
- Prepare a worksheet:

Prefix + root word = _____

un + employment , = _____

- List the prefixes (or suffixes) and root words under the appropriate heading. Have students write the new words. Ask them to say or write the new word in a sentence. Review spelling rules when appropriate.
- Prepare a worksheet:
   erode, eroded, erosion

   1. _____ is a big problem in Kansas.

   2. The wind will _____ the soil.

   3. The hill _____ after the big storm.

- List the root word and its variations. Develop completion sentences. Have students complete worksheet. Ask higher-performing students to write the words in new sentences.
- Prepare a worksheet:
   unknown, unemployed, undeveloped, development

   1. The man was _____ when the plant closed.

   2. The region was _____ and no one knew what was there.

   3. The resources were _____ to the travelers passing through the area.

   4. The _____ of a new road will help the area grow.

- List words that require discrimination of affixes. Develop completion sentences. Have students complete worksheet. Ask higher-performing students to write the words in new sentences.

PROCEDURE 8: REVIEW

Vocabulary words in this guide are reviewed in several ways:

   1. Context usage in subsequent lessons.
   2. Selected review on the vocabulary review worksheet
   3. The vocabulary review included in the chapter review lessons.

In addition, the following review procedures are recommended:

   1. Review important vocabulary words for a lesson before the *Reading* section should a significant time delay exist between the *Vocabulary Instruction* and *Reading* sections.
   2. Provide time for independent review:
      a. Have students keep a collection of study guides. A guide folder might be convenient (periodically reviewed).
      b. Have students keep a composition book of words, definitions, and/or sentences.
      c. Have students keep an individual file of vocabulary words. Use 3 × 5 cards.
         Suggested format:

Word _____

Definition 1. _____

   2. _____

Sentence _____

---

3. Vary your methods of review:
   a. Use partners
   b. Develop games

III. Study Guide Instruction
The following strategies are recommended for effective use of the study guide.

1. The study guide may be employed as a prereading tool to enable students to preview content material covered in the lesson. The teacher may guide the students in skimming the study guide prior to assigned reading activities.
2. The study guide can be used to reinforce reading comprehension and to draw the reader's attention to the highlights of the reading selection. Two strategies are suggested for completing the study guide. The first procedure would allow students to fill in answers to the study guide as they locate them during silent reading. The second procedure would instruct students to complete silent reading and then answer the study-guide questions. The second procedure would allow for an uninterrupted flow of reading. When using the study guide, it is highly recommended that teacher-directed instruction is used to help students master skills for locating answers. When the students are proficient in this skill, teacher-directed instruction can be discontinued.
It is critical to monitor the students' use of the study guide so that students are not filling in answers without comprehending the material. Immediate feedback correction of inaccurate responses and positive reinforcement are suggested. The study guide will only be a positive teaching tool if it is not used as a "busy work" activity.
3. The study guide is a comprehensive tool for reviewing the main ideas of a unit prior to the exam. The teacher may wish to provide direct instruction in how to use the study guide for review.

Sample Teacher-Directed Instruction Lesson for the completion of the study guides.

SKILL	TEACHER RESPONSE	STUDENT RESPONSE
When given a partially completed study guide, the student can use the text to locate information and record it on the study guide.	Teacher assists students in locating major ideas to complete a study guide after silent reading.	

SKILL	TEACHER RESPONSE	STUDENT RESPONSE
	Teacher distributes study guides to the students and instructs them to look at *Section 1*, which covers pages 40–43. "We have finished reading about the beginning of the Ice Age. In order to help you recognize important information, you are going to learn how to locate and record this information on your study guide. The purpose of the study guide is to help you to locate and record information. What is the purpose of a study guide?"	
		"To help locate and record information."
	Open your book to page 40. Read the first sentence in the study guide. "When you look for the answer, look for a sentence that is like the one on the study guide. Listen to this statement. The period of time before writing is called _____. Are you looking for a one-word answer?"	
		"Yes"
	"Notice the page number given after the first blank. The page number where the first answer can be found is page 40. Where can the first answer be found?"	
		"On page 40."
	"What important or key words are in the first sentence in the study guide? Listen to the sentence. The period of	

STIMULUS	TEACHER RESPONSE	STUDENT RESPONSE
	time before writing is called _____. The important words are *period of time* and *before writing.* What are the key words?"	
		"Period of time and before writing."
	"Are the key words, period of time and after writing?"	
		"No"
	"Why not?"	
		"The key words are period of time and before writing, not after."
	"Look on page 40 for a sentence with those key words. Is a sentence like that on that page?"	
		"Yes"
	"What is the period of time before history called?"	
		"It is called prehistory."
	"When you are looking for information to complete the study guide, use these clues: the page number given on the study guide and the key words. What clues can help you find information for the study guide?"	
		"The page number and key words in the sentence."
	[and so on]	

V. Reading

A single instructional procedure for assigning reading in the content area cannot accomodate the wide range of abilities present in most special education programs. It is recommended that teachers omit or expand the following procedures according to each group's performance level.

DECODING ASSISTANCE   Most students will require some assistance with decoding. Preview the lesson and make a list of the difficult words selecting those that contribute the most meaning to the passage. Provide instruction several days in advance if possible. Use one of the following procedures to present the word depending on its type: phonic (common letter combinations), morphemic (affixes: prefix or suffix), or irregular (no common pattern).

- Write each word on the chalkboard. Underline any common letter combinations or affixes.
- Have student volunteers attempt to decode each word or use direct-instruction methods to each decoding skill.
- Emphasize the letter combination of affixes as a decoding strategy.
- Identify irregular words for the students.
- Provide opportunity for practice.
- Test recognition using teacher, aide, tutor, or peer.

ASSIGNED READING
Higher-performing students: select the independent readers in the class. Remember that the more technical the material, the slower the reading. Then refer to the graphics and vocabulary study worksheet as they read.

- Have students silently read the assignment.

Option:

- Develop questions in advance. Have students answer them as they read.
- Encourage students to take notes as they read.

Lower-performing students: (Prerequisite: students must be able to count sentences and paragraphs in order to locate their place on the page.)

- After decoding, assign silent reading of one or two paragraphs.
- Do corrections after students have completed a sentence. Give phonic or morphemic (structural analysis) cues to assist decoding. Identify irregular words for them.

Suggestions:

- Avoid "round robin" sequencing that generates unnecessary anticipation.
- Ask comprehension questions after each paragraph for very dependent readers.
- Reduce the amount of reading by assigning only the most important paragraphs.
- Design and duplicate a study guide that presents basic statements from the assigned reading. Students may wish to fill in the study guides as they read.

Nonreaders: For very low or nonreaders, the goal is to present the lesson's concepts independent of the student's reading abilities. Instructional emphasis is placed on visual aids and guided discussions. Suggested procedures for the assigned reading are:

1. Read all or portions of the reading to the class. Ask questions to check the student's comprehension as you read.
2. Tape the selection in advance. Be sure to refer to illustrations, vocabulary, definitions, and comprehension questions when appropriate.
3. Use only the study guide as the assigned reading.

IX. Review Instruction

At the end of each unit, one lesson is used for review before giving the unit test. The review lesson includes the study of the text, vocabulary, study guides, and other worksheets, as well as new articles or audiovisual materials.

PROCEDURE 1:

- Use teacher-directed instruction to review the main ideas presented in the text, vocabulary, the study guide, or other materials included in the unit.

PROCEDURE 2:

- Begin a review by discussing the main concepts of the unit. The unit summary at the end of each unit will help students focus on the main ideas.
- Read the study guide to the students along with the correct answers or ask students to identify correct answers from their work.
- Review vocabulary by discussing definitions, using the word in context, or using synonyms.
- Use selected questions from the review worksheet to check understanding of concepts.
- Allow time for a question and answer period.
- Highlight news articles, audiovisual materials, or other information that has been presented during the unit.
- Assist students in scheduling a realistic amount of time for study during the homework session.

SUGGESTIONS FOR EFFECTIVE DISCUSSION AND GROUP WORK   Social studies offer excellent opportunities for students to develop skills in thinking and interacting with others. Developing such skills helps students become thoughtful, active, and cooperative citizens. Many students who are accustomed to an individualized instruction approach may not have developed effective discussion and group work skills. The following suggestions can help students acquire and apply these skills.

DISCUSSION:

Discussion is an important way for students to integrate and apply the information they have learned.

1. Involve students in planning guidelines. For example, talk about good listening behavior and identify specific behaviors that facilitate or hinder discussions.
2. Have students work in varied groups: pairs, small groups, the whole class, and so on.
3. Change the assigned seats periodically to promote a greater mixture of students.

4. Be sure topics are ones students know something about.
5. Introduce topics with questions or statements that encourage students to respond with more than recall of information.
6. Keep the discussion moving and on target when necessary.
7. Encourage wide participation. Try to avoid a monopoly of discussion by a few students.
8. Give students time to think before responding to higher-level questions.
9. Review when appropriate. Help students organize their thoughts by using charts, outlines, and so forth.
10. Vary the discussion length according to the situation.
11. Give the students guided practice in recognizing key words that promote comprehension of questions.
12. After a discussion, ask students to identify specific behaviors that facilitated or hindered participation.

GROUP WORK:

Learning to work well with others is an essential component of citizenship.

1. If your students have not had much experience with group work, begin with one small group. (Be sure the other students can work independently while you work with the small group.)
2. Provide instruction about the role of group members: group leader, recorder, and participating members.
3. Help students develop standards of behavior for group participation.
4. Rotate leadership and participating member roles.
5. Increase the number of groups until all students are able to participate in groups simultaneously.
6. Keep group activities short so students can complete a group task and go on to another.
7. Assign a task that can be accomplished by the group. Be sure that students have the skills necessary to complete the task successfully.
8. Before groups begin to work, review the task and procedures with group members.
9. Increase the challenge of group tasks as students gain proficiency in working in groups.
10. Continue to guide and work with students to improve their group skills.
11. Provide oral and written instructions to facilitate comprehension by all members of the group.
12. Model the role of group members and guide students through a group work activity.
13. Monitor students' performance to provide feedback and positive reinforcement.

STUDY SKILLS Students are expected to demonstrate competency in a variety of study skills throughout the course. These skills are infused into the course content and are critical to student's understanding of world history, geography, and economics.

Suggestions for developing instructional units for research and note-taking skills are described. This information is presented in a hierarchy of goals to enable a student ultimately to conduct independent research on any topic in the library. Areas covered are: locating information in a book, locating information in reference materials, locating information in the library and note-taking, outlining and summarizing.

This concludes the illustration of the information in curriculum guides that can be generalized for uses with a variety of school subjects. Lesson formats and strategies within formats are suggestions to teachers; they are not mandates.

Next is an illustration of one sample course: its syllabus, an excerpt from a unit of study in the course, and an outline of a lesson within the unit. Material included in this series was chosen for its value in illustrating (1) the kinds of information teachers need to define when teaching a course of study, (2) the kinds of information that can be collected for specific courses of study by local education agencies and put into curriculum guides for teachers, and (3) a place to demonstrate application of the lesson format recommended in the previous section. (Codes referring to worksheets, transparencies, and other resource materials were retained even though the actual documents are not included or explained. These codes can remind teachers that readily available supplemental instructional materials also save teacher time for meeting other specialized needs and can enhance teaching effectiveness.)

Excerpts from a secondary level course, Multilevel World History, Geography and Economics follow. As examples of a parallel course of study, they are organized into three sections: *Course description, unit of study,* and *lesson within the unit.*

*Parallel Course of Study: Course Description**

The Multilevel World History, Geography, and Economics Guide, 9–12*, was developed to provide an adapted program paralleling the district's curriculum. It enables students to acquire and apply geographic skills, concepts, insights, and values as they gain appreciation and understanding of the everyday living patterns and heritage of people living in the world's major cultural regions. It provides students with the essential historical background to understand, interpret, and evaluate current world conditions.

There is a total of twenty-one units in the guide. The first three units provide an introduction to the course, the text, and the use of the world atlas.

This course of study is organized into eighteen units that parallel the text. Each unit focuses on a specific period of time beginning with the Ice Age and progressing to life in the twentieth century and beyond. The units are introduced with a picture that illustrates the period of time being studied. Each unit also

---

* Adapted and used with permission. San Diego City Schools, pp. 3–21, 1983A, 103–9.

contains a map-skills section, key questions, checking-up questions and concludes with a unit summary and review workshop. A special features section is included in each unit and presents information about careers, citizenship, famous people, or past and present traditions. Sample pre- and post-tests are provided, but teachers are encouraged to develop more in-depth assessment measures based upon the information that was emphasized in the classroom.

Parallel Course of Study: A Unit of Study

The information presented here represent guidelines for teacher preparation covering one specific unit of study within a course (9–12) on world history, geography, and economics. This unit covers early civilization in Egypt, India, and Crete.

Course goal to be emphasized in the unit: Students will recognize the different cultures in world history in order to better understand the traditions, ideas, and motives of the world's people.

(San Diego 1983a, 103)

TEACHER PREPARATION

1. Read the entire unit in advance.
2. Select and plan vocabulary study and reading methods.
3. Read and select activities of your choice from the additional activities list.
4. Duplicate worksheets.
5. Consult the reference section at the end of each lesson for use of audiovisual materials. Preview the materials to determine their appropriateness for the class.
6. Collect and provide magazines and newspapers when necessary (San Diego 1983a, 104).

Unit 3: Early Civilization in Egypt, India, and Crete

LESSON	OBJECTIVES: THE STUDENT WILL:	WORKSHEETS/ WORKBOOK PAGE NO.	BLACK-LINE MASTER NO.	TRANS- PARENCY MASTERS
1.	. . . state the importance of the discovery of King Tutankhamen's tomb		3-1A 3-1B 3-1C	3-1A
	. . . interpret maps and graphs		3-1D	
	. . . identify knowledge they have about ancient civilizations			

Unit 3: (*continued*)

LESSON	OBJECTIVES: THE STUDENT WILL:	WORKSHEETS/ WORKBOOK PAGE NO.	BLACK-LINE MASTER NO.	TRANS- PARENCY MASTERS
2.	. . . describe agriculture in the Nile River Valley		3-2A	
	. . . describe three periods of Egyptian history			
3.	. . . explain the religious beliefs of the Egyptians		3-3A-3-3AA 3-3B	
	. . . identify the functions of temples and the duties of priests			
4.	. . . describe the role of nobles, scribes, and farmers		3-4A 3-5A 3-5B	
	. . . tell about life in the Indus Valley			
	. . . name two major religions that developed in India			
6.	. . . review the main ideas about early civilization in Egypt, India, and Crete			
7.	. . . identify important information about early civilization in Egypt, India, and Crete		3-7A	

Unit Test
(San Diego 1983a, 105)

Unit Overview

Unit 3 begins by developing the ability to interpret maps and graphs. Other river civilizations, such as Egypt, Indus Valley, and Crete are discussed. The effect of rivers on the development of agriculture is emphasized. Egyptian way of life and its contributions are studied followed by the life of people in Indus Valley and Crete.

UNIT OBJECTIVES
The students will:

- Interpret maps and graphs
- Describe the process of farming in Egypt
- Tell the history of Egypt
- Discuss the pyramids and burial rites of the pharaohs

- Describe the Egyptian way of life
- Discuss the civilization of the Indus Valley and Crete
- Identify how the beliefs of Hinduism and Buddhism affect lives of people today

Suggested Time Allotment   1½ weeks

(San Diego 1983a, 106)

Parallel Course of Study: One Lesson Specification

Below is one lesson taken from Unit 3 on early civilization in Egypt, India, and Crete. These guidelines for teacher preparation show the step-by-step elements a good lesson plan includes. Teachers adapting or developing lessons for their students in special education can include similar elements to insure a complete, well thought out lesson.

Lesson Format

The lessons can be divided into two major sections. The first section of each lesson is designed to assist the teacher in preparing for the lesson. This section includes: *objectives, materials needed for the lesson, a summary of the lesson,* and *background information*, which may be utilized to generate discussion. The second section is the instructional lesson which follows the repetitive format described earlier: *pre-reading, vocabulary, key questions, study guide, reading, activities,* and *homework*. Additional activities and audiovisual materials are listed as supplementary material at the end of each lesson. Review lessons are provided at the end of each unit to prepare the student for the administration of the unit test.

(San Diego 1983a, 107)

Lesson 1

OBJECTIVES

The students will:

1. Identify the knowledge they have about ancient civilizations;
2. State the importance of the discovery of King Tutankhamen's tomb;
3. Interpret maps and graphs.

MATERIALS NEEDED FOR THIS LESSON

Worksheet 3-1A, Pretest
Worksheet 3-1B
Worksheet 3-1C
Worksheet 3-1D, Study Guide
Transparency 3-1A
Transparency 3-1B

SUMMARY

This lesson will introduce the class to the civilization of Egypt, India, and Crete. The discovery of King Tutankhamen's tomb will be discussed, and maps and graphs on Egypt's land forms and climate will be interpreted.

BACKGROUND

This information may be beneficial when discussing the lesson:

- Nile River
  This is the longest river in the world, flowing over 4,000 miles in Africa. When the Nile flooded, fertile soil was deposited in the Nile Valley where most farming in Egypt still takes place. Construction on the Aswan Dam began in 1968, and its completion in 1971 ended the yearly flooding pattern. The Nile silt now collects behind the dam in Lake Nasser, which has caused Egyptian farmers to rely on artificial fertilizers. The Nile River is Egypt's chief natural resource.
- Population of Egypt
  Egypt has about 38½ million persons. Almost all of the people of Egypt live on 3½ percent of its land, which is located along the Nile River and on the Suez Canal.

Directions for Instructional Lesson

PREREADING

- Say to the class, "In this unit, you are going to study the people and their way of life in Egypt, India, and Crete. This pretest will help you determine your knowledge about these areas.
- Distribute, read, and administer *Worksheet 3-1A, Pretest.* Upon completion correct the pretest.
- Instruct students to open their book to page 82. Discuss the unit objectives with the class. Stress that cities grew and became more complicated during this period of time. Egyptian civilization, which lasted over 5,000 years, contributed to the way we live today.
- Direct the class's attention to the picture of the mask that covered the mummy of King Tutankhamen.
- Say to the class, "Were any of you able to see the treasure's of King Tut's tomb when they were on display in the United States? The treasures were shown in the art museums of large cities several years ago. Why was the discovery of King Tut's tomb important? (It was the first tomb that was found intact, (not robbed), which told us about Egyptian civilization.)
- Distribute, read, and discuss *Worksheet 3-1B* on the discovery of King Tut's tomb. *Note:* It is recommended that the information is read by the teacher to the class as they follow along due to the level of vocabulary words.

VOCABULARY

- Delta, source, cataract
- Select a vocabulary study method and provide instruction using *Worksheet 3-1C, Vocabulary Study.*

STUDY GUIDE

- Select a prereading strategy and provide instruction using Section 1 of *Worksheet 3-1D*, Study Guide.

KEY QUESTIONS

- Use *Transparency 3-1A* to review the key questions for this lesson.

READING

- Select a reading strategy and provide instruction using pages 84–86 of the text.

ACTIVITIES

- Complete section 1 of *Worksheet 3-1D*, Study Guide.
- Use the checking questions as guides for discussion on page 86. Use *Transparency 3-1B* to discuss the answers to the key questions.
- Summarize this lesson by stressing the importance of the Nile and the climate and location of settlement in Egypt.

HOMEWORK

- Assign students to select 10 cities and interpret their temperatures by using the daily newspaper section on weather.

ADDITIONAL ACTIVITIES

1. Instruct students to obtain a map of California or to use the encyclopedia to locate five cataracts in California.
2. Have students locate information on the climate of Alaska and tell how it is different from the climate in San Diego.

AUDIOVISUAL MATERIALS

- The following audiovisual materials may be incorporated into this lesson. The materials are available from the Instructional Media Center (MC).
(list of materials)

(San Diego 1983a, 108–9)

This concludes the discussion of parallel courses of study for students in special education. By presenting a course syllabus, guidelines for lesson formats, instructional strategies, a sample lesson for vocabulary instruction, a unit of study, and a lesson within that unit, teachers can see the parts of the lesson, such as prereading, vocabulary, study guide, and so on as they are applied at all levels in a parallel course of study. Teachers can then use these examples of sample applications as guidelines when developing a parallel curriculum in other subjects or at other grade levels.

Practical Academic Curriculum

A practical academic curriculum component, as defined here, is primarily—but not exclusively—classroom-based. In this type of curriculum, academic skills that are practical in nature are taught in the classroom using a traditional lesson format. These skills are then sometimes practiced for later use in natural settings. Compared to regular education objectives, these represent different but related objectives. Practical academic curriculum objectives, methods, and materials can either lead toward or interface in a variety of ways with objectives of regular, parallel, or life management curriculum objectives. Practical academic curriculum objectives, methods, and materials can even overlap those of parallel and regular curriculum.

Much of the practical academic curriculum is based on objectives developed from skills enroute to regular objectives or lower-grade-level curriculum. Teachers can never be sure students studying in this component will not be able to learn regular objectives at regular or reduced levels of complexities at some time in their lives. This should always remain an option. The most common reason for study in basic academic skills, however, is to learn practical academic skills and fundamental knowledge that assist with accomplishing major life activities (life management curriculum components).

If students can be taught some academic skills and knowledges that they can use both in school and in natural situations outside the classroom, they should be taught these skills. This is where the basic academic curriculum components feed into and support objectives in the major life areas of a life management curriculum (i.e., using skills in counting by tens, part of a practical academic component, in order to be able to divide allowance money and plan for spending it as part of a life management component. Distinguishing "where" questions from "who" questions, a practical academic component, in order to be able to ask for directions when trying to find some place in the community in a life management component.)

Sources. The process of task analysis, again, is the teacher's best ally both for determining content and for teaching a practical basic academic curriculum. The potential shortcoming of basic skills models is that they can result in teaching isolated splinter skills. "Students are able to read words, count, or compute, but are not able to solve real-world problems." (Wilcox, 1983, 362). To avoid a patchwork curriculum with pieces that don't match, teachers can use task analysis and ecological inventories to determine which skills enroute to higher-level skills and other related skills are (1) most feasible and (2) have purpose and fulfill a functional use when established as objectives for individuals or groups of students in special education.

Basic skills scope-and-sequence charts from different curriculum guides and textbooks in regular and special education are helpful resources. To begin pinpointing which skills to use, teachers can think of which enroute skills on those charts are important objectives for students who are unlikely to learn all of the skills on the scope-and-sequence charts.

Academic skill analyses in computer-managed instruction (CMI) can guide identity of enroute or subskills in a skill hierarchy. Computer-managed instruction is the use of computers to manage individual instruction programs. Properly programmed computer software is designed to help educators manage each student's activities as students pass through a program of instruction. Teachers do not have to be able to do the programming; programming is done by local experts or persons designing commercial software for these purposes. Programmers, with assistance from educators, break skills into component parts so as to track student accomplishment along a continuum. Student performance records are kept in databases on software. The Learning Tools IEP software[1] is a commercial example. It lists skills in sixteen developmental areas and compares student performances to a hierarchy in each area. From the information, the program devises IEP goals and objectives.

In considering the advantages and disadvantages of skill banks created from other special education teachers and personnel, it helps to ask certain questions: Can educator-users select the skills deemed high priority for a particular individual or group of students? Can other skill objectives be added to the program to customize it for different individuals?

Some computer databanks are standard and cannot be customized, but other commercial software programs allow users to customize skill lists to meet local needs. Teachers can modify, add, or delete. Certain programs are specific to one or more local education units or districts. Others provide access to many banks of skill breakdowns fed in from a variety of sources in virtually every school subject and for students with many different disabilities.

Commercial Publishers of special education material such as Janus[2], Curriculum Associates[3], New Readers Press[4] and, Science Research Associates[5] (SRA), Associates (DISTAR Reading, Math and Language Arts) provide skill-building books in academic skills that are practical for the population at large. These focus on common formats (job application forms, blank checkbook pages) and practical exercises (make up a grocery list, find a phone number in phone book). Within these curriculum trade books, the complexity levels have been simplified for students working in a practical academic curriculum.

Computer software programs teaching practical basic curriculum are abundant! *Good* computer software programs to teach practical academic curriculum are, however, less common. See Chapter 4 for recommendations.

District-developed curriculum guides are probably the most desirable sources of curriculum for student study because they are developed locally for local students. The first part of this chapter presented one district's curriculum component that is parallel but reduced in complexity compared to regular curriculum (parallel curriculum). Now we will look at that same district's corresponding secondary level multisemester courses in applied basic skills (practical academic curriculum).

Illustrations of Practical Academic Courses of Study

Course syllabuses are perhaps the best documents for capsulizing curriculum in any type of component. These are documents that highlight what is to be taught that school personnel and community members can use for education-related discourse. More details can always be provided if needed from more detailed curriculum descriptions. Syllabuses can also assist teachers learn about a student's past program of study. The course syllabuses presented here represents only the practical academic, or applied, courses.

The following examples of applied curriculum that correspond to practical academic curriculum components described in this text come from a district-provided teacher resource: *Applied Curriculum and Functional Curriculum: Updated Courses for 1986–87 School Year,* (San Diego, 1986).*

Applied Social Studies, Junior High School Level

Course Description:	This elective credit course can be taken for multiple credit in middle or junior high school.
Prerequisite:	None. (The course number and elective credit for this course can be assigned to students who have completed course work but have not mastered all proficiency requirements for a parallel or identical special education social studies course.)
During *odd*-numbered school year:	This course provides an academic focus introducing basic geographic skills with appropriate application of those skills to everyday living.
During *even*-numbered school year:	This course provides an academic focus introducing U.S. history concepts with appropriate application of those concepts to everyday living.

---

* Used with permission. San Diego 1986, 9, 10, 15, 16, 17, 18.

Major Outcomes:
During *odd*-numbered school year,
the student will:

- Identify current news figures.
- Identify purpose and usage of the newspaper.
- Identify major points of a city and county on a map.
- Identify and locate prominent features using a map key and major directions.
- Identify and locate continents and oceans on a world map.
- Identify time zones on a U.S. map.
- Study and discuss people as producers and consumers in the United States.

During *even*-numbered school year,
the student will:

- Identify current news figures.
- Identify purpose and usage of the newspaper.
- Identify and discuss the major historical events, places, and people that have affected the development of the United States as a nation.
- Identify the basic rights guaranteed by the Constitution and the Bill of Rights.
- Name and understand the significance of major national holidays and the national anthem.
- Describe personal/family background and cultural differences.

Basic Texts and Teaching Guides:
Odd year:

Kalsounis, *States and Regions,* Silver Budett, 1984.
Special Education Guide for Social Studies, 7–8, Odd, San Diego City Schools, Stock No. 41-S-8560 (selected units).
Teacher's Guide—Newspaper in Education Week, Copley Press.

Even year:

Bernstein, *America's Story, Books 1 and 2,* Steck-Vaughn, 1985.
LifeSchool: Occupational Knowledge "About Me," David S. Lake, 1981.

*Special Education Guide for Social
Studies 7–8, Even,* Stock No. 41-S-
8550 (selected units).
*Teacher's Guide—Newspaper in Edu-
cation Week,* Copley Press.

(San Diego 1986, 15)

Applied Social Studies, Senior High School Level

Course Description:

This elective credit course can be taken for multiple credit in high school.

Prerequisite:

None. (The course number and elective credit for this course can be assigned to students who have completed course work but have not mastered all proficiency requirements for a parallel or identical special education social studies course.)

During *odd*-numbered school year:

This course introduces basic legal rights and responsibilities. It also covers governmental positions, institutions, and community agencies.

During *even*-numbered school year:

This course introduces basic world history concepts.

Major Outcomes:

During *odd*-numbered school year, the student will:

- Identify current events and news figures.
- Identify and discuss key political people and their roles in city, state, and national government.
- Identify basic legal rights and responsibilities.
- Identify how to become a registered voter and the rights and responsibilities thereof.
- Identify the role of key people and institutions in legal proceedings.
- Identify agencies that serve the community.
- Identify and maintain personal documents.

During *even*-numbered school year, the student will:

- Identify current world news events and figures.

- Identify historical events on a basic timeline.
- Identify and locate continents and oceans on a world map.
- Identify local, national, and international signs.
- Identify and describe appropriate uses of various types of public transportation used throughout the world, including local areas.

Basic Texts and Teaching Guides:
Odd year:

Chan, *Getting Help—A Guide to Community Services,* Janus, 1981.
Lefkowitz and Uhlic, *Government at Work* and activity sheets, Janus, 1982.
Lefkowitz and Uhlich, *It's Our Government* and activity sheets, Janus, 1982.
LifeSchool: Community Resources, "Post Office," "Health Services," David S. Lake, 1981.
LifeSchool: Government and Law, "Legal Rights," "Assault," "Voting," "Social Security," "Personal Documents," David S. Lake, 1981.
LifeSchool: Occupational Knowledge, "Developing Confidence," David S. Lake, 1981.
Special Education Guide—U.S. History/American Government and Institutions, San Diego City Schools, Stock No. 41-S-8555 (selected units).

Even year:

Bernstein, *World History and You, Books 1 & 2,* Steck-Vaughn, 1982.
LifeSchool: Occupational Knowledge, "Cultural Differences," David S. Lake, 1981.
LifeSchool: Community Resources, "Traffic Signs," David S. Lake, 1981.
Special Education Guide for Social Studies 7–8, Odd, San Diego City Schools, Stock No. 41-S-8560 (selected units).
Special Education Guide—World History, Geography, and Economics, Stock No. 41-S-8515 (selected units).
(San Diego 1986, pp. 16–17)

Applied English, Junior High School Level

Course Description:

This elective credit course can be taken for multiple credit in middle or junior high school.

Prerequisite:

None. (The course number and elective credit for this course can be assigned to students who have completed course work but have not mastered all proficiency requirements for a parallel or identical special education English course.)

During *odd-* and *even*-numbered school year:

In this course students will learn oral/signed and written language skills as they relate to career education in the following area: basic academics, everyday experiences, personal-social relationships and occupational knowledge.

Major Outcomes:

During *odd*-numbered school year, the student will:

- Demonstrate organization skills to assist in completing assignments.
- Give and obtain information of increasing complexity (social greetings).
- Identify personal information and appropriately limit information provided to individuals in unfamiliar situations.
- Ask appropriate questions to obtain and clarify information given.
- Use the telephone/TDD for personal and practical purposes.
- Describe simple events and retell a short story or occurrence.
- Use the writing process to compose personal message and/or letters.
- Use correct mechanics and spelling to complete assignments and personal information forms.

During *even*-numbered school year, the student will:

- Identify broad categories of literature: fiction, nonfiction, article, poetry, and biography.
- Prepare and give a brief oral/signed presentation based on a short story or event.

■ Use library to locate references and check out books and demonstrate appropriate library behavior.
■ Alphabetize to the second letter and apply the skill to reference materials.
■ Identify, locate, and use multimedia resources for obtaining information.

Basic Texts and Teaching Guides:

Odd year:

Gottlieb, *Forms and Messages*, Steck-Vaughn, 1983.

Even year:

Life Schools: Community Resources, "Recreation," David Lake, 1981.
Special Education Edition Guide for Multilevel English I. San Diego City Schools, Stock No. 41-E-8605 (selected units, 1983.)
Walker, *Life Skills English,* Media Materials, 1984.
Writing Packet (K–12). San Diego City Schools, 1981 (selected units).

(San Diego 1986, 9)

Applied English, Senior High School Level

Course Description:

This elective credit course can be taken for multiple credit in high school.

Prerequisite:

None. (The course number and elective credit for this course can be assigned to students who have completed course work but have not mastered all proficiency requirements for a parallel or identical special education English course.)

During *odd*-numbered school year:

This course will teach oral/signed and written language skills relate to everyday living, including acquisition and maintenance of employment.

During *even*-numbered school year:

This course will teach oral/signed and written language skills as they relate to everyday living.

Major Outcomes:

During *odd*-numbered school year, the student will:

■ Read a building directory in order to locate needed services.

- Read schedules related to public transportation and media presentations.
- Read a newspaper to get specific information relating to world events and local activities.
- Use the writing process to compose a short letter and address the envelope.
- Complete simple forms related to employment.
- Use correct mechanics and spelling to complete assignments.
- Read and respond appropriately to classified and employment advertisements.
- Understand vocabulary relating to employment and workers' benefits.
- Identify appropriate communication behaviors when working with others.
- Speak/sign correctly to obtain employment information and present appropriate information in a job interview.

During *even*-numbered school year, the student will:

- Organize information for speak/signing and writing.
- Give oral/signed directions in a clear manner for use in the classroom and community.
- Read schedules related to public transportation and media presentations.
- Read, respond to, and appropriately use classified advertisements.
- Read a newspaper to get specific information relating to local and national events.
- Complete simple forms relating to personal documents.
- Use the writing process to compose simple paragraphs.
- Use correct mechanics and spelling to complete assignments.

Basic Texts and Teaching Guides:

Odd year:

How, *English That Works*, Scott-Foresman, 1982.
LifeSchool: Occupational Knowledge, "Job Search," "Job Application," Job

Interview," "On the Job," "Workers' Benefits," David Lake, 1981.
Special Education Edition Guide for Multilevel English I, Stock No. 41-E-8605 (selected units).
Writing Packet (K–12), San Diego City Schools, 1981 (selected units).

Even year:

Jew, *Using the Want Adds,* Janus, 1977
Larned, *Reading a Newspaper,* Janus, 1978
Special Education Edition Guide for Multilevel English I. San Diego City Schools Stock No. 41-E-8605.
Writing Packet (K–12) San Diego City Schools, 1981 (selected units).

(San Diego 1986, 10)

Applied Occupational Education

Course Description:

This elective credit course can be taken for multiple credit in grades 7–12.

Prerequisite:

None. This course focuses on transition from world of school and controlled environment to the world of school and independent living with an emphasis on work attitudes, behaviors, and tasks as they relate to seeking, securing, and maintaining employment.

Major Outcomes:
The student will:

- Identify reasons why people work.
- Evaluate personal skills, interests, and aptitudes for job success.
- Locate jobs which are appropriate to skills, interests, and aptitudes identified previously.
- Compile a personal data sheet giving complete information pertinent to making application for jobs.
- Complete job interview preparation.
- Demonstrate appropriate on-the-job conduct and appearance in a variety of role-play situations.
- Identify safety concerns on-the-job.
- Demonstrate understanding of uses of public transportation, including

reading a bus schedule, planning a journey involving at least one transfer, making travel reservations on train and/or plane.

- Demonstrate understanding of time schedules, constraints, and on-task behavior.
- Demonstrate social and personal maturity.

Basic Texts and Teaching Guides:

McKnight, *Entering the World of Work,* Kimball Vineyard, 1983.
McKnight, *Entering the World of Work - Activity Book,* Kimball Vineyard, 1983.
Career Education/Life Centered Skills, Stock No. 41-C-1200, 1982.
LifeSchool: Community Resources, "Public Transportation," David Lake, 1981.

(San Diego 1986, 18)

Summary and Conclusion

This chapter discussed parallel and practical academic courses of study specially designed for special education students. It explained that special education teachers use existing specially designed courses of study or develop their own. Illustrations from existing local education documents were included not as models but to suggest that concerted efforts at the local level can result in documents to guide curriculum and instruction.

A sample of general teaching guidelines for teaching *parallel* curriculum in the discipline of social science was summarized. A format for lesson organization was highlighted and explained. Four of nine recommended segments of lessons were illustrated in more depth. Strategies suggested in these guidelines were for generalization across the teaching of different subjects in the social sciences discipline.

Following the example of curriculum guidelines were excerpts from guidelines for teaching a single unit of study within one course in the social science discipline. The unit chosen was about early civilization in Egypt, India, and Crete. Illustrations included the identification of course goals to be emphasized in the unit, steps in teacher preparation for instruction, objectives of each lesson in the unit, and specifications of one lesson in the unit. The lesson format was consistent with the format recommended in the general curriculum guide.

Next, *practical academic* curriculum was introduced and explained. Teachers were taught to differentiate between parallel and practical academic curriculum. Parallel curriculum was described as having the same objectives as regular curriculum but student expectations of attainment were at reduced levels of complexity. A practical academic curriculum was described as stemming from the regular curriculum objectives as well, but the objectives were not the same objectives. When it is determined that it is not appropriate for students to learn portions of the regular curriculum, even at reduced levels of complexity, different but related objectives are selected.

The chapter concluded by describing how these, often derived from skills enroute to the regular curriculum objectives, result in practical or applied curriculum. Some sources of practical academic curriculum were identified. Descriptions of secondary-level practical academic, or applied, courses were given. With these formal local agency course descriptions were listed major outcomes and basic texts and recommended teaching guides.

A first step in taking a job in special education is to inquire about the availability of curriculum guides for parallel and practical academic curricula. Where none exist, a second question is appropriate. Teachers can ask what they are to base different components of student curriculum on? Though a good question, this may not receive a definitive answer.

To avoid operating in isolation in curriculum development, teachers might investigate the possibility of establishing a local education unit task force to work on curriculum development. More often than not, local education units have some system through which regular education teacher specialists take leadership in writing regular education curriculum guides. State departments and local education agencies even sponsor summer projects for the writing of guidelines and other resources for use in regular education. Special education teachers have rights to the same kinds of well-developed resources to assist them in employing the best practices possible in behalf of special education students. With these rights come responsibilities for contacting administrators in the local education units to increase their awareness of needs and possibilities. Collaborations in developing and updating specially designed curriculum can be exciting ventures for teachers of special education students.

Notes

1. Learning Tools
   686 Massachusetts Ave.
   Cambridge, MA 02139
   "Curriculum Management System"

2. Janus
   Special Needs Skill Center
   Study Skills: Strategies and Practice
   Language Skills Series
3. Curriculum Associates, Inc.
   5 Esquire Road
   No. Billerica, MA 01862-2589
4. New Readers Press
   Publishing Division of Laubach Literacy International
   Box 31
   Syracuse, NY 13210
   Economics: It's Your Business
   Economics: It's Your Business Workbook
   1986, Henry Billings, author
5. Science Research Associates (SRA)
   155 North Wacker Drive
   Chicago, IL 60606

References

Archer, A. 1979. Reading instruction in the content area textbook. In *Direct Instruction Reading* edited by D. Carnine and J. Filbert. Columbus, Ohio: Charles E. Merrill, 354–83.

San Diego City Schools. 1983. *Special Education Guide for World History, Geography, and Economics, 9–12.* San Diego: San Diego Unified School District.

San Diego City Schools. 1985. *Special Education Edition of the K–12 Course of Study 1985–1986: Extracted from the Official San Diego City Schools Course of Study, K–12, 1985–1986.* San Diego: San Diego City Schools.

San Diego City Schools. 1986. *Applied Curriculum and Functional Curriculum: Updated Courses, 1986–1987.* San Diego: San Diego Unified School District, Superintendent of Schools.

Wilcox, B. (1983). "A module on the design of high school programs for severely handicapped learners." In *A series of professional training modules on the education of severely handicapped learners: An update on educational best practices,* edited by L. Voeltz. Minneapolis, Minn.: Upper Midwest Regional Resource Center, University of Minnesota.

9

Life Management Curriculum

Life management curriculum is perhaps the most significant contribution of schooling to many students with disabilities. What is a major purpose of life management curriculum? What are some different ways it can be approached? What are some examples of existing courses of study in life management? How does this component provide a place in the curriculum for intensive instruction in disability-specific skills that students need in order to participate in the academic curriculum? What processes can tell which objectives will be powerful to individual students because their accomplishment can most help now and in the future? Once personal instruction priorities are identified, how can individualized curriculum and instruction be specially designed and executed?

Life management curriculum components take may forms. Curriculum options most commonly included involve instruction with the goal of teaching students with disabilities to participate as fully as possible in the major life areas. As introduced earlier, these major life areas are domains, environments or situations such as (1) domestic and family living, (2) education, (3) community living including recreation and leisure use, (4) work, and (5) communication. Life management curriculum components can be clustered into courses with titles resembling those in the core curriculum (i.e., "Functional Social Studies"). Life management curriculum can be described as leisure use, social skills, activities of daily living, language and communication skills, and career education including prevocational and vocational activities. It can encompass intensive training in methods for accessing curriculum and other specific skills most students with a specific disability need. And it can be highly individualized.

When basic academic skills and subjects are taught for immediate incorporation into natural situations in which their use is needed, they are considered to be part of the life management curriculum. This is because they cannot be separated from the activities themselves as they are when taught in the more traditional practical academic curriculum component. Then whenever students are unable to do the academic skills, which are commonly thought of as being necessary to completion of life management activities, they are taught alternative performance strategies. One such alternative performance strategy is giving clerks three one-dollar bills when the price shows two dollars plus change or five one-dollar bills when the total is four dollars plus change (Bigge, 1982). Thus students can participate without the academic skill of counting different portions of a dollar.

Goals and objectives making up life management curriculum components are generally identified on individualized educational programs. Specifics include goals and objectives for greater amounts and different kinds of instruction required for the individual to learn to perform ordinary self-help and independent-living skills and activities in usual ways (i.e., caring for personal hygiene, self-feeding, shopping, banking). Also included are goals and objectives so students can learn to participate fully in education life situations in different ways or perhaps with special equipment they have to learn to use (i.e., using braille for the self-help skills of writing at school).

Among the students in special education, some need more special life management instruction than others. For example, older students preparing for immediate transition to postschool environments may need more curricular emphasis in life management than younger students. Students with severe intellectual impairment may need to spend a greater portion of their school time in life management curriculum components than do students with less limiting disabilities.

Life management curriculum outcomes for students with disabilities—especially for those with mild and moderate intellectual disabilities—can look something like the list of curriculum outcomes The National Regional Resource Center Panel on Indicators of Effectiveness in Special Education (1986) lists. The panel included these self-help and independent living outcomes for students in special education:

- Applying problem-solving and decision making skills
- Communicating needs and feelings effectively
- Knowing about essential aids and equipment and how to acquire them
- Knowing about benefit programs and financial assistance opportunities and how to acquire them
- Understanding affirmative action, fair employment, and other antidiscrimination guarantees that affect them
- Advocating for legal, personal, or consumer rights
- Negotiating confidently with agencies or individuals to acquire essential benefits and services
- Understanding how earned and unearned income affects benefits eligibility
- Knowing about and understanding how to acquire personal care assistance to live independently
- Knowing about housing options and understanding how to acquire them
- Applying the principles of accessibility to homes
- Knowing about transportation options and how to acquire/use them
- Being comfortable [and appropriate] in social situations and using leisure time productively (National RCC Panel 1986, 6).

To the degree possible, the same outcomes are goals for students with severe to profound intellectual impairment, but they may be expressed differently. Most of the curriculum for students with severe intellectual impairment would take place in life management or other functional curriculum components. Curriculum and instruction is directed primarily toward use of "natural cues, consequences, and materials whenever possible, and varying trainers and settings to enhance generalization" (Mulligan and Guess 1984, 320). Much of the curriculum is based on an adult-referenced model: "Content is organized into domains that describe the broad categories of activities that characterize adult life: work, leisure, and personal management . . . with goals of developing content that is locally appropriate" (Wilcox 1983, 362–63).

Life management curricula are typically organized from three different orientations. A single student in a single year could participate in life management components with each of the three different orientations. Certain life management curriculum components are organized around teaching students to function in the major life areas the local education agencies have identified such as community, domestic, recreation/leisure, and vocational environments. In the first illustration to come, these are described in a way that relates to core-curriculum disciplines. More frequently, life management components are described by the identity of major life areas or natural environments (a variation in this orientation). Some Life Management curriculum components are organized around disability-specific needs. Instruction responds directly to the effects of specific disabilities and the instructional needs of persons with those disabilities and centers on the kinds of skills most students with this same disability need (i.e., learning certain response methods for use in school; learning self-help; learning socially acceptable behaviors). Finally, and just as important, life management components stem from goals and objectives that are unique to individuals. Though each of these orientations to life management curriculum is discussed here, the emphasis throughout is on an IEP team process for determining powerful priority goals and objectives for individuals requiring a life management curriculum.

Curriculum Organized Around Life Areas

Participating as fully as possible in major life domains or areas predominate life management curriculum outcomes for students in special education. As stated, one way to organize curriculum for groups of special education students is to focus on major life areas, which can be done in different ways. Two patterns, however, become apparent. One is to teach skills in several different life domains as they relate to a particular core-curriculum discipline such as language arts. The common thread is the core-curriculum discipline. A second way is to organize by category of major life domains such as the domestic domain. The common thread then is the domain. Both patterns of organizing curriculum are illustrated.

Core-Curriculum Disciplines

Specially designed life management curriculum is sometimes organized by disciplines and subject titles similar to those used in the core curriculum. The previous chapter described applied, or practical academic, curricula consistent with disciplines in the core curriculum: applied social studies, applied English, and applied occupational education. The local education unit that described these applied courses also have functional, or life management, course descriptions. In trying to decide on a system for describing functional curriculum, they used descriptions based on core-course disciplines and curriculum organized around major life areas. The one consistent with the core-curriculum disciplines is illustrated here. This organizational pattern relates to core-curriculum disciplines and includes courses such as "Functional Social Studies," "Functional Language Arts," and Functional Industrial Education." Examples of course descriptions* are as follows.

Functional Social Studies*

Course Description. Elective credit, multisemester course—grades 7–12. Prerequisite: None.

Students develop individualized social studies skills within the domestic, vocational, recreation/leisure, and general community domains. For example, within the domestic domain, a student may be expected to participate appropriately in family/group chores; with the vocational domain, a student may be expected to demonstrate skills necessary to obtain admission to a particular sporting event; with the general community domain, a student may be expected to demonstrate skills required for the use of public transportation.

Major Outcomes. Students develop social studies skills as specified on each student's IEP.

Basic Texts and Teaching Guides. Individual student skill inventories are adapted to meet the needs of each student.

Special Education Guide for Functional A Strand Courses, San Diego City School, 1983, Stock No. 41-S-8505, SS-46.

---

* Used with permission. San Diego City Schools. 1985. Functional Social Studies, p. SS-46; Functional Language Arts, p. ENG.-65; Functional Industrial Arts, p. INDED-106.

Functional Language Arts*

Course Description. Elective credit, multisemester course—grades 7–12. Prerequisite: None.

Students develop individualized language arts skills within the domestic, vocational, recreation/leisure, and general community domains. For example, within the domestic domain, a student may be expected to identify a variety of labels of typical household goods; within the vocational domain, a student may be expected to participate appropriately in filling out a variety of job applications; within the recreation/leisure domain, a student may be expected to choose age-appropriate leisure reading material; within the general community domain, a student may be expected to use a restaurant menu.

Major Outcomes. Students will: Develop language arts skills as specified on each student's IEP.

Basic Texts and Teaching Guides. Individual Student Skill Inventories are adapted to meet the needs of each student.

Special Education Guide for Functional A Strand Course, San Diego City Schools, 1983, Stock No. 41-S-8505, ENG-65.

Functional Industrial Education*

Course Description. Elective credit, multisemester course—grades 7–12. Prerequisite: None.

Students develop individualized industrial education skills within the domestic, vocational, recreation/leisure, and general community domains. For example, within the domestic domain, a student may be expected to appropriately participate with family/group in home maintenance activities; within the vocational domain, a student may be expected to develop skills for a specific job; within the recreation/leisure domain, a student may be expected to participate appropriately in a hobby requiring the use of a variety of materials and tools; within the general community domain, a student may be expected to demonstrate appropriate behavior when participating in a variety of job interviews.

Major Outcomes. Students will develop industrial education skills as specified on each student's IEP.

Basic Texts and Teaching Guides. Individual Student Skill Inventories are adapted to meet the needs of each student.

Special Education Guide for Functional A Strand Courses, San Diego City School, 1983, Stock No. 41-S-8505.

Major Life Domains

Skill or activity descriptions of desirable student outcomes or competencies by major life domains are perhaps the most frequently used pattern for defining life management curriculum. An excerpt from the Madison Wisconsin Metropolitan School District curriculum syllabus and guideline for moderately and severely disabled students provides a sample of skill lists ordered by life domains. Skill or activity lists presented as guides to teachers are preceded by teacher orientation to a philosophical framework and other helpful information. This example illustrates (1) how life management curriculum components can be described around major life domains, (2) the curriculum's philosophical basis, and (3) different aspects of this curriculum in terms of appropriateness for use with students requiring special education.

A Longitudinal Listing of Chronological Age-Appropriate and Functional Activities for School Aged Moderately and Severely Handicapped Students*

Introduction. This task force (teachers and parents) was organized to share curricular ideas and to articulate philosophical beliefs. The intent was to prepare guidelines for a longitudinal educational curriculum from which individualized educational programs could be developed. More specifically, educational plans should help delineate strategies to prepare each handicapped individual to function as independently and productively as possible in natural community, domestic, recreation/leisure, and vocational environments.

In order to assure that educational plans consider the needs of an individual in regard to these four major life areas, the task force felt that curricular content could be organized within them. Stated another way, everyone does and always will live somewhere; therefore, people need to learn to function in their domestic environment as independently as possible. People need to learn how to access and use the community resources which are available and to learn skills which allow them to participate in enjoyable leisure activities. In addition, adults need to learn vocational skills to increase and enhance their contribution to society.

The task force agreed on the importance of teaching skills in the environments in which they are used. Thus, part of the instructional day may be spent in nonschool environments teaching skills required for bus riding, grocery shopping, eating in public restaurants, etc. The demands of an individual's present and future natural environments determine what skills should be taught. The activities selected need to be chronologically age-appropriate as well as functional. This will enable each individual to function at his own level of independence, in a socially significant way within the environments that he and his nonhandicapped peers live.

For organizational purposes, the curriculum content contained in this guide has been divided into the following four major life areas [italics added]: *Domestic Domain, Community Domain, Recreational/Leisure Domain,* and *Vocational Domain.* Domestic activities have been delineated under the following headings: Personal Health Care [included as an illustration], Housekeeping, Clothing Care, and Meal Preparation. The *Community Domain* section of this guide categorizes activities under the headings of Stores, Restaurants, Transportation, Coin Operated Machines, Other Community Facilities, Public Bathrooms, and General Problem Solving Strate-

---

* Used with permission from Ford et al. (1980, 1–12).

gies. The *Recreation/Leisure Domain* is comprised of activities listed in a checklist format and is organized according to the settings where performance is most likely to occur: Home/Indoors, Home/Outdoors, School, Community, and Vocational. Finally, the *Vocational Domain* is divided into three parts: a Work Adjustment Inventory of job related skills; a listing of Specific Work Skills as they relate to given vocational tasks; and a Job Description which provides a brief delineation of the vocational tasks taught in each community-vocational setting to middle and high school students in the Madison area.

Within each domain, skills and activities are organized according to the student's school placement. Students in the Madison Metropolitan School District progress through elementary (kindergarten through fifth grades), middle (sixth through eighth grades), and high school (ninth through twelfth grades). For moderately and severely handicapped students the following chronological ages correspond with the various school levels:

Elementary School—Ages 5 through 12
  a) Primary—Ages 5 through 8
  b) Intermediate—Ages 9 through 12
Middle School—Ages 12 through 16
High School—Ages 16 through 21

Preceding each section, a brief statement of philosophy is provided for the elementary, middle, and high school levels. The philosophies include major considerations regarding the development and implementation of the curricular content at each level. In order to generate listings of suggested curricular content included in this guide, the task force utilized various strategies to inventory: (1) natural environments, (2) parents, (3) printed materials, (4) current teacher practices, and (5) student behaviors.

As previously mentioned, this task force recognizes the need to teach moderately and severely handicapped individuals in a variety of natural environments. Opportunities to verify and utilize functional skills in natural environments must also be engineered. However, it is not always possible or advantageous to provide all instruction outside the classroom. This guide provides nonexhaustive listings of a variety of natural environments and functional age-appropriate activites in the Madison community. It is intended to serve as a resource for educators, parents, and students to identify and then prioritize appropriate instructional activities. Each of these activities requires a variety of academic, communication, motor, self-help, social, and other skills. During the IEP process, it is intended that this guide may help identify functional needs for moderately and severely handicapped students. As various functional activities are prioritized this will provide a context for developing, adapting, and/or verifying skill requirements. Individual educational planning can then focus on providing appropriate instruction in the classroom and in natural environments.

This curricular guide is not intended to provide a "cookbook" for educators and parents who deal with moderately and severely handicapped individuals. It does not propose specific teaching methods, materials, or content priorities for individual students. The task force is fully aware that the individual educational needs of students can only be met through individualized educational planning and not through standardized and rigid curricular designs. The degree to which students participate in the activities suggested in this curriculum will depend upon several factors including (1) teacher and parent educational priorities, (2) student strengths and weaknesses (cognitive, physical/motoric, emotional, and social), (3) availability of community and school resources, and (4) requirements of current and anticipated future natural environments in which the students may function.

On the surface, many of the suggested activities contained in this guide may appear to be beyond the realm of possibility for many moderately and severely handicapped students, particularly those with serious physical and sensory impairments. However, before discounting possible student involvement in any activity, educators and parents must consider the principle of *partial participation*. Simply stated, the concept of partial participation directs educators and parents to consider adaptations in procedures, sequences, and materials that allow students to participate in activities to the maximum extent possible. For example, a student who cannot perform the variety of tasks necessary to independently search for and buy a list of grocery items may be taught how to select items from the shelf once the item has been pointed out by an adult and place the item carefully in the shopping cart. While this same student may not be able to calculate how much the food items will cost, he may be able to give the cashier a predetermined amount of money and receive change back. This partial participation is allowing the student to experience a series of very functional and fundamental daily living activities. Along with the concept of partial participation, educators and parents should also be cognizant of the varying levels of independence with which students may participate in activities simply because they may never achieve a completely independent level of functioning. Although some students will always require close supervision to cross streets safely, this does not justify the exclusion of this skill in a student's individualized educational program. Students should participate in activities with the maximum amount of independence that their individual skill level allows.

In the final analysis, it must be the *student*, not a curricular guide, that dictates *what* should be taught. The attempt here has been to provide a framework of curricular possibilities from which individual educational programs may be devised. The task force appreciated the opportunity to engage in the sharing of ideas and philosophies. Many outcomes were realized by this professional exchange, only one of which is this guide.

Domestic Domain

Components of a domestic skills curriculum should be a regular part of a student's weekly schedule. During the early elementary years, much of the instruction can occur as a natural result of classroom activities while other skills may be taught through role playing and structured and nonstructured play times. As the student progresses from the primary to the intermediate elementary level, environments other than the classroom may be more desirable to teach some skills (e.g., meal preparation, bedmaking). Teachers should be encouraged to investigate options for domestic skill training such as group homes, staff homes/apartments, and possibly even student homes when a community domestic site seems to be a more appropriate environment than the classroom. Since the overall goal is independence for the student in his current and subsequent living environment, it is essential to involve parents in the planning, implementation, and evaluation of each student's domestic program. As a student enters his last years of high school, it becomes especially important to antici- pate his future domestic environment upon graduation. Emphasis can then be placed on preparing a student for this specific environment as well as continuing to refine those skills necessary in any domestic environment.

A. *Elementary School: Philosophy*

At this level, instruction should be primarily directed towards: (1) practice of domestic activities as they relate to the natural requirements of the home and school environments; (2) frequent exposure to concept areas such as nutrition, wellness, family life, and social interactions appropriate to age and specific situations; (3) increasing independence in the performance of personal hygiene/grooming tasks; and (4) increasing student self-awareness of personal hygiene needs and routines.

As a student progresses through elementary school, he should be learning not only to perform the variety of domestic tasks suggested, but also to identify the *need* to perform these tasks (i.e., self-initiation). At the elementary level, many domestic skills can be taught as they naturally occur during the routine of a school day (e.g., wiping up spilled milk, dressing after swimming). Other suggested activities may be more effectively taught in a natural environment apart from the classroom or the school building (e.g., student's home, staff apartment, group home).

Special consideration should be given to determining *parental preferences* in terms of existing domestic routines, sequences, and materials/equipment available to the student in the home. This becomes increasingly important as the student begins to perform the domestic routines taught at school in the home.

B. *Middle School: Philosophy*

At this level, instruction should be directed primarily towards: (1) increasing the student's level of independence in performing domestic tasks including (a) expanding the student's use of tools and materials, (b) expanding the length of the domestic routines performed by the student, (c) identifying the need and initiating the perfor- mance of domestic tasks as part of the student's daily/weekly routine, and (2) demon- strating self-awareness in the areas of (a) nutrition, (b) family life including sex education, and (c) physical health and wellness.

Special consideration should be given to determining parental preferences in terms of existing domestic routines, sequences, and materials/equipment available to the student in the home.

If skills delineated in the following instructional sequence for middle school students cannot effectively be taught in the school facility, alternative community domestic sites (e.g., student's home, apartment, group home) should be utilized to teach these skills.

C. *High School: Philosophy*

At this level, the student is becoming an adult member of his household. Curricu- lar planning should continue to develop domestic skills necessary in grooming, hy- giene, health-education, family life including sex education, housecleaning, meal preparation, and clothing care activities. Sequencing skills and activities will be em- phasized including identifying the need to perform, select, plan, initiate, participate, maintain, and terminate activities. The student should acquire skills that allow him to perform some activities as independently as possible as well as those skills necessary to participate and interact with others in domestic activities. More specifically, the student should acquire skills which are necessary to meet the day-to-day needs and interests of the student as an individual, as well as those which allow him to become a contributing social member of a functioning household. In order for the educational program to be as preparatory as possible, postschool domestic environments need to be projected. Parental input is critical in determining and analyzing these post-school domestic environments for each student. The projected post-school domestic environment will affect the type of individualized domestic programming that should be provided for each student.

Domestic Domain Activities.

I. Personal Health Care—Elementary
  A. Toileting
    1. Indicate need to go or to be taken to the bathroom.
    2. Locate correct bathroom.
    3. Develop an individualized toileting routine.
    4. Recognize and use appropriate bathroom times within a schedule.
    5. Indicate the need to change wet/soiled pants.
  B. Dressing
    1. Identify clothing articles.
    2. Remove clothing articles appropriate to the situation (i.e., go to bed, come inside).
    3. Put on clothes in correct sequence.
    4. Put clothes on correctly (e.g., right side out, front and back correct, etc.).
    5. Develop/practice use of fasteners.
    6. Develop skills for footware (shoe tying, lacing, buckling).
    7. Choose clothing appropriate to situation, weather, and activity (e.g., choose everything you need to go outside in winter).
    8. Start to choose clothing that matches and/or "goes together" (e.g., stripes, plaids, colors).
  C. Grooming
    1. Wash hands/face (to include recognition of dirty versus clean).
    2. Comb hair.
    3. Clean eyeglasses.
    4. Use mirror to assure daily neatness.
    5. Brush teeth (consider use of electric tooth brush).
    6. Shower/bathe.
    7. Wash hair.
    8. Use hair dryer.
    9. Introduce deodorant usage/menstrual needs as necessary for individual students.
  D. First Aid/Safety
    1. Keep hands/objects out of mouth.
    2. Blow nose and dispose of Kleenex.
    3. Cover mouth when coughing, sneezing.
    4. Keep band-aids on, wash cut, keep dirt out.
    5. Introduce school nurse; talk about doctors, dentists, tools they use; and role play visits to doctor, dentist, hospital to lessen fear.

6. Recognize Mr. Yuk sign and poison as dangers and recognize items which are poisonous (e.g., cleaning fluids, house plants).
7. Recognize and report sickness or injury to adult.

E. Nutrition
1. Introduce wide variety of tastes and smells.
2. Present/select snack foods that are low-calorie and nutritious.
3. Classify foods into food groups.
4. Stress appropriate portions of food to eat.
5. Stress liquid/water intake.

F. Wellness
1. Develop daily exercise routine and a knowledge of what body parts each exercise strengthens.
2. Develop breathing and muscle relaxation methods.
3. Weight control.
4. Recognize and deal appropriately with emotions and feelings in self and others.

G. Family Life and Social Interactions
1. Recognize family members and types of families.
2. Discriminate boys/girls, men/women.
3. Locate/identify body parts and functions to include left/right on self.
4. Recognize signs of growth.
5. Recognize behavior appropriate to age in private (home) and public (school, community) locations.
6. Recognize family roles and responsibilities.

II. Personal Health Care—Middle School
A. Toileting
1. Review bathroom labels and expand to community bathroom labels (gents, lasses, damas, handicapped accessible).
2. Plan ahead for bathroom needs (e.g., go to bathroom before a trip, between classes, etc.).
3. Check appearance in bathroom mirror before leaving for class, work, etc.
4. Use variety of community bathroom facilities.

B. Dressing
1. Maintain neat appearance (e.g., clean clothes, zippers zipped, shoes tied, shirts tucked in, clothes not ripped, etc.).
2. Match outfits (e.g., color and design).
3. Choose clothing styles appropriate to age and current trends.
4. Determine daily clothing independent of adult supervision (e.g., weather, style, occasion, personal choice, etc.).
5. Determine when clothes need to be laundered and care for accordingly.

C. Grooming
1. Demonstrate skin care skills
   a. Cleanse skin.
   b. Moisturize skin.
   c. Medicate skin.
   d. Use make-up.
2. Demonstrate dental care skills.
   a. Toothbrush

      b. Floss
      c. Water pic
      d. What causes cavities, etc.
  3. Demonstrate hair care skills.
      a. Shampoo hair.
      b. Maintain daily neatness.
      c. Style/part hair.
      d. Dry hair with towel and electric hair dryers.
      e. Safety with electrical aides.
  4. Demonstrate shower/bath skills.
      a. Regulate water temperature.
      b. Shower/bathe safely and efficiently.
  5. Demonstrate shaving skills (personal option).
      a. Face
      b. Legs
      c. Underarms
      d. Razor safety
  6. Demonstrate nail care (personal option).
      a. Clean nails.
      b. File nails.
      c. Care for cuticles.
      d. Polish nails.
  7. Demonstrate menstrual hygiene skills.
      a. Use sanitary pads and tampons, including appropriate disposal.
      b. Change pads/tampons as needed throughout day.
      c. Carry items needed in order to be prepared.
  8. Use toiletries (personal option).
      a. Deodorant
      b. Mouthwash
      c. Cosmetics
      d. Colognes

D. First Aid/Safety
  1. Carry tissue, especially in community.
  2. Recognize emergencies and seek help (e.g., seizure, choking).
  3. Apply first aid for cuts and burns.
  4. Demonstrate wheelchair safety.
  5. Discuss medical personnel.

E. Nutrition
  1. Classify foods in four food groups.
  2. Estimate gross caloric content of foods in terms of weight gain or loss.
  3. Plan balanced meals using four food groups.
  4. Learn importance of carbohydrates, vitamins, minerals, and protein in diet.
  5. Select snack foods based on nutrition/calories.

F. Wellness
  1. Recognize reasons for and methods to control weight.
  2. Acquire various forms of exercise.
  3. Establish and demonstrate exercise routine.
  4. Demonstrate relaxation exercises.
  5. Recognize/channel emotions appropriately.

6. Develop awareness of body organs and functions (e.g., eyes, ears, lungs, stomach, etc.).
7. Develop awareness of smoking, drinking, and drug use and their effects on the body.

G. Family Life and Social Interactions
1. Identify sex organs and their functions.
2. Identify basic growth distinctions for both males and females.
3. Develop awareness of public versus private behavior.
4. Develop appropriate social/sexual interactions for age.
5. Discuss family change (e.g., birth, death, divorce, remarriage, foster families, group homes, etc.).
6. Continue to expand repertoire of information pertaining to family roles and responsibilities.

III. Personal Health Care—High School
At the high school level, emphasis should be placed on the maintenance of previously learned skills with emphasis on independence, rate, and quality. In addition to the previously taught skills (A–F) new information will be provided in the following areas [A–G continued from earlier years]:

G. Family Life and Social Interactions
1. Acquire strategies to deal with individual feelings.
2. Cope with environmental stimuli and peer pressure.
3. Continue to develop/demonstrate appropriate peer interactions.
4. Develop/demonstrate appropriate reactions to peer and adult pressure.
5. Learn about alternative life/family styles.
6. Obtain information about contraception.
7. Obtain genetic counseling.

Disability-Specific Curriculum

Students with unique needs arising from communication, behavioral, sensory and physical impairments are likely to require specialized instruction from teachers or other service providers. When special education teachers, teach braille communication skills or some other disability related skills, they are included here as part of a life management curriculum. They are, after all, skills students with disabilities use to manage their lives.

Instruction on such skills is so intense that it involves the time, specificity, and intensity equal to studying any other subject in a curriculum. There are areas of study that similar-age nonhandicapped students are not at all involved in or at least not for the same large blocks of curriculum time. Corn and Martinez (1977), for instance, report that four skill areas are commonly needed in a curriculum for students with visual impairments: (1) typing skills, (2) listening skills, (3) daily-living skills, and (4) orientation and travel skills.

1. Typing Skills—to provide alternatives to their own handwriting, which is hard to read and tiring to write, and for blind students, [relatively] unproductive.
2. Listening Skills—to allow students to make efficient use of hearing for listening to recorded texts and obtaining information from teacher presentations and class discussions. Tuning into sounds in the environment is also essential for the development of orientation and mobility skills by students with visual impairments. (Corn and Martinez 1977, 17).

Even though these skills are taught in the regular curriculum, they are included here in the functional life management skill components because they are not customarily taught as part of the regular curriculum as early, as intensively, or as fully, using all the specialized instructional strategies, as they need to be taught to students with visual impairments.

The other two skill areas a curriculum for students with visual impairments commonly requires—daily living skills and orientation and travel skills—seem more obvious candidates for placement as life management curriculum components:

3. Daily Living Skills—to provide independence and feeling of self-worth. These include the "how-to's" of daily living from good grooming to cooking a simple meal, to organizing and locating belongings.
4. Orientation and travel skills—to teach the basics of movement and travel skills as needed in different places. These skills are often taught by a special education service provider called an orientation and mobility (O&M) teacher (Corn and Martinez 1977, 17).

Each disability requires certain predictable disability-specific interventions. For example, personal and social adjustment, are a likely priority for students with behavior problems. Because communication is so rudimentary to all life management and so many students in special education need different kinds of intensive and specialized work in this area, we include it as a discipline within the functional life management curriculum. For students who have hearing impairment, developing their speech, auditory skills, speech reading, and signing language requires a major focus somewhere in the curriculum. Sometimes these topics are treated as any other basic subjects in the language arts discipline; at other times they are included as a life management curriculum component. Ideally, the communication skills in the life management component of a student's total curriculum would be taught directly and intensely for purposeful infusion throughout that student's entire curriculum.

Teachers' professional preparation textbooks, trade books, and literature by professionals are sources of curriculum for students with specific disabilities. Many texts about providing developmental and corrective curriculum and instruction to individuals with specific handicaps are available.

Comprehensive curriculum guides written for specific disability groups are resources available to teachers. Disability-specific life management curriculum components are often included as options along with identical, parallel, and practical academic components. Teachers should now be able to figure out life management components and their relationships to core curriculum even if they are grouped and described slightly differently. Teachers can determine if intensive skill training in student use of disability-specific communications skills are taught in life management or other components.

The *Texas School for the Blind Curriculum*[1] is one example of a total curriculum plan for students with one disability. The curriculum of the Texas School for the Blind is a comprehensive, skill-based curriculum for academic, visually impaired students and lower-functioning, multihandicapped students. The academic curriculum includes all state-required skills for K–12 courses leading to high school graduation; however, many of these skills have been modified to make them appropriate for visually impaired students. For example, map skills in social studies courses now refer to "visual or tactual" maps; a biology skill about genetics was revised to include knowledge of genetics "as it applies to the individual student's visual impairment, if applicable"; and skills in the use of adaptive communications equipment and methods, such as braille, are included in the language arts courses. In addition, there are compensatory skill areas that include functional living instruction, such as social skills and self-care skills, and skills unique to the population of visually impaired students, such as orientation and mobility. The alternative academic curriculum, designed for students functioning more than two years below grade level (but higher than first-grade level), has courses that parallel the academic courses. However, there are fewer skills per course, and there is a strong emphasis on functional living skills. The curriculum for the early childhood level focuses on communication, social skills, cognition, daily living skills, motor skills, perceptual awareness, and play skills. The curriculum for older, nonacademic students emphasizes vocational skills. A curriculum for deaf-blind students is being developed.

A student's IEP objective can identify an entire existing curriculum or designated parts. Certain objectives may be so individualized they do not appear in any existing curriculum materials. These are unique objectives developed as priorities for the individual. Extracting powerful goals and objectives unique to the individual student calls for an astute teacher and a workable process.

Individual-Specific Curriculum

To determine which curricular activities will mean the most for individuals with disabilities, our educational system provides many opportunities for discerning input. One such arena is the individualized educational program group that develops programs for students with special education and related services needs. Additional arenas include student homes and other kinds of school-based meetings between school personnel, parents and parent representatives, and a range of trained professionals.

Assumptions for Making Decisions

Many approaches to determining priority objectives for individuals exist. Several methods are presented here as an introduction to this challenging area in special education. Teachers and others involved can choose the most powerful potential objectives for a student in special education from the multitude available.

Making decisions on the basis of empowerment assumes that it is possible to select *more powerful* goals and objectives over *less powerful* possibilities for individual students in special education. More powerful goals and objectives empower learners to perform personally meaningful activities that could not be done without calculated intervention. Activities may be of any nature (i.e., highly academic, social, basic, self-help). This leads to the first of three supportive assumptions.

Supportive Assumption One. First is the concept that personally *meaningful* activities are more powerful objectives than those having no personal meaning for the student. Meaningful activities are those that students with disabilities can participate in as fully as possible that are the same school and nonschool situations enjoyed by their same-age nonhandicapped peers and other members of society.

Supportive Assumption Two. The second assumption is that it is the disabled student, when appropriate, and the persons who know the student well who are in the best position to help identify the present and future meaningful life activities for the student. Decision-making strategies are important for directing group processes that are to develop objectives for future home, school, and community life activities. Of all the activities that could be chosen, it seems reasonable that this group, working together, could identify the most personally meaningful activities. A decision-making process is essential as a basis for planning the upcoming year and future curriculum.

Supportive Assumption Three. The third supportive assumption is that, in most cases, objectives empowering learners to perform personally meaningful activities that generalize to more than one situation and to different people are more powerful than objectives that take the same time and instruction, but only teach students to perform activities in one situation or environment with a known other person.

Teachers need to learn to identify the student's personally meaningful *current* life activities, projected *five-year* activities (or some other projected number of years), and then for activities *one* year into the future. They also need to learn how to extract the powerful objectives for an individual from the many that are available. The process of making these identifications and choices, which is described here, will enable teachers to extract generalized objectives when they:

1. Take a leadership role in some systematic multi-discipline problem solving process to determine objectives powerful to individuals.
2. Identify and chart meaningful current major life activities of an individual student.
3. Predict and chart meaningful and seemingly feasible major life activities three to five years in the future.
4. Predict participation in life activities one year from the present.
5. Analyze information to determine potentially powerful instructional goals and objectives.

A Matrix-Based Process for Determining Powerful Curriculum Objectives

One effective way to move toward determining powerful priority goals and objectives for individual students is to use a matrix-based decision-making process. This organizational scheme can guide IEP group deliberations toward intelligent collaborative decisions about priority goals and objectives in behalf of students with many complex special needs.

A group facilitator, using the matrix-based decision-making process, introduces the concept and practice of organizing the large amount of student-related information on three printed matrices. The matrices are identical in format, but they represent different time periods in the target student's life. IEP team members can copy the same matrix and use it to define present student performance and predict future and desirable student performance in meaningful life activities. Members can label the three matrices parts I, II, and III. Part I is for recording information about present (current) student performance in life activities. Part II records projections of anticipated student participation in activities three years in the future. Part III is for determining new or expanded activities for a given student by the same time next year, a one-year cycle. Information on this third matrix is the basis for determining and developing "powerful" annual goals and short-term objectives, many of which are unique to the individual student. Figure 9.1 shows the three matrices.

A team's mutual involvement in completing these matrices expedites discussion of important information preliminary to deriving annual goals and priority short-term objectives. In the process, members need to extract goals of increased and appropriate student participation in a variety of current and future life situations.

The concepts involved in the matrix-based decision-making process to guide educational program planning are not new. The process integrates several practices different experts in the field of education for students with disabilities recommend. In essence, it is a form of ecological inventory. The principles of partial and full participation in current and subsequent natural environments is described by Brown et al. (1979) and Brown et al. (1980). Brown and his associates were pioneers in finding ways to apply current and subsequent environment and ecological inventory strategies to developing curriculum content. They also pioneered describing deliberate teaching of skills that can be generalized—that is, are

Figure 9.1 Guide to Identifying Meaningful Activities for Individuals

Part 1 Current Activities		Home	School	Community
	Self-Help			
	Work			
	Leisure use and Social Interaction			
	Application of Academic Learning			

Part II Activities 3 Years from Present		Home	School	Community
	Self-Help			
	Work			
	Leisure Use and Social Interaction			
	Application of Academic Learning			

Part III Activities 1 Year from Present		Home	School	Community
	Self-Help			
	Work			
	Leisure Use and Social Interaction			
	Application of Academic Learning			

applicable and usable in more than one situation (Gaylord-Ross et al. 1984, Horner, Sprague, and Wilcox 1982, Sailor and Guess 1983, Stokes and Baer 1977, Billingsley 1984).

The matrix process described here incorporates the importance of describing *home, school,* and *community* environments—and potential student roles in these from Clark (1979, 1980) and Schwartz (1980). It focuses on the concept of preparing for lifetime careers, not just vocational careers, with settings that include home, school, occupation, and community. Examples of roles and responsibilities (or activities) in lifetime careers might include being a student, worker, consumer, citizen, or family member.

The daily living skills and self-help activities included on the matrices stem from the work of Brolin (1976, 1978, 1983), Brolin and Kokaska (1979), and Kokaska and Brolin (1985).

With the matrix-based format, input is requested in three environments, or situations, of student functioning: *home, school,* and *community.* The parents provide information about home functioning; school personnel, about school functioning. Community participation information could come from parents and school personnel plus other informants such as club leaders, friends, and so on.

The information for each situation of student functioning (home, school, and community) is broken into four kinds of activities within each environment (see left-hand columns of the matrix): (1) self-help, (2) work, (3) leisure use and social interactions, and (4) application of academic learning. *Self-help* includes such self-care activities as communicating the need for help with personal needs such as toileting, eating, sleeping, medical care, cooking, shopping, transportation, and the like. *Work* includes paid work, unpaid volunteer work, and/or chores around the home. Additional work would include preparing for schoolwork, working at jobs outside the home, and doing some kinds of volunteer work. *Leisure use and social interactions* includes any time spent without obligations such as pursuing recreation, entertainment, or hobbies. It can be spent at home alone or with others. Also included are social interactions with nondisabled people such as talking in various situations, taking music lessons, joining conversations, and going to church or other group functions. The application of academic learning or *practical academics* means reading functionally to find one's way around a shopping center, taking the garbage out when full, feeding fish the correct amount of food, paying clerks in stores in correct monetary units, and so on. Table 9.1 summarizes activities in each of these four areas.

Identifying and Charting Meaningful Current Activities

The information on current student performance in major life activities is the basis for future projections of desirable student activities. Describ-

Table 9.1 Kinds of Activities

SELF-CARE
Self-help activities including communication of need for aid in caring for personal needs: toileting, eating, sleeping, medical care, cooking, shopping, transportation, and so on.

WORK
Paid and unpaid work including volunteer work: work chores around the home—with or without being paid an allowance, running errands, school work, volunteer work, paid work outside the home, and so on.

LEISURE USE AND SOCIAL INTERACTIONS
Any time spent without obligations: recreation, entertainment, hobbies; enjoying leisure time at home when alone; enjoying time with friends; joining conversations; taking music lessons; going to church, parties, and other functions, and so on.

APPLICATION OF ACADEMIC LEARNINGS
Using reading skills functionally to find way around town; using math skills functionally to pay for items; using writing skills functionally to write thank you letters; reading books to learn information, and so on.

ing current student activities depends on different kinds of assessment information. Presentations of student performance information typically range in degree of specificity. Most depend on criterion-referenced data from formal and informal observation. Part I, describing the student's *present* performance level and participation activities, just involves recording information from various members of the team. Each contributes helpful background information, describes current activities, and gives assessment results. Teachers might include a *brief* school history and summary of present school performance based on assessment and other data. Parents might include information about the student's special interests, their concerns, characteristics of the child in the home situation, and the child's performances at home.

This initial recording process does not involve making choices or decisions at this point. Yet it is a potentially valuable communication process. It provides people with a common background of information about the child. As people hear input from each other, they learn more about the child and may even notice the child is capable of doing things they did not realize he could do. Parents can learn, for example, that their child, who does not dress himself at home, gets dressed and undressed independently for swimming during physical education. Or teachers can learn that a student talks spontaneously at home but not at school. Gathering information about present levels of student performance and participation in different situations is also vital to evaluating and proposing future objectives and extracting the top-priority annual goals and objectives.

Predicting and Charting Life Activities Three to Five Years Away

Part II moves to the student's more distant future. Three-to-five-year projections were chosen as a way to expand everyone's view of the student. This jump from present to more distant functioning makes planning for the immediate year more relevant and effective. It is also valuable for parents to participate in this long-range process as it helps them work with the reality of their situation—one they might easily be tempted to avoid—and plan a practical future for their child. For example, the mother of a twenty-year-old man, who read at the first-grade level and had few other academic skills, said at an IEP meeting that she was looking forward to the following year when her son would be living in the dorm at the local university. What this parent did not see, even though she was an involved and caring person, was that her son would probably never be admitted to the university as a regular student given his current functioning and past performance. Professionals had not helped her look at the boy's future years before or at least had not done so consistently. No one had even instituted a transition plan and related curriculum. Earlier long-range projections might have enabled this parent to work with her son in making more down-to-earth plans, ones the youth could have learned to fulfill with pride.

To guide the process of projecting future activities, team members ask such questions as, What kinds of activities would other age-equivalent students be doing five years from the present (or three years from the present if three years is chosen as the projected time frame)? What would the family and others recommend for this particular student five years from the present. In order to do these and other activities, what rudiments or enabling skills is it most critical to teach in the meantime?

Predicting Participation in Life Activities for the Next Year

Members of the IEP team, including the student when appropriate, use assessment information, the student's current functioning (part I) and the projected three-to-five-year activities (part II) to begin part III. They might then ask, What does this student need to learn by a year from now that would contribute to accomplishing the projected three-to-five-year activities? Answers to this question are recorded in part III, and they become the basis for the IEP annual goals and short-term instructional objectives.

Determining Powerful Goals and Objectives

Having completed these three matrices (current, three to five years in the future, and one year in the future), everyone involved has a broader, more informed perspective for determining annual goals and short-term objectives for the disabled individual. Members can then consider potential objectives according to their degree of functionality. Function is the heart of any life management curriculum. A person's natural, required, or expected activities (or functions) become the foundation of any life management curriculum (as well as objectives in other curriculum components).

Types of objectives, according to their degree of functionality, as identified by Billingsley (1984) are *generalized outcomes and functional, functional only,* and *neither generalized outcomes nor functional.* Table 9.2 clarifies the differences between objectives that promote generalized outcomes and are functional, those that are only functional, and those that promote neither generalized outcomes nor

Table 9.2   Objectives and Their Degree of Functionality*

GENERALIZED OUTCOMES AND FUNCTIONAL

- By 6/83 when requested to or at appropriate time, P. will assist in dressing herself with 70 percent accuracy.

- J. will spontaneously initiate the sign for toilet at 100% accuracy.
- Tom will demonstrate the ability to shop at three different supermarkets

> Safeway (2427 River Road)
> U Mart (416 Santa Clara Street)
> Fred Meyer (3000 River Road)

for up to fifteen specific brand grocery items. Picture cards will be used as the grocery list. Performance includes traveling to the store, selecting items, paying for the purchase using a next-dollar strategy, and transporting purchases back to the school.

FUNCTIONAL ONLY

- Given the task of cleaning the table, P. will be able to carry her plate, glass, and silverware to cottage kitchen sink with verbal cue by 6/18/89.

NEITHER GENERALIZED OUTCOMES NOR FUNCTIONAL

- P. will match a numeral to a number of objects (through 17) by indicating the correct number after being given three or four choices. He will reach 85 percent accuracy on this activity within thirty consecutive class days.

Source: Adapted from F. Billingsley "Where Are the Generalized Outcomes," *JASH* 9:3: 188, Table 1, "Examples of Objective Types." With additions from B. Wilcox and G. T. Bellamy *Design of High School Programs for Severely Handicapped Students,* portion of Figure 4.7, "Illustrative IEP Objectives." (Baltimore, Md.: Paul Brookes, 1982) p. 59.

functionality. With these differences in mind, teachers can guide team delibera-tions towards objectives that result in generalized outcomes and are functional. Objectives with this degree of functionality are empowering.

To be considered a generalized outcome, Billingsley (1984) states that "per-formance should be observed (a) outside the training situation, (b) in the presence of a nontrainer when the presence of some manager was required for the task, or (c) in as-needed or spontaneous situations (e.g., "Judy will sign 'toilet' when she has to go to the bathroom")" (p. 188).

To be recognized as a *generalized outcome,* an objective is written to describe performances for generalization across situations and across persons: ". . . ad-aptation within natural environments requires a generalized outcome in order that skills may be performed in each appropriate setting and in the presence of persons other than the original trainer(s)" (Billingsley 1984, 186, derived from Brown, Nietupski, and Hamre-Nieupski 1976).

Billingsley (1984, 186–87) states that ". . . it seems probable that state-ments of generalized outcome will act to promote the cross-situational measure-ment of instructional effects. Unless generalization is prescribed by objectives, educators may find themselves evaluating pupil progress toward stimulus-bound performance."

Objectives stated as generalized outcomes are more powerful than functional objectives; in turn, functional objectives are more powerful than objectives that are neither generalized outcomes nor functional. Within these guidelines, how-ever, it is valuable to recognize that it is not always possible, for instance, to teach practical academic skills (functional skills) and simultaneously provide opportu-nity for generalized training. It is important to teach functional objectives because later, or in a different component of curriculum, they can be incorporated for use in different natural situations. Hopefully no major objectives for individuals will be neither generalized nor functional.

Application of the Matrix Process

It is important to focus on the process, not on the fact that the student may have a disability. The example used here involves a student, Tara, who is young and happens to be nonspeaking. Tara also has severe orthopedic disabilities.[2] The same process can be equally productive for students of any school age and any disability of any severity. It helps to try involving all the persons who share concerns about one child in a dialogue. The example shows how informal comments can provide foundation for the more formal aspects of the meeting to follow. The process may take longer than most meetings about the student, but the potential positive impact has a long-term beneficial effect.

Tara.   To introduce Tara, a five-year-old student who receives special education and selected services, we use comments from her mother. Tara's mother keeps herself well informed about Tara's program and about new advances in the field. Tara's father is also supportive, but today he is at work. Tara's mother has been interested in having Tara's program as academic as possible. She says about Tara: "Tara is our pride and joy. She's a happy child, though often frustrated—understandably so. Her greatest frustration, and ours, is her inability to talk. We work with her constantly to help her in this as much as possible.

"At *home* Tara spends an average of two hours at a meal. She is able to self-feed now with elbow assistance, feeding herself about 10 to 30 percent of the mealtime. It's impractical for us to allow more time for this during meals.

"Tara has just started being potty trained and is doing well. She is placed in her potty chair at regular times throughout the day. She seems happy with her new independence in this area.

"For communication, Tara uses each of several different communication board overlays. She has these on her lap tray, which we take off her wheelchair and bring in to be near her at home.

"We recently realized that we've been developing personal communication signals at home that won't help Tara communicate with others outside the family. Tara can communicate requests and statements to us—but the ways she does this are pretty much the same for each. Just degrees or nuances of her expressions clue us into her specific message. Then, too, we know her routine and anticipate her needs. We know what she means, but her teacher is helping us realize that we may be the only ones who can read her signals.

"Tara seems to learn how to communicate her needs as one of the last steps in learning something new. For example, we kept waiting for her to initiate communication about wanting to be toileted. We left her in diapers for four years before starting toilet training. Now we find that she has the control, and she does well with scheduled times. So now we are teaching her to request potty-time. And this has been the pattern with her—first learning the activity, then learning to request it. It seems to work for her. We just hope that she becomes more assertive about communicating her needs and wants *when* she needs and wants them!

"We see confirmations each day of Tara's brightness and awareness. We're not surprised that she has tested out above age level in everything except motor control, and we're really pleased she's doing so well. For Tara, we feel the sky is the limit as far as her potential is concerned."

Identifying and Charting Meaningful Current Life Activities.   A group process of putting information about Tara into a matrix is the first step in extracting the present or potentially meaningful participatory activities of the student. This first focus is current, or present, major life activities of the individual at home, in school, and in community situations.

A team leader and all team members collaborate to assist each other in formulating statements that reflect a synopsis of this information expressed in a way that everyone involved in the process can understand. Members help each other to pinpoint and clearly state activities and so fill in the matrix. The matrix format with its limited space forces members to consolidate and focus on the most important information. The staff invited Tara's mother to start because even though she liked the idea of the matrix-based process, she was anxious to "get her part over."

HOME. When asked to identify Tara's important home participation activities, her mother stated them. As Tara's mother reiterated those she thought most personally meaningful to Tara, a group leader wrote the major points on a large wall chart (see Fig. 9.2).

From the home (home/self-help on the matrix) perspective, Tara's mother mentioned these *self-help* activities as being most important: (1) self-feeding (though still limited), (2) helping in taking off and putting on zip jackets, shoes, and socks, (3) participating in potty training; soon to start pointing to a picture to indicate "potty," (4) moving (on floor) to desired toy and dragging it out for play, and (5) communicating desires by using communication board, especially at mealtime.

Other group members were interested to learn more about Tara's responsibilities at home. *Work* was the next area to describe. At first Tara's mother didn't think that Tara did any work at home, but when encouraged and given examples by team members, she identified work-oriented activities centered around self-improvement. Tara works with her mom on basic concepts such as letter-sound association and concepts of sizes. She works on speech articulation of a few sounds in attempts to make recognizable initial sounds and vowel sounds. Finally, Tara's mother reports that she works on therapy carry-over such as weight bearing and head position. Her mother could think of no job or work for which Tara took responsibility (i.e., telling her mom when a plant needed watering).

Sometimes parents have difficulty thinking in terms of *leisure and social activities* because they are so busy concentrating on the physical, learning, or behavioral disorders of their child. Tara has learned, though, to participate in some family-centered special times. Her mother says she listens and follows along when her father or sister reads to her. She also watches TV, entertains herself with a Casio keyboard or other toys when positioned on her side for doing so, entertains herself by scooting around on the floor, and rolls a ball by pushing it to a partner.

Academic activities were easy for this mother to describe as she takes her child's learning seriously. She is well educated and has extremely high expectations for Tara. She constantly reinforces and supplements school learning and Tara's communication abilities. Tara signals two or three picture words on the communication board (i.e., *more, please, yogurt, you feed me*). She sorts socks by color and size. She chooses between *right* and *left* during specific dressing activities. Tara's mother is most excited about her progress in forming her mouth to clue persons to the first sound of food and other things she is choosing (she

Figure 9.2 Current Life Activities

	A. Home	B. School	C. Community
Self-Help	1. Self-feeding (10%–30% of mealtime) — Finger feeds and spoon feeds with assist at elbow. 2. Dressing — Assists in removing and putting on zip-up jackets, shoes, socks, and plastic braces. 3. Toileting — Placed on potty at regular intervals during this potty-training period. Potty picture has been added to all communication board overlays — not yet accessed. 4. Moves by inching in prone position or by rolling — to proximity of desired toy or objects, then grasps it and pulls it out for play. 5. Communicates desires using communication bd., especially at mealtime.	1. Self-feeding on occasion — prefers to be fed. 2. Given a yes/no question — responds with yes or no signal. Teacher and aides must anticipate needs and wants, then phrase a yes/no question for her to answer. 3. Toileting — attends school with training pants. Placed on potty at regular intervals. Staff is beginning to encourage her to signal need by verbalization, manual sign, or communication board.	N/A
Work	1. Works with mother on Unicorn Board w/ communication overlays. 2. Works with mother on conceptual skills (i.e., counting, letter-sound association, letter order of alphabet, more and less gradations of size, same and different). 3. Works with mother on speech articulation of oral musculature. 4. Works with mother on therapy carry-over such as weight bearing, arm extension, head position.	1. Turn-taking with response on cue in class activities is asked of her. 2. Learning to identify shapes, colors, sizes, letters, sounds. 3. Accesses Apple computer with Unicorn expanded keyboard for work on concepts and communication.	(unpaid) Cooperates with live and videotaped sessions demonstrating use of augmentative communication devices. Cooperates with professors and other students who work with her on communicating.

	A. Home	B. School	C. Community
Leisure and Social Activities	1. Listens and follows along while being read to (1½ hr.+/day). 2. Watches TV — especially educational preschool programs such as Sesame Street (1 hr./day). 3. Entertains self with Casio keyboard or other toys when positioned lying on her side (or she can roll to this position from any other) (1½ hr.+/day). 4. Entertains self by scooting around on floor (1½ hr.+/day). 5. Rolls ball by pushing it, back and forth with partner.	1. Plays "Stop + Go" whistle game w/regular kids during mainstreamed recess. (She signals stop and go on comm. bd.). 2. Interacts w/ handicapped peers thru eye gaze, vocalizations, changes in body tone, facial expression, laughter. 3. Interacts w/ nonhandicapped peers silently through eye gaze (if she does not feel threatened), facial expression, laughter, body position + tone. 4. Enjoys rhythm and music activities.	1. Goes swimming with mother on Saturday mornings. 2. Goes horseback riding once a week. 3. Goes to concerts with mother. 4. Occasionally goes to temple with family. 5. Goes to the park. 6. Goes on walks with mom or dad. 7. Goes to visit family friends.
Application of Academic Learnings	1. Signals two- or three-word utterances on her communication board including: More please, and you feed me, yogurt-please at meals in requesting food. 2. Sorts by shape, color, size. 3. Chooses between right and left during activities such as putting on shoes or brace. Uses her right or left arm on request. 4. Makes proper mouth position for certain letters: "b month" (which could also make the sound if breath control coordinated) is made as a communication for a desired "b" thing such as bread.	Counts classmates to see how many lunches are needed. Use four pictures on communication board to signal yogurt, veggies, rice, and please on communication board.	Chooses to go into/out of swimming pool. Chooses biggest horse. Matches m sound on lips to choose music.

cannot yet coordinate both her breath stream and mouth position enough to say words or their beginning sounds.

SCHOOL. Next it was time for school-based members to add to the matrix. Individual team members filled in different kinds of activities at school. Since several special education and related services persons were involved, there was more information than space on the matrix. Thus the format made the participants focus on certain activities more than others for this problem-solving session. The group zeroed in on activities that seemed most important for Tara's current and future participation in school and other major life areas.

Tara's mother added a few comments as she is well informed about the school program and Tara's activities within it. (Read vertically under "School" on Fig. 9.2.)

COMMUNITY. Community participation refers to nonhome- and nonschool-based student participation. Educational programs are currently concerning themselves with student participation in communities more intensely than ever before. Tara's self-help activities in the community—in nonhome and nonschool situations—are extremely limited. Upon examination, the team could think of no self-help activity that this child did in the community. With further deliberation, though, they realized that she uses gesture and vocal responses with family to indicate yes and no to their questions when away from home and school. They also realized that she did not use communication boards outside the home and school. Again, the matrix was a tool, helping team members look at Tara's present functioning and functional needs in different environments. (Read vertically under "Community" in Fig. 9.2.)

Summary of Current Student Activities. The matrix now shows a thorough listing of Tara's current major life activities. In writing it together, team members made some important discoveries. Tara's teacher learned that Tara won't respond well to loudly voiced questions. She learned this from Tara's mother after expressing her frustration with the lack of Tara's response in class. Tara's parents found out that Tara is having great success with the new "Stop and Go" game at mainstreamed recess. The assessment specialist voiced concern that Tara is not showing what she knows at school. The physical therapist reiterated the importance of proper positioning and handling, especially in the classroom environment.

The only major obstacle to Tara's success with academics is her lack of a fluent and versatile communication system and her frequent reluctance to try indicating a choice on a communication board with her fist or to answer yes and no. This also blocks social interaction on the conversational level. Her shyness complicates the difficulty, especially since she is unwilling at present to let others know what she knows.

Predicting and Charting Tara's Life Activities Three to Five Years in the Future. The team moves to the next step, using the best information available to them at the time to hypothesize about probable meaningful activities for Tara in the future. This team chose a three-year instead of a five-year target because Tara is so young. There has not yet been enough time to gauge her speed in learning new materials, and her interests and social skills were only beginning to emerge.

The team considered two school environmental alternatives for Tara by the time she was age eight:

1. Tara could be mainstreamed into a regular class with a personal aide. This aide would help with schoolwork, feeding, toileting, and taking Tara to meet the bus for special needs children after school. The bus would then take Tara to a physical and occupational therapy facility where she would have physical therapy twice a week and occupational therapy twice a week. An itinerant speech therapist would meet with Tara at the regular school site three times a week, working with her as she tries to communicate in regular class activities.
2. Tara could be enrolled in a regular school-based special education program for students with physical disabilities. On-site therapy would be provided. The special education classroom would be her main base. She would leave this class for certain periods each day for various therapies and for mainstreaming into regular classes. She would be mainstreamed into specific activities for specific curriculum subjects and for opportunities to interact with nondisabled peers.

Tara's current classroom teacher said that she thought that Tara should be mainstreamed full-time if indeed a personal aide was a possibility. Tara's mother was open to discussing this, but she felt that Tara should have physical therapy as an integral part of her more energetic time of the day (during regular school hours, especially the morning). With a special education class as her base, she could receive an individualized program that would allow for therapy and give her more opportunities with computer-assisted learning. Tara would need intensive and specialized training in learning to participate fully in the school environment. She needs to be taught efficient use of several alternate response methods. Her mother felt that Tara would be better able to continue with her happy, achieving self-image if she were working at least part of the time at her own pace within such a classroom, away from the pressures of the regular classroom. Then through some mainstreamed hours Tara would gain a larger perspective on her peer identity. The psychologist agreed with Tara's mom that Tara's special needs in computer access, communication, and self-concept could best be met through concentrated, specialized instruction from a special education professional. The therapists collectively voiced their preference for and effectiveness with children who did not come to them worn out after a day of school. Also they could coordinate therapy goals to help Tara participate in the educational program with improved quality of movement.

The team anticipated that, considering Tara's current rate of learning and what she has tested out as knowing, she would be at or above age level in academic work in three years time. Though no one can really know how much her apraxia (motor problems with speech) may affect her in the long run, the team felt that with extra encouragement and special help, Tara would have every opportunity to achieve the highest potentials possible for her. This would not be possible, however, without a communication system that worked easily for her so she could relay most of what she had to say. The team stated that Tara would need well-matched augmentative communication systems with which she was relatively fluent by the time three years had elapsed. Communication devices would enable her to respond in a regular class discussion, to do her "written" schoolwork, and to hold conversations with peers and others.

Present performance information on Tara's current exploratory work with the voice output Light Talker microcomputer-based communication aid (activated by a head-worn sensor) interested the team. They thought this would be a viable and effective method of "oral" communication if she could access it easily and quickly. Speech output communication, even though computer-synthesized speech, would improve all areas in which Tara was currently inhibited. With this device, Tara would be able to make essential self-help requests, initiate conversations and interactions with others more effectively, and be able to respond and learn academics. She would not be slowed down by her response methods and could relay more information for each physical selection. The team's concern with an effective communication aid is a good example of a targeted three-year goal. Use of the communication system could be integrated into the curriculum and school activities by the three-year mark. Figure 9.3 shows how this goal is integrated into the matrix.

Predicting Activities for the Next Year. The various intersections of the one-year matrix resulted in the most intense dialogue (see Fig. 9.4). Team members frequently referred to the current activities matrix (part I) and the predicted three-year matrix (part II). For Tara to stay at age level or above in academic skills, and to gain ability in social and self-help skills, she will have to approach certain major challenges in the next year. Primarily these have to do with independence and speed in giving responses and her acceptance of her teacher, teacher's aides, peers, and others as interaction partners in communication. The group jumped first to the school/work matrix cell.

SCHOOL/WORK. From the information gained during the plotting of current activities, the team concluded that communication boards are not working as an output mode in the classroom for Tara to show the teacher what she wants. Due to her disability, she will only be physically able to accurately and consistently touch four areas on any communication board. Tara must learn to use an easier, faster response method with more response options within this next year. Otherwise, without at least one working response mode for Tara, the teacher would not be able to gear her academic learning to Tara's pace or conceptual level, and Tara would fall short of participating in activities projected as targets for her in the school/work intersection of the three-year matrix.

Tara's teacher and speech, physical, and occupational therapists concluded that perhaps the communication-board system with selection by pointing with her hands should not be the sole solution for communicating what she knows about her schoolwork. Tara experienced imprecision of motor movements, and it took extended amounts of time and effort to make a selection of only the four locations on her board she could touch with consistency.

Tara's mother stated that Tara was pretty clear in her communications if people knew how to watch Tara's face, gestures, and attempts at forming beginning sounds on her lips. The team acknowledged that the two of them did have a seemingly clear communication system worked out. People who do not know the child that intimately, though, need more precise signals from her. The three-year predicted activities of passing out songbooks at church and engaging peers in conversations and interacting in regular class activities were examples to work toward. The mother understood and joined discussions on which methods and strategies might be best.

Tara was concentrating so hard on the needed hand movements to point to a communication board that she could handle only a few cognitive tasks per lesson. It seems she could think much more readily than she could point with her hands. Thus eliminating unnecessary physical frustration might increase her motivation as well as enhance the speed at which she could learn and demonstrate her progress. Someone suggested the ETRAN eye-gaze as an alternative response method because Tara's eye control seems quicker and more accurate than her hand control. Team members looked at pictures of an eye-gaze ETRAN (see Fig. 9.5). The professional team hypothesized that Tara could learn to look at choices placed in four corner positions in an ETRAN in front of her quicker than she can touch four positions on a board of picture choices (communication board) placed flat on her lap tray. They also liked the idea that she could be naturally facing the person with whom she communicates as the person watches her eyes. They felt that using response choices representing concepts being taught and tested put on the ETRAN would be functional. They also felt Tara's physical indications by eye movement would be more physically accurate than her hand and arm movements. They concluded that her rate of making choices on an ETRAN would be faster, allowing more choices in a limited amount of time. Questions arose about portability and ease of teacher use. These legitimate concerns were addressed.

The team, including physical and occupational therapists, agreed they should add use of an ETRAN to Tara's repertoire of activities they predict she would want to be doing a year from the present. They would also set up a plan to collect data comparing the effectiveness of the two communication systems for use in school lessons. They would assess its possibilities for generalized use across school and nonschool situations.

Because Tara has easy command of eye-gaze and eye-shift, the team decided that Tara would use the ETRAN board eye gaze in class as one major response mode. She would continue to use her fist in direct-selection communication boards for other communications such as requests for toileting, playing games, and indicating what she wants from four choices in lessons.

Figure 9.3 Activities Three Years from Present

	A. Home	B. School	C. Community
Self-Help	1. Feeding — Feeding self 75% of mealtimes. 2. Dressing — Takes off shoes and socks, pulls down open-front jackets or shirts, once started over arms. 3. Toileting — 100% potty-trained. Will indicate need. 4. Mobility — Crawls in a more efficient manner. Operates electric wheelchair. 5. Wipes off face with washcloth. 6. Communication — Make recognizable (to family) sounds for certain words. 7. Gets into and out of bed (mattress on floor).	1. Have a way of getting attention. 2. Request help when needed. 3. Request help with toileting. 4. Request help with reading (page turning, unknown words). 5. Operate electric wheelchair.	1. Know survival signs appropriate to age level and experience. 2. Know address and phone number. Communicate this through aug. communication aid. 3. Maintain head in mid-line while on short walks through interesting territory. 4. Choose items on shopping expeditions by pointing and thus indicating this to salesperson.
Work	1. Put clothes in appropriate piles. 2. Pick up small toys and put them away in container (drops them into it). 3. Work with mother on sitting independently. 4. Work on supported standing (arms weight bearing on supportive surface, while mom helps keep legs straight). 5. Work on learning to spell with aug. comm. aids.	1. Works on spelling w/augmentative communication device. 2. Demonstrate to regular teacher she can read her reading lessons. 3. Works math on computer. 4. Respond in class with communication device during individual or in-class activities and discussions.	(unpaid) Cooperatively participate in augmentative communication demonstrations. Pass out songbooks in church school (indicates to children they pickup songbooks from her tray) as people come in door.

	A. Home	B. School	C. Community
Leisure and Social Activities	1. Play with computer games (including drawing) by self with access through augmentative communication device. 2. Entertain self by crawling around, getting toys out, and playing with them. 3. Play with musical instruments without assistance, especially drums, Kalimba, Casio. 4. Read with page-turning by self if book is set up for this. 5. Listen to music. 6. Watch TV. 7. Play with clay, watercolors, or other art materials.	1. Engage peers and others in simple conversations through augmentative communication device or aides. 2. Interact dynamically with regular kids during mainstreamed recesses by playing games she can play (i.e., hangman and guessing games, with communication device or electrical wheelchair mobility games such as follow the leader, chasing balls.	1. Swim with assistance (may float in supine position unassisted but with help close at hand). 2. Attend movies with parents or other adult friends. 3. Ride horseback with assistance once a week. During ride keeps head up (3/4 up for entire ride of 1/2 hour). 4. Go on walks with adult friends and to concerts or movies with same. 5. Go shopping with mother. 6. Take similar age friend to the movies.
Application of Academic Learning	1. Help mother choose coding for communication device options (if Light Talker then helps mother choose functional categories and symbol sequences for certain messages). 2. Play problem-solving games on computer with nondisabled children. 3. Draw on Apple computer screen with software that has phonetically cued commands. Such as D for draw, R for right, U for U-turn. (see Delta Drawing). Uses augmentative communication device or adaptation such as Unicorn keyboard to access computer.	1. Do school work on grade level. 2. Use computer to practice math. 3. Use computer to write answers, sentences, and short reports.	1. Find locations of certain buildings by their <u>add</u> or even addresses. 2. Read prices under $10.00 and tell parent how many dollar bills should be given to pay for groceries. 3. Read words on cereal boxes in store.

Figure 9.4 Activities One Year from the Present

	A. Home	B. School	C. Community
Self-Help	1. Self-feed half of mealtimes with built-up spoon, bring utensil to mouth to remove food. 2. Assist with undressing, kick off shoes, pull off socks, put arm through sleeve if set up supported. 3. Request help with toileting: by direct selection of potty-chair picture on communication board; also use "T" sign.	1. Use of ETRAN to show what she knows in school lessons. 2. Use eye-gaze and vocalization to attract teacher or aides or other children's attention. 3. Make requests through communication board with direct selection in class with aide and teacher.	1. Indicate need for bathroom when away from home and school. 2. Choose between items mom gives her permission to buy in grocery: use eye-gaze at object in front of clerk. 3. Look toward direction pushers should take wheelchair at corners on way to grocery store.
Work	1. In side-sitting position: grasp toys and other objects off floor and release them near floor when finished playing with them. 2. In side-sitting position while bearing weight on extended arm: rotate other arm out to reach for object, grasp it, move it, and let go. 3. On adapted rocking horse: rock and maintain balance through bearing weight on arms and grasping with hands. Also by pushing off her feet for rocking and balance.	1. Work on concepts and skills: (Reading) a. recognize letters (graphemes to phonemes). b. match picture to initial letters. c. match fifty words with corresponding picture cards. d. identify fifty words. e. indicate temporal sequence of sets of 3 pictures. f. classify pictures by functional category. g. reproduce block or bead patterns. h. identify rhyming words. i. identify ten initial consonants. j. demonstrate understanding of <u>more</u>/<u>less</u>. (Math) a. seriate six objects by size, length, and area. b. sort by two attributes. c. write numerals to ten. d. match numerals with number of objects.	1. Demonstrates use of adaptive equipment for videotapes and conferences. 2. Copy words on computer to make signs using the software Print Shop.

	A. Home	B. School	C. Community
Leisure and Social Activities	1. Sort small toys into boxes set out on floor—grasps objects, drops them in the appropriate box. 2. Lie on side and play with Casio keyboard. 3. Play with toys from ring sitting position supported by adult. 4. Read certain words in story books. Where is the word <u>cat</u>? 5. Choose which music to listen to.	1. Use computer with nonhandicapped peers. 2. Initiate game with nonhandicapped peers during recess. 3. Choose activities to do alone.	1. Swim with assistance: supported by mother in supine float position or forward or upright positions. 2. Go horseback riding with assistance. 3. Go to children's music concerts and performances (such as Pickle Family Circus). 4. Go on walks with adults, sister, or respite worker. 5. Go shopping with mother.
Application of Academic Learning	1. Make spontaneous two- to three-word utterances even if words are not intelligible. 2. Group presented items according to their function (chair, tie and a rubber band, spoon and fork). 3. Direct family member to draw with home computer (selects <u>D</u> for draw, <u>R</u> for more cursor to the right).	1. From groups of three ambulatory students, indicate how students should line up according to height. 2. Signal "stop" after three crackers have been placed on her plate and the plates of other students. 3. Indicate beginning letters of school, store, and home street names.	1. Indicate beginning letter of names of school, home, and grocery street names. 2. Discriminate names of animals on signs at zoo cages.

Figure 9.5   A person facing Tara can see her make a selection by gazing at a corner of the ETRAN.

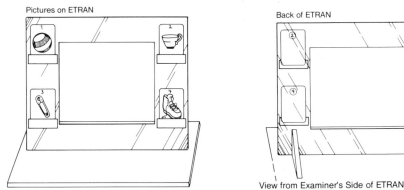

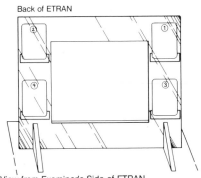

View from Examiner's Side of ETRAN

School/self-help: In regard to Tara's future independence, which can only be gained by allowing different people to feed her, Tara's parents spoke of their decision to involve her father and others more in feeding and dressing routines even though this separation from her mother currently upsets Tara greatly. The father will take over feeding and dressing Tara approximately 25 percent of the time. Since 240 respite hours have recently been granted by a social service agency for use over the next year, Tara's parents will also be able to go out and let respite workers care for Tara on a regular basis.

Tara will also be continuing to work on prereading and premath skills, computer-assisted learning, and expressing more complex utterances. Teachers and aides will encourage head control along with proper positioning.

Refer again to all the completed matrices. By looking at the completed matrices (current, three years in future, and one year in the future), the team has a broader and more informed perspective for determining annual goals and short-term objectives for Tara.

Determining Instructional Objectives From One-Year Matrix.   Teams can use the one-year matrix in either of two ways to determine potentially powerful *short-term instructional objectives*. Reading *vertically,* the team can summarize the skills and activities that are important for full or partial functioning within rather than across situations: home, school, or community. Reading *horizontally,* the team can summarize by kind of activity, what skills and activities are priorities for full or partial functioning across home, school, and community situations and persons. This IEP team chooses to approach the task by reading horizontally and looking at one kind of activity and present or future need across home, school, and community situations.

It can be assumed that team members used the identified activities that they deemed meaningful for Tara to learn and do during the next year. Reading across the self-help activities, for instance, team members identified meaningful self-help activities for the home, school, and community situations. With little or no editorial changes, these identified activities can be turned into statements of short-term instructional objectives:

SELF-HELP/HOME ACTIVITIES

1. Self-feed half of each meal with built-up spoon.
2. Kick off shoes, pull off socks, and pull arm out of sleeve (with assistance).
3. Request need for toileting from picture on communication board or by making "T" manual sign.

SELF-HELP/SCHOOL ACTIVITIES

1. Use "T" manual sign as one signal for toileting.
2. Use eye-gaze and vocalization to attract attention of teacher, aide, or children in the classroom.
3. Make requests for basic needs through communication board in class with teacher and aide.

SELF-HELP/COMMUNITY ACTIVITIES

1. Indicate need for bathroom when away from home and away from the aide at school.
2. Choose between two items mom gives her permission to buy in grocery in manner that is understandable by clerk.
3. Look in direction pusher should take her wheelchair at each corner on way to local grocery store.

Generalized Objectives From One-Year Matrix.   This team could stop here and feel quite confident that they have identified some things which are important for Tara to learn over the next year. They have the choice of stopping the process by using the activity statements on the matrix as the short-term objectives. In doing so, the team could feel confident they have been more selective than is usual in determining short-term objectives for a particular student. The objectives, however, are mostly functional in nature.

Using the information on the one-year matrix, the team has two other options: each can result in objectives that would be more powerful for Tara. Use of these options result in objectives that have both generalized outcomes and are functional.

The first option involves restating each of the activities on the matrix. All it takes is identifying natural situations in which it would be helpful to the child to be able to demonstrate the objectives and the different persons with whom they could be demonstrated in the different situations. Restated and more powerful objectives are as follows:

SELF-HELP/HOME ACTIVITIES

1. Self-feed half of each meal with built-up spoon.
   Generalization objective: Demonstrate ability to feed self half of the amount of her lunches at home, in school, and at picnics.
2. Kick off shoes, pull off socks, and pull arm out of sleeve (with assistance).
   Generalization objective: Demonstrate ability to assist with self-undressing when helped by any of four persons (mom, dad, therapist, and aunt) and to do so at home, in therapy, and at the swimming pool.
3. Request need for toileting from picture on communication board or by making "T" manual sign.
   Generalization objective: Demonstrate ability to use "T" sign of the American sign language or indicate the potty picture on the communication board to request of any of three persons (dad, school aide, aunt) need for toileting when she is at home, in classroom, on playground, and at swimming pool.

SELF-HELP/SCHOOL ACTIVITIES

1. Use "T" manual sign as one signal for toileting.
   Generalization objective: See number 3 above.
2. Use eye-gaze and vocalization to attract attention of teacher, aide, or children in the classroom.
   Generalization objective: Demonstrate ability to use eye-gaze and vocalization to attract attention of different persons at school, at home, and in the community.
3. Make requests for basic needs through communication board in class with teacher and aide.
   Generalization objective: Demonstrate ability to initiate practiced requests of different persons (teacher, aide, aunt, respite worker) in home, school, and community situations.

SELF-HELP/COMMUNITY ACTIVITIES

1. Indicate need for bathroom when away from home and away from the aide at school.
   Generalization objective: Demonstrate ability to indicate need for bathroom to different persons in school, at relative's house, and at church.
2. Choose between two items mother gives her permission to buy in grocery in manner that clerk can understand.
   Generalization objective: Demonstrate ability to indicate in a generally

understandable way which of two items mother is holding Tara wishes to buy at a checkout stand at different groceries.

3. Look in direction pusher should take her wheelchair at each corner on the way to local grocery store.
   Generalization objective: Demonstrate ability to look in the direction a pusher should take the wheelchair at each corner on walks to familiar places and in hallways to familiar school destinations.

Generalized Objectives From Different Matrices.   The second option for identifying generalized and functional objectives involves review of information across activities, across situations, and across years. In this instance IEP team members look at information on all the matrices or use some other source of this kind of information about a child. They go on to search for information that, if included in objectives, will enable Tara to enjoy partial or full participation in at least one (and hopefully more than one) of the one-year activities across all situations. Such a carefully chosen objective would simultaneously make a significant contribution toward attaining one or more of the three-year projected activities.

The team noticed that one obvious repeated pattern was the skill of *requesting wants and needs*. This activity was directly identified in the current matrix, the one-year and three-year matrices. The *implied* need to learn the activity of requesting her wants and needs was identified in several other places on these matrices as well. The lists show the activities the team extracted that led them to this conclusion.

CURRENT YEAR MATRIX

Self-help/Home	#3: Place on potty at regular intervals; picture symbol for "potty" added to picture board but not used. #5: Communicates desires using communication board, especially at mealtimes.
Application of Academic Learning/Home	#1: Signals two or three word utterances on communication board (*more, please, You feed me,* etc.).
Applications of Academic Learning/School	#2: Uses four pictures on communication board to signal yogurt, vegies, rice, and please.
Applications of Academic Learning/Community	#1: Chooses to go into and out of the swimming pool. #2: Chooses biggest horse.

ONE-YEAR MATRIX

Self-help/Home	#3: Requests help with toileting by direct selection of potty-chair picture on communication board; also use "T" sign.
Self-help/School	#2: Use "T" manual sign for toileting. #4: Make requests for basic needs through communication board using direct selection in class with teacher and aide.
Self-help/Community	#2: Chooses between items mother gives permission to buy in grocery stores through eye-gaze in front of clerk.
Application of Academic Learning/ Home	#3: Directs mom to draw with computer drawing game: What letter does *draw* start with? D? or R?"

THREE-YEAR MATRIX

Self-help/Home	#3: Be 100 percent potty trained—will indicate need.
Self-help/School	#2: Request help when needed. #3: Request help with toileting. #4: Request help with reading (page turning, help with unknown words).
Self-help/Community	#4: Choose items on shopping expeditions by indicating choice to salesperson.

While team participants were highlighting with a marker the repeated activities relating to indication of wants and needs, one member made an observation about another related and repeated activity pattern. The special education teacher noticed that the student act of attracting attention is a desired activity directly stated on the one-year and three-year matrices. It is also implied as an underlying, or enroute, skill in several places on the one-year matrix (i.e., attracting attention in order to request help in toileting, making requests from choices on communication board, notifying others she wants to look at TV, inviting other students to come and play, interacts with a clerk at a store). Furthermore, the speech clinician pointed out, this can be seen as an act that would enable Tara to attract attention independently *when* she wants it and *of whom* she wants it. At present well-meaning parents and professionals anticipate Tara's requests. Because they come to her at the appropriate times, she has no need to signal someone's attention in order to communicate something to them. People cue her and thus leave her little responsibility: "Tara, it's lunch time. Show me *lunch* on your communication board." Tara obviously cannot become self-reliant about making requests for basic wants and needs until she can attract others' attention and have them come within range of her communication aid (in other words, come close enough to read what she indicates).

Optimal self-reliance in increasing degrees of participation in different situations with different persons (including her parents) remains the ultimate goal for Tara. Tara will need some generalized attention-attracting behavior skill to obtain attention from others in order to request her basic wants and needs. Attracting attention is also an enabling skill to several other activities—some related to request making and some not.

Formalizing Powerful Goals, Objectives, and Related Instructional Plan. It is this second way of analyzing matrix information that these team members choose to determine potentially powerful goals and objectives. The next steps are (1) writing goals and short-term objective statements, (2) determining curriculum, (3) determining performance objectives, and (4) developing instructional plans.

GOALS AND SHORT-TERM INSTRUCTIONAL OBJECTIVES: In formulating the instructional objectives, the parents decided to limit the objective about initiating communication to persons Tara knows. The resulting short-term instructional objective reveals the team's conclusion.

ANNUAL GOAL: Increase initiative in request making.

Short-term instructional objective:
1. Given situations in different environments, with different familiar people, Tara will attract attention and initiate communications of her personal requests.

The team has followed a time-consuming but educationally positive process for determining certain priority and powerful instructional objectives for Tara. Collectively they extracted some generalized objectives that will be powerful for Tara. They exerted extra team effort to identify current and future activities that (1) are (or will be) personally meaningful to Tara, (2) empower her to perform similar personally meaningful activities in different situations and with different people, and (3) if possible contribute to accomplishing certain future goals and objectives. Feeling highly satisfied that they have given careful consideration to

Tara's educational program—not only for immediate year ahead but for several years to come—the team leaves details of related performance objectives and instructional plans to the teacher and speech pathologist.

Performance Objectives. After consultations with concerned team members and the family during the week following the formulation of the annual goals and short-term objectives, the special education teacher developed performance objectives and instructional plans. (The performance objective reflects the language of instruction in the "Environmental Manipulations" portion of the *Comprehensive Communication Curriculum Guide* (Klein et al. 1981):

PERFORMANCE OBJECTIVE: Given natural situations for communicative interactions in home, school, and community situations, Tara will demonstrate the ability to use some acceptable means of signaling attention of persons known to her (teacher, aide, similar-aged nonhandicapped peer, parent) and making self-motivated requests of them. Performance includes: attracting attention, making a request, waiting for a response, and thanking the person. She will complete at least three or four components five times in each of four different interaction activities by December 1 [assuming that the short-term objective was identified the previous September]. Specifications of acceptable student performance are:

- *Acceptable means of signaling* will include eye-gaze, vocalization, and raising of the arm.
- *The request methods* will include direct eye-gaze, eye-gaze to areas of an ETRAN, and use of communication board.
- *Requests* in natural situations will include requests for pushers in games, someone to take Tara to the bathroom, bus driver to honk the bus horn to announce her arrival at home, and, to generalize even further, requests to swimming teacher for chosen activity.

For instruction and data-collecting purposes, Tara will perform these four components, or subtasks, of the interaction activities:

1. Attract attention (attention seeking)
2. Make request (requesting)
3. Wait for response (awaiting response)
4. Thank persons if request was granted or give some other appropriate response if request was not granted (acknowledging response to request)

Determining Curriculum. Once objectives are determined and formulated for a student, the teacher plans curriculum, instruction, and ongoing assessment of student progress. Whenever possible and helpful, teachers prefer to use existing curriculum as guides in this process. In this case, notes from her professional preparation program gave the teacher the most help. Her course notes recalled the *Comprehensive Communication Curriculum Guide* (Klein et al. 1981), which she knew had been field tested with students like hers. She outlined the material with the objectives and sample applications from the curriculum. For her own purposes, and so that she could inform others, the teacher identified the source of the curriculum, identified pages from which she derived instruction, and outlined the parts she would be using. This documentation is important not only as a guide to the current teacher, but it also provides the source of an ongoing consistent curriculum for this child from year to year. [For the record, the teacher wrote:]

Curriculum component:	Life Management: self-help, communications
Curriculum source:	*Comprehensive Communication Curriculum Guide* by Klein et al., published 1981 at the Early Childhood Institute, University of Kansas, Lawrence, Kansas
Pages:	"Initiations" as outlined here from pp. 74–78; "Environmental Manipulations to Facilitate Spontaneous Use," pp. 79–84.

Instructional Plans.   Specifically, the instructional plans to accomplish the short-term instructional objective (and related performance objective) during the next four months are as follows: To begin, a different communication board will be used for each situation. To foster generalization, however, the thank-you symbol will be the same on each. Only the pictures for the requests will change.

INSTRUCTIONAL PLANS
Initiation and Response Activities
1. "Stop and Go" game request:
      During the regular lower-grade recess time, Tara will attract the attention of a chosen child, make a request for the child to push her in a "Stop and Go" wheelchair game between the two of them, await an answer, take part in the game if the child consents, and end the request sequence with a thank you.
      Setup: A large circle is chalked off on the playground. Children who flock around Tara are told that the game is a little different now. The children must wait for Tara to call them to play. Before they can play, they must wait on the circle line for Tara to look at one of them and "call" them and raise her arm. If she picks a child, then the child can go to her, and she will give him/her a message on her board. Students play

with Tara by pushing her when she puts her hand on *go* and stopping when she puts her hand on *stop*. After she picks someone, other children left are told to go play and come back to the circle line when they see Tara in the middle again if they still want to play. (For safety, the pushers are closely supervised.)

First-time recess: Aide stays with Tara in center of circle, helps her to get attention following this sequence: looking at the child she wants to play with, making a sound, lifting her arm. Initially the aide prompts Tara through these actions, telling her what to do, and waiting for Tara to follow through. Aide also helps the other child wait for Tara's communication. Tara is to put her hand on or near the section on the communication board that says "Do you want to play?" Then she is to indicate the space on the board that has a picture and says the rest of the request: "Stop and Go". Tara awaits the answer, which is usually *yes*, and they play the game for a few minutes. The aide will interrupt the game at some point and say: "Let's pretend the game is over. Tara, touch *no more*. Touch *thank you*. Let's try that, Tara." Tara will—and then the aide tells the child who is helping—"Now when she hits the request *no more*, you'll know the game is over, but don't leave until she touches *thank you* after you stop playing. Please encourage her to look at you right after she indicates *thank you*. If she doesn't use the *thank you*, then call me over and I will help her learn to use it, OK?"

Successive occasions: Prompts gradually fade out, aide moves to further and further distances but stays near enough to keep track of quality and safety of student interaction.

2. Toileting request:

In class when Tara needs to be toileted, she will seek the attention of a classroom aide, express her need, await consent, allow herself to be cared for, and then thank the aide. Tara is currently toileted at regular times at school. For initiating response, she will be asked: "Do you need to go potty?" by the aide, and the aide will say "Show me on your board." (School personnel recommended a change to a phrase with bathroom in it; parents felt it was important to stick to what she is used to.) Tara will be asked this every five minutes during the usual toileting time until she responds by selecting the potty chair picture on her communication board. This is the first sequence.

Successive occasions: Successive sequences will require progressively more signals from Tara. The following will be added one by one:

- Tara will stare in aide's direction.
- Tara will vocalize while staring in aide's direction.
- Tara will raise her arm when aide looks her direction.

When the aide comes over, the aide will initially ask her what she wants—waiting for Tara to show her (but not telling her to show her on the communication board). Tara will need to indicate this on her own. Eventually, the aide will just come over upon request, and Tara will touch this square. At first, the aide will be easily summoned by any effort Tara makes; then only by very clear, complete signals as proposed above.

3. Horn-honking request:

At the end of her school day (if the bus driver is willing), when Tara goes to meet the bus with the classroom aide, Tara will seek the attention of the bus driver, express a desire for the driver to honk the horn (upon her arrival home) a certain number of times, await the driver's response that he agrees to do this, and then thank the driver. The bus driver will first be asked to participate in helping Tara learn to make requests. If driver is willing, the aide will initially prompt Tara through the attention-seeking sequence. The communication-board direct-selection request will be: "Horn" (picture of horn), "home" (picture). Then the aide tells the driver Tara wants to request how many times he will hit the horn upon her arrival home. On this cue the driver asks, "How many times shall I honk the horn, Tara?" Tara indicates a number between one and four. If she indicates a number more than four, the bus driver will tell her it is too many and to choose again. When she arrives home, he will honk as requested. Tara will be prompted by her mom or dad when she is greeted to indicate thank you (for honking) on her board.

Successive occasions: On future occasions, prompting will be faded out. The bus driver will be warned, however, not to initiate the communicative interaction by asking her about the number of honks before she has indicated this.

4. Swimming:

At her Saturday morning swim session, Tara will seek the attention of the swim teacher, while in the water, and make a request for a desired swimming activity. She will then await the response, engage in the activity if granted, and then thank him or her. At swimming Tara's mother encourages her to call the aide over by prompting the sequence currently being used at school for attention seeking. When the aide comes over, Tara's mother will tell her that Tara has something to tell her. The aide will get an *ETRAN* board adapted to float on water and let Tara choose the next activity. Tara will choose by eye-gaze or direct selection via pointing with her arms or legs (love that freedom of movement in the water!).

Successive occasions: Interaction is repeated, with prompts gradually fading out entirely. The ETRAN board could automatically be brought over whenever Tara calls the aide. (Other options on the board might be a picture of a little girl getting out of the pool or a picture of a little girl looking a little blue and cold.)

Reviewing progress: Present performance data suggest that Tara is a pretty smart young lady. Therefore, it is not anticipated she will have trouble learning these generalization skills. If she does, however, it will be important to control the stimuli which cue her that a certain action is expected on her part: for example, using the same eating tools at home, at school, and at picnic; giving similar verbal cues prior to her pulling off her socks when helping undress herself; and direct the wheelchair pusher in a variety of hallways instead of in hallways and sidewalks (stimuli cues about where to turn on sidewalks are very different than clues for making turns in hallways).

If not included as goals and short-term instructional objectives on an IEP, these cues should be included in goals and objectives somewhere in the rest of a pupil's program. It is valuable to remember that each student's curriculum extends in many ways beyond IEP goals and objectives.

Summary and Conclusion

This chapter covered curriculum components termed life management curriculum. Life management curriculum focuses on teaching students to function as effectively as possible in domains such as home, community, education, vocational, and leisure. Four course descriptions of life management curriculum gave examples of curriculum organized by relationship to topics of regular education disciplines (i.e., "Functional Social Studies"). A second sample life management curriculum introduced the basic philosophy of choosing age-appropriate functional activities, stating that it must ultimately be the needs of the student, not the curricular guide, that determines curriculum choices. Continuums of specific skills and activities in each domain suggested possible life management objectives. Both of these curriculum examples focused on preparation for major life areas in one way or another.

The concept of developing components of life management curriculum specific to a disability was explored briefly. Readers were reminded that students have to get needed intensive instruction in learning ways to access academic curriculum when their specific disability interferes with access in the usual ways. In order to assure that the training be given appropriate emphasis in a total curriculum, it was suggested that the life management components of curriculum might be the place to teach the things that all students with a particular disability are likely to need to learn. This introduced the final discussion of an individual-specific curriculum, designed—using a matrix process—to match the needs of a particular student with disabilities. The matrix process involves three submatrices, each having four activity areas: self-help, work, leisure and social interactions, and applications of academic learning. These four activity areas intersected with three situations in which activities commonly take place: home, school, and community. Submatrices are: present performance, anticipated performance in three to five years, and anticipated performance in one year. The entire step-by-step process was explored using the example of Tara, a bright five-year-old girl with severe orthopedic disabilities, and her family. The need to choose curriculum objectives that are highly functional and generalized was stressed as the process of determining objectives using the matrix was described in detail. The triple-matrix approach functions like a magnifying glass, enabling IEP team members to focus intelligently on what a student needs to learn based on current performance. Then the team can synthesize all the information into a cohesive curriculum that is the most empowering possible for that individual student.

Until such time that special education teachers have existing curriculum guidelines and curriculum guides from which to draw, the challenge in their jobs will be compounded unnecessarily. Teachers have a responsibility to their students and themselves to inquire about possibilities for developing or updating curriculum for special education students in their local education units. Life management curriculum for special education students as a group and to meet disability-specific needs are probably the easiest places to begin.

It becomes apparent that it is not practical for every teacher and planning team to complete a matrix-based decision making process to determine powerful goals for each student. Time is the complicating factor. This is not to say, though, that the plan can be used as a "mind set" for providing direction to decisions about objectives unique to individuals. The process can be conducted over time and without the physical presence of the matrices. The memory of the matrices and their uses, however, can structure information seeking and guide the process for determining objectives that are meaningful, generalized, and functional.

Notes

1. Used with permission. *Texas School for the Blind Curriculum*
   Texas School for the Blind
   1100 West 45th Street
   Austin, Texas 78756-3494
2. Tara case presentation information summarized by Shana-Carol Robinson.

References

Bigge, J. 1982. *Teaching individuals with physical and multiple disabilities.* Columbus, Ohio: Charles E. Merrill.

Billingsley, F. 1984. Where are the generalized outcomes? An examination of instructional objectives, *JASH* 9(3): 186–92.

Brolin, D. E. 1976. *Vocational preparation of retarded citizens*. Columbus, Ohio: Charles E. Merrill.

Brolin, D. E. 1978 and 1983. *Life centered career education: A competency based approach*. Reston, Va.: The Council for Exceptional Children.

Brolin, D. E., and Kokaska, C. 1979. *Vocational preparation of handicapped children and youth*. Columbus, Ohio: Charles E. Merrill.

Brown, L., Branston-McClean, M., Baumgart, D., Vincent, L., Falvey, M., and Schroeder, J. 1979. Using the characteristics of current and subsequent least restrictive environments in the development of curricular content for severely handicapped students. *AAESPH Review*, 4(4): 404–24.

Brown, L., Falvey, M., Vincent, L., Kaye, N., Johnson, F., Ferrara-Parrish, P., and Gruenewald, L. 1980. Strategies for generating comprehensive, longitudinal, and chronological age-appropriate individualized education programs for adolescent and young-adult severely handicapped students. *Journal of Special Education* 14(2): 199–215.

Brown, L., Nietupski, J., and Hamre-Nietupski, S. 1976. The criterion of ultimate functioning and public school services for severely handicapped children. In *Hey, don't forget about me! Education's investment in the severely, profoundly, and multiply handicapped*, edited by M. A. Thomas. Reston, Va.: Council for Exceptional Children, pp. 2–15.

Carney, I., Miller, J., and Snell, M. 1983. A module on instructional technology for severely handicapped learners: Skill acquisition. In *A series of professional training modules on the education of severely handicapped learners: An update on educational best practices*, edited by L. Voeltz. Minneapolis, Minn.: Upper Midwest Regional Resource Center, University of Minnesota, pp. 349–432.

Clark, G. 1979. *Career education for the handicapped child in the elementary schools*. Denver, Colo.: Love Publishing Co.

Clark, G. 1980. Career preparation for handicapped adolescents: A matter of appropriate education. *Exceptional Education Quarterly* 1(2): 10–17.

Corn, A., and Martinez, I. 1977. *When you have a visually handicapped child in your classroom: Suggestions for teachers*. New York: American Foundation for the Blind.

Ford, A., Johnson, F., Pumpian, I., Stengert, J., and Wheeler, J., eds. 1980. *A longitudinal listing of chronological age-appropriate and functional activities for school aged moderately and severely handicapped students*. Madison, Wis.: Madison Metropolitan School District, Specialized Educational Services, pp. 1–12.

Gaylord-Ross, R. J., Haring, T. G., Breen, C., and Pitts-Conway, V. 1984. The training and generalization of social interaction skills with autistic youth. *Journal of Applied Behavior Analysis* 17(2): 229–47.

Horner, R. H., Bellamy, G. T., and Colvin, G. T. 1984. Responding in the presence of nontrained stimuli: Implications for generalization error patterns. *JASH* 9: 287–96.

Horner, R. H., Sprague, J., and Wilcox, B. 1982. General case programming for community activities. In *Design of high school for severely handicapped students,* edited by B. Wilcox and T. Bellamy. Baltimore, Md.: Paul Brookes, pp. 61–98.

Klein, M. D., Wulz, S. V., Hall, M., Waldo, L. J., Carpenter, S. A., Lathan, D. A., Myers, S. P., Fox, T., and Marshall, A. 1981. *Comprehensive communication curriculum guide.* Lawrence, Kans.: Early Childhood Institute, University of Kansas.

Koskaska, C., and Brolin, D. 1985. 2d. ed. *Career education for handicapped individuals.* Columbus, Ohio: Charles E. Merrill.

Mulligan, M., and Guess, D. 1984. Using an individualized curriculum sequencing model for teaching communication skills. In *Early language intervention: An introduction,* edited by L. McCormick and R. L. Schiefelbusch. Columbus, Ohio: Charles E. Merrill.

National RRC Panel on Indicators of Effective in Special Education 1986. *Effective indicators for special education.* Lexington, Ky.: Mid-South RRC.

Sailor, W., and Guess, D. 1983. *Severely handicapped students.* Boston, Mass.: Houghton Mifflin.

Schwartz, E., ed. 1980. *Participant's guide: Institute on career education for the handicapped.* Project RETOOL, Birmingham, Ala.: University of Alabama.

Stokes, T., and Baer, M. M. 1977. An implicit technology of generalization. *Journal of Applied Behavior Analysis* 10: 349–67.

Wilcox, B. 1983. A module on the design of high school programs for severely handicapped learners. In *A series of professional training modules on the education of severely handicapped learners: An update on educational best practices,* edited by L. Voeltz. Minneapolis, Minn.: Upper Midwest Regional Resource Center, University of Minnesota, pp. 349–432.

Wilcox, B., and Bellamy, G. T. 1982. *Design of high school programs for severely handicapped students.* Baltimore, Md.: Paul Brookes.

C H A P T E R

10

Reporting Achievements and Documenting Educations

Evaluation and grading document a student's achievement throughout the course of instruction. Evaluating, grading, and contributing to the cumulative records of a student are responsibilities of special education teachers for which the procedures are often unclear and even controversial. What are certain basic premises of evaluation and reporting? What are possible evaluation and grading practices with special education students in areas of their curricular study? What is minimum competency evaluation, and what are current questions about its use with some students in special education? What practices exist for evaluation of special education students for promotion and graduation? Why is it important to document the education of students while it is happening and after it happens? What kinds of information is important for cumulative documentation of student educations?

Evaluations are appraisals of student competence, progress, effort, and comparison with others (Carpenter et al. 1983). They are conducted for many reasons including assessment of present performance levels and readiness for future units of instruction. Information from evaluations guide teachers and communicate student progress to others. Evaluations are based on student outcomes and efforts in activities such as written reports, tests, classroom projects, mastery of stipulated competences in specified skills, and mastery of the objectives on individualized educational programs.

Teachers use *grading* systems to communicate their evaluations. Grades are symbols (letters, numbers, words) that represent value judgments about the relative quality of a student's achievements on course objectives during a specified period of instruction. The varied and valid reasons for evaluating students include the following:

- To assess each student's present level of performance.
- To assess student readiness for future units of instruction.
- To determine the quality of a student's work compared to that of others.
- To assess the effort put forth by each student.

Evaluation helps teachers select courses of study, plan learning activities for each learner, and communicate student progress to students, administrators, parents, and employers.

Grading of nonhandicapped students brings up certain issues, but grading students with disabilities is even more complex and rife with differing points of view. Special education teachers will quickly encounter many of the issues involved with evaluating and grading their students. Grades give a general message of a student's achievement, but how should this message be interpreted? Students in full- or part-time special education can achieve much, but if their work is compared to a regular education classmate, grades may not adequately show that achievement. Also teachers use different evaluation strategies. For example, one teacher might give a low grade at first so that the student will strive for something higher, whereas another teacher might give a high grade at first to reward beginning efforts. Also a remark given on either a report card or an assignment can be interpreted in several ways. In some instances, a teacher might base a grade on ability or competence, but the students could understand that the grade is based on their effort. Parents can get the same report of grades and either correctly or incorrectly assume that it compares their child's achievements to those of nondisabled peers. And then, to complicate matters more, administrators and employers usually look at grades to get a sense of a student's "future performance."

Evaluating student progress in any field of study is a vital component of education, and grading is the most common tool for communicating that evaluation. Since part of the evaluation process must necessarily be of a subjective nature, though, one report can receive widely varying interpretations. Also the traditional letter system of making evaluations may not be best suited to the needs of special education students. This is because grade evaluations can be based on a range of criteria including the mastery of achieved competencies, the fluency of the rate of progress, the degree of effort that the student has put into the task, or the degree of success with which students accomplish their own individualized instructional programs.

Within specific grading systems, teachers can choose among several optional grading processes. A competent teacher needs to be aware of as many options for evaluating and grading as possible and the different practices available in making awards. After studying the different systems and the options within each, teachers need to define which are to be used in each component of a student's curriculum.

When teachers use a traditional grading and reporting system, this implies that students in special education can be graded in one or more subject areas in the same way that similar-aged students in regular classes are being graded. Historically, students who receive average scores on tests or schoolwork are assigned a letter grade of C. Within this grading system, a letter grade of C signifies that students have achieved average scores on norm-referenced tests. A student who exceeds average levels receives A's and B's. Slow-learning, slow-progressing students, though, often receive F's and are admonished for their lack of effort and attention to the assigned task. This means that traditional progress reports often do not reflect a handicapped student's achievement accurately.

To keep special education in step with society, its assessments must be referenced to the needs of its students. But it is also desirable that, as far as possible, special education be referenced to regular education and not left to drift off in any direction. Where regular education goes, special education must go too, albeit at its own pace—and possibly by divergent routes. Thus in a curriculum component with objectives that relate to regular objectives but are different enroute objectives, grading may also need to be somewhat different. Since more emphasis might be on practical, applied skills, the grading here may be based on accomplishment of inventories of skills.

One of the major challenges regarding evaluation within special education involves deciding how much a student's handicap should be taken into account. Carpenter et al. (1983) discuss issues about grading as it pertains to students with and without handicaps. If a student's handicap is determined to be no factor in a certain course (with the same requirements as other students), that student may justifiably be graded according to the established policies for grades. If, however, a student's handicap hinders ability to perform as well as others, mitigating factors may prevent equal comparison. Carpenter et al. raise such questions as, "If Marty's handicap leads to reduced proficiency on the same objectives as other students, should her ability have an effect on her grade?" "Should she be evaluated by the same standards as Judy who has no handicap?" They remind readers that answers to such problems often rest in the purpose or message intended by the grades. The purpose of each grade should be clearly stated. They also suggest that one grading mark limits the range of messages that can be communicated.

Evaluation is an important cog in the wheel of education that provides feedback to the student, teacher, and parent. Evaluation is basic in shaping the future course of any type of education. So that teachers may "know" the students better, that each child's education can be progressively planned, and that the students themselves graduate with a comprehensive and referenced record. A system of comprehensive, cumulative documentation must go hand-in-hand with consistent and efficient evaluation.

Students should receive some kind of regular, site, or program-developed progress reports. In regular education, grading is the most common system used to communicate student evaluation. Report cards, midterm grades, progress reports, and parent conferences are the major reporting systems (Butler et al. 1984). In special education, it is the IEP used at regular reporting periods that monitors student growth with respect to individual goals and objectives in special education (San Diego Unified Schools 1984–85).

Reporting and accountability practices for special education students include evaluation and grading in areas of study, minimum competency evaluation, evaluation for promotion and graduation, and cumulative documentation of educations. These topics cannot be discussed without identifying issues accompanying each. Teachers, parents, and others cannot be involved in behalf of special education students without considering these kinds of practices and issues.

Evaluation and Grading in Areas of Study

Traditionally, special education concern about evaluation and grading has focused around the annual IEP process. The IEP process, however, does not usually represent a student's entire curriculum, and monitoring student progress through the annual IEP process often is not enough. The process is limited in the degree to which it provides records about student performance outside areas directly related to the goals and objectives listed on the student's IEP form.

Other frequently used options for special education student evaluation and reporting are (1) contract evaluation and grading, (2) criterion-referenced evaluation, (3) completely individualized evaluation, (4) IEP evaluation, and (5) variations on traditional grading. The descriptions of approaches and identity of issues here are meant to be introductory in nature. These approaches offer starting points. Teachers can choose from among these the most appropriate options for individual students in particular situations.

Contract Evaluation and Grading

In contracting systems, the teacher and individual students explore the objectives and materials for learning; cooperatively they decide which of the prescribed activities a student or group of students will be able to accomplish during a specified time period, a week, month, or year. In regular school, contracting is usually based on the traditional school texts in the different subjects and sometimes on the usual units of study, such as a social studies unit. A contract made between each student and teacher on an individual basis creates a learning environment in harmony with the needs and interests of individuals within a class.

Grading decisions are also decided cooperatively by both teacher and individual students, and symbols indicate student achievement. Usually the teacher and individual students decide what grade—A, B, C, or D—the student will receive if she finishes certain objectives at certain preagreed upon levels of proficiency. Students are spurred on by the contracting method of learning because they understand at the course beginning precisely what is required for successful completion. Evaluation of achievement in this system is not one student measured versus others; this evaluation is based purely on performance of set task(s).

The value of this system is that students have input into their learning activities and the grade they can achieve. When this system of grading is used with special education systems, this fact should be noted in any reporting system that informs parents and others of student performance. Persons interpreting the grades need to know that they do not show comparison of any one student with other students.

Criterion-Referenced Evaluation

The criterion-referenced approach differs from the contracting system in that the student does not have a hand in determining either the learning content or the grading system. Under the contract system, the teacher and pupil have equal input in deciding what is to be learned, what activities will aid the pupil in learning the skills, and what the grade will be in keeping with achievement. Pretests and post-tests are seldom used with the contract method of evaluation. But with the criterion-referenced approach, checklists and other criterion-referenced instruments are used for evaluation. In this case, the number or percentage of skills or subskills completed to a certain criterion on an identified list of skills designate the terms of evaluation. Sometimes the evaluation is simply in terms of satisfactory or unsatisfactory performance. At other times, a point system is used. Teachers using a criterion-referenced evaluation specify a system such as five points for an F, ten points for a D, twenty points for a C, thirty points for a B, and forty for an A. When this is done, the evaluation documentation should clearly state that these letter grades are based on a modified grading system and do not compare this student's performance with that of any other student. An objective might state that the student would complete at least 80 percent of the total items selected for mastery from the district "Functional Skills Curriculum." This criterion of 80 percent completion might relate either to a semester or a full two-semester course.

Teachers can choose from several other variations on criterion-referenced evaluations (Dick, 1983, 4):

- *Satisfactory/unsatisfactory*—useful when the instructor needs to determine whether a student's performance meets a certain standard. S/U grades can reflect minimal competency, that is, 80 percent of the test items correct, or maximum competency, that is, 100 percent safe operation of equipment.

- *Written evaluations*—very helpful and worthwhile because they are specific and detailed. Teacher's comments should be sufficiently factual and well-documented. Written evaluations can be coupled with traditional grades.
- *Skill reports*—checklists of competencies or objectives students have successfully completed. These can also be attached to traditional grade reports.
- *Self-evaluation*—teaches students to assess their own performance and behavior. Students fill out checklists, write evaluations, and discuss their evaluation with the instructor.

Contract grading can be added to the alternatives. If desirable, results of these reporting systems can be converted to traditional letter grades that stand for levels of competence students have reached.

Completely Individualized Evaluation

Under completely individualized instruction and evaluation, the teacher has no preconceived ideas as to the details of the body of knowledge an individual student should master. (This approach is *not* to be confused with individualized education programs, or IEP.) To some degree, evaluation here is structured by the teacher using the books and materials available in the classroom to motivate a student to explore these materials. Once a student chooses a topic for learning, she or he can pursue this particular topic. Each student reviews the materials in the classroom and the library. Then the teacher and student set up the student's objectives. To use this evaluation method, teachers need to have large quantities of different kinds of reference materials about subjects that interest particular students. But the teacher chooses the materials not only because of the topics but also because of the modes in which the information is presented to students with disabilities. In individualized instruction and evaluation, each pupil can select his learning problem for mastery from any topic of learning such as cultures, specific animals, or certain kinds of music and musicians.

Since the learning methods and materials are completely individualized, the performance level can be evaluated by a speech, a drama, sets of pictures or objects with accompanying explanations, or any other method of student presentation. Throughout study, teachers are available at all times to direct and guide students and to assure that students are learning the basic skills that comply with appropriate grade-level expectancies.

This method allows high student input, but it differs from contracting methods because in a contract method basic subjects and competencies form the focus of the learning objectives and evaluation. In contracting, the teacher usually decides before meeting with pupils the competencies that should be mastered during a specific time frame. The teacher and the student then decide how and when the student will master the contract.

In completely individualized instruction and evaluation, the objectives of school subjects and competencies are achieved, but in a less direct manner. Social studies skills and knowledges are learned and practiced through use. Likewise English skills are mastered while studying the learning problem the students select as they talk about the content and write appropriate compositions. For example, penmanship and computer word-processing are learned and practiced through organizing documents and providing graphics for their studies. Spelling study is based on words learned and needed while the student is working on an individual problem.

Teachers use either single or multiple grades in this approach. As with other grading systems, teachers can give grades based on one or more of the following areas: ability, effort, or achievement. Teacher and student could also make up their own scale for each area used. For example, if measuring competency and using a traditional A, B, C method, a C might signify average according to what students without disabilities might be expected to achieve. A grade of C for effort might signify average effort according to that particular student's abilities and expectations and what can be expected of that student. In this system, no F grades are used. Instead, an N is used, which means "needs to improve." Where an N is given, teacher and student discuss the areas in which improvement is required, and they make plans that may include more specific direct study of, for example, how to look up information or how to write complete sentences.

The grading system would also include the kind of *written evaluations* and *self-evaluations* described in the criterion-referenced evaluation system. A teacher would write periodic descriptions of an individual student's weaknesses and gains in relation to stated objectives. In addition, the teacher includes notes of social, physical, and mental growth. Then such a log is passed on to a subsequent teacher.

IEP Evaluation

Within an IEP evaluation system, teachers and others use annual goals and instructional objectives to measure performance. Grades based on IEP goals and objectives take into consideration students' learning styles, academic strengths, and weaknesses. Within IEPs, a wide variety of systems can be used as various descriptions of present performances and annual goals and objectives. Any evaluation system that IEP team chooses as appropriate is acceptable on the IEP. Examples of objectives might include to complete regular art class with a grade of C or better, to improve in reading from grade 2.6 to grade 3.0, or to pass any fifteen of the twenty-five subtasks in a special community-based assignment.

Any modifications in testing procedures, (e.g., oral tests or untimed tests) and in the awarding of grades, (e.g., multiple grades or shared grades, discussed below) should be written into the IEP. This will ensure that the parents, students, teachers, other professionals, and school administrators are in agreement with the testing and grading modification used with handicapped students.

Schulz and Turnbull (1983) suggest a global IEP-based scale. The proposed scale could be as follows:

A = Student surpasses the expectation of IEP.
B = Student meets IEP expectations.
C = Student performs somewhat below IEP standard expectations.
D,F = The student performs significantly below IEP standards and expectations.

(Schulz and Turnbull 1983, 132)

If such a scale is used, it is a modification of the local district standards of grading and therefore should be described on the IEP.

Within IEP instruction and evaluation, the criteria for each objective or standard of performance against which student performance is measured will be either norm-references or criterion-referenced. Norm-referenced objectives and criteria compare a student's performance with that of fellow nonhandicapped students at the same grade level. Criterion-referenced objectives are stated using expectations of student progress in relation to some defined standard (or criterion).

Basing grades upon attaining objectives in the IEP can be a helpful alternative to regular teachers who have special education students integrated into their classes. As regular teachers individualize instruction more and more, it becomes clear that some students are not working on the same level as their peers. Sometimes it is a problem to explain this variance to other children in the class and to parents. But questions about differential grading practices decrease when individual work is based on IEP objectives because these are readily explained to classmates and to the parents. The IEP system assumes that the regular teacher and the special education teacher exchange information about classroom practices in both places before formulating curricular expectations and establishing grading procedures.

Either integration or mainstreaming has become an integral part of the IEP process since PL 94-142, the Education for All Handicapped Act of 1975. Regular education teachers find themselves in a dilemma concerning whether to grade mainstreamed students using standard testing and grading procedures. When evaluating a student with special needs, a teacher is confronted not only with wanting to provide individualized instruction, but also with wanting to keep the grade inflation to a minimum. The type of grading the teacher uses especially becomes an issue because poor letter grades add another negative element to affect the low self-esteem and insecurities that many special needs students already feel.

Schooling within the regular education components is assumed to have primarily the same objectives for special education students as those pursued by regular students taking the same curriculum. Thus the grading policy and procedures a school district as a whole uses would also apply for special education students unless otherwise specified (on IEPs). Traditional grading procedures and reporting are frequently the letter grades of A through F. Some mainstreamed students in special education may, however, require modified time elements in order to complete their work. This and other variations on traditional grading are noteworthy.

Variations on Traditional Grading

In components of curriculum where students are attempting to meet regular objectives at reduced levels of complexity, teachers might use the traditional A through F grading approach, and the students would receive lower grades to reflect their lower performances. In this case, when students are trying their best, this grading system may seem unfair. So, many professionals incorporate shared grading, systems of multiple grades, letter grading with subscript numbers, or alternate assignment grades along with standard grades.

Shared Grading.   Shared grading, often used in mainstreaming, is a system of evaluation within which two or more teachers discuss and decide what grade a share-graded pupil should receive for a grading period (Kinnison et al. 1981). The professionals involved might include a regular teacher and a resource teacher, or a special education teacher and a teacher in the field of art, music, or vocational education.

Multiple Grades.   Teachers can give students multiple grades as part of the evaluation process. "The premise is to reward the student for progress made even though all areas of achievement may or may not be at a satisfactory level. Final grades for each student would be an average of all the multiple grades. One type of multiple grade involves three areas: ability, effort, and achievement" (Kinnison et al. 1981).

> *Ability* reflects the student's growth in the content area being studied based upon expectations of his or her ability to grasp the information presented.
> *Effort* reflects the teacher's judgment as to how hard the pupil tried.
> *Achievement* is a comparison of a student's achievement to others' in the same class or classes.
>
> (Kinnison et al. 1981, 98)

Letter Grades With Subscript Numbers.   Subscript numbers indicate the student's level of achievement in designated areas of learning (Kinnison et al. 1981, 89). For example, C_4 means the student's performance was at C level or average, but instruction was given at the fourth-grade (lower grade) subject level.

Differential Grading.   Lewis and Doorlag (1983) demonstrate differential grading by presenting three strategies for differential grading of one student mainstreamed into a fourth grade class who is successfully completing math assignments at the third-grade level (See Figure 10.1).

Alternative Assignment Grades Plus Standard Grades. Kiraly and Bedell (1984) recommend a generic school policy for grading main-

Figure 10.1   Differential Grading

✔✔   **TIPS FOR THE TEACHER**

Differential Grading

Report cards are a major way for teachers to inform parents of their child's progress in school. However, with mainstreamed special students, grading performance is often difficult. How should the teacher grade Judy who is mainstreamed into the fourth grade class and is successfully completing math assignments at the third grade level? Here are some alternatives:

1. State the student's current grade level in the academic subject and grade the student's performance at that grade level.

    Judy, Grade 4
        math grade level ___3___
        math performance at grade 3 level ___B___

2. State the student's current grade level in the academic subject and grade the student's work behaviors rather than skill performance.

    Judy, Grade 4
        math grade level ___3___
            works independently ___B___
            completes assignments ___B+___
            neatness ___B___

3. State the student's IEP goals and objectives in the academic subject and indicate which have been met and which still require work.

    Judy, Grade 4
        Goal: By the end of the school year, Judy will perform math computation problems at the 3.5 grade level: ___in progress___

        Objectives:
            1. Judy will add and subtract 2-digit numbers with regrouping with 90% accuracy: ___Achieved___
            2. Judy will write multiplication facts with 90% accuracy: ___Achieved___
            3. Judy will multiply 2-digit numbers with regrouping with 90% accuracy: ___in progress___
            4. Judy will write division facts with 90% accuracy: ___in progress___

---

streamed handicapped secondary students. They suggest that the school performance of mainstreamed students be evaluated and graded by the teacher of the
class the student attends. The regular teacher and/or special education teacher
would provide students with alternative assignments and special assignments
would have two grades: (1) a grade on its own merits taking into consideration
the abilities of the student, (2) a second grade that would indicate the student's
placement within the class. This second grade would be recorded as a standard
grade for comparison with the rest of the class. The assignments could be
measured by adapted or modified means such as oral presentation or multiple
choice questions. The ultimate decision is whether or not the student passed the
assignments. Results are reported formally and informally to special education
teachers and reported to parents as a written progress report, not as a standard
grade.

Minimum-Competency Evaluation

Riding the crest of the accountability wave in all of education is
the practice of minimum-competency testing. This is a move towards teaching the
basic skills, knowledges, and attitudes considered essential to students for survival as citizens. A minimum-competency approach to education is based on
creating a set of minimum requirements for grade-level achievement, promotion,
and certification. It begins by defining and listing basic skills, knowledges, and
attitudes that are required for successful performance of other skills essential for
survival in today's world. A minimum-competency approach establishes standards for both promotion and graduation in elementary and secondary schools.
Hence, it makes both local education agencies and educators accountable for
instruction in traditional subject matter areas.

The major evidence demonstrating the need for minimum-competency teaching or some other altered educational program is the number of high school
graduates who cannot read, write, and figure well enough to function adequately
either in society at large or in post-secondary education. Advocates of minimum-
competency teaching believe that this approach will enhance the ability of students to interact effectively with their respective environments.

Minimum-competency testing (MCT) programs are viewed "as a rational
and systematic response to a general public desire for programs that are economi-
cally efficient, socially uniform, accountable, and traditional." (Nickse and Mc-
Clure 1981, 59.) Minimum competency thus pressures students to acquire basic
minimum skills and thereby become employable job candidates, informed consumers, and educated citizens.

Minimum-competency teaching and testing pressures students to master at least most of the testable skills required for promotion and graduation. Its testing programs identify students whose performances are behind schedule and thus are in need of remediation. Such testing programs divide students into two groups—those who have acquired the necessary skills and those who have not.

Minimum-performance programs characteristically consist of three steps: (1) development and communication of minimum objectives of education for each grade, usually stated in behavioral terms, (2) planning and conducting instruction pointed toward fulfilling the stated objectives, and (3) measurement of students' performance as related to the planned objectives. (See Monjan and Gassner 1979, 16–17.)

Measurement of student performance is usually in terms of competencies that define what local authorities have decided are minimally acceptable. These measurements generally center on reading, written expression, and arithmetic. The testing instruments are most frequently in the form of "objective" tests.

Strengths of Minimum-Competency Teaching and Testing

Paralleling patterns of industrial management, schools employ minimum-competency programs as a "nuts-and-bolts" approach to educational management. Through using industrial concepts, schools promote an educational system that is anchored on measured outcomes in terms of increased efficiency. Such programs induce schools and teachers to provide more instruction in the basic skills and to identify students who need remediation work in those skills. They also provide a consistent database for monitoring statewide progress in education.

Minimum-competency programs, then, make school diplomas meaningful by ensuring that their holders have acquired at least a minimum ability to read, write, and compute. They also help employers identify diploma-holding job candidates as those who have at least some basic skills.

Questions About Minimum-Competency Testing and Teaching

A lack of agreement exists, even among educators, first, in regard to the nature and meaning of competency and, second, in regard to the types and levels of competencies that are needed. Competencies can be described as behaviors, skills, powers, or understandings, but they could also be the ability to solve problems and think creatively. Based on what meaning "basic competency" has, there is great difference in how the competencies are pursued and evaluated.

Why Test for Certain Skills?   Why do we teach and test many of the skills currently included on minimum-competency tests? Who determines which skills are essential? Bracey (1983) questions skills currently taught under the MCT program and thus evaluated as "basic," to which he ascribes little worth. Teaching multiplication of fractions is one example. Bracey questions teaching this skill at all. Out in the world, almost everyone uses calculators and the decimal system to carry out such calculations. Thus education seems to be out of step with the rapidly changing society it feeds. If such a discrepancy exists in the case of regular education, then who can say that the skills taught will, in fact, be essential to any of the students taking minimum-competency tests?

What Should Be Taught That Is Not Taught?   Many educators puzzle not only over the value of an MCT education but also are concerned about what is *not* being taught that should be. For example, students often lack the ability to apply their background knowledge of a subject to a passage of reading. Yet pupils will read and retain materials at a far higher level of proficiency when the subject is interesting and relevant to them. Merely teaching reading, per se, in isolation, does not develop the more involved skills a child needs in order to read in an informed, analytical, and inferential manner.

How Valid Is Minimum-Competency Instruction?   How valuable is an education that narrows its emphasis to a limited number of skills identified as minimum outcomes for everyone? While some educators ask this question, courts are making decisions questioning the validity of the proof that even the minimum-competency skills have actually been taught (Bracey 1983). Thus, in order to stave off malpractice suits, professional educators might steer teaching to become more didactic and channeled. Hardly creative of an environment in which students can develop educational skills, this approach could result in a regressive step to teaching by rote. This in turn would produce citizens who function by rote. All of this brings up the issue of uniformity, which can lead to stagnation.

Elkind (1983) sees this problem as analogous to those that industry faces. He observes that modern industry recognizes the worker is not a robot and that workers need motivation, challenge, to feel involved, recognition, and input into the system. These conditions appear to be lacking in some MCT programs, where the student is more akin to a robot—performing, unenthusiastically, isolated tasks of a repetitive nature, controlled and led by a teacher, with little or no room for free thought, expression, or development. Students may be taught the basic skills they may indeed pass the uniform tests, but do they actually *learn* those skills, and learn them in such a way as to be competent in the areas of life to which those skills are supposedly directed? Mechanized testing, multiple testing, and so on, is geared to a pass or fail, skill mastered or not mastered mentality, with little room for inquiry, conceptualization, and student problem solving, all of which develop real, as opposed to paper, skills.

Is Minimum-Competency-Evaluation Discriminatory? Does minimum-competency testing discriminate against certain minority and handicapped students? "As it happens, most of the states have chosen a cutoff point that passes almost all of the white English-speaking students" (Lazarus 1981, 190). For borderline students, minimum-competency testing makes diplomas not just meaningful but actually all-important. In fact, they may even make the diplomas more important than the education they supposedly represent. To the degree that schools deny diplomas to numbers of non-English-speaking and handicapped students, the schools thereby limit those students' future employment opportunities.

Subtle discriminations can occur as a result of increasing emphases on using minimum-competency results as evidence of teacher and administrator accountability. Having students in class who cannot keep up and who lower test score averages can negatively affect the reputations of the teachers involved, which is unfair. Pressure on these students is unfortunate. According to Elkind (1983), their failure is more humiliating than ever. Students who fail to achieve are seen as letting everyone down—their peers, their teacher, the principal, the superintendent, and even the school board. Because of all of this, teachers may be highly reluctant to accept certain special education students.

Minimum-competency education does appear to improve schooling programs quickly and inexpensively. But this approach may also be an oversimplified response to a complex challenge. This approach to education may, in fact, reflect an effort to solve certain educational problems without first understanding the basic nature and root of those problems. Minimum-competency education "enacts into law, albeit in a muted way, the philosophy that a certain kind and amount of education is correct for everyone" (Lazarus 1981, 189).

Doesn't MCT need to encompass more comprehension, deduction, listening and speaking, interpretation, reasoning, and thinking skills within the learning of knowledge? Shouldn't teachers not only teach knowledge but also, and most important, instruct in the skills that will enable students to use and manipulate that knowledge. This can all be done on a "basic" level and would undoubtedly prove far more efficacious than teaching unrelated "basic" skills. Such an expanded approach would instill multiuse, generalizable skills and knowledges. Some skills regarded in the past and now as basic would disappear to be replaced by new basic skills; others would endure. Educators need to constantly weigh and evaluate the value to individuals of the skills tested in minimum competency tests. As teachers, "we need to know more about the cognitive aspects of instruction— how teaching styles influence learners' attention, understanding, and motivation" (Nickse and McClure 1981, 223).

To sum up, teachers and administrators need to strive for more consensus on the goals of education. Also, evaluating students by their competencies, broadly defined, is superior to most other criteria for evaluation. Furthermore, educators do need to identify students whose programs are at risk and help enhance their programs promptly and effectively; minimum competency testing does ascertain which students need special help, and it also provides a motivation for giving them that help.

Evaluation for Promotion and Graduation

Regular students completing programs at junior high, middle school, and high school levels are often awarded official diplomas or some other certification of completion. Students in special education programs also need some form of certification showing what they have achieved. "Grades and promotions are based on students' achievement of goals and objectives (academic, vocational, social, self-help) specified in their individual IEPs" (National Regional Resource Center Panel on Indications of Effectiveness in Special Education 1986, 5–19). Although the need for some form of certification remains the same, students in special education may require alternatives to the regular diplomas or promotions.

Junior High Promotion

Junior high promotion requirements, as well as high school graduation requirements and any variations thereof, are described by the administrative regulations of local education units. Two regular education promotion options that can apply to certain special education students are described below:

Regular Promotion with Certificate of Promotion. Successful completion of designated course credits entitles students in junior high school and other students completing these credits to receive a certificate of promotion. The following examples are requirements of a local education agency.

I. Credits. Ten semester credits earned in the ninth grade, including two credits each:
- in English,
- in physical education, and
- in either science or social science.

Regular Promotion Contingent Upon Completion of Credits. In cases where students lack the credits required for promotion from junior high school or middle school to high school, they can be conditionally promoted. Such promotion is contingent upon completing the requirements in summer school. The schools must notify both the student and the parents of this impending conditional promotion. Award of a regular certificate of promotion can then follow based on satisfaction of the requirements.

High School Graduation Requirements Within the IEP Approach

"Eligibility to graduate and receive a diploma is contingent upon the successful attainment of curricular goals and instructional objectives contained in an individualized educational program (IEP)" (Ross and Weintraub 1980, 202). This situation applies when students are unable to attain the skills necessary to fulfill standard graduation requirements and considerable curricular alterations have been set forth in the individual IEP. A transcript outlining the courses and/or competencies attained accompanies this type of diploma.

The IEP approach has both positive and negative aspects. The positive aspects, according to Ross and Weintraub (1980) include:

- The reasonable accommodation of graduation requirements to meet the unique educational needs of handicapped students eliminates potentially discriminatory practices.
- Since attaining the goals and objectives of the IEP demonstrates successful completion of a particular requirement for a handicapped student, it will ensure that the IEP is carefully reviewed when the student is not progressing at the anticipated rate.
- This approach sets forth criteria for measuring the minimum competencies of a handicapped student.
- Evaluation of the student occurs on a case-by-case basis.
- Potential employers can determine a graduate's course of study by requesting a student's transcript.

The negative aspects of the IEP approach include:

- To the same extent that this option is flexible with regard to student needs, it can become a source of confusion and friction over whether educational standards and the standard diploma are being diluted.
- Critics of this approach might regard it as discriminatory against nonhandicapped students.

(Ross and Weintraub 1980, 202)

Alternative Ways of Applying the IEP Approach to High School Graduation.   Several alternate ways of applying the IEP approach to high school graduation exist. Three are described here: the curricular approach, competency requirements in basic skills, and alternative experiences.

THE CURRICULAR APPROACH. A specialized curriculum, with its own standards for all students participating in it, is one approach for students in special education (Ross and Weintraub, 1980). A specialized curriculum is set to meet particular educational needs, abilities, and interests of students such as vocational education, basic skills, life management, or college preparation. A minimum-competency test or other standard sets levels of achievement. Each curriculum has its own requirements for graduation. A student could receive a diploma attesting to achievement of the essential standards of his or her prescribed curriculum. In this way, "all students would have access to a program leading to a diploma. This policy has the advantage of securing the doctrine of equality of education access" (Ross and Weintraub, 1980, 203).

This approach has some negative aspects. According to Ross and Weintraub one is the need for validation of competencies for each curriculum track. A second negative aspect is that "the policy could have the effect of lowering the standards of certain curricula by focusing more on the access of certain classes of students to the program than on their performance once admitted to the program" (p. 203).

COMPETENCY REQUIREMENTS IN BASIC SKILLS. Students must demonstrate achievement in basic skills at a prescribed level in designated board-approved competencies in order to receive high school diplomas. Special education students can meet regular or differential standards such as those discussed in earlier chapters. Such modifications in competency requirements must be designated on each student's individualized educational program (IEP). If alternatives to the usual requirements are used, credit for taking required courses is a second part of the graduation requirement that must be addressed in an IEP.

ALTERNATIVE EXPERIENCES. In this approach, credit for graduation can be gained through alternative educational experiences. Provided that the alternative experiences relate directly to educational goals, experiences such as the following can benefit special education students (adapted from Dick 1983, 5):

- Work-training programs allow students to explore career interests in occupational fields in a program not offered through the regular or special high school curriculum. The school can often provide course work pertinent to these career courses and coordinate a work-experience program with employers that enables students to obtain on-the-job training in an occupation of their choice.
- Work-study programs afford students an opportunity for earning income while attending school at least half time. Such programs may be offered in conjunction with cooperative vocational education or special education.

- Students with employment experience can obtain credit for work experience as a substitute for class attendance and credit requirements. The district could award credit if the student's work experience resulted in learning outcomes that relate to the student's educational goals.
- Students aged sixteen or more with two full years and ten credits of completed high school including demonstrated job proficiency or one credit in a vocational course might graduate early. A diploma could be granted after successful completion of the equivalent of two years of vocational or on-the-job training, such as in a vocational rehabilitation program.
- Students could be allowed to demonstrate their knowledge and skills by passing a performance test in lieu of attending classes in required or elective courses. Not only could the required course be challenged for credit, but credit units could be granted upon passing.
- Students might be permitted to independently complete the requirements for credit in required or elective course areas. This option may be particularly necessary for students who are frequently absent during school hours.
- Handicapped students who are accepted into an accredited post-secondary institution after three years of high school could be granted a diploma following successful completion of two semesters of college.

Differential graduation standards based on applied learning is another kind of alternate experience. Barret (1983) proposes that minimum levels of proficiency in career education, vocational education, work experience, and independent living skills be accepted as the basic curricular framework for the development of differential standards for graduation for learning handicapped students for whom an IEP team determined (that) regular proficiency standards are inappropriate. (Differential and unique proficiency standards were discussed in Chapter 2 of this text.) This proposal responds to concerns that high school education for learning handicapped students has deteriorated into remediation of fragmented components of proficiency examinations rather than an opportunity to gain competencies in the applied sciences which will enhance their chances to become productive members of society" (Barret et al. 1983).

Alternatives to Regular Diplomas for Completing Regular Requirements

Students in special education receive standard diplomas and other certificates of recognition upon completion of their schooling. Long before students reach the point of completing their program, it is important to determine what standards and requirements they are striving to meet and what they will be awarded when they meet them. The IEP is the standard place for recording this determination. Certificates of record include regular diplomas, certificates of attendance, and letters of recognition.

A Regular Diploma for Completion of Special Education Programs.   For students with disabilities so severe that they require educational programs consisting primarily of specially designed instruction, diplomas are awarded for completion of a special education program that parallels regular curricular areas (Dick 1983). Students enroll in a special education English program and a special education social studies program, and so on. In doing this, students acquire the required units of credit in subject areas. "Defining requirements in terms of area of study instead of required courses allows a flexibility needed to accommodate varying needs of students. Thus, consumer survival, self-help skills, and other activities of daily living usually needed by special education students could satisfy the requirements for graduation. Diplomas would be awarded to handicapped students who complete a Special Education Program without differentiation. Differences between a Special Education program and the regular school program would be noted on the student's transcript of record" (Dick 1983, 5).

The Special Education Diploma.   A special education diploma is issued to handicapped students who successfully achieve goals and objectives written on individualized education programs but do not fulfill other graduation requirements. Such an approach enables students to receive a diploma, and it enables school districts and employers to identify students who have passed minimum-competency tests and have completed standard courses from those who have not (Ross and Weintraub 1980). Ross and Weintraub identify two negative aspects of the special education diploma:

- This approach can give the appearance of special treatment for handicapped students who fail the minimum competency test.
- A differentiated diploma may discriminate against a handicapped student and thus potentially give rise to challenge based on Section 504 of the Rehabilitation Act of 1973.

(Ross and Weintraub 1980, 202)

A Certificate of Attendance Based on Minimum-Competency Test Failures or Exemptions.   Handicapped and nonhandicapped students who are unable to pass a state level minimum competency test (MCT) are given a certificate of attendance in lieu of a diploma. Afterwards, they may retake the test a certain number of times until their twenty-first birthday. If they pass, they then receive the graduation diploma (Serow and O'Brien 1983). Students can take the minimum competency tests a year or so before graduation so that if they do not pass, they can participate in intensive remediation.

The impact of failure can be traumatic for some students in special education, particularly those with mental retardation. Some students even withdraw from school after MCT failure (Serow and O'Brien 1983). In light of this, it is important to ask whether certain categories of students—for instance students with retardation—benefit in meaningful ways from MCT participation. If it seems that certain students will never be able to attain the requisite level of competence even with intensive remediation and careful and frequent testing opportunities, "then the forced participation of EMR students in MCT programs may not be only pointless from an academic standpoint, but even harmful to their psychological and social development. . . . perhaps the fairest and most realistic policy would be to exempt only those students classified as mentally retarded" (Serow and O'Brien 1983, 83).

Letter of Recognition.   In courses of study in which practical, applied, and life management activity objectives predominate, letters of recognition can designate completion of this more functional and applied course of study. For an example of functional and applied skills courses of study, refer to the San Diego Unified School (1984–85) description of these curriculum options in previous chapters.

Certificate of Attendance Without Minimum Competency Test.   Certificates of attendance are "issued to all students who participate in education programs for a required period of time, but who fail to meet a specific graduation requirement, including a Minimum Competency Test, if such a test is mandated" (Ross and Weintraub 1980, 201). This would apply to both handicapped and nonhandicapped students. Certificates of attendance are sometimes considered demeaning to students who may not be able to compete successfully because of their disadvantaged circumstances. To assure that these students are not precluded from further education and related services, policymakers will need to describe the courses of study that each student has completed and send that documentation on with the student.

Documenting Student Educations

Some verification of the content, nature, and general outcomes of every student's educational program seems a reasonable expectation. Such general records provide overviews of current, future, and past programs, and they guide planning. Documentation of a student's education consists of a day-by-day or periodic, and yearly record of educational experiences and achievements.

Documenting the curriculum and other school activities of special education students in a cumulative form is probably more difficult than keeping cumulative records for nonhandicapped students. Certain aspects of a student's special education curriculum are documented in the IEP, and the information about student experience and curriculum performance can be considered cumulative because IEPs are developed every year. This, however, may not be adequate information because it does not, clearly show the overall structure and content of a student's total curriculum. As with regular education courses of study, the purpose of the cumulative performance record is to identify the major objectives upon which a student's curriculum was, is, and probably will be based.

Daily and Periodic Records

Daily and periodic records document an education as it is happening. Records provide information for program planning and decision making and analyze the effects of environmental arrangements on behavior over time. They are used to provide answers about student performance as they participate in curriculum. More specifically, data is gathered frequently throughout the year to provide answers to at least these questions: (1) Is the student progressing toward the objectives in all components of his curriculum? (2) Is the student progressing as specified in goal and objective statement in the IEP? (3) When will the student be ready to advance to the next step or does he repeat previous tasks? (4) What has been found out about the student through recording of performance information? (5) What has the student achieved in the past, and what does data suggest that she is capable of achieving in the future? (6) If curriculum and instruction do not result in data that is satisfactory, what different arrangements, or adjustments, appear to be necessary? (Henderson and Erkin 1987, McLoughlin and Lewis 1986, Rowntree, 1981)

A major purpose of documenting an education as it is happening is to indicate any need for change. Different arrangements and adjustments might include the need to improve the teaching-learning situation. Reasons for change can be as constructive and enlightening as the change itself. Change could involve considering or reconsidering student placements, curriculum content, goals and objectives, timelines, instructional strategies, materials, resources, instructors, monitoring systems, response methods, presentation modalities, and student interest. It is essential that the measurement, data collection, and data-reporting systems complement each other. Student performances can be recorded on line graphs, bar graphs, student self-rating forms of behaviors (i.e., self control behaviors), checklists, forms to record accuracy and rate data, and event-recording forms.

Many resources describe data collection and different organizing schemes for handling information about student accomplishment. Some are identified in Chapter 2 as examples of criteria used to determine student accomplishment. They can serve as focus to this introductory discussion of record keeping (i.e., accuracy, cumulative counts, duration, and rate).

Recording information on a day-by-day basis or periodically is a first essential step in processing assessment information on students. Guerin and Maier (1983) identify this as a critical step and conclude that it is the recording methods and the ease with which others can recover information that affects the likelihood that the data will be used. They identify four considerations in selecting a recording procedure to assure likelihood that data will be collected and used (adapted from Guerin and Maier 1983, 57–58):

1. Use recording procedures that are as simple and as efficient as possible.
2. Have students or aides, when appropriate, participate in the recording process.
3. Record information so that it accurately represents the critical elements of the history or event. The elements need to be clearly and precisely identified, labeled, stated, or described. Categories, whenever possible, should be described in behavioral terms so events can easily be recognized and confirmed.
4. Use a recording format that does not require the transfer of the raw data to another form.

Teachers need to monitor student progress and achievement systematically on an ongoing basis, using both formal and informal methods, including test results, grade reports, attendance records, and other information to document an education as it occurs. Summaries of daily and periodic records then form the bases for documenting year-to-year courses of study.

Records of Courses of Study

A review of the regular education curriculum will show that a student's education is well channeled and therefore able to be well documented. The primary content, at least, is public information, and the course of study is universally defined (with allowances for individual differences, of course). But the curriculum of each student in special education can vary considerably from any other students in special education and from students in regular education. The nature of the portion of a student's curriculum that is special education is much more unpredictable and therefore is not subject to compiling data about it in a cumulative, analytical way. In regular education, the goals and objectives are structured and set out in printed courses of study, textbooks, lesson formats, term reports, and, of course, tests and examinations. These last two are the process for determining whether the goals have been achieved. Based on such a structured framework, the job of tracking each student's progress is made comparatively easy. Special education, however, does not follow such a fixed pattern. Teachers may not have easy access to information other than that on the IEPs of current students.

Can the IEP, alone, fulfill the following vital functions? (1) Can it enable the receiving teacher to learn as much as possible about the student and the student's total curriculum? (2) Does it aid in program evaluation research—that is, to check how efficacious programs were, to see which techniques worked over time and with which individuals? (3) Does it furnish a post-school individual with a meaningful and relevant record of his education?

The meetings to draw up IEPs generally occur only annually. Reassessment takes place throughout the year, but it will not necessarily be documented so that a new teacher can benefit from the information.

In many cases, there is little communication, if any, between the sending and receiving teacher. Yet it is essential to the relevance of goals set and plans made that a receiving teacher know the student's school history. Records form the backbone of that knowledge. Cumulative records would also facilitate devising an overall, say, five-year plan, which could be continually adjusted and reassessed in the light of newly gathered information. Allen (1943) says the cumulative record should function primarily as a guidance tool rather than merely as an instrument for official record.

A cumulative record system must necessarily be concise for the sake of convenient access to several years accumulation of information and analytical study of it. Ideally, records could be in the form of a one or two page document, a brief certification of the IEP goals achieved, with what regularity and at what level, and any other courses of study followed and with what degree of success.

This brings up a traditional legal and ethical dilemma—the need to know versus the right to privacy; quite rightly the law is concerned with seeking a just balance between the two.

Under PL 94-142, parents have the right of access to their children's records and the right to limit the release of information about their child to persons not directly involved in their child's education. Parental consent is required before nonauthorized members of staff can view the records. Such legal provisions are necessary to afford protection from indiscriminate access by curious adults and insensitive peers.

An assumption is made here that the since a purpose of a primary cumulative record is to provide teachers, parents, and the students themselves with some documentation of an education undertaken over several years, an ongoing system to describe and preserve such a record has benefits. It is further assumed that it is worthwhile for local education agencies to find some acceptable and helpful way to document courses of study for students in special education from year to year.

Documentation need not be long and involved. It can record the most salient features and refer teachers and parents to the locations of more specific details. Record summaries could at least identify the components of a student's course of study, as well as extracurricular activities and salient and nonconfidential pieces of information about a student's participation. Records could include the identity and sources of curriculum content used in different components. The kind and nature of education and services provided to the student could also be mentioned. Finally, salient and nonconfidential information about methods and accomplishments involved in successful student performance could be highlighted.

Curriculum components into which each year's course of study can be classified are:

1. Regular education curriculum: no special education
2. Regular education curriculum: with special education
3. Parallel curriculum
4. Lower grade level curriculum
5. Practical academic curriculum
6. Life management curriculum
7. Other curriculum

Each component in which a child participated could be listed. This would be accompanied by descriptive information such as the subjects studied in each component, the names and sources of curriculum, the nature of services received, and student performance. These different descriptive data are discussed in more detail in the next sections. First, however, readers are introduced to two components in addition to the standard components in which student participation might be identified: participation in enrichment activities and in extracurricular activities.

Information About Enrichment Curriculum Activities. This component corresponds to electives in regular education. Teachers need to be sure that when appropriate, their students have opportunities to study subjects of special interest to them and to perhaps even "audit" exciting units of study or courses in regular education. This component encourages teachers to build in curriculum and activities for students that are highly motivating and that spark students' self-initiated study and problem-solving.

Extracurricular Activity Curriculum. Some see extracurricular activities as outside the realm of the traditional curricular components, but here these are regarded as an integral part of what makes up a child's total curriculum. It is, after all, in these extracurricular activities that students most often pioneer their attempts to use skills both functionally and in more than one situation and with different persons. We prefer the word *cocurricular* for the term *extracurricular*. Cocurricular components include such activities as participating in assemblies, field trips, school clubs, dances, and other activities beyond those that are classroom oriented.

Descriptive Information

There are different kinds of descriptive information that identify each curriculum component in a student's curriculum:

- Curriculum subjects, skills, areas, domains.
- Names, descriptions, and sources of curriculum.
- Nature of services (i.e., special education, related services, and regular education services.
- Information about student performance *or* location of that information.

Curriculum Subjects, Skills, Areas, and Domains. Course identification information might include the names of the basic academic subjects and other school subjects (i.e., math, science, handwriting), skills (i.e., special disability-related skills such as Braille writing), curricular areas (i.e., gross-motor skills, prereading), and domains (i.e., domestic, recreation/leisure). These are introduced in Chapter 1 and illustrated throughout the text.

Names, Descriptions, and Sources of Curriculum. Whenever students are studying from an existing course of study, the teacher can name that course of study or relevant parts of it for the record. Then if someone wants more specific information about what students are studying or have studied, he can refer to that course of study. An example might be a fifth-grade course of study for the local school district. By doing this, teachers need not spend hours listing objectives because they can assume that if students satisfactorily complete identified parts of the course of study, they will have also completed the objectives therein. This is true for almost any existing teaching resource such as a board-approved curriculum for regular education, special education, and other existing curricula or components.

Three kinds of records can help assure cumulative, ongoing, *multiyear*, descriptive information, covering the important aspects of each student's curriculum. The first and simplest is to identify the sources of any existing or prepared curriculum and its related objectives. The second is to keep lists of major objectives and skills by years and by subject or discipline for any teacher-generated curriculum. The third is to keep lists of those major objectives and skills accomplished as part of the IEP process. Then at any time, interested persons, when appropriate, can review records of a student's schooling for the present or past years.

EXISTING CURRICULA. When using existing regular and special education curricula or their components for keeping records, identify the name and source of the curriculum, the date of the book or document, and the range of pages covered. (When referring to regular education curriculum, it is sometimes necessary to clarify whether objectives were met at regular levels of complexity or if outcomes were based on different objectives because they were skills enroute to regular objectives.) If not clearly stated in the name of the document, also name the discipline or subject and grade level when given.

TEACHER-GENERATED CURRICULA. A teacher-generated curriculum is often the most crucial and important part of a student's schooling. The benefits, however, can often become lost or diminished due to poor or nonexistent record keeping.

Teachers who are specialists in the education of students with disabilities generate special curricula to meet the special needs of particular groups or individual students. With the best of intentions and all their expertise, teachers can carry out fine plans with their students only to have two possible unfortunate results. If each previous teacher has not used some system for recording major skills that were the outcome of their instruction, future teachers may repeat the same subjects, bore students, and bypass the opportunity to teach students new material. And, second, since there is little connection between what students have already learned and future learning, students do not have the benefit of a truly cumulative curriculum.

It is a professional responsibility to be able to describe different components of any students' curriculum and to be able to produce information about student performance in the different curriculum components. When teachers are not using existing recognized curriculum sources, it is only reasonable that they commit whatever curriculum and form of student evaluation they are using to writing. Then new teachers can refer to the name and location of these printed descriptions. In this way the material will be available to subsequent teachers and are describable as a part of a student's schooling.

INDIVIDUALIZED EDUCATION PROGRAMS. The actual IEP document itself describes part of an ongoing record of schooling for every student in special education. Accomplishment of the short-term instructional objectives and, in turn, the annual goals, documented in the IEP's performance objectives and instructional plans provide a precise record of that portion of each student's schooling.

Until objectives, statements of instructional approaches, and outcomes can be added to descriptions of past courses of study, there is no way to describe special education student courses of study in entirety. Different state and local educational units have different interpretations as to whether or not goals and objectives on active IEPs can be made available as general information as other objectives in student programs are. If law determines that IEP goals and objectives are to be confidential for the period of time for which they are active, we recommend that—if legal and local policy permit—they be added to the appropriate *multiyear* performance records as soon as they have been accomplished and are no longer part of active IEP. Parent permissions may be necessary before doing this.

Local education agencies can use this process to compile records of student schooling over several years. Such accumulations might take the form of names of (1) existing curriculum documents, as written or modified, (2) teacher-generated and teacher-described curriculum and identification of major skills and activities accomplished or in progress but not identified in any printed course of study, (3) IEP objectives completed and cumulative still in progress, and (4) combinations of any of the above.

Special Education and Related Services. Information about educational and related services can be spelled out in terms of those provided by special education, related services, and regular education. Special education teachers generally have primary responsibility for specially designed instruction or *special education services. Related services* are provided when it is established that they are required to help a student benefit from special education. Descriptions of needed modifications in response methods, presentation modalities, and conditions would be described in these records. In each case, roles and responsibilities of service providers can be described in addition to identifying the student's major accomplishments.

For each curriculum component making up part of a student's education, one or more of these sources (sped; rel; reg. ed.) provides the services. Policy should assure that comments about the nature of the services are kept general enough so they do not violate student rights but are of a helpful nature to those involved with the student. Certain services are classified by one local education unit as a special education service and by another as a related service. Career/vocational education is one example. In some local educational units it is treated as a school subject; in others as a related service. Whether regarded as special education or as a related service, it can be identified as supporting students in one or more curriculum component. One other potential question of placement arises when several sources, perhaps even nonschool sources, collaborate in the behalf of students. The vocational domain in a life management curriculum component is one example. Special education teachers, related service behavior specialists, and outside employers could all be providing service. In most cases, such services are meeting the unique needs of handicapped students in one or more life management components with implications for participation in other components. Thus, teachers should choose the documentation that most characteristically represents what happens to students.

Areas of a student's programming that are not special education and related services should, of course, be described as such. After special education and related services are noted, teachers can continue the process for describing the nature of regular education programs that are used. Descriptions of regular education services might be the same as those used for students not in special education, or they may differ slightly to denote any special objectives of the regular teacher for meeting the individual needs of particular students.

Information About Student Performance. Evaluation information describing a student's progress and achievements in the educational program completes the picture of a student's annual course of study. Evaluation is a possible grey area in protecting the confidentiality of student records. Parents, new teachers, and other authorized persons could certainly search IEPs and inquire about student performance in each curriculum component from others who have worked with a student, but this is a time-consuming approach. And when one is inquiring about previous years, it may not be productive.

Most professionals and parents realize that evaluation information about student performance merits confidentiality. Report card grades, competency test results, certificates of promotion and graduation awards are part of official school records. Authorized person can refer to these. Locations of teacher–generated curricula are not so easily located for retrieval by a student's new teacher. Cumulative records can identify the nature and location of these records by curriculum component(s) and area or areas of study.

Summary and Conclusion

Now comes the time every textbook author awaits—writing of the summary and conclusion of the final chapter and restating the intended outcome. The final hope is that all this makes a positive impact on the preparation of teachers and the education of students in special education.

Grading systems to communicate evaluations and other documentations of student courses of study are evidences of the education so precious to all students including those in special education. This final chapter introduced some of these and reviewed grading and evaluation practices with students in special education. Minimum-competency testing as it pertained to special education students was discussed and issues identified. Alternatives to junior high promotion and high school graduation were enumerated and described. Finally, a case was made for ongoing documentation of courses of study on each special education student. This was followed by a proposal that certain kinds of salient information on student courses of study and related information be kept in cumulative records. The chapter proposed that cumulative records would expedite the job of each teacher receiving a new student and assure that previous curricula be continued or at least followed by programming related to the previous programming.

Documentation of curriculum and other school activites of special education students in a cumulative form is perhaps more difficult than keeping cumulative records for other students. Some aspects of curriculum of special education students are documented in the student's IEP. Information about student experience and performance in the curriculum can be considered cumulative because IEPs are developed every year. This, however, may not be enough information and may not be presented in a way that can easily be obtained by studying each student's IEP curriculum each year and over the years. In addition, the confidentiality of IEPs raises issues of recording the information in any other format or making it more easily accessible.

Every student and parent deserves a right to some systematic documentation and cumulative recording of the schooling of students in special education. Teachers can benefit from having cumulative records covering the most important parts of past schooling for their students to build on—not just what is on an IEP.

Furthermore, teachers will be more effective in planning and teaching if they have a record for themselves and for others, descriptions of the major components and content of the regular education and special education provided to students during each school year.

Some verification of the content, nature, and general outcomes of every student's educational program on a yearly basis seems a reasonable expectation. Such general records can provide overviews of current and future programs, and can guide effective educational planning.

This book is dedicated to teachers who make changes so special education students can continue to learn and then show what they know and can do. Special education student participation in the full education to which they are entitled depends upon their engagement in a curriculum and accompanying instruction that is powerful, describable, assessment linked, and accessible. This text was designed to give special education professionals the foundations in the specialized competencies they will need for their demanding important work. But this text represents only a beginning. More specialty training, more practice, more study will be required. Most of all, a wholehearted creative response to the challenge of teaching students with special needs will keep the dedicated teacher on track— learning, sharing ideas and strategies, and building on the foundation this text offers.

References

Allen, W. 1943. *Cumulative pupil records—A plan for staff study and improvement of cumulative pupil records in secondary schools.* New York: Columbia University Press.

Barret, P. 1983. Recommendations for inclusion of career education, vocational education, work experience, and independent living skills on the differential standards for graduation for special education students. A Policy Paper. Sacramento, Calif.: Differential Standards for Graduation Committee: Project Workability.

Bender, W. 1984. Daily grading in mainstreaming classes. *Directive Teacher* 6(2): 4–5.

Bracey, G. W. 1983. On the compelling need to go beyond minimum competency. *Phi Delta Kappan* 64(10): 717–21.

Butler, S., Magliocca, L., Torres, L., and Lee, W. 1984. Grading the mainstreamed student: A decision making model for modification. *The Directive Teacher* 6(2):6–7.

Carpenter, D., Grantham, L., and Hardister, M. 1983. Grading mainstreamed handicapped pupils: What are the issues? *Journal of Special Education* 17(2): 182–88.

Dick, M. 1983. Alternatives in evaluation and grading of special needs students. *Missouri LINC paper #823.* Columbia, Mo.: Missouri University, College of Education.

Elkind, D. 1981. *The hurried child: Growing up too fast too soon.* Reading, Mass.: Addison-Wesley Publishing Co.

Guerin, G. R., and Maier, A. S. 1983. *Informal assessment in education.* Mountain View, Calif.: Mayfield Publishing Co.

Henderson, H. S., and Erkin, N. 1987. *Number facts masters: Teacher handbook.* Daly City, Calif.: Mastery Programs, Ltd.

Kinnison, K., Hays, C., and Acord, J. 1981. Evaluating student progress in mainstreamed classes. *Teaching Exceptional Children* 13(3): 97–99.

Kiraly, M., and Bedell, J. 1984. Grading the mainstreamed handicapped student. *National Association of Secondary School Principals Bulletin.* 68(472): 111–15.

Lazarus, M. 1981. *Goodby to excellence: A critical look at Minimum Competency Testing.* Boulder, Colo.: Westview Press.

Lewis, R., and Doorlag, D. H. 1983. *Teaching special students in the mainstream.* Columbus, Ohio: Charles E. Merrill.

McLoughlin, J. A., and Lewis, R. B. 1986. *Assessing special students.* 2d ed. Columbus, Ohio: Charles E. Merrill.

Monjan, S., and Glassner, S. 1979. *Critical issues in competency based education.* Elmsford, N.Y.: Pergamon Press.

National Regional Resource Center Panel on Indicators of Effectiveness in Special Education. 1986. *Effectiveness indicators for special education.* Lexington, Ky.: Mid-South RRC, University of Kentucky.

Nickse, R., and McClure, L. 1981. *Competency based education: Beyond minimum competency testing.* New York: Teachers College Press.

Ross, J. W., and Weintraub, F. J. 1980. Policy approaches regarding the impact of graduation requirements of handicapped students. *Exceptional Children* 47(3): 200–3.

Rowntree, D. 1981. *Developing courses for students.* N.Y.: McGraw-Hill.

Salvia, J., and Ysseldyke, J. E. 1985. *Assessment in special and remedial education.* 3d ed. Boston: Houghton Mifflin Co.

San Diego Unified School District. 1985. Comprehensive model of curriculum and placement CAC presentation (includes state requirements and entry level guidelines). San Diego, Calif.: San Diego City Schools, 4100 Normal St., Rm. 2014, San Diego, CA 92103.

San Diego Unified School District. 1984–1985. *Course of study, K–12.* San Diego City Schools, 4100 Normal St., Rm. 2014, San Diego, CA 92103.

Schulz, J., and Turnbull, A. 1983. *Mainstreaming handicapped students,* 2d ed. Newton, Mass.: Allyn and Bacon Inc.

Serow, R., and O'Brien, K. 1983. Performance of handicapped students in a competency testing program. *Journal of Special Education,* 17(20): 149–55.

U.S. Office of Education, Department of Health, Education and Welfare. Part II, p. 42482, paragraph 121a.129. Education of handicapped children, implementation of Part B of the Education of the Handicapped Act. *Federal Register* 42(163): 42474–42518.

Vasa, S. F. 1981. Alternative procedures for grading handicapped students in the secondary schools. *Education Unlimited,* 3(1): 16–23.

Wentling, T. 1978. Teaching special needs students: Measurement and evaluation. *Industrial Education* 67(5): 29–30.

Index